ABOVE THE REICH

ABOVE
THE
REICH

DEADLY DOGFIGHTS,
BLISTERING BOMBING RAIDS,
AND OTHER WAR STORIES FROM
THE GREATEST AMERICAN
AIR HEROES OF WORLD WAR II,
IN THEIR OWN WORDS

COLIN HEATON and
ANNE-MARIE LEWIS

CALIBER

CALIBER

An imprint of Penguin Random House LLC
penguinrandomhouse.com

LIBRARY OF CONGRESS CATALOGING-IN-PUBLICATION DATA

Names: Heaton, Colin D., interviewer. | Lewis, Anne-Marie, editor.
Title: Above the Reich : deadly dogfights, blistering bombing raids, and other war stories from the greatest American air heroes of World War II, in their own words / Colin Heaton and Anne-Marie Lewis.
Other titles: Deadly dogfights, blistering bombing raids, and other war stories from the greatest American air heroes of World War II, in their own words
Description: [New York] : Dutton Caliber, [2021] | Includes bibliographical references and index.
Identifiers: LCCN 2020041524 (print) | LCCN 2020041525 (ebook) | ISBN 9780593183885 (hardcover) | ISBN 9780593183908 (ebook)
Subjects: LCSH: World War, 1939–1945—Aerial operations, American | Air pilots, Military—United States—Interviews. | Johnson, Robert S., 1920–1998—Interviews. | Doolittle, James Harold, 1896–1993—Interviews. | Olds, Robin, 1922–2007—Interviews. | Haydon, Edward Ross, 1920–2012—Interviews. | LeMay, Curtis E.—Interviews. | World War, 1939–1945—Personal narratives, American
Classification: LCC D790 .H43 2021 (print) | LCC D790 (ebook) | DDC 940.54/49730922—dc23
LC record available at https://lccn.loc.gov/2020041524
LC ebook record available at https://lccn.loc.gov/2020041525

Printed in the United States of America
1 3 5 7 9 10 8 6 4 2

BOOK DESIGN BY TIFFANY ESTREICHER

*Dedicated to the men of all nations, friend and foe,
who fought and died for the mistakes of others*

CONTENTS

ABOVE THE REICH

FOREWORD

How can contemporary readers unfamiliar with combat aviation quench the desire to understand the great aerial battles of World War II? They can, of course, turn to the enduring major references or to biographies and autobiographies. I, for example, was so inspired by reading General James H. Doolittle's *I Could Never Be So Lucky Again* that it motivated me to join Ed Rasimus to write *Fighter Pilot*, the story of my father, Robin Olds. Throughout the year I worked on the manuscript, I always kept "Jimmy's" book on my desk along with two by Walter Boyne, *Aces in Command: Fighter Pilots as Combat Leaders* and *Beyond the Wild Blue: A History of the U.S. Air Force, 1947–1997*.

Coming from a family of pilots (such as my grandfather Robert Olds and father, Robin), with diaries, letters, and hundreds of documents at my disposal, I was, admittedly, something of a special case. Today most of the curious are likely to turn first to movies or documentaries about aerial warfare. But while great filmmakers perhaps allow us to imagine how the scenes appeared and the action unrolled, every story starts with spoken or written words. Films need scripts; computer graphics need descriptions. To that end, we will always be beholden to our storytellers, those who document and record the original voices of the men and women who witnessed and participated in great historic moments and managed to survive. Nothing can beat firsthand stories. And this important new book by Colin Heaton and Anne-Marie Lewis is full of them.

Heaton's masterful compilation of personal interviews plunges us into the moment, taking us back to original historical events as seen through the eyes of five remarkable United States Army Air Force pilots. His narratives faithfully capture the exploits of my father, Robin Olds; Curtis LeMay, the protégé and navigator of my grandfather, Major General Robert Olds; Robert S. Johnson, one of our highest-scoring aces in Europe during World War II; Edward "Buddy" Haydon, an accomplished aerial battle pilot and my father's close personal friend; and Jimmy Doolittle, whose feats are so famous they perhaps eclipse all the others'. What a gathering of eagles!

It is an understatement to term these narratives, all told in the subjects' own words, as merely important to the legacy of American military aviation. We can more accurately describe this outstanding work as absolutely essential to our understanding of the history of World War II.

Christina Olds
May 2020

———

They're nearly all gone now.

In early 2020, of the hundreds of World War II veterans I've known, met, or interviewed, representing a half dozen nations, I remain in contact with one. When I was secretary of the American Fighter Aces Association in the eighties and nineties, collating and archiving their experiences, we had as many as four hundred members. Today there are fewer than two dozen.

We can track the growing attrition by the literature. When my book describing the Marianas Turkey Shoot of World War II—*Clash of the Carriers*—was published in 2005, one-fourth of the contributors were already deceased. When my history *Enterprise: America's Fightingest Ship and the Men Who Won World War II* was released seven years later, fewer than half were still alive. And when my study of *US Marine Corps Fighter Squadrons of World War II* was published in 2014, only one of my "flying leathernecks" remained.

Everyone who writes World War II history has experienced similar loss, which is why Colin Heaton and Anne-Marie Lewis's work is so valuable. The variety of subjects they have recorded spans services, nations, and conflicts. Very few interviews like these could be conducted today because the subjects have, in aviation terms, "departed the pattern."

Therefore, those of us who knew and recorded the deeds—and equally importantly, the thoughts—of the survivors represent a rare chronological link. A bridge across time. We have long since lost all the World War I veterans, and I knew only four Great War airmen. Absent the dedicated work of colleagues who focused on first-generation aviators, we would have little to access a century later.

Of the five subjects in this volume, I knew three: Jimmy Doolittle, Robin Olds, and Bob Johnson. I wrote the first posthumous biography of Curtis LeMay and cannot believe that I passed up a prior chance to meet him. When I was dining at the storied Nieuport 17 restaurant in Tustin, California, with Marine Corps Medal of Honor ace Ken Walsh in the 1970s, LeMay was seated across the room with friends. Ken offered to introduce us, but I was reluctant to intrude.

The memories come flooding back. "General Jimmy's" precise, British manner of speaking: "aeroplane" and "chap." Robin's deceptively soft voice concealing that up-front, red-meat brand of leadership. Johnson's slight build, seeming in conflict with the Thunderbolt's large cockpit. I can only regret that I never met Edward Haydon, as his story, too, is obviously well worth reading.

The factual accounting of military figures gains in importance as myth and legend increasingly grasp the public's mind. Examples flourish. Gregory Boyington did not shoot down twenty-eight airplanes, and he has never been the US Marines' leading ace, however reckoned; the corps' scandalous treatment of Medal of Honor fighter pilot Joe Foss should shame the corps—but does not. Foss should rightly be the leading Marine Corps ace in World War II, not Boyington. George Gay (Battle of Midway) was not "the sole survivor of Torpedo Eight," though he made that claim for a half century. The Tuskegee Airmen did not have a perfect record on bomber escort and produced no aces. Other examples abound.

As Colin Heaton and Anne-Marie Lewis will attest, the mantra takes greater importance today than ever: do it now.

Barrett Tillman
April 2020

———

Colin Heaton is one of the foremost experts in the area of World War II oral history, having interviewed in the 1970s, 1980s, and 1990s many key German and American personalities of the war. His new book presents new, primary source material on some of the greatest leaders the United States Army Air Forces (now the United States Air Force) has ever produced. Heaton here focuses on General James "Jimmy" Doolittle, General Curtis LeMay, Colonel Edward Ross

"Buddy" Haydon, Lieutenant Colonel Robert Samuel Johnson, and Brigadier General Robin Olds, presenting the first-person recollections of these five American Air Force leaders when they were in the twilight of their lives and full of recollections and analyses. Their personal and personable narratives offer military enthusiasts an intimate understanding of their upbringing, their military service, their thoughts as leaders and fighting men, and their reflections on the history they helped to create.

An overview of these men's lives shows shared traits generally ascribed to "the American spirit." All had rambunctious youths characterized by boxing, football, fighting, risk taking, and a desire for adventure. And in some respects, they all displayed the American spirit of the pioneer or immigrant who, desirous of a better future, is willing to undertake whatever is necessary to strike out for new beginnings. Later in life, all led from the front and distinguished themselves at every duty station: Doolittle's raid on Japan on April 18, 1942, changed the tone of the Pacific War. LeMay flew at the head of his bomber formations during runs on Nazi Germany and later orchestrated the bombing of Japan; Haydon, Johnson, and Olds all took bold action in aerial combat as fighter pilots. As Olds tells us here: "World War I taught us something important: whoever controls the air controls the battlefield below."

The subjects of this collection led the way in shaping modern aerial operations and strategy in World War II, and their actions roundly proved Olds's theorem correct. To give but two examples: In 1944 Doolittle took over the Eighth Air Force in Europe and led it to victory over the skies of Germany. An excellent leader with a PhD from Massachusetts Institute of Technology (MIT), he intimately understood the machines his men had to fly to achieve the Allied victory, and was able to best deploy such assets. LeMay perfected defensive bomber formations, using "square" rather than the old V formations, and then took over the Twentieth Bomber Command in the Pacific that eventually had the responsibility of dropping the two atomic bombs on Japan that brought the war to its conclusion.

The interest in *Above the Reich* does not stop at developments in aerial warfare in World War II. Frankly discussing their military service during the Cold War, the Korean War, and Vietnam, Heaton's interview subjects offer readers detailed and intimate views on how warfare evolved in the jet and nuclear ages. Their testimonies also reflect on the United States' new enemies, the Soviet Union and the People's Republic of China, and reveal the strategic thought that shaped the way they and other military leaders considered how post–World War II aerial assets should be deployed and used in the Cold War confrontation with Communism.

Not surprisingly, none pull any punches when it comes to evaluating Capitol Hill politicians and "armchair generals" at the Pentagon far removed from those who are required to execute disastrous orders and take the fight to the enemy. While Robert McNamara, US secretary of defense from 1961 to 1967, is particularly excoriated for incompetence during the Vietnam War, their commentary overall illustrates the crucial importance of well-informed leaders who do everything possible to thoroughly understand conditions at the front before making decisions that cause needless death and loss.

Bryan Mark Rigg
May 2020

A MAN TOO
HARD TO KILL

———— ★ ————

Robert Samuel Johnson

R obert S. Johnson grew up during the Great Depression in Lawton, Oklahoma, during the dust bowl era. High unemployment and a long drought destroyed farming, increasing the misery. His life of poverty did not prevent him from deciding to become an aviator. He eventually became a fighter pilot, serving with the Fifty-Sixth Fighter Group, known on both sides of the English Channel as "Zemke's Wolfpack," so named for its colorful, blunt leader, Colonel Hubert A. "Hub" Zemke.[1]

The Fifty-Sixth Fighter Group produced some of the highest-scoring ace fighter pilots in the US Army Air Forces in the European theater of operations (ETO). Including Johnson's own twenty-seven victories, his fellow fighter pilots were credited with destroying 985.5 enemy aircraft: 674.5 shot down and 311 destroyed on the ground, the most victories of any fighter group in the Eighth Air Force. Johnson scored his victories in eight-nine combat missions (a ratio of 3.17

sorties, per victory) and was the first American pilot in the ETO to break America's top World War I fighter ace Captain Edward Rickenbacker's score of twenty-six, achieved in World War I.

When I first spoke to Bob Johnson by telephone in 1986, he seemed quite keen on doing an interview. We spent many hours talking about his life as I took copious notes. Nine years later, on the way to Lake Wylie, South Carolina, where he had invited me to his home to finally meet face-to-face, I stopped to get a bite to eat at a local restaurant before checking into a hotel. As I walked in, there sat Robert Johnson, eating his dinner. "Damn," he said as soon as he saw me. "You must be anxious. I thought I was going to see you tomorrow."

The situation was more than a little uncomfortable. I did not want to intrude on his meal, but he asked me to sit down, and I did. We spoke about arbitrary things, but nothing related to the interview; I would save that until the next day. He did say that he wished his wife, Barbara, were still alive to meet me, because she had enjoyed hearing my southern accent on the other end of the line. She had seemed to be a very nice lady, one I wished I could have met, too.

Johnson was looking good for a man of his years: short but still solid and strong. I spent a couple of days with Bob, who was entertaining and energetic. He was pleased to show me the war memorabilia he'd collected over the course of his lifetime. One of his prized possessions was a painting depicting his encounter with the Luftwaffe ace Egon Mayer, titled *Not My Time to Die.*

We stayed in frequent contact until 1998, when I graduated from Temple University with my master of arts degree in history, and landed in Glasgow, Scotland, at the University of Strathclyde. I called him from Glasgow a couple of weeks before Christmas, and he said he was taking a trip and would let me know when he returned. I had been waiting to hear back for almost a month, when I was contacted by an attorney, who informed me that Bob had passed away on December 27.

My contact information was in Bob's personal effects, which included a signed copy of his memoir, *Thunderbolt!,* which he had planned on sending to me when he returned. I still have and treasure his book today.

After his postwar work as an advisor for the aviation industry, Johnson traveled around the country visiting high schools to educate young people about why America became involved in World War II. He was long active in promoting knowledge about the history of aviation, stimulating younger generations' interest in those who served and fought for freedom, and educating civilians about the sacrifices of those who never returned, regardless of nationality.

A quiet, straightforward man, Bob's mild-mannered demeanor belied the killer instinct and intense focus required of the fighter pilot to achieve success, or even survive during active duty. If the highest praise one may receive is from one's enemy, Johnson has been highly praised indeed: in the opinion of Luftwaffe lieutenant general Adolf Galland, *General der Jagdflieger* (general of the fighters), "Robert Johnson was one of the best pilots in the war. Meeting him proved to me that the war was a contest between good men thrown together in a very bad situation. Had he flown as long as our men, he would probably have over two hundred victories."[2]

A close look at the statistics shows that Galland assessed Johnson's skills correctly: with 275 victories, ace Lieutenant General Gunther Rall's sortie-to-victory ratio mirrors Johnson's ratio almost perfectly—the major difference being that Rall flew several hundred more missions.[3] Had he had more opportunities to report on missions, Johnson's projected ratio shows he quite possibly would have had a much higher victory record. Galland's recognition of Johnson's achievement and his high respect for the American aviator's talents is moreover a prime example of the code of chivalry among pilots. Those who have engaged in combat and survived understand that despite the differences and against all odds, in a dogfight they are there to fight for their country: it is not personal, it is duty.

My interviews with Bob Johnson were conducted over a span of twelve years, from 1985 through 1997, in person, by telephone, and by written correspondence. This is his story, in his own words.

ROBERT SAMUEL JOHNSON

I was born on February 21, 1920, in Lawton, fifty-two miles north of the Red River in southwestern Oklahoma. I grew up in a very rural area during the Great Depression, when life was really hard for everyone. We were in what they called the dust bowl, and those kids who did not get an education were going to have a hard life later. I did all the boyhood things that rural American boys did. Our parents would drive us for four, maybe five hours to the Wichita Mountains and let us go. We fished and also hunted the occasional coyote, prairie dogs, and those sorts of critters.

I used to practice shooting flowers in the fields, perfecting the use of windage to hit them as the wind made them bend back and forth. I got pretty damned good with that rifle. I used to practice shooting birds—crows, pigeons, doves, anything that gave me a gunner's eye. Leading a target became second nature. A couple of friends who hunted with shotguns were surprised when I could nail a bird on the fly with a rifle just by estimating the range and adjusting the point of aim to lead my targets. It's as much instinct as it is acquired skill.

I was also in the Boy Scouts, and I loved going out and camping, sleeping in tents, and learning survival skills. Not sleeping in a bed, maybe for days at a time, never bothered me. We used to swim and sleep under the stars, cook rabbits and fish, living the rough life, or so we thought. I would have to say that at that age, we were pretty self-sufficient compared to city boys I later got to know in college and the military.

I got into boxing due to bullying, especially at school. I was very small and short for my age, and we had guys who targeted guys like me. Up until about the fifth grade, I got thumped a lot, until I finally decided that I was going to pound the cornstalk out of the next guy who tried me, just to make a point. I was in eighth grade when one of the worst bullies, this idiot named Ben, was asking boys for money. All but one guy gave it up, but this one guy a little bigger than me decided to fight. Ben won because the other guy landed a punch but didn't follow it up. Ben nailed him and took his coins.

Ben walked around and saw me. He knew me and walked over and demanded any money I had. I told him that I did not have any, and he loudly proclaimed he would see for himself. That was all I needed. I allowed him to get close, then gave him a left punch to the nose, a right to the gut, and another left back in the face. He went down, but as he tried to get up, I was on him. I pounded that fool so hard he was not moving, and a teacher came in and pulled me off.

They dragged me to the principal's office and sat me down. They then revived Ben and brought him in and started cleaning the blood off his face. He was crying. The principal and teacher both looked at me, all seventy pounds, and then looked at this other guy who was a foot taller and outweighed me by at least forty pounds. I could see that the principal was trying not to laugh. He knew about Ben—the boy had been in trouble many times for his shakedowns.

The principal asked me why I beat him up. I told him that he had already hit some other boys and then he came for me. He wanted my money. I said that I was going to make him earn it. The principal turned his head, but I could hear him trying not to laugh. He told the teacher to take Ben away to the school nurse. I sat there, and he told me that he did not allow fighting in school, and he would have to tell my dad. I said that was fine—that my dad would rather have me in trouble for defending myself than in a hospital.

My dad came to the school and was informed of the situation. I could tell that even while he was agreeing with the principal that fighting in school was a bad thing, the look he gave me was, "It's okay, I know you did what you had to do." So, I knew I was not in trouble with him. I got suspended for a day, and Ben was out for a week because other students came forward to complain about him taking their money and hitting them.

That was really the beginning of my boxing training. I knew that I was going to have to fight through life, and my dad suggested that I be trained for it. I went to the local gym and learned from an old guy who had been a sparring partner for some professionals. He had also been a boxer himself. I learned that the guy who hits first and hard often wins the fight if you follow up. "Inflict, confuse, and complete" was what he said. I studied the most vulnerable areas of the body, where to hit, and in what sequence. I got really good at it.

I started boxing in the ring in tournaments, and I learned something about myself. When I was hit, I got mad, and then I didn't care how big or bad the other guy was—only one of us was walking out of that ring. It came to a point that I didn't really have to think about where or how I was hitting a guy; it was all instinct and mental, muscle memory. Every human being has the same basic configuration. I just kept hitting the exposed and vulnerable areas. I seemed oblivious to the hits I was taking, and I never really felt them until the fight was over. Yet despite my promise as a boxer, I did not want to do that for a living.

The first real fight I had was when I was sixteen. I was up against a pro in his twenties who had a lot of experience. He also had a well-earned reputation as a tough guy and a dirty fighter. We were about the same weight, 120 pounds or so, and he was a foot taller. He was a battle-scarred guy who looked like a fighter. The guys running the club and even people in the crowd did not want the fight because they believed it was unfair, and I would be badly injured.

Well, the referee gave us the instructions, the bell rang, and this bigger guy came out. I went for the gut punch and missed, but my following right punch caught him square in the chest. I threw all my weight into it, and he fell back against the ropes, then fell down face-first and was out for the full count. Then he got up complaining, and I told the ref to let him come on. He threw a few left jabs that didn't connect, and then he went for a right hook to my head. I ducked and hit him in the chest again, and this time he went down and stayed down.

The ring doctors came in and took him out, and he never fought in the ring again, from what I was told. I had hurt him badly. That was when I learned that no matter how big or imposing an opponent was, he could be defeated. I never forgot that. I think that confidence I gained was what carried me well into my later years. To be a fighter pilot, you have to be aggressive, and you must have confidence. Add experience to that equation, and you can become a formidable fighter.

I knew I wanted something beyond high school. You have to remember that maybe half the kids never even finished high school. They went to work on the farms or in factories if such work was available. I decided I was not going down that path. I went through high school and played sports, mostly football. At less than 150 pounds, I was one of the smallest guys on my high school team, whereas the other guys were 70 to 170 pounds heavier. I still played for three years as a back, starting out. My coach moved me around to blocking and center. I still did a lot of boxing while in school and continued when I went to Cameron College, which is now Cameron University.

My dad and football coach knew I wanted to go to college, and after speaking with them and a few others, I decided to study engineering. They said that engineers had the best chances of getting good jobs even in the worst of economic times. It was while I was in college that I decided to join the armed forces and fly. That interest started early. I was sitting on my dad's shoulders at Post Field near Lawton one day. I had always been, as most kids were in that day, interested in becoming a cowboy or a railroad engineer. I loved trains—they just excited the hell out of me. But when I saw airplanes, all that changed.

This air show was in 1928, and I knew right then that my ideas about my future were changed forever. This air show was a military event, and they were flying the old wood and fabric-covered biplanes. They had three fighters flying in the old V, or "vic," formation, and they did all kinds of stunts, twisting and turning below five thousand feet. Then and there, I changed my goal from cowboy or engineer to army aviator. Hell, by hook or by crook, I was going to become a pilot.

Growing up I had a couple of good friends, Joe Reed and Wayne King. We were like the three musketeers and had been classmates for what seemed like forever. I was fortunate because both of their dads owned their own airplanes and ran a small flight school at one of the small airports near Lawton. It was a grass airstrip with an old hangar and about fifteen planes—old ones that would probably not be allowed to fly today.

Joe's dad owned the flying school. He had been an army pilot in World War I, and he still held a reserve status. He was also the town postmaster, while Wayne's dad was the chief instructor. Joe Reed's postmaster job was a full-time position, and he had little time to train student pilots. I used to sit and watch as their dads took them for flights in the Jenny [training aircraft] or other planes, while I had to sit out and enjoy the view. But my time was not wasted, because I spoke to pilots, collected flight manuals, and listened to them talk. I was on an early intelligence-gathering mission.

Having friends with that kind of connection, after the spark of seeing the air show, I made my plan. I asked if I could work around the field, doing odd jobs just to earn flight time. My offers were never accepted, and I suspected it had something to do with my mother [who would have had to give permission]. Well, that plan didn't work out, but then opportunity knocked again.

Back in those days, barnstormers and acrobatic pilots traveled the country, and when I applied for a job at Cameron College, where the shows were often held, I was able to get my plane rides as payment. We did all kinds of things: helping with the concession stands, escorting people to and from the planes, walking the fields to make sure that no debris could damage tires or blow up into a propeller, and making sure the ground was free of holes where wheels could dig in. If we found any, one group marked them with a flagpole, and another came behind and filled them in. This really paid off for me, for sometimes I did get a ride.

I managed to see and get into many types of planes, and one day at a show, a Ford Tri-Motor flew in. It was the biggest plane I had ever seen up to that time. It was used as an airliner back then. This thing had all kinds of lights on it, like a flying Christmas tree. My dad was with me as this pilot took the Ford up and landed many times, giving paying customers rides. Once as he flew over, he dropped fireworks that exploded and lit up the entire area—Roman candles and things shooting many bursts of colored flares into the sky. It was marvelous.

When he landed after that display, my dad looked at me and asked me if I wanted to go for a flight. Man, I can tell you, at that moment, it was the greatest day of my life! My dad paid, and I got in and could smell all of the aromas that would later become so familiar to me. Oil, gas, lubricants—all the smells that I equated with absolute freedom. I sat down and placed the seat belt strap across, and I remember my excitement at the noises: the hum of electric starters, the flick of the switches, and the grind as the motors turned over. As the engines revved up, shaking the plane like crazy, I felt like I was in another world. Then came the release of the brakes, and the plane slowly rolled forward. The roar of the engines increased, and we were picking up speed.

I looked out the window at the crowd passing by as we gently bounced along the ground before we lifted off. We climbed into the fading daylight, and night fell. I could see the lights of the city and the changing colors of the sun, which had gone down. We flew for fifteen minutes, and the plane banked, the engine pitch changed, and we headed to earth. It was dark, and I couldn't see the ground clearly, but felt the slight *thump* as we touched down—no bouncing—and taxied to a nice, easy stop. I was hooked.

I started flying when I was thirteen. I flew whenever I could and got my first license, which I still have, the day before I turned sixteen. I earned my flight-time money working at the Lawton Cabinet Shop, where I'd worked part-time after school since I'd been about eleven. When summer came, I worked full-time, up to sixteen hours six days a week. I had to lift large, heavy wooden beams and guide them into the big saw that cut them into boards. This was hard work for a full-grown man, but it toughened me.

My dad was very proud that I stayed at that job for several years, becoming an assistant manager, but still making $4 a week. My dad was an honest, hardworking, churchgoing man, and my mom was the standard-issue midwestern housewife. A strong work ethic was crucial in my family, but then again, we were all that way growing up. Having any job during the Depression was a godsend.

I had to pay $1.50 for fifteen minutes of flight time, so if I spent $6,

I could get an hour and a half with the instructor. Every Sunday, when not working, either before or after church, I was there at the airport. My first plane was a Wiley Post trainer—a biplane. This had a unique cockpit where the student and pilot sat side by side, which was different from Jennys and other aircraft that had cockpits one behind the other. Merle Donnley was my instructor. The first time up, he let me have the stick and rudder. Ironically, I was hit by a crosswind that rolled us over on the right side, but without any training or experience, I applied left rudder and stick and brought her level. Merle was very impressed that I had a natural instinct. To me, it made sense.

My third lesson was in a Travelair biplane, bigger and more powerful. Merle said, "Let's go!" and I took off without any problems. I learned, however, that this plane did not land like the Post. I was overshooting the runway on landing, going back around a few times, starting my approach sooner and farther out, but the crosswinds would drift me off center. After several tries, Merle finally took the controls from me and landed. It was decided that I would stay with the Post until I had more experience.

Later, Mr. King became my instructor. With him, I did all the things that all combat pilots would learn and live by: slips, slides, split-S maneuvers, rolls, touch-and-goes, vertical stalls and recovery from spins, inverted flying, flying around pylons, and, finally, deadstick landings. I was good, and I knew it, but I also learned never to get cocky enough to think you cannot make a mistake. It only took one error in judgment or a second of inattention to detail to end your flying career or your life.

About seven hours after my first flying lesson, I was allowed to go solo, despite my less than spectacular flying that day. For some reason, my head was not wrapped around it, but King let me go. I flew the circuit, did all the great things I always did, but this time alone. I finally landed—one of the nicest touchdowns I ever made—and my instructor was there smiling. I was now a pilot with my student license. This gave me the opportunity to sometimes fly with an older professional pilot, Tedo Swain. I'd do short trips with him, and he'd let me log flight time, so by the time I was sixteen, I had thirty-five hours.

When I started Cameron Junior College at age eighteen, the dean, Dr. Clarence Breedlove, asked if I wanted to register for the civilian pilot training program. He knew I had my student license and loved flying. He did not have to ask twice, but I asked him how much it would cost me. When he said about $50, I was crushed, but I told him that I could sell my car, a 1929 Model A, and get another part-time job, as I had left the cabinet company and was working at the grocery store. It had better hours anyway.

Well, he told me not to sell the car; he would loan me the money. I guess when he saw potential as an educator, he wanted to allow the student to exploit it. I can say that he was one of the three people who really changed my future forever. As soon as the civilian pilot training program was started, about 1939 or 1940, I went through that also.

Just before this, I had met a beautiful lady, Barbara Morgan. We dated, such as it was, and I knew that she was my girl. Being with her took me out of the flying fever for a few months. I had lost focus, but she said, "If it's important to you, then finish it. You only live once, Bob." She was always supportive, and that was one of her great charms.

I took on a lot of extra part-time jobs, as a fireman, working in a ladies' department store and the grocery store, and doing odd jobs like building and repairing fences or fixing cars. Soon I was able to repay the loan with interest. It was a matter of pride for me, and that loan paid off in many ways. My instructor at the time was Duane Huscher, a really interesting guy. He had a Taylorcraft high-wing sport plane that also had a side-by-side cockpit configuration. Nice plane and bigger, more powerful, than the Post. After more hours in this plane, I completed seventy-five hours' total flying time.

In 1941 I turned twenty-one. The world was ablaze. There had been civil war in Spain, the Chinese had been fighting the Japanese for a decade, the Russians too, and Russia had gone to war against Finland. German U-boats were sinking ships every day, it seemed. American pilots had gone to China to fight the Japs, and others went to England to fight the Germans. Then came the time when Adolf Hitler was overrunning all of Europe, taking Belgium, France, Holland, Norway, Greece, Yugoslavia, Crete, and Albania, and several countries had joined up with Germany: Romania, Hungary, Bulgaria, and Italy. All we young men knew war was coming, so our entire football team decided to join the military.

We scattered to the army, navy, army air forces, and marines, everywhere. I had already signed up at Fort Sill, Oklahoma. I knew that I was totally qualified, and I had no worries—by then, I had a hundred hours' flying time. Forty-six of us were to be evaluated. The physical included blood work, urine samples, eye exams, head-to-foot orthopedic exams, psychological tests, and an interview with the flight surgeon. After the first day, there were only nine of us left. The next day, there were only six of us. The flight surgeon told me to have my tonsils removed and then await orders. As the waiting dragged on and I kept reading about the air war in Europe, the AVG [American Volunteer Group, better known as the Flying Tigers] guys, I was envious.

We were not yet in the war, but everyone I knew said it was only a matter of time. Let me tell you, every day for several weeks, I eyeballed that mailbox like a dog in front of a butcher shop window. I wanted to fly and fight, whether we were in the war or not. "Screw that," I thought, so I drove to Oklahoma City to see what was going on. I got there, and a sergeant looked at my file, pulled a folder, and said a document was missing. He pulled out a sheet and told me to get it signed. Off I went to where I was supposed to go and came back with the document. On November 11, 1941, I stood with over a hundred others and took the oath of military service.

The next day, we left on a train for Kelly Field in San Antonio, Texas. This was my introduction to military discipline. I almost felt that there had been a great mistake. I was there to learn to fly, but I ended up cleaning floors and latrines, drilling with rifles, marching, and running in something called "cadence." I wondered if they were throwing me into the infantry. We had a lot of studying to do: the Articles of War, Geneva convention, army rules and regulations, that sort of stuff. We were enjoying the first few days off when over the one radio we heard Pearl Harbor had been attacked. We heard President Roosevelt address the nation, and we knew we were at war. It was on now!

After ground school, which was really basic training, we moved on to Sikeston, Missouri, a few days after the Pearl Harbor attack, for primary flight training on several different planes. This was where I made the acquaintance of Frank K. Everest, who later became one of the world's greatest test pilots. We called him Pete.[4] He flew combat in Europe, China, Burma, and throughout the Pacific, and became a legend like Chuck Yeager. We all started our training flying in the Fairchild PT-19.[5] My flight record as a civilian was well known, and I was advised to "forget everything you know and start from scratch." I tried, but pilots are kind of like career criminals—old habits are hard to break.

During flight training, we had to follow every command immediately. No hesitation, no second guessing. If the instructor said, "Left roll, dive, climb, and level," we did it then and there. I excelled in the Fairchild PT-19 and moved on. The next bird was the open-cockpit Stearman, which I flew when it was five degrees below zero in December 1941. The Stearman was a very easy, fun plane to fly, perfect for training students. It was a very forgiving plane that allowed you to make mistakes within reason without cracking up. I learned many more maneuvers in this training program, and I also learned to hate the slow roll. It seemed quite unnatural to fly that way; I never liked it. I preferred a snap roll if one must, just to get it over with.

We were washing out guys at a horrific rate, and we had a few deaths. One poor guy died in a whiteout, impacting during a snowstorm, killing himself and the instructor. Another death was probably due to mechanical failure: the engine died, and I guess they just spun in. Some washed out for psychological reasons or other medical issues. Vertigo or violent air sickness also quickly eliminated candidates. Others just lost their nerve. The numbers dropped dramatically.

During this training, we focused heavily on formation flying, mock dogfights, and such. Pete got into trouble during a solo mock dogfight when he decided to ambush another trainer. He was on his ass, dogging him, and they even dropped to the deck, which was against the rules. Buzzing was frowned upon, and the trainer turned to engage him. Pete slipped, slid, and maneuvered away, over and around, and was always on this guy's tail.

When Pete pulled alongside to laugh at the other pilot, he realized he'd been harassing one of our hard-ass instructors. Pete took off with the instructor right behind him, but Pete pulled some things out of his ass, shook him off, and went back to base. Back in the barracks, he told us what had happened. He was sure that he was going to get dropped for showing off and not flying the regulation altitude. Ironically, he was instead congratulated on his flying. I'm pretty sure that was when they entered "fighters" into his jacket, which was how recommendations were made for bombers, transports, or fighters.*

---

* Pilots were often selected for fighters, bombers, or reconnaissance duty based on their strengths and weaknesses, with instructor evaluations being the major deciding factor.

My next new flight instructor, Phil Zampini, was a far different creature than my first instructor, Lieutenant H. E. Fulk. Zampini was senior and very detailed in everything he said and did. It was his job to reduce the numbers; to find a reason to eliminate students in order to conform to the limited quota. He was efficient and did his job, and men left for the slightest mistake. Somehow I survived the cuts, and he took a liking to me. He then taught me stuff that was not part of the flight curriculum. "These things can save your life, so learn," he would say to me. I learned a lot from him, to be sure.

I'd read in the *Army Times* that there had been a change to the regulations regarding married personnel as flight cadets. You could now be married and apply. Barbara and I wanted to get married, but we'd had to wait due to the restriction when I began my training. In those days, you had to get permission to marry from your commanding officer, and if you were in training, it went to a board. Well, I knew what I had to do. I went to see the commander, Major Rockwood, and asked permission to get married. He said he would send my request along to the Cadet Board with his positive recommendation but that I should not get my hopes up. I would see the board that evening. "Man, that was fast," I thought.

I was confident enough to send a wire to Barbara telling her to come to Sikeston so that we could get married. But later that evening, I was told no. The board did not recommend that I get married. "Well," I thought, "too bad, because she is already on the way. I'll just take my chances." All my fellow cadets knew about the wedding and were going to attend. I still do not know how the officer cadre never learned of it.

Barbara arrived on February 21, 1942, my twenty-second birthday, and we went with another cadet and his fiancée, who acted as our witnesses. The following day I was to leave for Randolph Field, Texas, for the next session. I was introduced to the North American BT-9

Yale, which was a completely different animal from all the other planes I'd flown. At this time, I was also trained on instrument flying and introduced to the Link Trainer. This was a box that encased you and was more like sensory deprivation. It was blind-flying training, totally on instruments. Then we flew the BT-9s with a canvas cover, and, being in the rear seat during flights, we had to take control and correct the aircraft, following the instructor's commands in the headset.

My instructor was a sour guy called Lieutenant M. R. Burgess, and my rapid reactions left him rather white-knuckled because I had great reflexes and started anticipating him. I had to stop that, and I did. During one of the final phases, I asked him to sign my flight log once we had landed, and he insinuated that I might not even graduate. Finally, one day he received orders, and he was gone. I was one happy man, I can tell you.

His replacement was a huge Irish monster named Lieutenant T. M. Maloney, an excellent pilot and instructor whom I liked a lot. I then had Lieutenant Farnell who, unlike Maloney, was smaller than I was. Farnell was my formation flight instructor, and he scared me. He flew so close to the other aircraft, even the other instructors' eyes would get as big as baseballs. But he was good, if a little unorthodox, and I learned all the great formation flying tactics from him. I mastered takeoff, landing, tight turns, and maneuvers in tight formation. Throttle control was critical, and you had to get the feel of it. There was a manual, and there was training, but a pilot has to have feel.

I initially trained as a bomber pilot, thank God, because we ended up in England, where we had to fly instruments and in close formation. We started night flying on instruments. After all this training, we were now groomed for the types of aircraft we would be assigned to. Bomber, transport, and fighter pilots would go on to advanced school. Most of us wanted fighters, since that was where the glory was, but we were told not to get our hopes up. The arguments were thrown around, and there was a lot of justification for going into multiengine aircraft. After the war, there would be more flying opportunities—we could be commercial airline pilots and such. It made sense. Although I wanted fighters, I guess pragmatism kicked in, and I signed up for bombers.

In May 1942 I was at Kelly Field to learn how to fly bombers. I was then evaluated, eventually as a multiengine pilot. We also flew the [North American] BC-1 and [North American] AT-6 Texan, gathering experience in the low-wing, all-metal monoplanes. All had retractable landing gear and were not very forgiving if a pilot was inattentive. But we never had any twin-engine planes to train on, which I thought was odd. We trained again on instrument and radio-beam flying in all kinds of weather, and eventually I racked up three hundred hours of flight time. Our last major requirement was a formation flight cross-country to Douglas, Arizona, and back. On return, we received our wings on July 2, 1942. Boy, that was the proudest day of my life next to the day that Barbara married me.

After graduation, I requested to fly Douglas A-20 Havoc twin-engine medium bombers, with duty near home at Oklahoma City. My second choice was Seattle, Washington, and my third choice was Florida. But wherever people are needed, that's where the bodies go. When my orders came in, I was assigned to fly Republic P-47 Thunderbolts in Connecticut. I was going to fly fighters! I was happier than an Irishman on Saint Patrick's Day with an open bar. My world seemed to be just perfect. I wrote home to tell my family that I had finally made it.

I was assigned to a new unit, the Sixty-First Squadron of the Fifty-Sixth Fighter Group. I was tickled to death, and our group was the first to get the P-47. We started flying the B model, which killed a couple of boys in training. They figured out that manipulation of the throttle control, especially when landing, was probably the problem. In many other aircraft, you cut the power and glide in, almost gliding into the landing without much difficulty. With the P-47, you had an aircraft that weighed seven tons dry, the heaviest single-engine fighter of the war, and it was not a forgiving aircraft. In landing, you had to maintain a certain RPM and altitude to maintain control. If you lost power, that big bastard Pratt & Whitney was a hard thing to fly, let alone land, unless you had a lot of runway, because you would not have much surface control maneuverability at low speed. It pretty much required a straight shot in unless you were a very experienced Thunderbolt pilot.

This was where I met and became good friends with Neel Kearby, a great pilot. We would be in England together, and he would later be the first guy to take P-47s to the Pacific. He scored twenty-two kills and got the Medal of Honor, but sadly, he was killed in a ground attack mission over there. He was a good man, and Barbara and I both liked him very much. It seemed the war just ground up the best and spit them out—the best of us and the enemy, too.

The number and sheer volume of manuals on the P-47B were incredible. We had to pass written tests as well as the flying proficiency exams. It was like being students again but without the hard-core, boot camp discipline. The atmosphere was informal and relaxed, which in my opinion was the way transition schools should be, especially for fighter pilots. I sat in the cockpit for hours learning everything there was to know, with First Lieutenant Gerry Johnson as my instructor pilot.[6]

He became a great pilot in Europe and eventually a POW. There were four Johnsons in our group and three in my squadron at various times. We were called the "Redneck Rodeo" and the "Johnson

Brothers," although none of us were related. Once, when I later received a big ass-chewing in England, Gerry came to me as my flight leader and asked me not to get into trouble unless they had my first name correct in the MP [military police] report. He did not want to be confused with me. I had sort of developed a reputation.

We went on to fly the P-47C and later D models. Flying the "Jug" required total concentration, especially since the stall speed was 105 miles per hour, which was the average cruising speed of the planes I'd flown before. On my first flight, I learned to keep pressure on the right rudder to keep her straight due to the massive engine torque. I know for a fact that a couple of our training pilots' accidents were due to this very factor. A ground loop was not the best way to impress the flight instructors.

Well, my first flight was almost my last. I was almost at takeoff speed when the canopy release snapped and popped back, slamming the canopy bar into my forehead. I saw stars and all. I radioed the tower, chopped the throttle, and applied the brakes to slow down and pull off. I closed the canopy and then revved up the engine to take off again. I thought it was locked, and when I hit eighty-five miles per hour, the same thing happened. The canopy lock did not engage again, so it rolled back, and again I took a whack to the noggin, but I said screw it. I reached takeoff speed and pulled back on the stick, even with the air rushing into the cockpit.

I closed the canopy again, retracted the gear, and increased the throttle. The roar of two thousand horsepower is not something that fails to impress. I increased power again and pulled the nose up, and it screamed higher into the sky. I knew that I had a real racehorse here. Our flight reached ten thousand feet rapidly in comparison to all the other planes we'd flown. The big, thick-bladed propeller ate into the air, pulling that big bird like an angel. Sure, she was a big bastard, well built, but that engine was a dream.

Landing this thing the first time was also an exercise in panic. I came in, reduced power, lowered the landing gear, and hit the flaps. The right flap worked, but the left stayed up, forcing the plane into a left turn at low speed. This is when you either come to terms with your skill or become a statistic. I raised the one good flap and the landing gear and increased throttle. I radioed my problem to the tower, and was told to manually cycle to hydraulic equalizer and then work the flaps again. The assumption was that I was not getting equal pressure to the flaps. If that were the case, then what about my hydraulics to the other control surfaces? I followed the instructions, but the left flap would not fully extend, so I went with half flaps and came in. It was a perfect landing under imperfect conditions. I was past scared; I was pissed off.

We learned that any new aircraft could have problems that were not yet worked out. The R-2800 engines were new, and my flight, like many others, would lead to vast improvements in all the parts of the Thunderbolt. The hydraulic issues were just one concern. I'm convinced that the men who died in training on the P-47 did not die because they were bad pilots. They died because of problems like these. I was lucky enough to have my issue detected early in my approach. Otherwise, I would have inverted and pancaked, no doubt, and I would not be here telling you this story.

We lost eighteen or nineteen pilots and just as many fighters in transition training on the P-47. It's also true that our runway was not the best place for this fighter. It was about three thousand feet long, but it was ringed by houses and high-tension wires. Rob Roberts came in and badly damaged a house with his landing strut due to these conditions. He managed to land perfectly, and the fighter was fine, but the bathroom in the house had ceased to exist! Rob was unaware of the damage he'd done to the house, and he took a lot of ribbing about that for months to come.

We learned just how good the P-47 was when we engaged in mock combat with our navy adversaries, and they flew the Chance Vought F4U Corsair, which had the same engine. These engagements proved invaluable to us all. This was where you learned the strengths and weaknesses of your aircraft, as well as improved your abilities as a pilot. Learning about tight turns, fast rolls, and teamwork was essential. The Corsairs were more maneuverable, like our enemies would be, so we learned how to exploit our two advantages: the ruggedness of the airframe, and those eight .50s [.50-caliber machine guns] that could throw out 7,200 rounds per minute. I would later see just how effective those suckers were.

In September 1942 we received our new commanding officer, Major Hubert A. "Hub" Zemke, who became a legend and even perhaps the greatest fighter leader in the US Army. He had learned fighter tactics in England and Russia, and his experience and knowledge went into creating Zemke's Wolfpack. I found out after the war that the Luftwaffe boys all knew who we were. German intelligence had dossiers on all the best American and RAF units and pilots, as Zemke, Gerry Johnson, and Francis S. Gabreski found out during interrogation when they became POWs. The Germans knew about me, Walker "Bud" Mahurin, and Dave Schilling—everyone.[7] Gabby Gabreski said that they even had his service record, and they knew everything, including where he went to school as a kid in New York. I found that incredible. We knew some things about a few of the top German pilots, but for the most part, they were just names that meant nothing to us. I learned a lot more later from a British pilot.

One of the things we learned about was something we had never heard of before called "compressibility." If you put this big fighter in a dive in the thin air at higher altitude, you might not be able to pull out of it. Many pilots in various types of fighters had found this out, but few had lived to tell about it. I learned my lesson at about thirty-two thousand feet. I rolled her over and put her in a high-speed dive. At about fifteen thousand, I tried to pull out but could not move the joystick. I pushed against the instrument panel and tried with all my strength, and it was the worst feeling I had ever had. I thought I was a dead man.

Once I dropped to about eight thousand feet, there was enough air to provide resistance, so I lowered the flaps and adjusted the trim to get as much air resistance as I could. It worked, but the g-force against me made me gray out. My vision blurred, and my head felt like it was coming off. I was soaked with sweat despite the bitter cold of winter. My heart was pounding so hard I could hear it. Lesson learned.

Some pilots crashed and walked away, totally destroying the fighter. The Jug was that rugged—a design feature that would save my life on more than one occasion in combat. Milton Anderson, another good guy, learned just how rugged it was when he once lost power on takeoff. His engine blew, and, with his gear still down, he put the nose down to maintain airspeed. He cartwheeled across the water in Long Island Sound, the wings and tail folding up and wrapping the cockpit like a shroud. I knew he was dead. We just wanted to get his body. But there he was, strapped in the cockpit, and he got out and swam to shore as we stood there watching him. It was incredible, really.

On November 24, 1942, we received our orders for England. We spent weeks getting ready, working sunrise to sunset taking airplanes apart and crating up everything right down to the field markers. It was around Christmas, and I was with Barbara, who was going back home to Oklahoma. I hated to see her go, and she really hated that I was going to war, but she clearly understood. As I watched the train pull away, I decided I was not going to die in this war. I was coming home. A couple of days later, we shipped off to Camp Kilmer, New Jersey.

We left the United States on the original *Queen Elizabeth* ocean liner late on the night of January 5–6, 1943, and arrived in Glasgow, Scotland, on January 12. Some of the guys got very seasick. It was very cramped quarters, as there were twelve thousand guys or more on the ship. The funny thing is, we were fourteen to a cabin that was designed for two occupants. That gives you an idea, I guess. The food was horrible.

My biggest fear was getting torpedoed. I sat in my cramped quarters and wondered—if that happened, an entire fighter group would be lost without ever firing a shot. I'd read reports about German subs sinking ships all over the East Coast. On the night of January 9, my fear was almost realized when a ship right next to us took a couple of torpedoes. The explosions racked through the ship, and we felt the shock wave. The next night we had a man-overboard call, but that was simply a way of stating the obvious. He was gone; no stopping to retrieve anyone. That was when we knew the war was for real.

After arriving in Scotland, we had a few days, and I saw my first Spitfires. We then boarded the train to England and saw P-47s. After we got situated, we met a British pilot in London, a nice guy who had been fighting in fighters, Hurricanes and Spitfires, since 1940. He was a sergeant, only twenty-one years old, and already an ace with seven kills. He had been shot down twice: once, he bailed out in the channel, and the other time, he crash-landed at his base after getting nailed. We were commissioned officers. He had to salute us, which he did in snappy British fashion, but to us, he was the superior man. He'd been in the Battle of Britain, and flown over France, Holland, and Belgium. We wanted his intel, for sure.

Our friend was a wealth of information. He told us the weak and strong points of the two primary German fighters, and this is the kind of stuff you pay for. We bought the beer, and he gave us all he had. He told us everything about the Messerschmitt 109—he had actually test-flown a captured and repaired Messerschmitt. He told us about the Focke-Wulf 190s, and how they were a very dangerous and different kind of animal. He also told us he had spoken to a German fighter pilot who had been shot down. On that very same mission, the German had shot down two of our British friend's colleagues and had forced our new friend to belly in due to damage. The German had followed suit and crash-landed right near him after his radiator was shot out.

The guy spoke perfect English, had gone to school in England, and had a dozen or so kills. Our friend said the German claimed that twenty or fifty kills for a German pilot was nothing, and a few of their guys had over one hundred kills. We were stunned at this information. This was the first time I'd heard of Adolf Galland, Werner Mölders, Wolfgang Falck, and the like, although I would meet Galland and Wolfgang Falck long after the war.[8] This RAF pilot was a real vault of information, and we loved the guy. He also recommended a hotel, and we followed his sage wisdom.

I found out that first night what the "blitz" was all about. I was almost asleep when explosions blew me out of bed. I looked out the window and saw explosions and thousands of tracers from the antiaircraft guns and heard the rapid *thump-thump-thump* as the tracers disappeared into the black sky. The searchlights, hundreds of them, were sweeping the sky, crisscrossing each other in a dazzling light show. "So, this is war," I thought to myself. I could only imagine what the civilians were going through.

We took sightseeing tours all over the city until our planes were ready; I loved Saint Paul's Cathedral and Westminster Abbey. Poets' Corner was always my favorite place. I was standing on historic ground far older than our own country. Our B model planes were given to the Fourth Fighter Group, whose three squadrons had already been in the war for a couple of years as the Eagle Squadrons [American volunteers], flying the Supermarine Spitfire for the Royal Air Force [RAF]. We instructed them on how to fly our planes, and they showed us a little bit about flying combat. Later, in early February 1943, we received our own planes, the new P-47C model with the improvements I mentioned earlier.

We were on a Royal Air Force Hurricane base near an RAF Spitfire unit. They were flying the Mark V version, which was legendary even then. When the Brits saw our big Jugs, they said we were dead men. They told us we could not dogfight with the Germans—not even the Spits could match them in firepower. They could outturn the 109s and 190s, but the 190s were faster and could climb and outdive them. They [190s] could also take a lot more damage than a 109, as they were rugged and had air-cooled radial engines. The four .20-millimeter cannon and two cowling-mounted machine guns were to be feared— but not as feared as the Germans flying them.

One of the Fourth Fighter Group guys we spoke with was Colonel Donald Blakeslee, who was an excellent fighter pilot.[9] Although he was American, Don had gone to Canada and trained and flew with the British for over a year before being brought into the US military. We asked him and his men about the warnings we had received from British pilots about the Luftwaffe fighters and pilots. Blakeslee was very similar to Zemke; a man of few words and to the point:

"Boys, come into this war thinking you're a cowboy and going to bag a lot of Germans, you will die quickly. These German pilots are no fools. They have a lot more experience, and many have a lot of kills. They did not get those Iron Crosses by being faint of heart or not knowing their business. Learn all you can before you get into the air against them, because once you're there, it's too late."

We also spoke to a couple of other guys in the Fourth Fighter

Group who landed at our base in Spitfires. They still had their old planes, and their Spitfires looked beat up all to hell. One came in slightly smoking. When the pilots got out and lit their cigarettes, one guy's hands were shaking like crazy, and he could hardly hold the lighter. He looked like he'd been ridden hard and put away wet.

I wanted to talk to this guy, and so did the others. Come to find out he had flown over thirty sorties with a couple of kills, a seasoned veteran. He told us that they were on a bomber escort mission, picking up B-17s returning from a strike, when their seven-plane formation was bounced by two Fw 190s. They were the only two to make it back so far, but they knew that three of the guys went down, and they'd seen one parachute.

"Did you guys get those two 190s?" I asked. He looked at me and took a long drag on his cigarette. "No," he said. "We were totally outclassed. They were yellow-nosed bastards. Watch out for them; they are the best in the German air force. Some of those guys have dozens of kills on their rudders. Don't fuck with them. Run like hell unless you bounce them from altitude, and if you attack, fire and keep running, and don't look back."

Blakeslee was standing there and echoed the warning. "Listen to him. The only way you are going to get these guys is teamwork and luck. Maintain high altitude. If you get separated from your squadron, or even your flight, you're not coming home. I saw a German shoot down four Spitfires all by himself in a two-minute fight, and I don't think anyone put a bullet in him. Then he climbed and was gone. He and his wingman shot down seven planes. It was over that quick. This is what the real war is about." No more sobering talk had ever occupied my time. We Fifty-Sixth guys just looked at each other.

Zemke agreed with Blakeslee and had further words of wisdom. "There are two fighter groups over there," he told us, "and these guys are there for a reason. They know when the escorts have to turn back, and then they knock the living shit out of our bombers. But a few of these guys will come looking for you, too. These are the ones to worry about. I spoke to an S-2 [military intelligence below division level] guy, and we know where their bases are. Bombers hit them on occasion, and we can escort them, but remember: they're over friendly territory. Shoot them down, and they're right back in the air. You go down, and it's all over. Always work as a team—no less than four ship elements—and always coordinate. Communication is the big thing. Be aware and be in contact *always.*"

Long before we even saw combat, we had our asses chewed for low-level flying. Gabby, myself, and a few others had been doing mock dogfights with Hurricanes, and that was a blast, but then we buzzed the neighboring village. It was not the first time, and the locals were complaining about having their homes rattled and livestock scattered from the roar of our engines. One complaint was that P-47s were flying so low the local mailman on his bicycle had to hit the deck when two fighters passed just a few feet over his head. He was able to get a couple of the call letters on my fighter.

Well, that was a dressing-down we did not need. After Zemke finished, he laughed his ass off. But he finished it off with a warning: "Do not at any time even entertain the thought of doing it again." We also had a small problem with rowdiness in the barracks. At Kingscliff [RAF air base], some of the guys—no names, mind you—liked to practice their shooting skills with their service pistols. Eventually there were a lot of .45-caliber holes in the walls and ceiling. We heard about that later in another ass-chewing we did not need.

On April 4 all sixty-four fighters took off for our new base at Horsham Saint Faith, near the city of Norwich. Our squadron leader, Major [later Major General Loren G.] McCollom, called us all in, obviously upset. He brought up the bullet holes in the old barracks and wanted names. He went down the line, asking for one of us to cough up the guilty ones. Dick Allison was the guy who started it, usually when drunk, but he owned up. He would come in late, throw the lights on, and empty his pistol, scaring the hell out of us. We finally had enough of that bullshit, and we all decided to give him a taste of his own medicine. We sat up one night, waiting for him. We were going to fire the pistols and a rifle into the ceiling to scare him. He did not come, so we got bored and fired into the ceiling anyway. Some time passed, and then as we lay there in the dark, the door burst open, and Dick walked in shouting and firing his pistol. That bastard was good at the ambush.

When Major McCollom finally got to me, I admitted that I'd fired a few rounds. But in my defense, I assured him I hit the bull's-eye, a knothole in the wood that was perfectly removed. He was not amused. In the end, seven of us all shared responsibility for the damage and got two weeks' restriction for this escapade. This was the start of my reputation. But the war was still young.

The guys from Jagdgeschwader 2 [JG-2, Richthofen] and Jagdgeschwader 26 [JG-26, Schlageter] were the two premier Luftwaffe fighter units on the Western Front based in France at that time. Most of the guys were around Abbeville, right across from us. That was JG-26, and these guys were real hotshots. That was how I received my combat and aerial gunnery training—against the best the Germans had.

On April 8 some of our guys went up with the Fourth Fighter Group pilots to get some experience. I couldn't go, but when they came back, they seemed to verify what we had been told. Two Spits had been flamed, hit-and-run, with no German losses. My first mission in the P-47 was April 13, 1943. This was a massive operation: we were to join an entire wing of Spitfires flying above thirty thousand feet, with us at twenty-five thousand, but we had no contact with the enemy. A couple of days later, they went out again, and I was the watch officer—no flying. The Fourth Fighter Group tangled with those Abbeville boys and lost two more.

My next mission was on April 17, but, again, no contact. April 29 was a day to remember: the entire group except me went up again and again got involved with JG-26, which Galland had commanded for a while—these were the guys to be feared. We lost two planes and two pilots [who became POWs], and three P-47s written off due to damage. Not a single German had been shot down. Morale was not at its best, I can tell you. This is not like losing a football game.

————

The next mission of note was May 3, 1943, when we went up in force. I was happy as hell to be flying.

These were "Ramrod" missions, our name for bomber escort before turning back. This was really where a fighter earned its pay, keeping those guys alive. I hated the thought of being in one of those big-assed targets. We met with the bombers right as the flak came up. It was madness: the whole sky turned black, and we were high cover also; about two hundred P-47s and Spits in the air. The fighters usually stayed away until we turned back, then slammed into the bombers. Most often, we only got to grapple with the enemy fighters as they attacked the stragglers when the bombers were on the return trip.

The radio came alive as someone called out the one call that makes every fighter pilot lock on: "Bandits, eleven o'clock low!" Then the calls kept coming all over the place as the fighters ignored us and ripped right into the bombers. Yellow-nosed 190s and 109s. Zemke hit the rudder and peeled over, so three of us stayed with him close behind. Two roared past in front of Zemke and past me. I panic-fired; hit nothing. Two more that had attacked from above dived away right in front of me while my guns were still firing. I damaged those two, saw the hits, and pulled up, but stalled and fell away. I recovered but was at twenty thousand feet, well below twenty-five thousand for safety.

I'd really screwed up. I was all alone.

After a few minutes, I saw some P-47s and raced to get to them for protection. I was feeling a lot better until I realized that the planes I was catching up to headed north were instead four Fw 190s! They had not seen me, so, sweating even more, I peeled left and gave it full throttle, remembering Zemke's words of wisdom about always maintaining contact. I also remembered to never look back. I had no chance against these four guys, even if I got two of them. I may be hardheaded, but I'm not stupid.

I made it back to discover Zemke had reported me as missing in action because they thought I'd been shot down by the two fighters that had passed me on the first attack. The two I hit that forced me to climb were followed by the other two, and my Jug lost speed so fast, the 190s flew past me and broke off. The rest of the flight broke and headed for home due to fuel, and they lost sight of me. I knew none of this. I got my ass chewed, but I learned something valuable: never leave your wingman, especially if you are covering him *and* especially if he is your group leader.

May 19 was a "circus" [decoy aircraft ahead of the main force] to draw enemy fighters. The bombers would be escorted, and we would fly around looking for the enemy. We were over the Dutch coast when the call came out: two enemy fighters high on our six [the six o'clock position, directly behind the pilot], but very far away. We could outrun them, so they were not a threat, but I had a feeling they had radios and were calling their friends. I later learned that they were decoys hoping to get some of us to peel away. Soon we were hit from above.

We were at thirty thousand feet, and flashes erupted all around my fighter. My dumb ass thought it was flak until I rolled right, looked back, and saw the 190s. I started a split-S and then went into an inverted dive, and the German started to do the same maneuver in the opposite direction. Had I completed the maneuver, he would have ended up right on my tail. My decision to race west was the smartest move in my life. If I'd pulled out, the German would have had me. So far, we had lost several planes and pilots, without a single victory for the group.

June 12 saw our first kill in the melee with the Abbeville boys, when Captain Walt Cook nailed one. I had failed to take advantage of an opportunity, and I was kicking myself for being afraid of getting chewed out if I broke formation again. The next day, we took off from our base at Horsham Saint Faith at 0900 hours for a sweep over Ypres, Belgium, which was just about the extent of our range. We were flying southwest to rendezvous with the returning bomber group.

At about twenty-seven thousand feet, we saw about twenty Fw 190s flying at approximately twenty thousand feet. A dozen of them were in one tight formation. There was a four-plane formation on the near side of their group. Our group leader, Lieutenant Colonel Zemke, was leading seven P-47s. He screamed in and shot down one of the 190s, then hit another but only damaged him, and then shot down a second one for sure, hitting both from the flank diving in. They never saw him coming in on them.

Well, I increased the power and streaked right past my squadron leader and flight commander, First Lieutenant Gerry Johnson and Major Gabreski. I remember hearing them screaming in my headset, but to be honest, I could not, and still to this day cannot, remember what they were saying. I was in the zone. As a boxer, you get into that area where you see the weak spot in your opponent. That is the spot you concentrate on. This Fw 190 had a weak spot: behind the cockpit midway to the tail section. Being an air-cooled radial engine like ours, it could take more damage than a liquid-cooled engine like the 109 or a North American P-51 Mustang [serving as a fighter and fighter-bomber]. He did not see us, and I knew I could hit him in his ass.

Well, this was when I got inspired. I got one of the very first enemy aircraft destroyed by our unit, and I broke all the rules and regulations to do it. I was supposed to fly top cover in the rear, but I flew past Zemke to shoot down the leader of an eight-plane formation of Fw 190s. My back was to the sun, I had a height advantage, and I had eight .50-caliber machine guns. I closed on the flight of 190s fast and focused on the flight leader. There was no reason to lead him, so I just let his wings fill the gun sight. I closed and fired, and the noise and shaking of my guns scared me. I thought I'd been hit, but the 190 broke apart, and I continued to shoot past and pulled left and up, climbing away from anything on my ass. The pilot could not have survived. He was screwed.

I saw more enemy fighters about a thousand feet below us and headed north. The rest of the 190s broke away, scattered, and ran for the deck, headed east. This day really stands out. We were fighting quite a few of them, and I passed by one 190 and his wingman so close, and I could clearly see the pilot. He had a white scarf and blue eyes, and his rudder must have had fifty kills painted on it. Our wingtips were probably ten feet away at the point we zoomed by each other, going in opposite directions. I learned later that he was probably Egon Mayer.[10] We would meet again very soon under quite different circumstances.

After I saw my kill break apart, I heard congratulations over the radio. But I was sometimes an idiot, like all young men. With more experience, I might have been able to shoot down two more. My fuel gauge said I needed to think about turning back, but I started chasing the remaining fighters, although the rest of the group had already headed to base. I mathematically calculated I could hang around for about ten more minutes before I had to go.

What I had not thought about was the fact that I was all alone, and if I had unwelcome visitors, it might end badly for me. At that moment, I felt kind of lonely and vulnerable, and I knew I'd be in trouble when I landed. It also occurred to me that if I bailed out that I would become a prisoner, which was not what I had in mind for R & R [rest and recreation].

I arrived back at home base late because I'd broken contact to go looking for more enemy planes and was called in to Zemke's office on arrival. Gerry Johnson, Gabreski, and Hub Zemke were there waiting for me. I knew that this was not going to be a good visit. They each took a few minutes to point out my stupidity, my lack of discipline, my failure to follow orders, and my luck at not being killed. Then they congratulated me on the kill.

I think Zemke was a little disappointed that he did not get a third kill on that mission, but he had two. He was a great leader, though. He was rigid in his application of discipline but had no problem throwing the book away and letting us do our own thing if he felt his superiors, who were not flying combat, were in the wrong—a mindset that also caused Zemke some problems of his own. After this first victory, I got a reputation as some sort of wild man. Other pilots would say, "Don't fly with Johnson, he'll get you killed."

Our missions started out escorting bombers to the maximum range of our endurance. At first, we just flew over the French coastline, and we engaged the Germans pretty regularly. Occasionally we met the enemy over the North Sea, and sometimes they came over to visit us. They would strafe the fields and that type of thing. As time went on, and we extended our missions, we sort of got to know each other better, you could say. We could just reach the German, Dutch, or Belgian borders before we had to turn back.

Later, they decided to make me a flight leader and then a squadron leader. I felt that even though I was a leader, the other guys were as good as I was, and we decided that if they were in a good firing position, they should have the lead. On one flight of eight boys, we had the four leading aces in Europe. Then we got aggressive, and everyone got competitive. We competed not only against the guys in our squadron but against other squadrons. Later, it was our group against other groups, that kind of thing. We had Gabby Gabreski, myself, Jerry Johnson, Bud Mahurin, and Joe Powers,[11] who was one of our leaders at that time. And, of course, Zemke and Schilling. We had a good crew, for sure.

We felt pretty cocky, but Zemke always tried to ground us in reality by reminding us that we were not immortal. "Stupidity is a great equalizer," he would say. He reminded us, too, that although most of us had been flying combat for about a year—some, like me, much less, and some, like Gabby, even longer—some Germans were in their fourth year of combat. He also said some had a hundred kills or more, and if we thought the enemy was not that dangerous, we should "look at the growing missing in action and casualty lists.

"I don't like writing letters to families," Zemke said. "I really hate the idea of writing to people, telling them that their father, son, or husband died because his head was up his ass. Don't make me write a your-head-was-up-your-ass letter. I will come find your corpse and kill you again if you do." He was serious. He'd gotten into a lot of trouble by doing things his own way, and I think he knew he would never make general; he had far too many political enemies. But as far as we were concerned, he was the best CO anyone could have.

———

May and June were rather busy, but I could not get any kills. We also had a hard time getting into action because the Germans wanted our bombers. They really did not seem to care much about us. They knew we had to turn back and leave the bombers unprotected. This period until early 1944 was a dismal time for the bomber guys. They had to fly twenty-five missions in order to be rotated home.

I spoke once with a bomber pilot who had just completed half that, I think. He said every man in his group knew that mathematically only three out of ten crews would survive at the current loss rate. I thought that was a high ratio and that he must have been mistaken. But then we saw the After Action Reports and lists of aircraft that failed to return. In fairness, I never met a bomber guy who blamed us. They knew we could only go so far until we had to leave them. Hopefully, they would make it back from their bombing runs to be escorted to base on the return leg.

Some missions clearly stand out for any pilot. The one that is clearest in my head took place on June 26, 1943. Forty-eight P-47s took off on a very nice, warm day. We were up in force going to meet a bomber formation coming back from hitting targets at Villacoublay, in the region around Paris. We'd heard over the radio that they'd been hit pretty hard. We were at rather high altitude, at around twenty-five thousand feet, if I remember correctly. We were nearing the rendezvous, looking for the bombers, when we were hit rock hard by a bunch of Fw 190s. These clowns had been at much higher altitude.[12]

They stormed in at max speed and hit us. I felt *thumps* in my plane, and it shook all seven tons of it. A 20-millimeter shell exploded in my cockpit, entering from the left side, striking my left hand and severing my hydraulics. I'd taken off without my goggles, which I'd sent for repair, and now I had hydraulic fluid all over the place. It was in my eyes and mouth, and my flight suit was absolutely soaked in it; you have to remember this stuff is flammable, somewhat like gasoline.

For a few minutes, I could hardly see a thing. More shells hit me, sounding like a hailstorm against my fuselage, then something banged into my head. The armor plate behind me had stopped a heavy shell, but it still knocked me forward to where I strained against my straps. The canopy had chunks shot out of it and my engine was thumping on most but not all cylinders. I felt like I was in a bathtub being hit with a bunch of sledgehammers.

I put that big-ass bird in a dive to get away from all that crap hitting me, but nothing happened: no aileron control, elevators shot, with the rudder barely functional. I became separated from the rest of the group and did not know how much longer my Thunderbolt would be airworthy or when the engine would quit. I had no surface controls and had to manhandle the rudder. I also suspected my flaps were gone.

I tried to open the canopy slightly so I could bail out if I had to. That canopy would not budge an inch. It had been hit bad enough to jam it shut. Unless I could finally get the thing open, I was going to have to ride the rodeo down, if you know what I mean. This very depressing feeling fell over me as I headed back to England. I kept looking around for friendly planes, but there was nothing. Being a flying target and unable to hit the silk depressed me even more.

Just when I thought things could not get any worse, I heard more thumping in my plane. Something nicked the tip of my nose, and I started to bleed, then I felt pain in my right leg from a bullet. Later, when they dug it out, the bullet had split in half, and I still have those two pieces. I'd been hurt worse playing football and boxing, but I'd never been that scared in my life, I'll tell you that. I was always scared—that's what made me move so quick.

Bang! I was hit again, and the fighter went into a nosedive without me doing it. Smoke started pouring in from the engine, but then it stopped.

Bang! More shells hit me, and I had a cockpit fire. A burst of flame came at me and singed my forehead, but that went out. I knew I could not dive again to get lower because I might not be able to recover due to the damage. Climbing was out of the question. Trim tabs were my only real option for maneuvering.

The next burst I felt shot away the throttle control. I now had an engine in high gear that I could not control.

I tried lowering the gear, but only one wheel came down. I started to yaw [swing sideways, left and right] so I retracted the one good wheel and figured I would try again if I made it back. Then more hits and another fire. Luckily, that went out too, but there was more smoke and the smell of melting rubber.

Another hammer blow to the left side threw me against the right side of the cockpit so hard it knocked the wind out of me. Then a real fire started. I was burning, and the smoke was so thick I could not see anything. But the wind whistling into the cockpit from the shattered canopy sucked it out. This whole time, I had been pressing the Mayday button.

I tried the canopy again: no joy, it was still stuck fast. The next blast of enemy fire ripped my oxygen mask off. The fire, I learned, was my oxygen bottle that had been hit. Then the engine oil exploded and covered the windscreen, and there was an explosion under the cowling—more oil—and something hit the windscreen so I could not see in front of me at all.

I was hit again and lost all control. I started tumbling again, and these black shapes passed by me. I'd just fallen through the bomber formation and come very close to hitting one of them. I continued to lose altitude. The glass on the instrument panel shattered like shrapnel and showered me as more rounds hit.

The fire grew and started burning my legs from under the control panel. I finally managed to get the canopy slid back about six inches. The bevel must have been dented by a shell; that's why it wouldn't go back any farther. I knew I was going to die, and I just became calm about it. I thought of Barbara and how I'd forgotten to write her in the last few days. Then I panicked again as the fire grew larger, and I took my feet from the rudder bar and put them on the control panel, getting leverage to grab the canopy bar and haul back on it. No good that time, either.

Then the fire was out; just thick black smoke. I put my mask back on, although there was no oxygen, and I was below ten thousand feet anyway. Then the smoke cleared, and I took it off.

Knowing I had to get out, POW or not, I stood on the seat and lifted. I could stick my head and one shoulder through the Plexiglas, but nothing more, so I sat back down wishing I had a hammer to break the rest of the canopy apart. By instinct, I grabbed the throttle, and somehow it worked to some degree, and I could throttle back. Then I smelled gas. Man, things just kept getting worse. I used my handkerchief to wipe my nose and eyes, which did not really help. It was soon covered in hydraulic fluid and blood.

And then things got even worse. I was looking around trying to locate any friendly planes, when I saw the plane that had probably been whacking me, but I was not sure. This beautiful light-blue, light-and dark-green, yellow-nosed Fw 190 closed on me. He was less than fifty yards behind me. Then he slid up beside me on my left and looked me over. I looked at him, and he looked at me. White scarf, blue eyes.

"*Damn.*"

I was thinking he was the same guy I'd seen before. The fighter looked the same, too. I remembered the markings and looked at the rudder. There were over fifty black vertical bars on the rudder. Of all the damned Germans to be in this situation with, I had to get an expert ace who apparently knew his business.

Then he slipped in behind me, and I just hunkered down behind my armored seat. I heard the bullets hitting the fighter, but no cannon shells. I guessed he was out of those. The last of the glass in my instrument panel flew out, and I saw sparks as the bullets hit my wings. "Great, blow me up," I thought. More bullets struck against the armor behind me. I was finally able to look out to the side of my broken canopy and saw him peel away for another run, so I pulled what I had and turned in his direction and fired. I was firing blind without a gun sight. I missed, of course.

Then he flew above me and slowed, slid over, and dropped right beside me on the right side. We looked over at each other again, and we were no more than five feet away from wingtip to wingtip. He pulled up beside me so he could see me clearly, looking my fighter over. He just slowly shook his head. I couldn't tell his facial expression until he took his oxygen mask off. We were at eight thousand feet anyway when he removed his mask. He did not smile, he did not grimace, he just stared. He shook his head three more times and tapped his head. I guess he saw even more damage. Then he nodded, gave me a wave with his left hand, and five seconds later pulled right and rolled away.

I thought he had left, but then I saw that he was behind me again. Once again, I could hear and feel the hailstorm of bullets, but then it stopped. He throttled up and came up beside me on the left again. We were over Dieppe, France, which at the time was a bastion of flak batteries. At my altitude, kids with rifles could have taken me out. Then he dropped behind me again and fired. More bullets hit the poor damned plane.

He pulled alongside for a third time. He could have given me a broadside and finished me, but he didn't. It was then that I realized what he was doing. He was actually escorting me over the coast to the channel! I could not believe it. He stayed with me for about ten minutes, until I was well within Air-Sea Rescue range. I knew I could be saved if I ditched and could get out. I opened the throttle and he did the same, staying with me as a wingman. I thought, "No one is going to believe this when I get back." Then I realized I'd been cursing at him, using language that would make a sailor cry, the whole time just talking to myself and screaming at the German. He could not hear me, but the guys back at the base heard it all. They knew my opponent's plane from my running commentary. In my panic, I'd kept the radio button pressed during the entire event.

Well, Mayday Control kept me on the radio, and, thank God, that still worked. I told them I had no instruments, no forward visibility, had regained throttle control, but hydraulics were out. Over a half hour later, they told me I was over Hawkinge Field, but my eyes were swollen and still burning, and I couldn't see anything. The only instrument that worked was my fuel gauge. Because of the small size of the field, they directed me to Manston [a large air base northeast of Kent, less than seven miles from Hawkinge]. I repeated my situation to them. Finally, I dropped the gear on their call and started to bank. I could see the field on my left but nothing forward. I just went in on instinct. I made a perfect landing, although I had to lay on the barely working left rudder to avoid crashing into a line of parked Spitfires.

I took a deep breath, then shut the fuel off, the engine off, everything electrical. I did not want to blow up after getting through all of that. I was perfectly parked between two Hawker Typhoons, as if I'd planned on lining up with them. Amazing. I crawled through the small hole in the canopy and pulled my parachute out, but it took a few minutes to squeeze through.

Later, I heard that the Sixty-First Squadron lost First Lieutenants Louis T. Barron[13] and Merle Eby,[14] and another guy, Robert Weatherbee,[15] who were all killed in action in the attack. Roger Dyer from the Sixty-Third also died. Five others made it back with heavy damage, and I think all of those planes were write-offs. Ralph Johnson had to bail out over the channel, but he was picked up and made it back to base.

I did not get my second kill until August, although there was a lot of activity. But I did get to fly the Spitfire V and IX models. They were fine-performing aircraft—not as fast as my Jug, but they could turn like hell. I learned in the Mark V not to snap roll and dive because the carburetor forced a stall until you leveled the plane. The Mark IX really had no roll rate, and it could not dive, but it could turn and climb like a banshee.

Soon we moved to Halesworth on the North Sea. We had just set up shop when [Brigadier] General [Ross G.] Hoyt arrived to decorate some of us. He gave me the Purple Heart, and Ralph Johnson and Charles Clamp [crash-landed at Manston] also received theirs. I had never even thought about it, really. Ralph earned his for the battle where he had to bail out. I missed a lot of missions for various reasons, and once I had to abort a long-range escort when my generator failed, and that pissed me off.

August 17, we had the 108-gallon belly tanks for an escort to Regensburg, in Germany. Fw 190s and Me 109s were all over the bombers, and they were going down like crazy. There must have been a hundred fighters in the attack formations.[16] We saw them hitting the bombers, and then a Messerschmitt 110 [twin-engine fighter-bomber] attacked, firing rockets. I had never seen this before, so Frank McCauley [5.5 victories] and I winged over and closed in on him. I was inverted, and I could see tracers from our two Jugs striking this guy, but the B-17 gunners hit him, too.

The sheet of flame was a couple of thousand feet, and then the plane just broke apart, and the pilot tumbled out through the long flaming torch. I passed within fifty feet of him when his parachute opened. It was an unbelievable sight. I circled, and saw his chute was on fire, and at twenty thousand feet, his canopy evaporated. "Long way down," I thought. "Long time to think about being dead." That mission cost us three pilots. Voorhis H. Day, Robert M. Stultz, and Arthur Sugas [shot down by Captain Johannes Naumann of Sixth Staffel, or "Squadron" JG-26] were gone, listed as MIA. The only upside was that we got seventeen kills as a group.

The next day, I had another kill flying with Jerry Johnson, who'd got three the day before along with [Glen D.] Shiltz, our first triple-victory pilots. Jerry called out a 109, and I went after him. He tried rolling, but I fired where I thought he would go, and he flew into my bullets. He just exploded. I flew through the fireball, which was going to be real hard, since I was in a compressibility stall. I had no control over the aircraft, but I had been there before and knew what to do. At four thousand feet, I pulled with all I had and blacked out. I came to confused and then realized I was in a power climb. Later, I would see that the stress had bent the wingtips, and the aluminum skin was rippled from the g-force that blacked me out. We had nine kills for the mission.

On October 8, 1943, I was on a mission when my wingman and I became separated from the rest of the squadron. We were returning, looking for some friendly airplanes to fly home with, when we came across some bombers we decided to escort back. We saw a plane not too far away a couple of thousand feet below us. I peeled over, went into the dive, and fired. I called it out for the confirmation. I had just shot down a Messerschmitt 110, my fourth kill, and I was feeling pretty good as I pulled up. Every fighter pilot looks to get that fifth kill to make ace. I was no different, but I did remember that "buck fever" can get a guy or his wingman killed. I'd become smarter since my ass-chewing.

As I pulled up from that dive, I saw four Fw 190s attacking the bombers. Then I saw an Fw 190 screaming at the bombers, shooting, with a P-47 blazing away right on him; then another 190 closing in behind the P-47. They were all shooting. I continued pulling up and then rolled over upside down so I could watch them some five thousand feet below me. I continued my dive inverted, shooting while I pushed the nose forward to give the necessary lead for my bullets to intercept the leader. His number three or four man pulled his nose up, shooting at me as I was coming down. I continued the attack, and just as I hit the leader, knocking him down, I felt a *thump* in my airplane. How badly I was hit, I didn't know; I was very busy.

After that, I leveled out and looked around. I'd pulled up right into the path of a group of Bf 110s and Fw 190s that were coming in behind the four fighters I'd engaged. I immediately threw the stick left and dropped the nose. Nothing happened when I hit the left rudder, and then I knew that my rudder cable was shot away. I had no rudder control at all, only trim tabs. This was very bad.

The main thing was to get clear of that cluster of enemy fighters. I dived away with the throttle wide open. My wingman got banged up a bit, but there was no great damage. Soon I saw some friendly P-47s and joined up with them. My first thought was to bail out when I learned how badly damaged I was, but I also knew the farther northwest I was, the better my chances of escape if I bailed. Once I saw friendly fighters, I felt better. I was still nervous, but I pulled up alongside them and found that I could still fly, even with thirty-five feet of rudder cable piled up in the cockpit. The planes were from the Sixty-Second Squadron, part of our group.

To be polite, I asked permission to enter the fold, and they said, "Sure, come aboard." Ralph Johnson turned out to be leading that flight. All of us pretty much knew each other. Zemke made a joke that he was certain "the redneck Johnson clan had covertly occupied the Fifty-Sixth Fighter Group with subversive tendencies." I still had the throttle wide open, and Ralph yelled over the radio, "Christ, Johnson, cut it back!" I was running away from them and thought my engine would overheat.

I chopped the throttle back, and we returned to England, landing at Boxted, the first base we came to. Ironically, we would later be stationed there as a group. There was a little opening in the clouds below, and I saw there were some runways. There was a bomber and a Piper Cub–type airplane ahead of us, and we let them land first. They said, "Bob, since you're banged up, you go in first."

I thought about it and responded, "No, I have plenty of fuel, and if I mess it up, none of you will get in. I'll just stay up here and come in last." They all landed and got out of the way. I came in a little hot, but still had aileron control—no problem there. I came in gear down, saw it was locked, and touched wheels first, then the tail wheel dropped. I had to hold the left rudder cable in my hand so I could get to the brakes. The minute I touched down, I cut power. I was pulling on the cable, using the brakes, and was able to stop. I pulled off the runway in case anyone had to come in behind me. I climbed out and walked the entire perimeter of that base because the fog was so thick, I couldn't see a thing.

I later found the other guys at the control tower waiting on me. The next morning, we looked at the airplane, which was only fifty yards from the tower, but I'd walked about two and a half miles in the wrong direction to get to that point. That was how bad visibility was on the ground. We had some guys come over and put a new rudder cable in it. There were only five holes in the fighter, but they were 20-millimeter rounds, and one had severed the cable. There was a dent in my armor-plated seat that absorbed a shell. I never felt the hit. That was how ruggedly built the Thunderbolt was. It was fifty years later before I found out that my fifth victory was Hans Philipp, a 206-victory ace from the Russian Front.[17]

On October 10 we had a Ramrod mission to Münster, Germany, escorting bombers. I took some flak—not too bad, but enough to make me nervous. Just as we saw the bombers, someone called out, "Forty bandits!" That got my attention. We dropped our near-empty belly tanks to lighten up. Then a large force of Germans streaked right into the bombers, guns just blazing. We had a great altitude advantage and bounced them.

Jerry Johnson flamed an Fw 190. I saw an Me 110 with two 190s going for the bombers and turned into them. The 190s saw me and pulled up, but I went after the 110. I fired and hit the rear gunner, and when the pilot banked left, I fired again, and the plane broke up. Like an idiot, I flew through the debris field. I could feel and hear parts of that 110 hitting me, so I gave full throttle and climbed. I looked over and saw dozens of Germans firing guns into the bombers, and some were firing rockets. Fighters and bombers fell to earth together as dozens of parachutes filled the sky. It was an incredible sight.

Then I took off after three 190s that were going after the rear of the bomber formation. I was gaining fast—maybe too fast to effectively score a kill—but I just wanted to disrupt their attack. One of the 190s saw me. Being above me, he dropped and turned into me; the other two stayed on the bombers. I finished the dive from the Me 110 kill and started climbing into the 190. I gave him plenty of lead as he came down, and my rounds hit his wings and exploded the canopy. I inverted and started my dive to avoid a stall with him screaming under me, and I saw a fire had started to burn his fighter.

I heard hammering as one of the other 190s came in and chewed my tail up. The rudder cable was gone, so I just hauled back on the stick and started another climb to get altitude. I saw a 110 firing, but he did not lead me properly and missed. I hit the rudder anyway, but there was no response. The guy then fired rockets, but they raced right by me—big bastards, too. I leveled out at thirty thousand and took stock of my situation. Screwed, with few options, and depending upon my P-47—a familiar position for me to be in by now.

I rolled the canopy back and unstrapped to bail out, but then I remembered that this was Germany and changed my mind. I grabbed the rudder cable coiling up on the floor of the cockpit, managed to get about thirty feet of it, and began pulling once I felt resistance. Nothing happened. I then saw that the rudder trim tabs worked, and I knew I had a good shot at getting home. I still had ailerons and elevators, so that was good, too. I spied a 190 in front of me and slightly below, so I dropped the nose, opened her up and closed the distance, and fired. The German plane simply disintegrated—there was no fire, nothing, just parts falling to earth, and no chute. As I climbed back for safety, Ralph Johnson and another P-47 caught up with me, and I made it back safely.

On a mission to Wilhelmshaven [Germany] on November 3, 1943, I managed to bag another 109 with those underwing rockets. When I fired, he exploded. On November 26 I took off on my first mission as a flight leader, a hop to Bremen. I'd not been in the air long before my fuel gauge showed I was losing gas at a rapid rate. Instead of leading the Sixty-First Squadron, I had to turn back, and that really pissed me off. I somehow had damage to the fuel tank that had not been detected, or I'd picked up a hit from random flak crossing the channel. Either way, I was gone, but the same thing happened to another pilot. [First Lieutenant Stanley B. Morrill, in the Sixty-Second Squadron. He lost fuel even faster and ran out trying to return. Morrill was killed when two B-24 Liberators collided upon return to Halesworth.]

On December 11, 1943, we had a Ramrod; forty-eight of us going as escort as over six hundred heavies prepared for a maximum-effort strike. We were assigned to the Third Bomb Division. We had just rendezvoused with the B-17s: we were at thirty thousand, and they were a mile below us and about four miles away. Then just before we hit the coast, we heard "Bandits!" and twelve enemy fighters were spotted just above us and a few miles out. They did not attack right away but seemed to be waiting. Once they were aligned abreast, they came after *us*, not the bombers. We knew the drill: this was a trap to draw us away from the bombers. The Sixty-Second Squadron engaged the 190s, while the Sixty-First and Sixty-Third stayed on to close with the bombers.

We connected with the "Big Friends" [the nickname for heavy bombers; fighters were "Little Friends"] and made our turn south toward Emden while increasing altitude. I'd just finished my turn when I saw two 190s coming at us. We broke, but one P-47 collided with another, and they both broke apart. As I rolled and looked over, I saw two parachutes, but there really was not much left of the two men drifting down. I felt sick. Ed Kruer and Lawrence R. Strand both were lost, just like that.

Shaking that image out of my mind, I scanned ahead and saw forty twin-engine fighters and about sixty single-engine fighters above and behind them going for the bombers. They attacked head-on, hitting the bombers hard. [Authors' note: due to Curtis LeMay's defensive box formation for heavy bombers, the Luftwaffe created a course for the new head-on attack method created by fighter aces Egon Mayer with 102 victories and Georg-Peter Eder with 78 victories.] I saw two fighters, a 109 and a 110. I went after the rocket-firing bastard. He saw me and went to the deck, and I followed him, closing in slowly. We were just off the deck when the 110 tried to slip, but I had him and fired. He broke apart.

December 22 was another good day for me and a good day for a B-17 that had some trouble. The bomber was aborting when I saw two 109s that must have seen him, too. I had Joe Perry on my wing, and we had altitude, so in we went. I closed in and killed one guy, and his friend decided to run.

The thirty-first was also good. I heard the call that there were enemy fighters, but since I could not see any, I assumed I was above them, and I rolled. I saw two Fw 190s tear into and explode two B-17s. They swung around for another head-on pass, but I was onto them. I rolled into a dive from altitude and closed quickly. They tried to slip into a cloud bank, but I flamed one. The other turned, but I got him, too.

On January 1, 1944, we received these new, big-as-hell, thick, paddle-shaped propellers specifically designed and built for the P-47. We had a chance to test them on another Ramrod to Münster on January 5. The new prop was a dream, and I realized—we all did—that with the 2,000-horsepower Pratt & Whitney engine and the propeller, we could outclimb the Fw 190A [first series of the Focke-Wulf fighters, later versions were the D and Ta 152] and all Me 109 models without fear of getting caught hanging. Once, I even outran a Spitfire IX in a climb, like he was standing still.

January 6 was another eye-opening day for me. We were over Koblenz, Germany, when we dived in on fifteen 190s. Gabby locked on to a German, and I also had one I wanted, but this guy turned out to be one of the best pilots I ever fought against. My guy turned into me and then snapped upward to the right, flashing past me, so I banked hard to get on his ass. I caught up to him, and he started twisting, rolling, slipping and sliding. Every time I fired a short burst, it was if he'd anticipated the shot, and he managed to evade my bullets as I closed in. He never made the same move twice in a row, so I could not anticipate where he would end up. This lasted for a few minutes, and then he screwed up. He rolled into a dive and continued his crazy maneuvers, but I finally fired from less than fifty yards away and flamed him. He did not get out.

One of the closest calls I had was when we had a couple of days off in London. Our train collided with a train that had stopped in front of us, and another slammed into the ass end of ours. Many people were hurt, and nine were killed on our train, but we pilots were uninjured, just shaken up a bit. When we returned to base, Zemke had gone stateside, and Dave Schilling was in temporary command. He stood us down, and we had more free time. Excellent! We felt we had earned it.

I got my twelfth kill on January 20, but that was when a new pilot, Allen E. Dimmick, was hit and killed by a 190 that I then managed to get. On January 30 I scored number thirteen, and in February I scored two in a single mission. Then we got a new pilot, a Polish fellow who flew with the RAF, Boleslaw Michel "Michael" or "Mike" Gladych.[18] He and Gabreski were old friends: Gabby had flown with the RAF Polish Squadron, since he also spoke Polish. Those two together were worth the price of admission, really. He [Gladych] had a remarkable history indeed.

Mike was an ace in Poland in 1939, and after the Germans invaded the country and won, he took off for Romania. The Romanian police caught him and put him in jail. With some inside help, Mike and the other expatriate Poles escaped. Most headed to France, some to Russia. The Gestapo put out a bounty on them, and they tracked Mike down near Lyons. The Gestapo guy was an assassin whose job was to kill, not capture, Mike, who was well known. He and Mike got into a fight, and Mike killed him, but he was blind after a blow to the head that knocked him unconscious. He woke up in an insane asylum, where the doctor managed to restore his sight. He had apparently been placed there in a case of mistaken identity.

Mike had shot down three Me 109s when he landed a Spitfire at Manston, fracturing his skull and collarbone, and he still bore the scars of that flight on his face. The strangest thing of all is that he was unconscious during at least the last fifteen minutes of the flight due to his concussion. He was found unconscious when his fighter landed, all on its own. Gabreski saw it, and the Poles, being Catholic, began thinking that Mike had some kind of God protection—angels on his wing, so to speak. They all wanted to touch him for good luck before every flight. Whenever we saw him, it was a reminder to us all of what we were fighting for.

Gabreski said that the Poles and Czechs were the bravest and toughest pilots flying with the RAF. Meeting Mike, I believed it. This guy was a complete damned madman. He heard of my story about the German pilot who could have killed me. He had one of his own: a similar event when flying Spits.[19] Later, flying in my Sixty-First Squadron, he had another similar experience. After the war, he met the pilot who had spared his life twice. Talk about luck.

Now, I have met many men I would consider brave, real heroes. But until I met Gladych, I had never met a man who did not know fear. Fear is one of those things that make us contemplate a dangerous action; think about it in order to affect a positive result with minimal risk. When it came to Germans, Gladych displayed none of that. He was a focused, one-minded killing machine, simple as that. I saw this guy throw himself into battle like a rabid boxer. There could be fifty Germans, and he would go at them, blazing away. Once, I called to him to ask if he needed help as I led the rest of the squadron in to support one of his solo attacks. He had about ten Germans around him; two were smoking. He saw us coming and said in his thick Polish accent, *"Go avay! Day are mine!"* That's what I'm talking about: no fear, just anger and a quick mind.

Some of our later work was ground attack, but the boys really got more involved in that kind of thing after I was gone. On March 2 Gabby, Powers, and I decided to strafe this airfield. There were no planes but a lot of buildings. We went in and just shot the hell out of the place, and the Germans were definitely interested in shooting us down. With our new drop tanks, we got more missions deeper into Germany, and on March 6 we had a Ramrod all the way to Berlin. Some of the guys had contact, but my flight did not until we were over Dummer Lake, just west of Hanover. There we ran into the largest number of fighters I had ever seen. So much for intelligence saying the Luftwaffe was on its last leg.

It was eight of us against what looked like two hundred Germans: fifty in the first group, more than that in the second, and twice as many specks in the sky farther north and east. They came at us head-on, and we just got tight and opened up with all weapons. Knowing Gabby was to the right a few miles, I hit the radio, letting him know that we'd found them. Then we realized why there were so many Germans: there were 1,200 heavy bombers headed back to England. That was the magnet.

Most of the Germans were Fw 190s, and many fired rockets nonstop—bright flashes of red and black, then nothing. Once a rocket hit a bomber, it was all over. I tried to engage these fighters, but once I had a good target sight, I had to clear my wingman's tail to avoid getting hit myself. Bombers and fighters were going down. The sky looked like a mushroom field: parachutes all over. I saw a B-17 above starting its death spiral, and then men were bailing out. Then I saw two 109s, and it looked as if they were shooting the men in the parachutes. I'd heard of this happening, but I'd never seen it. I decided that one of those bastards was mine.

I gave full throttle, roaring on high mercury, and closed in on one, but he must have seen me. He cut power, and I followed suit, so as to not overshoot, and I lowered my flaps a bit. I was gaining big-time, but if I overshot, he would have me. I closed in and fired, he pulled left, and I fired again—good hits—and then he jinked right and went into a dive. That fool had no idea, and I followed him. He leveled out, and I finished him off with solid hits in the cockpit. Smoke, fire, then impact. He was one dead Kraut.

Then a really odd thing happened: we were low enough to see the airfield below, and that sucker was packed with every type of Allied fighter and bomber we had. These had to be captured planes, along with a shitload of German bombers, fighters, and dive bombers. I called in a strafing attack, and we all joined in. We shattered and scattered planes and mechanics. Then we pulled up to fifteen thousand feet, and I saw a 109 streaking down to hit two of our guys. I called for them to break, and the German followed. I got on him and finished him. Later, we learned that sixty-eight heavy bombers had gone down, and we'd lost a pilot and fighter when Lieutenant Andrew B. Stauss from my squadron bailed out after Zemke scored three kills.

We all got our heads together and thought about the day's events. We all agreed on a plan, and Zemke endorsed it: to send our P-47s ahead as a screen to engage the enemy before he hit the bombers. Two days later, we tried it, and Mahurin scored three kills. The Germans really got a bloody nose, not expecting us to be thirty to forty miles ahead of the bombers. I got two kills.

Gladych got one, I think, but his story was even better. He went after a 109 and shot him up but had two 190s on his tail. Knowing this, he headed straight to the German air base below. He was maybe twenty feet off the ground when he began strafing aircraft, the 190s on his tail. Caught by surprise, the German gunners opened up and shot down their own two planes. Despite the great day, we lost five pilots. Sad indeed.

On March 15 we engaged about a hundred Germans on another bomber escort. The top cover went for the bombers, but others were up above. My guys climbed into the 190s as they dived down on us almost head-on, and both sides had guns blazing. We took hits, and they also got hit. One guy passed by me so close there could have only been inches between our wingtips, and I saw his eyes above the oxygen mask. We hit the all-call button, and almost immediately a group of [twin-boom twin-engine] Lockheed P-38 Lightnings screamed through us to get to the 190s. They also passed really close by; so close it was frightening, really.

A 190 flew right in front of me, and I blew him up. He was so close I thought I could read his instrument panel. No sooner did I pass over that flaming garbage than I saw a 190 on a P-38's ass, hitting him. I rolled and got on his tail and knocked him down.

We were in very deep shit, and I was pushing every button I could find on my radio, including SOS. I gave the location and description of the Germans, and in just a matter of minutes, we had scores of planes: P-47s, P-51s, and P-38s. It was a big turmoil, but we lost only one bomber that day due to flak. When we could find no Germans in the air on the way home, we would usually drop down and strafe anything of military value: airfields, marshaling yards, trains, boats, anything like that. The Ninth Air Force later took that habit up as they pushed ahead of our ground forces.

During the battle, I thought I'd lost my wingman, who was on his first mission. But there he was, Second Lieutenant Herbert R. Holtmeier, and he was okay. Suddenly the sky was clear—no enemy and few friendlies. Then I saw six P-47s climbing, so I radioed I would cover them. At that moment, I spied a single 109 sneaking in on their six. I was ten thousand feet above him, and I went after the guy. I had never had a triple, and I wanted one. I was on him when he slipped into a cloud bank. I pulled up and banked, and then there he was, so I closed in and fired. He was gone. Then it dawned on me: since I now had twenty-two kills, I was the top ace in Europe! I beat Mahurin by two!

We learned later that by using our advanced attack screen and engaging, and with the P-38s answering our call, not a single bomber took a hit from a German fighter. We shot down twenty-four, losing one pilot. Three months after this mission, I was credited with another kill that I'd claimed as damaged, so I had four kills on this sortie. I also realized that I was at about 175 hours of combat. At 200, we were sent home. I was just getting good at this job, so I went to see Zemke. He knew what I wanted, and he granted me an extension. He also handed me my promotion to captain. What a great day that was for me.

I learned that Jerry Johnson and Bud Mahurin were lost on March 25 while I was on pass in London with [James E.] Fields and [Evert G.] Everett [both pilots]. The day before, we had lost three other good men. They said that Jerry Johnson was shooting up a train that turned out to be a flak train, and they nailed him. The guys flying overhead said he bellied in, exchanged pleasantries with a French farmer, and headed ass over heels south toward the Spanish border. Mahurin dropped off the radar after shooting down a Do-217, whose rear gunner shot out his engine, and he bailed out. They were still laughing when they described how he was running in his parachute before he hit the ground. When he landed, they saw him cover over three miles. He was listed MIA until he later showed back up, having evaded the Germans.

———

Once D-day was over and I was gone, the push to Germany was on. [Robert S. Johnson had already been ordered back to the United States.] Ground attack missions became just as frequent as bomber escort duty. More than other fighters, the P-47 was really built for ground attack. In addition, once we had auxiliary fuel tanks, our range increased greatly. We had maybe another thirty minutes of flight time unless we engaged enemy fighters and had to drop the auxiliary tanks. We started off using the fuel in our extra tank and then switched to the internal tanks. You did not want to get caught in battle with a few hundred extra pounds on your aircraft.

Ground attack missions were the most dangerous, no doubt about it. When you went in to strafe or drop a five-hundred-pound bomb on a point target, you were exposed to all the evil Hitler had to offer. I know that many men who were not religious got religious pretty quick after their first few ground attack missions. I saw some planes come back that looked like scrap. I could not believe that they actually flew that garbage back. Jimmy Stewart [not to be confused with the actor and bomber pilot] brought back a third of a telephone pole stuck in his wing after strafing the airdrome at Lille, France.[20]

Light flak could get you more easily, although you were pretty safe from the heavy 88-millimeter and 105-millimeter flak guns that really whacked the bombers. Machine gunners could get you if you attacked troop convoys, trains, or airfields. As I said, most of the ground missions started after I left, and I think that is another good reason why I am still alive. An awful lot of guys who flew aerial combat with me ended up as POWs or were badly shot up doing that kind of business.

On a long-range escort, bombers going to Poland, on April 9, we met the bombers over Denmark. We also met the Germans. Fw 190s came from everywhere, going for the B-24 Liberators. Sam Hamilton and I had sixteen 190s coming right at us, and we did not flinch. As they came down, we met them in a climb, then fired. They scattered, and I banked hard and started chasing them. My belly tank would not release, so I was stuck with this thing under me adding drag and reducing my airspeed. Hamilton chased some to lower altitude, and I had two on my tail.

I was busy trying to shake these guys off when Hamilton called that he was in trouble, so I rolled and saw him three miles below me with two 190s. I went down and saw him dealing with one in front and one behind him. I was closing in when he shot down the one in front. I spooked the guy behind him, and when he turned, Hamilton got him, too. Then a third one came in to get Hamilton, and I went into a right tight climbing turn into him. I was climbing at full throttle, and he tried to catch me but stalled out. That was when I turned, rolled, and went after him, but he had already turned and was heading right at me. I fired, he weaved, and then I got two strikes on him. He headed for the coast with me chasing him. He must have been badly damaged because the canopy rolled back. As he was climbing out, I fired, and the bullets knocked him back in the cockpit. Good kill, and he was a damned great pilot, too.

April 13 was another Ramrod. Near Munich, I saw three Fw 190s trying to creep into the bomber formation. I called them and led the planes into an attack. I lit up one 190, and he disappeared into the clouds, but then I saw him, or at least his plane, again. He'd bailed out, and my wingman almost flew into the dying Focke-Wulf. Then, not long after, I spotted another 190 far below, sweeping over the deck along the canals. I swooped down and wanted to get him from behind, but he saw me and turned into me. That's what I would have done. He fired and slid to his right, I slid left, skidded, and fired, and he ran right into my rounds. I got him, too. I now had twenty-five air victories.

We were sometimes grounded due to bad weather, but that kept the Germans down, too. Things started to pick up in May and June. We were often paid visits by high-ranking brass, including General James Doolittle and many others who wanted to meet successful units and pilots. We got a lot of press when the big brass came by the bases. Sometimes we would meet bomber pilots and crews. Hearing their stories made me realize just how serious our job was.

I'm often asked about my most memorable missions, and I have to say that, eliminating those where I scored great victories, one Ramrod mission to Berlin was the most vivid and horrifying event I ever saw in my life, before or since. I was flying high cover when I saw a P-51 chasing a 109. I dropped to a thousand feet above them in case the Mustang got unwelcome visitors. The 109 pilot was good, but his plane was not—the Mustang was eating him up. It was maybe just over a hundred feet behind him when he finally jumped from the fighter. I was close enough by that time to see the German pull the ripcord on his parachute.

Then the unthinkable happened: the Mustang could not avoid the flipping German. He crashed into the propeller, crushing the hub. The torso stayed on spinning wildly, as the arms, legs, and head flew away piece by piece. The Mustang pilot rolled the canopy back to jump, with pieces of that German still on the front of his plane. His windscreen was covered in blood and body parts, but I got beside him and gestured him to stay; it could still fly. Then another P-47 got on his left side. We motioned that we would escort him home.

We finally crossed the channel and escorted him back to his home field. He lowered the gear and flaps and just set it down. We circled until he got out, to see if he was all right. When he did climb out, he took one look at the bloody aircraft and started throwing up. We waggled our wings and went home. On the way back to base, I kept thinking, "That guy is going to live with that image for the rest of his life." I was just a witness, but it still comes back to me sometimes. I can only imagine what it would be like if it had happened to me.

On May 8 we did a Ramrod to Brunswick, Germany, with almost a thousand bombers: B-17s and B-24s. I just happened to look at the formation inbound to the target when I saw a flash, and a B-17 suddenly exploded. Then I saw fighters coming down from very high altitude. I called it out, and we all banked left at full throttle. An Me 109 came down through the formation right under me, and I turned to get on his tail. He cut power, so I did the same and stayed on him. Then he increased power and rolled over into a dive, almost the worst thing to do against a P-47. I caught him and fired, and he disintegrated.

I rejoined the rest of the guys who were still upstairs, and we went to the bombers. Then the radio roared out, "Bandits! Three o'clock low going into clouds!" I looked but could not see anything. Two P-47s went into the clouds to find them and almost immediately came screaming back out with three 190s on their asses and closing. I told them to turn right and climb full power, and they started to leave the three Germans behind. I rolled from above and got in behind the 190s, locked on to the lead, and fired. A few hits, and he broke off, but I then fired on the second guy—a definite cockpit kill. Then fire as it rolled over and exploded below.

When I landed, I had twenty-seven kills. I taxied to the edge of the apron, holding up two fingers. I had broken the golden twenty-six victories held by Rickenbacker, and the ground crews went nuts. I got out, and all kinds of brass were there, reporters, everybody. Generals and mechanics shook my hand, but the most important thing was Zemke's smile. "You proved me wrong; you're not dead. Pack your trash, Johnson, and get the hell out of here. You're going home."*

I flew a total of ninety-one missions and got my twenty-sixth and twenty-seventh victories, a Bf 109G and an Fw 190, on my last mission, May 8, 1944. Later, they gave me credit for an additional airplane, which made number twenty-eight. In 1994, however, I was informed that they had gone through and recounted the records, and I was officially credited with twenty-seven. They gave me credit for

---

* "Once Bob got those two kills," Hub Zemke recalled later, "I knew he was headed for a ticker tape back home. I hated to lose him, but he had lived through so many close calls, I think it was about time to get him the hell out of there."

the two in one mission and Ralph Johnson one. Actually, it should have been reversed: I got one. I did not fly on the day of the double victory for Ralph.

From the Fifty-Sixth Fighter Group, only Francis Gabreski scored more kills than I did. We were very competitive, as all fighter pilots are. Gabreski continued to fly after I'd left. He went down on July 20, 1944, soon after scoring his twenty-eighth victory, and became a prisoner of war. He went on to become an ace in Korea with 6.5 victories. Hub Zemke was also shot down and taken prisoner, but I was already gone by that time, too.

Regardless of how successful we were or how competitive, Hub always said that he would nail any man's hide to the wall if we risked or lost a fellow pilot due to seeking a kill. I remember a meeting we had not long after my ass was chewed for the first kill. "Gentlemen, I want you to be aggressive. Kill the bastards and protect the bombers. That's what we are paid to do. But if you ever leave a fellow pilot in danger or lose him or sacrifice a bomber for a kill because your kill is more important, I will court-martial the living hell out of you. I do not want you to be confused about this." He was serious, too!

Later, many of the guys went on to fly Mustangs, and most loved it more than the P-47. Hub Zemke liked the P-51 because it had great range, but he put one in a dive like he was still in a P-47, and when he pulled out, he ripped the wings off that airplane. That was how he became a POW. Ironically, years later, he admitted that going down and becoming a POW probably saved his life, because he had later gone to command the 479th Fighter Group flying the P-51D after I left, and they were the greenest boys in the theater.

Until I left our base on May 8, 1944, I was kept in a rest and recuperation home, where I damned near went nuts. There was nothing to do; it was a miserable place. I left for home on June 6. They did that so I could be around there for D-day, but I was not aware of that event until it happened. [D-day was kept top secret until the final hours and was on a need-to-know basis.] That was how tight security was. I tried in every possible way to fly combat for two more weeks when I arrived at the rest home. Their answer was, "No, go home and get fat." I was never allowed to fly combat again.

I had a chat with General James Doolittle and asked him what I could do to stay, since others had flown a hundred missions and extended. Chuck Yeager did it, and Gabreski was allowed to stay. He said that the order came from Washington. Since I'd been the first fighter pilot in Europe to break Rickenbacker's record, I was something of a show piece. I would join Richard I. "Dick" Bong from the Pacific, who also broke Rickenbacker's record.[21] We were to tour the country together with movie stars and such, selling war bonds and keeping people's spirits up. They did not want to take the distinction of breaking Rickenbacker's score from me. That's probably why I am still here.

Dick Bong had shot down his twenty-seventh plane two weeks before I got mine, and he was already home when I returned. He was a quiet guy who did not like all of the publicity and questioning by the press. When I walked in, he ran up to me. "God, am I glad to see you!" he said. "Take a little of the pressure off me!" Both of us had been reserve officers, and we were given regular commissions and assigned new planes.

The first thing I did when I came back was get together with Barbara. We were invited to the White House because President Roosevelt wanted to meet me. He was very nice to us. We also had tea with Eleanor Roosevelt, and she and Barbara got along very well. I then received a list of things that I had to do as part of my tour. Barbara and I were invited to Congress, where a joint session of the House and

Senate gave me a big standing ovation. It was pretty humbling for a small-town Oklahoma kid.

As part of my tour, I went to the Republic Aviation plant in Farmingdale on Long Island, New York, where I met thousands of workers who were building the P-47. I spoke with them and thanked them for building a plane that had saved my life on many occasions. You could see the workers really appreciated seeing a guy who proved that their work was critical to the war effort. I flew across the country giving talks at universities, businesses, political gatherings, what have you. We hobnobbed with celebrities and movie stars and did a few gatherings with Bing Crosby, Bob Hope, Betty Grable, and others.

We were primarily trying to boost support for the boys still fighting the war over there, selling war bonds and the like. Bong hated every minute of it. One time, we were in a hotel waiting to go downstairs for another of the never-ending press conferences. Bong had taken about as much as he could. "Screw that, Bob, I'm out of here," he said, and he went down the fire escape wearing a civilian overcoat and jumped into a taxi. I did not see him again for several weeks. When I did meet with him again, we were on our way to gunnery school.

They had a new computing gun sight they wanted us to try out, and Bong did really well with it. I found I could do pretty well, too. The logic was that it would save a pilot up to five seconds to lock on to a target and minimize range and deflection error, compensating for those factors. I joked to Bong, "One day they will have planes that fly themselves." Damned if I was not right. Within a year, they were flying remote-controlled heavy bombers as drones, and today in 1995 it is very common to have pilotless aircraft. I would not be surprised if pilotless fighters and bombers fly combat one day. Such is technology.

A few months went by, and Bong and I had to make decisions. He wanted to go back to his unit, and so did I. Somehow he managed to pull some strings and get back into combat, and he finished the war with forty kills and earned the Medal of Honor. I was told that I would be assigned noncombat duties. My life just dragged on until I was appointed as an advisor to the aircraft industry. I felt I could do more for the pilots that way than if I was stuck on some base in Okinawa as an Air Force officer. When I left to work for Republic Aviation, I stayed in the reserve.

The first thing I did was work on the standardized cockpit for pilots, rather than for engineers. Since the guys who were building the damned planes were not the guys flying them, why not include a pilot's perspective? Our improvements allowed pilots to better see the weather outside and to view the entire instrument panel just by slightly dropping their head or raising their eyes. I spent eighteen years with Republic Aviation before it was bought out by Fairchild Aircraft Company. I was just about to go over to Northrop Corporation when someone talked me into the insurance and securities business. From a financial standpoint, I am very happy they did. I have basically retired but remain available to some of my old clients.

After the war, we got to know many of the enemy pilots. Adolf Galland, who was a very good friend of mine and whom I had known since 1949, flew the Me 262 and loved it. I told him that I always wished I could have shot down one of those critters. But he still swore by the 109, although, compared to a 190, it was easier to shoot down. I have met many of the other guys [Luftwaffe aces]—[Gunther Rall (275 victories), Erich Hartmann (352 victories), Gerhard Barkhorn (301 victories), Johannes Steinhoff (176 victories)]—and I worked with Wolfgang Falck [7 victories and Father of the Night Fighters] when he was a consultant to Republic. All of them had their favorite planes. They were all great men, and I hated the fact that we had been forced to be enemies.

Nowadays, since Barbara died, I travel quite a lot. I enjoy it, but sometimes the pressure gets to be too much. I'll give you an idea of what I'm talking about: I was at Oshkosh, Wisconsin, for the air show last week; then I went to MacDill Air Force Base for the last flight and breakup of the Fifty-Sixth Fighter Group. Two of the squadrons are out at Luke Air Force Base in Arizona now and may be coming back. I hope they do. I came home for a couple of days, then I was off to Knoxville, Tennessee, for a P-47 fighter pilots' reunion. That's the way it's been going.

I'm also still on the lecture circuit, going around to schools talking about World War II, what happened and why. Generally, I get my expenses paid, but I never ask for money. Unfortunately, they keep me pretty busy. I tell young people today, "Look forward to where you want to go, what you want to be, and work with that. What can you do to improve the world? First, as you go through school, find your favorite subjects and push those interests to the limit. Drive to be the best! You have to realize that you are going to be on your own one day and, in fact, will have people depending on you. If you're nothing but a bum, who can you help and what can you do?"

You have to fight for what you want. I always fought for what I wanted. Life has taught me many lessons. I guess you could say I'm a fatalist; a strong believer that when your time is up, you're gone, out of here. Why worry about that?

STRIKING THE FIRST BLOW FOR FREEDOM

———— ★ ————

James H. Doolittle

G rowing up tough in impoverished circumstances, Jimmy Doolittle overcame his humble beginnings in the mining camps of
Alaska to become America's first genuine hero following the
entry of the United States into World War II. An early competitive
air racer, he also earned university degrees, including the first PhD
awarded in the field of aeronautical engineering. His intelligence, in-
genuity, and courage were often tested, but never as fiercely as when
he recruited, trained, and then led his men on the April 16, 1942,
mission to bomb Tokyo, the first of the air raids on Japan by the US
Army Air Forces during the Pacific campaign.

Accomplishing what was then believed impossible, Doolittle led
sixteen twin-engine B-25 Mitchell medium bombers launched from
the deck of the aircraft carrier USS *Hornet* in a mission for which he
was awarded one of the first Medals of Honor of the war. While the
mission inflicted minimal tactical damage, it resulted in massive

strategic repercussions. [Authors' note: This was only four months after Pearl Harbor.] First and foremost, it proved the Japanese home islands could be successfully attacked, an event that had never before occurred in the country's entire two-thousand-year history. The raid thus dispelled the Japanese myths of invincibility and the protected, sacred nature of the Japanese homeland, and simultaneously validated the "Billy Mitchell theory" that the bomber was a decisive factor in modern warfare, even if only psychologically.[1] It greatly bolstered US morale and that of our allies, demonstrating abroad that the United States was committed to the war effort and proving to Americans themselves that they were not defeated after Pearl Harbor. Finally, and crucially for later battles, the successful bombing of Tokyo forced Japan to hold back 20 percent of its military assets. These assets, which would have otherwise been used against the Allies in the Pacific and Asian theaters, were instead maintained as a defensive force in case of enemy attack or invasion.

Doolittle also commanded the Eighth Air Force in Europe in the last year and a half of the war. Whereas General Curtis LeMay devised the defensive bomber box concept that saved aircraft and lives, Doolittle conceived the plan to kill the majority of the German fighter pilots who engaged them. It is often said that there is no higher praise than the respect of your adversary. In the words of Luftwaffe general of the fighters, Lieutenant General Adolf Galland (who became great friends with Doolittle after the war, and whom I personally interviewed in 1984): "Doolittle's tactic of the three-fold attack, using fighter-bombers and fighters to attack our airfields, roads, and railways ahead of the bombers, and also using them in waves as escorts, was what did the most damage to us. He was the man who really won the air war for you. Everything else was just adding to the casualties."

In the flesh, Doolittle was a quiet, thoughtful man. Despite being ninety years old when we began our discussions in 1986, his mind was clear and his recollections almost photographic, from our first tele-phone conversation to our initial face-to-face meeting a few weeks later. At his home in California, he greeted me with a firm handshake and made me feel as if he were seeing an old friend after a long ab-sence, although it was, of course, the first time he had laid eyes on me. His house was a comfortable place for historians, who were always welcome. When he required a reference, he went to a bookshelf or a drawer to pull out a letter, photograph, or document. He was accom-modating and gracious with his time, especially in follow-up calls.

Doolittle and I discussed many things off the record, including various veterans whom I'd interviewed or who were on my contact list while I was out west, and he was direct in his warnings about "certain people" should I interview them. However, unlike Curtis LeMay, who had no trouble giving "the dirt," so to speak, on certain persons he loathed, Doolittle never really had anything bad to say about anyone; not even Dwight Eisenhower, who he knew did not like him. He was a true gentleman in that respect. I will always remember how he pronounced certain words, especially the way he said "aero-plane" as the British do, instead of "airplane," as most Americans pronounce it. He was one of a kind.

Doolittle was presented with the Presidential Medal of Freedom and his fourth general's star in the years prior to his death in 1993. For decades, the surviving Doolittle Raiders, as they became known, held a reunion every year to commemorate the raid, the group of brave young Americans who carried it out, and the leader who for-ever altered the United States and demonstrated the fighting spirit of its air warriors. The year 2013 marked the last of such public events because so many of the participants had passed on to rejoin the ranks of those who'd walked before them and left their indelible marks on history.

One thing about the man was clearly evident: Doolittle was a renegade from the start, believing that there was always a better way to accomplish a task or a more effective way to complete a mission. He continuously pushed his men to be their best, while never slowing down his own pace, even though he was twice their age. When America needed a real hero, he was there. Successively a miner, racing pilot, aeronautical engineer, war hero, air force commander, tactician, strategist, and Medal of Honor recipient, he lived a life stranger and more remarkable than the best fiction.

JAMES H. DOOLITTLE

I "dropped in" on December 14, 1896, soon before my father moved the family from California to Alaska on the heels of the gold rush. I was an only child, and growing up in Nome and the mining towns around there was an experience. You had to be tough in many ways just to survive. There was no electricity, and we burned wood and coal to stay warm and cook. The wood came from crates and shipwrecks, and some shipments from the United States. You have to remember that Alaska was not a state back then, and life there was very primitive. It was a dangerous area for certain, with a lot of crime and everything else you could imagine.

There were saloons, prostitutes, gambling—everything. The real Wild West. There was no law to speak of; everyone carried weapons, and they used them. Gambling was rampant, and crime increased with the growing population. I was always in fights with other boys. I was short for my age, and that made me a target. After a while, I had a reputation, since I adopted a "strike first" mentality early on. That probably saved my life many times over the decades. I always believed that it was better to be proactive than reactive—the latter people tended not to last as long. I became really good at fighting—not just boxing, but also the dirty tricks that can help you in a tight spot. I would call those the "Dark Arts of Survival."

Well, my fighting ability was not matched by my academic performance. I was not a very good student, which I think was due to my attraction to hunting and the outdoors. I did later get a job selling local newspapers to make some money. In 1908 we moved to Los Angeles, where we had some relatives, and the warmth and modern world were a marvel to me, really. I could not believe that you could have lights on demand, and food to eat without growing it or shooting it. My parents wanted me educated, so I enrolled at Borendo Elementary School and then attended Los Angeles Manual Arts High School in 1910. That was an interesting time for me, as I had some friends who were fellow students who became quite famous also.

Goodwin Knight,[2] who was later a California governor, and the moviemaker Frank Capra, whom we all know, of course, were friends of mine.[3] We met at school and remained friends from those days forward. One thing I found interesting was that I was only in one fight in high school, unlike back in Alaska, which was several every week. I took down this big bully who was trying to take money from students. Without hesitation, I gave him a right-and-left combination to the jaw and kicked him in the right knee. I heard it "pop," and from that day forward, I had no more problems and a lot more friends.

I never had a lifelong interest in flying as such, but I went to Dominguez airfield, which is today in Compton, just outside Los Angeles. This was 1910, while I was still in school. That was when I first saw Glenn Curtiss and other famous aviators.[4] I then decided to make a glider, and I followed the instructions in an old *Popular Mechanics* magazine. My mother sewed the fabric for my biplane adventure, although I think she was somewhat reluctant to provide me with any encouragement.

This thing was really more like a hang glider, and I took it to a small bluff with a fifteen-foot rise. I ran and jumped, but the tail struck the ground and sent me crashing. Undeterred, I decided that what I needed was more speed. I had a friend tow me behind his father's car with a rope, but I never got airborne and was dragged quite a way. My glider was totally destroyed, but I was very lucky myself, as I only had some bruises and a few scrapes.

Well, I can tell you that still did not stop me from flying. I had a hard thought, and then I decided to take the remains of my damaged glider and build a monoplane glider, with bicycle wheels for landing gear and a small engine. That just did not take off either, so I gave up. Then I decided to take up boxing, since I was a good fighter. I wanted to learn the technical aspects of the sport. Professional boxers were real heroes back then, like today, and the famous guys made a lot of money, and I really liked making money. That was usually because we never had much of it.

I had a coach, Mr. Forest Bailey, who was one of our teachers, and he taught me the finer points and more technical aspects I mentioned. He was hard on me, but he was right to be hard. He would always correct an error in form or style, and he finally told me that I had the right attitude but not the skill, and skill could be improved. I worked hard at it. I entered a few amateur boxing matches and won fights. I won the West Coast Amateur Championship in 1912 as a flyweight.

Later, as I put on more weight, I entered the bantam class. I did exhibitions with Eddie Campi,[5] Kid Williams,[6] and a few others who were real draws, and I did all these fights in fast company. Bailey told me that my stamina was excellent, and I had a temper, so when I was hit, I just had blind rage, which often won the fight due to my unrelenting series of punches. However, in some cases, I got mad and lost my technique. That was when I learned the calm, disciplined fighter always has the advantage over the rage warrior. Let your enemy frenzy himself into a sucker punch. Be a thinking fighter, know where to hit, and how not to get hit.

My greatest problem was that I did not leave my anger and fighting in the ring. I once went out, and some guy was giving me a hard time. I do not remember what it was about—a girl, I think. Anyway, he said he was going to beat the hell out of me and threw a wild punch, and I just launched. Two punches, and he was down, and I hit him again while he was on the ground just for good measure.

Well, someone called a cop, and I was immediately picked up. It was sort of hard not to be identified, and I was arrested for disturbing the peace. They could not charge me with assault, as it was self-defense. I spent that weekend in jail, and my parents had to sign me out. Facing my mother after that was worse than the weekend in jail.

My mother and I had a long talk about my fighting, and she wanted me out of boxing. So, somewhere during this entire, disturbing process, she decided to buy me a motorcycle. Well, I can tell you that it did not work out as well as she had hoped, because now I had a way to get around to all the boxing matches! I really became good as I gained more weight and learned how to control my anger and study the science of boxing. I was stunned as to how much mathematics, especially geometry and physics, played in being a good fighter. I studied math, all the higher levels, and applied that discipline to my fighting. I finally became a professional fighter under the name of Jimmy Pierce because fight results were posted in the newspapers. There were not many Doolittles, so that would have been a dead giveaway.

There were many benefits to boxing, and not just the money and fame. That was how I met my wife, "Joe," my name for her, Josephine. Her family was not very enamored with me, I can tell you. Even my own mother told her, "Joe, you can do better; you are a wonderful girl." She was not a fan of my lifestyle; she felt that I was becoming a street thug. That family was a hard group to sway, I can tell you. I was badly outnumbered all around, but we worked it out. I decided that I needed some time away to let things cool down before I burned too many bridges, so I returned to Alaska for a few months, just to clear my head. I did not know where I was going or what I wanted to do, but I knew I wanted to marry Joe and make both of our parents proud.

I pulled my head out of my rear and returned to Los Angeles and enrolled in Los Angeles Junior College in 1915. I did well academically, which shocked and pleased my mother. Then I went to the University of California to study mine engineering, as my math skills were through the roof, and I knew I could make a great living. This was also where I continued boxing for the school and as a professional before settling down to my studies. Joe did not like me fighting. She was always afraid I would get hurt.

I explained to her that mining was even more dangerous, and she said, "Yes, but you will be an engineer, not a miner," and I had to agree with her on that logic. Well, I guess I made a good enough impression, as all the parents felt that I was on the right course to being a decent human being, and Joe and I were married on December 24, 1917—Christmas Eve, of all things. I told everyone that was because I wanted to marry her quickly, and she told everyone that it was because I had a bad memory and needed a reason to remember our anniversary.

I went to work for the Sierra Mining Company one summer to gain some practical experience, and while I was there, we had two guys killed in an accident. There were many things that awakened me to the dangers of shaft mining. I studied the problem. Many times, the old wooden shaft supports would just rot and get weak, and if they failed, it was like a house of cards. I suggested that they consider using iron, bolted into sections to make it stronger, and it would last longer.

They were concerned about cost, but I did a simple math equation to prove that it was more cost effective in the long run, and the miners' union was not really a group that wanted to have to strike. They would do that if they felt that their safety concerns were not being addressed, and the strikebreakers could come in. All of this would cost a lot more than spending a few hundred dollars on stronger shaft supports. They agreed.

When we entered World War I, I returned to school, continued my studies, and reported for ground flight training. I took to the courses, which included meteorology, Morse code, aerodynamics, mathematics, mechanics, and navigation, and I delved deep into it. This was great because I had been unemployed, and they paid me $50 a month. After graduation, I went to San Diego for flight training in Jennys, which was rigorous and, at that time, not very dangerous. There were some accidents, but I had no problems. I graduated on March 5, 1918, and was the proudest I have ever been. The day they pinned my wings on me, I thought about that damned glider back when I was a kid.

After that, I went to Camp Dick, Texas, which was kind of a punishment for me. There was nothing to do, no planes, nothing. It was a penal colony without the flogging or bread and water, in my book. I felt forgotten, along with dozens of other guys just itching to get into the fight in Europe. My next stop was Dayton, Ohio, and then on to Lake Charles, Louisiana, the whole time without flying. Here at Lake Charles, we had a reprieve. This was all right with me, since we did our advanced training in the [Thomas-Morse] S-4C Scout, which I liked better than the old Jenny, since it was faster.

This was where we learned formation flying, fighter tactics such as they were back then, stall recovery, loops, and simulated ground attacks, that sort of thing. I liked it. I was really into it. Sometime during all of this, I was notified that Joe had been told that I was dead. I was stunned that that could even happen, but it was almost understandable. This was when a former Lafayette Escadrille fighter pilot had returned from the war.[7] His name was James R. Doolittle, and he had been killed in Buffalo, New York. Some moron reporter caught wind of it and told Joe that it was me. She knew me better than that, and despite some confusion, I called her and proved she was right. I was too tough to die in an accident, but dumb enough to walk away from one and try it again.

After many weeks of that, I went to Rockwell Field in San Diego. This was a nice place, but I ended up being stuck there as a gunnery instructor, which I guess is the same as being the ticket taker at a great theater showing a good film that you never get to see. We used the Jenny with a top-mounted Lewis machine gun firing over the propeller for training; pretty simple, really. However, one day, I proved Joe right about being too tough to die when I had a midair collision while flying with a student pilot. This fellow came up at us in a Scout and removed my landing gear, which was a little unsettling. The crash damaged the propeller and lower wing, but that poor fellow lost his head, literally. We lost his plane, but I landed without much incident. However, Joe read about this incident in the local paper.

I assured her that, yes, it was a bad accident for the other pilot, as he was killed, but that I was absolutely fine. Then, believe it or not, I had another accident (not my fault, either): a collision with another errant pilot. My prop tore off a student's tail section, and we lost both the plane and the pilot, and again I was able to nurse the old bird back down without further incident. That was very sad—we had another memorial service not long after the previous one, and I was involved in both. I almost began to think I was close to being immortal, I guess. I was never even injured in either event.

Not too long after that, I was assigned to the Mexican border as part of our security flights. I think we had about two dozen altogether, due to Pancho Villa's raids. This was not long after General John J. "Black Jack" Pershing's mission to monitor and secure the border and capture or kill Villa, but this was a crazy assignment; it made absolutely no sense whatsoever. We could not fire on the Mexican bandits even if they fired on us, and we actually had a pilot killed by ground fire.

I promised myself that I would do everything possible to protect my pilots and crews from such ridiculousness if I ever rose to command status. So I improvised, and instead of shooting them, we flew low to stampede their cattle and just raise general hell, and I kept thinking that all of us doing some nice strafing runs—especially if they were on our side of the border—could eliminate that threat once and for all. Hell, just killing all of their cattle would have put a major strain on their morale and logistics, but no, we could not shoot the cattle, either. After all of this stupidity, I returned to Kelly Field a year later. After a few long-range flights and temporary assignments, I went back to Dayton.

On Why He Stayed in the Army and Did Not Return to School: I really enjoyed flying, and it was something I was good at. When you enjoy doing something and are damned good at it, you should stay with it. Besides, I felt safer at the controls of an aircraft than in a deep mine shaft. At least in a plane, you can have some measure of control over your fate. I also liked the military life, as it suited me.

I never did barnstorming. That would not have been allowed, although the army allowed us to set new speed and altitude records, which made the aviation corps look good in the press. The guys who did barnstorming were the guys who got out of the service and tried to make the best living they could. The first show I did was in San Diego, and it was a big one—over two hundred airplanes—and we had a great time.

During this time, I made friends with some of the senior officers, and these men had friends in very high places. One night they were discussing government funding for the army aviation program. One of them, a major, said that he "had it on good authority Washington was going to cut the funding drastically," which would have meant that many of us pilots would go to the cavalry, artillery, or infantry, if not into civilian life. That really disturbed me, but as I knew this was a privileged conversation, I could not really discuss it with anyone, not even Joe.

Yet it was true. There were some struggles in Congress about restricting funds for the air branch. Once the war was over, for whatever reason, the powers that be decided to cut back heavily on military spending, which I have always considered to be a bad strategic move. Many of us felt that we should always be prepared for the next war, since there always is one, but the civilians, most of whom never served in uniform, never really understand that.

Well, we also went on a nationwide tour with many different types of aircraft in 1919, and this was the most fun time of all. I did get into airplane racing, which was wonderful. I practiced for the Schneider Trophy [Schneider Cup] competition, which was open only to seaplanes, and I flew my first one in 1925. This was a very prestigious event, by the way, and many careers were launched by this and the Pulitzer Races. I actually won the Schneider that year, and it gave army aviation a real shot in the arm.

I had other air incidents apart from the previous events I mentioned earlier, and the next one was all my fault. I was being stupid one day, and I dropped down and buzzed a couple of guys on the ground and did not see the fence I hit until it was too late, totaling my plane, and my CO grounded me for a month. I walked away from that one also, no problem. I guess that was when I really believed that I had a charmed life. This is not to say that I thought I was invincible, though.

My next crash was just as less impressive, during our attempt to take three Jennys cross-country. As luck would have it, none of the three made it. I ground looped mine in a freshly plowed field upon landing. The prop was bent, but we had a spare, and the tail was quickly repaired, so we returned to our base at Rockwell without further mishap. The next crash was when I was chasing ducks in a Jenny, and I crashed the tail on a ridge. That was lightly embarrassing, and painful when I reported to my CO again. I was pretty certain he was getting tired of seeing me on such a frequent basis, and, I can assure you, that feeling was mutual.

The next embarrassing event was a crash in Florida, where I was taking off on the beach, and a wheel stuck in the sand. I was turning around, and a wave hit the landing gear, flipping me over. The plane was a wreck, and Joe was there for that one. I did eventually finish the flight from Florida to California. Now that I remember, in 1924 I broke the tail on a Fokker [biplane trainer] but landed it. I later crashed another Jenny at MIT, but I was again unhurt. That guardian angel was really working overtime, I guess. Ironically, in all my flights, I made only three parachute jumps from aircraft. Some would say that was three too many.

I had my detractors, of course. My CO, Colonel Harvey B. S. Burwell, had many reasons to be irate with me. Once, I pulled a stunt that was completely illegal, doing some wing walking and other things, and Cecil B. DeMille caught me on camera. My CO found out about it really quick. He saw the film of me sitting there on the landing gear under John McCullough's plane, and he grounded me for another month.

Then, as if my bad luck runneth over, I was on duty during this period, so the only enjoyment I had was riding my motorcycle. I saw a plane coming in to land, and I drove in its path, so the pilot had to go around. I did it again as a joke—not too smart. The pilot happened to be my CO, so there I was, grounded for another month and restricted to base. I had some time to think about all I had done, and the last event was really idiotic, but I just had so much fun doing it. While restricted, I gave my wife a plane ride, which was against regulations, and if I had been caught, that would have been the end of me for sure—career, everything. But I was always a risk taker. I think any good combat or test pilot has to be. It makes you push the envelope, push yourself, test all the limits of machine and man.

I had been thinking a long time that aircraft designers and pilots should work together to make the best aircraft possible. Bob Johnson and I spoke about this at length during the Second World War, when he was flying with Zemke's crew—and what a bunch they were—and even long after that. He went on to work as a consultant for Republic, which later became Fairchild Republic, and that was a very good thing for military aviation.

So, using this logic, I thought that I should better my own understanding of aerodynamics from the scientific point of view. I believe that this was the best decision I could have made. I also believed that with proper training and preparation, a pilot could fly in any kind of weather; and with the development of newer instrumentation, instrument flying was to become all-important, and I wanted to prove it.

After I received my bachelor degree, I was accepted to MIT for the master's program, which I started in 1923. I must say that without Joe's help as both a wife and a secretary, I could not have accomplished the course in the time I did. God bless her for that. Many years later, when I was a command officer, I used to say, "Damn, I wish Joe was here to type up all of these reports." My thesis was to test and explain stress loads on aircraft, using a combination of mathematical and personal observations and calculations relative to g-forces placed upon both the pilot and the airframe.

This had not been done before; at least not to that extent. I finished my master's, and the thesis was later published. I suppose I became a sort of celebrity abroad, but here it was basically ignored. [Authors' note: according to the interviews conducted with Adolf Galland, Dietrich Peltz, and Hannes Trautloft, the famous German aircraft designers Professor Dr. Wilhelm Emil "Willy" Messerschmitt, Hugo Junkers,[8] and Kurt Tank[9] each had a copy of Doolittle's thesis, which greatly influenced their careers. Doolittle was well known to the Germans long before he became an enemy.]

Then I began to think about a doctoral program, since I still had another year on my leave from the army. I submitted my proposal on wind velocity's effects upon aircraft performance, and MIT gave me the nod. However, my first draft was rejected. They wanted more formulas and fewer personal observations in order to reinforce my finding, which was something of a setback, but I chose to make it an obstacle to overcome. I managed to break the dissertation and defense record at that time, and I finished in 1925. Again, Joe was there through it all.

Well, regarding Joe, I have to say that she was one of the best soldiers I ever knew. With her sons and husband off fighting in World War II, she became active in several charities, giving speaking tours, that sort of thing. She even made a lot of money from her speaking engagements, but, you know, she never kept anything above her own living expenses. With the money she was given by various groups and corporations, she created the Doolittle Fund. This was part of the Air Force Aid Society that helped widows and children of airmen who were killed, a very worthwhile organization.

Joe and Bee Arnold (wife of General Henry H. "Hap" Arnold) ran that operation. Joe was heavily involved in the support network of wives and returning airmen who had been terribly wounded and were undergoing rehabilitation. She spoke with the young wives, helped them through the turmoil, being as much a mentor as a guidance counselor of sorts. I can't tell you how proud I was of her when I learned of these things later.

One of her shining moments was when, in 1944, she christened the aircraft carrier USS *Shangri-La,* named for the place where President Roosevelt had stated to the world our Tokyo flight had originated from.[10] Ironically, not everyone was fooled, but it was so implausible that I think we kept it a secret from the world longer than most of our other military secrets. Perhaps the only secret given greater security was the atomic bomb.

During this time, there was a lot of testing going on. It really was the birth of the golden age of aviation, and I felt so privileged to be a part of it. Technology was advancing in every area—not just airframes and engines, but in pilot testing, instruments, newer emerging radio technology, and even parachutes. The gains made in testing—and this was private-sector money, for the most part; not government funding—undoubtedly saved thousands of lives in years to come, and of that, I am very proud.

I did test flights for altitude and distance, testing the endurance of various aircraft models. I guess you could say that we were the first test pilots, in a way. We tried every gimmick we could think of to get funding for long-distance flights, but we met a lot of resistance. There were other tests I did, such as flying with the turn-bank indicator invented by Elmer Sperry, the same fellow who invented many aviation milestones, including the famous ball turret on our bombers, the artificial horizon, and the gyroscope.[11]

I was also pleased that I had completed an outside loop. I wanted to know how much stress a plane and especially the pilot could take. Flying under the hood was another innovation, and it was a great way to prove the worth of instruments flying over great distances and in inclement weather. [12]

There is something that I should mention that really tells the tale about how silly, jealous, myopic, and outright ridiculous the military can be, but something I followed with great interest, and it had a great influence on me. That was the fratricidal war between the army, navy, and even the ground army versus the air service; and Congress even got involved. I am talking about Billy Mitchell.[13] I mention him for a few reasons, and not because I flew the medium bomber named after him. I speak about him because he saw the future that I just mentioned.

Mitchell knew that no ship was unsinkable from the air. He was a brilliant man, highly decorated from several countries, and he was an ultimate perfectionist. When he proposed to the military branches that he could sink a ship from an airplane, they laughed at him, and, even worse, the navy did all they could to prevent him from even trying to prove it, lest they be wrong. Because that would prove the viability and necessity of having airplanes, especially bombers, which would drain funding from the navy. They wanted to build more battleships and new aircraft carriers, and get their own planes.

Therefore, common sense would dictate, at least in my mind, that the navy should have had a vested interest in letting him do his experiment. If he failed, then their position on funding and their pride would be intact, and the army could not justify begging for more money to build an air arm for bombers. On the other side of that particular coin, if he succeeded, then the navy would be able to justify their requests to Congress for aircraft carriers and bomb-carrying airplanes to sink enemy ships. It was a win either way, at least in my mind. But then, you had a lot of egos involved, and that was where he got into serious trouble.

When Mitchell set up his test run [July 21, 1921], he selected the aircraft, and the target was the captured enemy battleship *Ostfriesland*. And he sure as hell sank that thing, shocking many a nonbeliever, I am sure. Well, he proved his point, and suddenly every aircraft designer began working on plans for land- and sea-based bombers. This was where we came up with the medium and heavy bomber designs for the Air Corps, and the navy had its own series of dive and torpedo bombers, most built by Curtiss. It really started an aircraft building revolution, but we were not the only people watching.

The Japs and Germans were also very interested, and they began their own line of bombing-capable aircraft as a result. The results of this were seen in the Japanese expansion in Asia, and the German use of the Stuka dive bombers and other medium bombers in Spain.[14] The British had always been way ahead of all of us in the concept of building bombers, and we had a lot of catching up to do.

As time went on, we accomplished many great things, and so many aircraft designers began starting their companies. We had everyone trying to get government contracts, and to do so, they needed top pilots to prove the value of their designs when submitting proposals. Then the Great Depression hit us, and the aircraft industry took a nosedive. There was no government funding for long-range flights, they were not buying aircraft in large numbers, and there was hardly any money to even train new pilots. But the airplane designers did not stop; they just worked without any money and often in abandoned warehouses or other buildings, and without a workforce.

Then, as if things were not already bad, Japan invaded Manchuria, then the rest of China. Spain was in a terrible civil war—drawing every nation in Europe into that nightmare, to some degree—and this turned out to be the perfect proving ground for Hitler's air force. All of us pilots who understood history and could see the signs knew that another war was coming. We did not know when or where it would start, or, to be more precise, expand, but we knew that our nation, especially the air forces, would not be ready.

When the war in Spain finished, everyone sat back and relaxed, acting like "This is it, the European problems are over," but I knew better. The Japanese were still doing their work in China, so we kind of went to sleep at the wheel, but Pearl Harbor changed all of that, I can tell you, and you know what happened. The entire military establishment was taken off guard, which I could not understand. Japan had been a constant threat to everyone, and they had blinders on the whole time.

It was understood that there had to be some sort of response, if for nothing else than to lift American morale. But more important, it was necessary to show the Japanese that they were not untouchable. Exposing their vulnerability was in itself a major part of the operation. I was under no illusion that we would strike any major blow with regard to tactical, let alone strategic, damage with our bombers. The purpose was psychological all the way around, and I think it worked. I know it worked for our nation.

That mission against Japan also gave the British, Dutch, French, Australians, New Zealanders, and many others—especially the Chinese and others under Japanese occupation—some hope also. All those other nations had been fighting Germany and Italy for a couple of years, and now Japan. I do not think that anyone with a rational mind thought we were not going to get involved in World War II at some point. They just perhaps did not believe it would be due to something like Pearl Harbor.

Training for the Tokyo Mission: Well, this story is legendary now, but back then it was one of our most secret operations. We practiced every method of flight planning and preparation. This included navigation, short takeoffs, applying proper trim and fuel mixture for sustained long-range flight, as well as fuel conservation. Back in those days, we did not have real-time intelligence to enable us to comprehend the enemy situation rapidly. For us, anything within a few days was good intelligence.

Following training and the various qualifications and selections of aircrews, including the practice runs at Eglin Field [now Eglin Air Force Base, Florida], the plan was hardly complicated. Once the navy, in particular the USS *Hornet*, closed to within four hundred to five hundred miles of the Japanese home islands, we would launch the strike with the B-25s. The plan was to hit the heart of Tokyo in one pass, then run along the south coast and head to China. The destination was Chuchow, where we would land, refuel, and head to Chungking, which was another 800 miles but well within our range, which was 2,400 miles if all went well. The longest distance we were intending to fly was 2,000 miles, and we modified the bombers for this, basically making them flying gas cans. Once the mission was over, we were to fly the airplanes to Burma and hand them over to our forces there.

Weather is always a factor in any military operational planning. The good thing was that we were able to compensate for many factors, such as rain and high winds, once we were airborne. The navigators would have a hard job compensating for drift and calculating airspeed, since there would be no landmarks until we reached Japan, and then none after that until we reached China, almost one hundred miles away.

The weather that day was not promising. The seas had been very high, and we were in a storm with high seas that lasted all through the previous day. The rain had been heavy, and winds were also high. This was a concern. The morning of the raid, the USS *Enterprise* sent out a scout plane, and it had seen a Japanese fishing boat, which the pilot believed spotted him. This, of course, altered our flight plan, and we had to launch early. Later, another Japanese vessel was spotted from *Hornet*. Then another vessel was sighted, and Admiral William F. Halsey ordered the USS *Nashville* to sink it. We had intercepted a Japanese radio transmission from one of the boats, and this was not welcome news, I can tell you.

Last-minute changes to a well-laid plan are never good, especially when the launch forced us to take off much farther out than we had planned on. Since we were not scheduled to take off until that afternoon, the alarm informing us to launch at 0800 was a shock. We were lucky, since the speed of the *Hornet* coupled with the thirty-mile-per-hour headwind meant that we should have plenty of lift.

The deck was pitching up and down, and the most important person in our lives during this process was the deck launch officer. We focused on him, and when the deck cleared a swell and rose, that was when the signal to take off was given. When my crew and I were in the B-25, we fired up the engines and checked instruments. The mechanics, especially Sergeant Paul J. Leonard, had meticulously gone over the planes.[15] Nothing was left to chance. Dick Cole and I were confident in our crew.[16] Our navigator was Hank Potter, who was an outstanding individual and navigator.[17] With him, we had no doubts that we would find all of the known points. Having such a crew is a great comfort. After we lifted off, I knew that the others would have no problems, since after every bomber took off, those behind it had more deck space to gather more airspeed.

Taking off from the carrier was pretty much the same as taking off from a runway. The greatest differences, of course, were the short airstrip, which required going to full power, and full flaps to catch every piece of air you could, then getting the landing gear up immediately to reduce drag. I had the math down to a science. My greatest concern once I cleared the deck was hoping that we did not have heavy headwinds reducing our airspeed, increasing drag, and forcing us to burn more fuel, since we were going to fly almost twice as far than I had calculated.

The bombing was pretty uneventful, with the exception of a Japanese boat that we passed right over, since we were flying at 200 feet, which also used up a lot more fuel than flying at a higher altitude, but we needed to avoid any coastal radar if they had it, so there was no way anyone looking up would not be able to identify us as being non-Japanese. Following this, with the weather and visibility getting better, we flew alternate headings to avoid Japanese forces that might have seen us and to prevent further detection.

As we neared Japan, I decided that an approach from the north would be the best, as we could continue on the southerly heading I had planned for. This would also hopefully allow us to avoid the antiaircraft batteries. The only aircraft we ever saw were some biplane trainers, I guess. We spotted nine fighters later, but they did not approach us, which meant that we were probably not expected. As we raced over the tops of the buildings, I saw the factories that were our targets. I climbed to 1,200 feet and ordered the bomb bay doors opened, and our bombardier, Fred Braemer, let our ordnance go.[18]

We carried only four five-hundred-pound bombs, due to the weight restrictions and to compensate for the weight of the fuel we had to carry. Like I said, this was not a major tactical or strategic strike like what would come later. Then, as we headed for the coast, we had another problem. Hank Potter determined that we would run out of fuel long before we reached the Chinese mainland, so I had to make plans for ditching. Looking out, I knew that water was probably cold, and after seeing sharks below, I rapidly thought about an alternative plan.

We were lucky that the headwind turned into a tailwind, and that is always a plus when you are trying to gain time and cover more distance on limited resources. I thought that with these factors, we might be able to make the mainland. If so, then we would jump. The weather was closing in again, and rain and fog were making visibility difficult. We tried to reach Chuchow on the radio, but that did not work, so we jumped out after I placed the aircraft on autopilot.

Dick Cole was so stiff from the long flight, I was wondering if he would be able to get out of the copilot's seat. We flew for thirteen hours, and that says a lot about our aircraft and the marvelous work performed by the mechanics. It also says something about American workmanship. I do remember that I had forgotten to lower the flaps prior to bailing out, but hindsight is worthless once you are under a parachute.

The jump was very smooth, and I landed in a soft rice paddy, muddy but unhurt, and I thought about all of the other men and hoped they would have the same luck. As I looked, I saw a light in a house and went toward it. I stated that I was an American—in the Chinese we were taught—but the people inside locked the door and turned out the light. That tended to make you uncomfortable. Besides, I always had reservations about trusting the Chinese with keeping secrets. Chiang Kai-shek was not known for his ability to maintain security discipline, and I was hoping that there would not be a reception committee for us.

Well, I was freezing, as it was cold, raining, and I was soaking wet—a bad combination. I was also very hungry. None of us had eaten in at least sixteen hours, and a few guys had nothing for over a full day, as they were seasick. When your body is low on fuel, as we are endothermic creatures, and then you are in a cold environment, hypothermia can sink in quickly. This also affects your mind, your judgment, your muscles will not work like they should—all dangerous factors. I really hoped none of my men were floating in the ocean. That would have been a death sentence.

I knew that my men would be in at least similar if not worse circumstances, and this was my greatest concern. I walked until I met a man who spoke no English but seemed to understand me, and I followed him to a military garrison. There was a Chinese major who wanted my Colt .45, which I refused to hand over. I told my story, and the officer and his men followed me to where I had landed. After seeing that the parachute was gone, I pointed to the house where I had knocked. There the farmer and his wife denied anyone knocking, and said they heard no plane and saw no parachute. The major accused me of lying, until a couple of soldiers came out of the house with my parachute. This eased things a bit. I was in no mood to be screwed with by this major, and I knew how to use that .45 pistol.

After that, the major knew I was telling the truth. It was not like I suddenly decided to take a vacation on the southernmost ass-backward part of China dressed like I was and landing by parachute. He sent his soldiers out to find the rest of my crew, and the only injured man was Potter, who'd sprained an ankle. I have to say that I was very relieved, knowing that Cole and Leonard were fine also.

We later found the wreckage of the Mitchell, but there was nothing much to salvage. I felt that the entire mission had been a failure. I knew that none of the other planes could have made it to the airstrip at Chuchow. I thought that I might even face a court-martial. I recalled just how far they were willing to go to court-martial Billy Mitchell in 1925, and that was just for insubordination. [Authors' note: please note the circumstances: that Mitchell was court-martialed for having made several statements to the press strongly critical of the US Department of the Navy and the US War Department, accusing them of "incompetency, criminal negligence, and almost treasonable administration of the national defense."] I had just lost a squadron of expensive bombers and probably most of their highly trained crews.

Paul Leonard could see that I was very depressed. I mean I wanted to cry, but you just can't do that when you are the leader of men—men who are still looking up to you for leadership, and still in possibly very hostile country. Dick Cole assured me that he could never see anything like that happening. Leonard was ever the eternal optimist, and he tried to cheer me up. His comments were almost prophetic. He told me that they would make me a general and give me the Medal of Honor. I thought that he had perhaps landed on his head.

The remaining crews were collected that had managed to reach Chuchow, and out of all the destroyed aircraft, from ours we managed to salvage only a motion picture camera and a still camera. Each bomber carried those, but the others in the other aircraft were destroyed. Dick Cole was worried, just as I was, that our men had ended up in the sea—or, even worse, may have been captured or killed. As for the other crews there was much that we would not know for a long time. We found out through intelligence and some of the guys who were later returned.

One crew had been captured by Chinese guerrillas, more than likely the Communists, and they were bound and robbed. Later, everything was ironed out. We also heard that eight of the men had been captured by the Japanese. This was loosely depicted in the 1944 film *The Purple Heart*. We also met an American missionary named John Birch, who had managed to evade capture. He helped us out, and we eventually reached Chuchow by various means. We knew from another crew that one man had died bailing out. Sadly, Birch was killed by the Chinese Communists after the war, and the John Birch Society is named after him.[19] He was a fine man, I thought. I also learned that five of my men were in Russia.[20]

All of us who survived met Generalissimo and Madame Chiang, and we were all decorated by the Chinese government.[21] It was a very moving moment. This was around April 30, and I had just been promoted a couple of days earlier. I kept thinking how crazy this was. I was almost robbed, if not incarcerated, by a Chinese major; some of my men had been roughed up by Chinese; a Chinese farmer and his wife would not help and then lied about the event; and here I am getting a medal from Madame Chiang for what we did. I told Paul and Dick that if the rest of the war was going to be so nuts, we were going to have a wild time indeed. Shortly afterward, I was ordered home.[22]

To make a long story short, the press went wild about the event after it was over, and President Roosevelt wanted to see me, so I went to the White House. Joe and I were met by General George C. Marshall, and since I had never been placed in handcuffs upon my return, I felt all would be okay.[23] This was when Paul's prediction came true. I was promoted to brigadier general from light colonel on the spot by the president, passing a grade, which was rare. [Doolittle also received the Medal of Honor.]

I felt proud of my boys also. They had done all of the hard work. It was really their moment to shine. Of course, it was still not until much later that it was disclosed that we had launched our bombers from an aircraft carrier. That was still top secret. Also, the Japanese went on a rampage all through the province where we had landed, killing practically every man, woman, and child to make a point.*

That was perhaps the greatest tragedy of our mission. The thought that our mission had cost the lives of thousands of innocent people

---

* Historian Dr. Bryan Mark Rigg joins the majority of historians in establishing the number of Chinese killed at 250,000. Bryan Mark Rigg, *Flamethrower: Iwo Jima Medal of Honor Recipient and U.S. Marine Woody Williams and His Controversial Award, Japan's Holocaust and the Pacific War* (Addison, TX: Fidelis Historia, 2020), 832n94.

preyed upon my mind, and I still think about it. We are a nation that goes out of our way to not harm civilians, even those of our enemies, and then something like this happens. However, given what the Japs had done in China before we landed, and what they did throughout all of Asia expanding their empire is less well known when compared to the Germans, but it was mass murder and torture on a scale that would have impressed Hitler.

All that horror was in retribution against the Chinese for helping us. I have read estimates of at least a quarter of a million people, perhaps even more, being murdered. They also exacted their revenge against our captured men, which I learned later. Bill Farrow,[24] Harold Spatz,[25] and Dean Hallmark[26] were executed. Bob Meder[27] died in prison, and Bob Hite,[28] Chase Nielsen,[29] George Barr,[30] and Jacob De-Shazer[31] survived to return home. Those men endured absolute hell for over three years, and they are the real heroes, along with the men who died. The loss of these men has always stayed with me. When people talk about atomic bombs and their justification, they come to mind. In all, twenty of us who survived the raid did not survive the war. Very sad for me.

Well, the raid did many things. First, it gave the American people hope and a sense of pride. Second, and equally important, the raid placed the Japanese on notice. They could be reached—perhaps not in the immediate future en masse, but eventually, and I think even the Japanese people realized this. The next thing it did was to show our allies that we were in the fight, and we were going to go at it head-on. The psychological impact of the raid, both for us and the enemy, could not be underestimated.

This was manifested by the fact that the enemy pulled back several of their top fighter units from the front to defend the home islands, which would make our job easier later. I also always believed that part of the ferocity of the Japanese in fighting us in the Pacific theater was partly due to the knowledge that we would come, at any cost, by any means, and our raid in 1942 proved that early in the war.

Upon Returning from China, and Meeting with Roosevelt: I went on a speaking tour, part of a war bond drive. I spent a lot of time meeting Hollywood celebrities who were also supporting the war effort. The entire nation was geared for this war, top to bottom. This lasted awhile, and I flew a B-25 around the country, especially to factories and places like that. But in the back of my mind, I still thought about my missing men and their families.

The Japanese never signed the Geneva convention of 1929, so there was no prisoner of war notification or registration, as we had with the Germans and Italians. If our men were captured, and they were killed, we often never knew about it unless information leaked out somehow. In most cases, we had men in captivity who were listed as missing and presumed dead for years who were still alive, unknown to us, and not released until after we invaded places like the Philippines, and when Japan surrendered.

I must say that the most difficult task following the raid was writing letters to the families of the dead and missing. That was always the toughest part of being a leader. The men you lead understand the risks, but their wives, parents, and children may have a harder time understanding. You try to soften the blow as best you can and hope that it works out. Joe was very good at this, working with these families. I think what she did for the nation was just as important, if not more important, than what we did in the military.

After the war bond tour ended, I was called in and later worked on the preparations for the placement of our forces in Britain and for planning the air war against Nazi-occupied Europe. This was the catalyst for the creation of the Eighth Air Force on January 28, 1942, but it was all on paper at that time. This was when Brigadier General Carl A. "Tooey" Spaatz went to England with the advance party. He had a monumental task ahead of him, from logistics, to intelligence, to staffing, not to mention securing the aircraft, bombers, and fighters—that sort of thing. I was also stunned that right after our raid, Congress could not throw enough money at us to train more pilots and aircrews; very different from a few years ago.

Well, General Douglas MacArthur chose Lieutenant General George C. Kenney to head air operations in the South Pacific, when many people thought he would choose me. That set me free to go to Europe, but then the decision was made to invade North Africa as the second front. Joseph Stalin was apparently very upset by this, as he wanted us in Europe immediately to relieve the pressure he was under, and I understood that.

However, logistically and materially, we were not up to that task. If we had bases in Algeria, Morocco, Libya, and Egypt, for example, that would provide many advantages. We could then hit European targets from the south, while also hitting them from the north in Britain, as well as invade the continent from two directions, actually adding pressure on the Germans and therefore relieving the pressure on the Soviet Union.

I was placed in charge of the Twelfth Air Force. I had a meeting with Major General George S. Patton, and we went to London to meet with Lieutenant General Dwight D. Eisenhower, who was in charge of Operation Torch.* Patton was a complete and total warrior, and that was very clear from our first-time meeting. I understood him, I

---

* Operation Torch was the code name for the American invasion of North Africa. Launched on November 8, 1942, Allied troops hit the beaches in Algeria and French Morocco, which were administered by the Vichy government, thus under German control by proxy.

understood his mind, and he reminded me of Curtis LeMay. He was a total warrior; a win-at-all-costs type of officer. I was a little less ruthless in my personal application of war doctrine, but Patton, Le-May, [British] Air Marshal Sir Arthur Harris[32]—those were the guys I would fear if I were their enemy.

Regarding North Africa, we always had logistical problems, such as fuel and ammunition. You must remember that Hitler's U-boats were rampaging around the Atlantic, and we were losing transport ships faster than we could build them at that time. The U-boat threat was always Winston Churchill's greatest fear, starving out Britain, and he was also fighting the war in Asia as well as in North Africa, and in the air war over Europe.

One problem was having enough qualified personnel, especially among ground crews. Another gripe I had was the effective area of operations. We had too many aircraft too close together—a real lesson learned from Pearl Harbor—and our fighters were based too far away to effectively coordinate air cover and rendezvous, especially given the variable weather conditions. Perhaps the greatest concern was the division of assets between the Pacific and our theater of operations. We had to focus upon one or the other first; defeating Germany was the most critical in everyone's mind, for a variety of reasons.

Finally, Winston Churchill and Franklin Roosevelt agreed [to focus on Germany first], and we were given top priority on fuel, ammunition, and personnel. As I said, that meant naval resources had to be allocated, so the British decided to take the lead in securing the Atlantic Ocean, and we took the Pacific—which was obviously the only option, as we had aircraft carriers, and it would be a carrier war. The Royal Navy would handle the U-boat problem, along with our aircraft patrols and theirs, mostly from the Royal Navy Coastal Command.

But there were other problems, political issues that were X factors.

Then there was the Vichy French problem.[33] We had no idea what would happen once our forces stormed their beaches in Morocco and Algeria. Then there was the working relationship with the British. Now, depending upon which general you spoke to, the situation was different. Patton's problems with the British were legendary, but I tended to get along fine with them—at least the RAF. While in England preparing to go to Gibraltar prior to Operation Torch, things worked out well. Later, when I was back in England, I had no great problems.

Interestingly enough, on the way to Gibraltar, we were spotted by a flight of Junkers Ju-88s, and that made things exciting, especially when they attacked us head-on and shot out an engine that was barely operable and wounded the pilot of our B-17.* We had some injuries, and we damaged a German medium bomber. After that, I always reflected upon how simple and easy our lot must have been when compared to what our boys flying over Germany a year later were going through.

Our objective was Tunis, the capital of Tunisia, as the British, under General [later Field Marshal] Bernard Law Montgomery, were pushing hard from the east, but we were unable to get too far too soon. However, I was promoted to major general, despite Eisenhower's feeling toward me, on November 20. This promotion helped me out with my command. As I said, I had no great personal problems with the British, but our lack of communication and their general attitude that we were somewhat backward tended to create operational misunderstandings. We needed and obtained a higher headquarters element to coordinate all tactical air operations. This made life a lot easier.

---

* The Junkers Ju-88 was a twin-engine fast medium bomber, also used as a converted night fighter to great effect.

We were also fielding new aircraft, and upgrades of existing designs, as were the British. This was true of bombers and fighters, even transports, which people tend to forget about. I also wanted a dedicated photographic reconnaissance unit, flying fast fighters into enemy territory to get pre-mission pictures for intelligence and targeting purposes. Then we would send them in after the bombing raids to take photos for the bomb damage assessment [BDA]. We had P-38 Lightnings, and the RAF gave us a few Spitfires, and all of these aircraft were stripped of guns and armor plate and turned into flying gas cans with a camera. We needed the range and speed to get that particular job done.

The Martin B-26 was a tricky plane to fly, and many guys had been killed in it; therefore, it had developed a reputation. I took Sergeant Paul Leonard with me, and we traveled to the various B-26 bases and demonstrated the proper handling and ease with which the Marauder could be flown. After that, the trust factor among pilots rose considerably, and the men were not reluctant to fly in it. Poor Leonard probably wondered when he would finally get rid of me, having dragged him from the Pacific to China, to North Africa, and then to Europe. But he was extremely loyal to me. Unfortunately, sometime later Leonard was killed during a bombing raid. That was the saddest letter I ever wrote, the one to his wife.

Perhaps the greatest decision factor of the war other than dropping the atomic bombs was the January 1943 Casablanca Conference, which decided the next stage. That was when President Roosevelt stated publicly (and, I should mention, without consulting Churchill, who was present) that nothing short of unconditional surrender would be accepted from the Axis powers. From what I have been told, Churchill did not want to go that route, knowing that an enemy would be more inclined to surrender if they felt they had some reprieve and acceptance with regard to a negotiated peace treaty, sort of like the Versailles Treaty after World War I. Churchill knew that men like Benito Mussolini[34] and Adolf Hitler, let alone Hideki Tōjō,[35] would never capitulate under those terms, if at all.

This was when it became total war, but Stalin [who would never leave Soviet territory during the war for fear of being overthrown while absent] was apparently happy with the deal. So, the greatest outcome of the conference was the ultimatum that Germany, Italy, and Japan would have to accept unconditional surrender. You also have to remember that Bulgaria, Romania, Hungary, and Vichy France were part of the Axis, too, even if operating as auxiliary or satellite allies. Now, this was a great political move, and I think necessary, but it may have also extended the war, especially for the Japanese. I am certain that senior Germans who may have considered negotiating once Hitler was gone changed their minds after the conference.

The second part of that was the Pointblank Directive, which placed enemy targets on a prioritized list according to military necessity. We would invade Sicily and Italy as part of the second front, which Joseph Stalin had been screaming for. In my opinion, one of the greatest accomplishments was the Pointblank Directive, which called for the combined American and British bombing of Germany. U-boat yards and pens, aircraft manufacturing, petroleum, ball bearings, railroads, bridges—anything that was of use to the enemy was to be systematically destroyed. These were also broken up into strategic and tactical targeting operations, which would be determined over time and during the course of events, such as the requirements of the Allied advance through Europe.

Operation Husky, the Invasion of Sicily: From our air force's viewpoint, it was a good operation, although the airborne contingent had severe difficulties. Once Patton and Monty got into gear, it was only a matter of time. The big test would be Italy. Even while the fighting still raged for Sicily, we were bombing Italian targets, especially ports and airfields, with special attention being paid to railways. However, this was not indiscriminate bombing like British night missions.

We had specific targets to hit and, even more important, specific targets *not* to hit, such as the Vatican, several monasteries, and abbeys. We did not want to destroy Old World art and treasures. This was actually a great way to practice precision bombing, and we became very good at it. It also helped with the wartime and postwar public relations campaigns, but there was a drawback: the Germans knew what we would not target, and they set up defenses in those landmarks.

Regarding Early Problems: Lieutenant General Ira Eaker had launched his mass raids into Germany in August through September 1943 and had lost so many bombers due to the lack of effective long-range fighter escorts that missions into Germany were halted. This was a total departure from the initial bomb runs against French targets, mostly against coastal targets, such as ports, airfields, and U-boat pens. They first had to fight through the German fighter units stationed in northern France and then contend with additional fighters based closer to Germany, and then there were the antiaircraft defenses.[36]

Then there were the "milk runs" into France that were not so easy, especially after the Luftwaffe waited until the short-legged fighters (like the P-47 Thunderbolt) turned back, then tore into the bombers. They would also tackle the fighters as they were near the extent of their fuel, one group attacking with a fuel advantage, while the others would engage the bombers. You usually had Me 109s attack the fighters, while the Fw 190s would go for the bombers due to having heavier armor and armaments.

The Schweinfurt-Regensburg raids were expensive: about 120 aircraft [64 lost on the August 17, 1943, mission, 60 bombers lost on the mission, more written off for 82 bombers lost on October 14, 1943, which became known as "Black Thursday," and the rest damaged or written off postmission]. And then there were the other missions. Fighters based in the United Kingdom as part of the Eighth Air Force would have to turn back at the Belgian and Dutch borders due to fuel concerns, and the Luftwaffe knew this. They waited, often circling until the escort fighters turned back, and then they hit the bomber formations like wolves into a flock of sheep. This would be the case until we got the P-51 D model.

The losses of so many bombers and their crews forced a halt to long-range missions into Germany proper until things could be reassessed. That was one of the opportunities that Curtis LeMay took advantage of, as he led many of these raids. LeMay was always bumping heads against his superiors, except me because I agreed with most of his ideas. He was intelligent, dedicated, and innovative when it came to bomber operations.

The Eighth Air Force was not the only one suffering. The Ninth Air Force lost more than fifty B-24s hitting Ploesti [oil fields and refinery in Romania]. They flew from the bases in Libya and were wiped out by the fighter and flak defenses, and there was no fighter escort. We were learning the hard way that the bomber does not always get through, despite conventional wisdom.

Eaker pleaded for the new version of the North American P-51 Mustang to be deployed. He had to wait until January 1944 for that to happen. During this period, as missions into Germany began commencing again, we bombed targets such as Augsburg from our Mediterranean bases, and the losses were also stiff. Shortly thereafter, the Twelfth was divided into two units, the Twelfth and Fifteenth Air Forces, to split the role of tactical and strategic bombing, especially in the ground support role. The Ninth was always focused upon the tactical bombing role, especially against Italian targets—and, later, German, Austrian, and Balkan targets—with some heavy bombers performing strategic operational missions.

I commanded the Fifteenth. Our first mission was to La Spezia, a port on the Italian coast. Our raid to Wiener Neustadt [the Henschel aircraft factory], a fighter production facility, cost us eleven bombers, but we took out some fifty enemy fighters and knocked out the plant for almost two months. That was a good day. Later, on January 3, 1944, I surrendered my command of the Fifteenth to Major General Nate Twining and assumed Eaker's Eighth Air Force command in England. This was in preparation for Operation Overlord, the invasion of Normandy, taking the war to northwest Europe, launched on June 6, 1944.

It was a great time. I had the materiel assets to do what I wanted, and Ira had done such a great job from top to bottom. I was hoping that I would be at least competent. Spaatz became air force commander, and shortly thereafter, I was promoted to lieutenant general, with my headquarters in High Wycombe.

Did Doolittle Win the War? To be honest, I think that is not true. I assumed control of the Eighth when it was just beginning to receive the large amount of materiel and support that would have arrived anyway, whether I was there or not. There were others more competent than myself, with Eaker being a prime example, who would have done no less and probably more.

I arrived at the time we received the P-51D long-range fighters, and this gave our bombers greater range and protection, so therefore results were more dramatic. It was the Mustang that made me look good, and the brave men who flew it protecting our bombers. Prior to that, we had British Supermarine Spitfires, Lockheed P-38 Lightnings, and our Republic P-47 Thunderbolts for escort, but they had limited range. I also decided to visit every base and meet the men. I think that men need to see their commanders and look into their eyes. They need to know that their commanders care about them and are willing to share the risk, or have been there and done it themselves. It's all about credibility. This increases morale, which is very important. LeMay would lead his bombers on missions as often as he could, as both a colonel and a general. Patton followed the same doctrine.

Another thing I did was change the mission of the fighter pilots. They had been denied authority to pursue enemy fighters for fear of leaving the bombers alone. Now that we had plenty of aircraft, I ordered fighter leaders to actively hunt down and destroy enemy fighters on the ground and in the air. The kill ratios among our pilots rose dramatically, and Luftwaffe losses soared from that point forward. They could never recover in planes and, more important, highly skilled pilots. I also ordered ground attack and strafing missions to work the German transportation system over. If it moved, could fly, or supported the German war effort, I told my pilots to kill it in place. This decision to alter the tactic of the air war brought success, but also criticism. I felt the end would justify the means. History would decide that.[37]

Spaatz thought I was wrong, and he told me so in very specific terms. Another thing I did was create a scouting force, where a pair of fighters would head out ahead of the bomber formations and provide accurate weather and visibility reports in almost real time by radio. This saved time and fuel, since many groups turned back when the weather became unbearable, despite the most favorable meteorological reports, and they had no visibility, which was the prudent thing to do. This proved invaluable. It also gave us decent intelligence on air defenses on many occasions.

On His Decision to Raise the Number of Missions to Be Flown by Aircrews: Yes, I believed that if a crew rotated after twenty-five missions, it was a waste of experience. New crews coming in would have to adapt, and this would reduce effectiveness. I eventually raised the tour for bomber crews to thirty-five missions, since our losses were dropping, and our productivity rating rose. The results we achieved as a result are probably where historians get the idea that I was the reason we won the war on that front due to our effectiveness. It was really just a culmination of many things; sort of a coalescing of factors that just fell into place at the right time.

On His Greatest Challenges with the Eighth: The first thing I noticed were the high rates of illness and frostbite among the crews. We tried to alleviate this by giving the crews better electrically heated flight suits and windows for the waist gunners, since the subzero cold and wind created the problem. The other problem was the weather.

Another problem was having better pre-mission intelligence. We had photo reconnaissance aircraft, and before we planned a mission, we would look at the previous mission photos as well as photos of intended targets. Then we would assess what had to be done, how many aircraft [required for missions], that sort of thing. I wanted every group commander to know to the letter what was expected. This included the fighter units. Rendezvous were planned to the finest detail. I wanted no bomber formation to lack fighter escort, and I also wanted the lead fighter groups to pound and strafe to their hearts' content to soften up the enemy on the ground.

We also placed greater emphasis on secondary and alternative targets in case weather forced a group to abort the primary target. All crews were debriefed upon their return, so the boys had a long day all the way around. I also wanted a more effective turn-around time on the aircraft—maximum effort from all echelons, including ground personnel. I must say that these guys repairing and working on the planes were the real reason for our success, and I feel they have not had their full due in the history books.

Regarding His Creation of Shuttle Missions: I proposed the idea that our bombers taking off from England fly on to western Russia, where they would rearm and refuel. Same for the fighter escorts. It would give the men a break. Plus, it also confused the Luftwaffe, as they were wondering where the formations were going. With the limited range of their fighters, they could not follow. What they did after a two-hour battle was land, refuel, and rearm, and catch the bombers on the way back from their targets.

Once the shuttle mission was created, it changed that to a large degree in our favor. It saved planes and aircrews, no doubt. I even spoke to General Adolf Galland about the missions several times, and he agreed that they inhibited the German flak and fighters from wreaking even more damage upon us. It worked well and was well coordinated with the Fifteenth Air Force based in Italy. We called it Operation Frantic, and the first mission from England was on June 21, 1944. It was led by Archie Old and Donald Blakeslee.[38] The Fifteenth had already flown the first missions on June 2 with no loss to enemy action. Old had more than forty aircraft destroyed and about twenty-five damaged. We lost fifteen P-51s, as I recall. They flew from Russia to Italy on the twenty-sixth.

The Soviets were a strange group. They kept demanding a second front, so we obliged, first in Africa, then in southern and western Europe. But when it came to helping defeat German industry, they were not as helpful. I read many reports from leaders of missions that described the cold reception they received from their hosts. Our weary crews received little active support unless it was to refuel their planes quickly and get them the hell out of there. Then we had the problem of interned crews and aircraft.[39]

Donald Blakeslee was one leader who came to mind. After the first shuttle mission on June 21, 1944, he walked into my office. He did not have an appointment, he did not call, he just landed, took a car, and drove to my headquarters, and stormed in. My aid tried to intercept him, and Don pushed him aside. I heard him yell, "Where is the damned general?" I walked out and saw him, and we already knew each other. Along with Zemke, he was arguably the best fighter leader in the air force. I motioned for him to come in, and he did, and slammed the door.

"General, not to be disrespectful, but who in the hell is in charge of protocol and talking with those damned Russians? Those were the most unappreciative, arrogant, and suspicious bastards I ever met. Are you sure we are fighting against the right people? Hell, I had some of those Communist bastards pointing guns at me! What hell is going on?" Well, as you can imagine, I was somewhat stunned, as I had absolutely no idea this would be the case. Later, I had other reports that were even worse and confirmed what he'd told me.

I told him, "Well, they are a strange breed, I know; they even held some of my men from the Tokyo raid who landed there. Let me make some inquiries and see what we can work out," and he thanked me, saluted, about-faced, and stormed out, muttering "Damned Russians" as I heard the outer door close. I called higher and had a memo written up, hoping that the powers that be might be able to solve this problem at the political level.

Not long after this discussion with Blakeslee, I had another meeting with Churchill, and I brought this situation up to him. He was very candid about his feelings about the Soviets in general, and Stalin in particular: "General, may I say that I understand the consternation being felt by your pilots. I have never trusted those people, although I know that [Roosevelt] had a different viewpoint. I am working best that I can with my personnel to try and ease things considerably, so just bear with me.

"Stalin is no better than Hitler, in my personal opinion—perhaps worse in many ways. I find him quite disturbing for many reasons. I would say one thing to you, and that is to make sure your pilots never trust those Russians. I have the disquieting feeling that when this war is over, we will be in a new one against our eastern allies." I thought years later, when Stalin reneged on his promises at the Yalta Conference, how true those words were.

After the war, this became a severe issue, one that Ira Eaker took up personally. I can tell you that Major General Curtis LeMay was no friend of the Soviets. I think Curtis would have been just as happy planning targets in Russia once Germany surrendered. That is not to say that he was not a great commander and leader. He just saw things differently, and, in hindsight, like Patton, saw things more clearly than the rest of us. I would have to say that of all my plans, this was the one that just failed, in my opinion. The Soviets did not want us there, and they never hid their displeasure at our boys being on their soil. I would say the Cold War was already in effect.

———————

Regarding His Directing "Big Week": Well, February 1944 was a busy month, but from the nineteenth to the twenty-fifth, I had planned a series of saturation missions: a thousand strong bomber formations escorted by hundreds of fighters to strike as deep as possible into the heart of Nazi Germany. I felt that if we could destroy the German fighters in the air by luring them up, their losses could not be replaced, especially among the pilots. It was basic math. Galland knew that also. In addition, it would further our Pointblank Directive, thus limiting Germany's ability to wage effective warfare. All of this was to reduce German assets prior to Overlord. Big Week proved effective and justified my decision, because we had minimal losses.

The Germans paid a high price in both planes and pilots. After Big Week, German aircraft production was rapidly reduced. General Galland told me he lost a thousand pilots between January and April

1944, with more than four hundred going down during Big Week. I would also state that you could estimate our effectiveness by the thousands of German motorized vehicles we captured intact, without any damage. They had simply run out of gas.

One of the headaches I had to endure was the constant petitions from the fighter pilots who wanted to stay and continue flying combat duty. I understood their reasoning: these were aces who did not want to lose out in the scoring, and, to be sure, they were adrenaline junkies. I liked that; we needed men like that who were warriors to their marrow. I could approve a few depending upon the circumstances, such as Gabreski and Yeager, who wanted to stay after their required missions were finished.

But then there was the situation with Robert Johnson. He had just scored his twenty-seventh victory and was about nine missions short of a hundred for rotation. He and I had a chat about that, and I liked him a lot and still do to this day. He was a great pilot and a wonderfully humble person. I had to inform him that his orders stateside were beyond my ability to address; this came from General George C. Marshall through Hap Arnold, then to Eisenhower. That was too much weight for me to even try to intervene, but I tried anyway. I was told by Eisenhower, "No, Johnson goes home, and that is the end of it."

So, I had to break Bob's heart. He looked as if I had just grounded him, which is the worst thing short of capture or death for a pilot, especially a successful fighter pilot. I had the same situation with Jimmy Stewart, who was flying B-24 Liberators. He really was a warrior also. I could not believe how humble he was, being a big movie star, wealthy, and famous. He was willing to give all that up to continue flying. Same with Clark Gable, whom I knew well. Both men received their orders home from much higher authority. Given who they were, I did not even think about petitioning for their extensions, as that would have been career suicide.

I could see it now, either Stewart or Gable getting shot down and captured, or killed, and the newspapers back home having "Doolittle Kills Movie Stars" on the front page. I would have had to go back to Alaska if that happened. We knew that Hitler had placed bounties on both their heads. I also learned that actor Sterling Hayden, who had become a Marine Corps officer, was working with General Donovan's OSS [Office of Strategic Services] under the name John Hamilton, doing dark things in the Balkans. I thought to myself, "What a strange war indeed."[40]

On Why Doolittle Was Not Allowed to Fly Missions in Europe After Taking Command of the Eighth Air Force: There were two reasons for this. First, I had been briefed on Ultra, the code-breaking system that read German Enigma messages. No one knowledgeable of this was allowed the risk of being captured. The war effort depended upon complete secrecy, as history has proven to be the case. Second, I had been thoroughly briefed on the plans for Overlord, so I had a double whack against me. I still flew in England, but my active participation in the war was over.

There was one exception.

On D-day, I took a P-38 with Pat Partridge as my wingman, and we flew over the beaches and channel. I will never forget the sight: thousands of ships, landing craft, and support vessels. It was incredible. Despite our losses, D-day went off without a hitch for our boys. But later, I was called on the carpet when a bombing mission had gone wrong.

Several bombers dropped their loads short while supporting the ground advance, and about a hundred men were killed, with another five hundred or so wounded. One of the dead was US Army lieutenant general Leslie McNair.* I took the responsibility, but I always felt

* McNair would be the highest-ranking American officer killed in the war.

that those were not the kinds of missions we should have been doing in large strategic bombers anyway.

This was tactical work and should have been treated as such. I felt sure after my ass-chewing from General Walter Bedell "Beetle" Smith that I would be replaced, so I spoke to Tooey Spaatz. Somehow I kept my job. The ironic part was that Ike wanted these missions continued, and more Americans died as a result, but the losses were considered acceptable. There would be many more problems that would arise. They always did. War is not perfect.

––––––––

Dresden was just one of several cities bombed to prevent German reinforcements' arrival at the front. The Soviets wanted Dresden bombed, and I ordered the strikes. The British had already been busy there. It was later we learned about the high number of civilian casualties, and that was indeed tragic. David Irving wrote in his 1963 book *The Destruction of Dresden* that we intended to kill civilians.[41] I think he got the entire scenario wrong. We never intended to bomb any civilians, and that was a British operation.

You had to understand that the RAF Bomber Command bombed primarily at night, and they performed area bombing, not precision bombing, which was impossible at night. In addition, they did not fly in tight formations, like we did. Their formations arrived and departed in a staggered trail formation. Flying ahead of the bombers were often Pathfinder aircraft (the nickname given to the first aircraft over the target): bombers that would locate the intended target and drop flares and pyrotechnics to mark the target. Then the rest of the following bombers would drop on that marker.

Even if that marker landed right in the middle of a logical target, the bombers had many variables to contend with, such as crosswinds and flak, and there was always the threat of German night fighters engaging them. All of these factors could throw off a bombardier. And the British targeted civilian centers in Harris's "dehousing" plan, meant to demoralize the population and kill the workers supporting arms production. That was not to my way of thinking. LeMay thought it was a great idea.

The entire premise of our planning was strategic in nature, hitting military and economic targets. Terrible things happen in wartime; of that there is no debate. But to think that any American commander would simply bomb civilians is unacceptable. Not even LeMay went that far. At least his targets had to have some kind of military value to justify the expenditure of ordnance. We are not bred for that. Even Hiroshima and Nagasaki were military targets, and the Japanese were warned in advance.

Plus, we never believed that simply bombing the population was the way to win a war, unlike the British and Arthur Harris—and the Germans, I suppose—unless as a result that population rose up in defiance of their government to force their capitulation. That was not going to happen in Germany or Japan, I can assure you. It is easy to criticize from the comfort of a typewriter. I still think dropping the atomic bombs was the right thing to do. It shortened the war and saved Allied lives. That in itself is justification. They started it, and we had the God-given right—no, the moral duty—to end that war the quickest way possible. Do I feel bad about civilian casualties? Yes. But American lives were at stake, so that is all that needs to be said. End of story.

Regarding His Opinion of Fellow Senior Officers and Others: Well, I have to say that Spaatz and Eaker became good friends of mine early on just after World War I. Hap Arnold was a colonel then and commander of Rockwell Field. Although we all had our differences of opinion later, we all respected each other. Now, Curtis LeMay was a great leader and a true warrior, but I did not get to know him until much later. I think that Arnold was perhaps the greatest man in our air force, Billy Mitchell notwithstanding. He was a true leader and innovator, and he cared about what his subordinates thought. Although he was a general, he would never think twice about asking a lieutenant his opinion on a matter. He used to talk with enlisted mechanics without fanfare. He was like Omar Bradley: he had a knack for obtaining unquestioned loyalty from his men. That is a rare gift. Hap Arnold was a great leader, and he encouraged his generals to correspond with him directly on any and all matters. This was truly a great benefit in many ways.

Eisenhower was a good leader, although I was always under the impression that he never really liked me or had a lot of faith in me. I think his professional opinion changed later, but his personal opinions were his own. As far as Mitchell went, he was truly the best long-range planner and supporter of air power. His court-martial was a political sideshow; he ruffled too many feathers with his hard-line beliefs that the next war would be defined and won by air power above all else. The fact that he was proven correct only adds to his credibility.

But Mitchell was also a visionary with regard to his prognostication of Japan's future attitude toward us, and he even stated that war between our two countries was inevitable. This, among other factors, contributed to his demise. It was a shame to lose such an officer.

George Patton was a completely different type of officer from most others I ever knew. Patton was the ultimate warrior, and I mean Spartan in his attitude toward combat. He was fearless, and he never shied away from a fight, whether with superiors or the enemy. He and Bradley were both excellent men, but as different as night and day. Patton would risk outrunning his supply lines to beat an ally like Montgomery to secure an objective and risk the casualties to do it.[42] But he would do it if he felt it was the right thing to do to save lives later and shorten the war. Plus, he just liked killing Germans.

I met with King George VI and the queen [who made Doolittle a Knight of the Bath]. Well, I don't really know why, but it was an honor. I always got a good chuckle about that. I could never see myself arriving at a function and being heralded as "Lord Doolittle." Joe made a joke out of it, and perhaps that was one of the reasons Eisenhower had a dismal personal opinion of me. Many of our senior officers had a tense relationship with our British allies, but I never had a problem with any of them. Perhaps the only tension that existed was with Harris over his desire to have us join in the night bombing campaign, which I was against. Luckily, Arnold, Spaatz, and even Eisenhower were against that, so I was not alone.

Something of interest that I think should be mentioned, if only due to the unique circumstances of the event, was when I met British actor David Niven.[43] I have to say that he was one of the most entertaining men I ever met, and a very good story and joke teller. He had been a Sandhurst [the Royal Military Academy of Great Britain] man, commissioned, then left to star in films in Hollywood. When the war broke out, he joined the commandos—tough group—and he was a frequent guest of Churchill's and the royal family.

One night at a dinner, we sat near each other. Niven found out who I was, regarding the Tokyo mission, and he asked a British general to move so he could sit next to me. Well, Niven was something like a major at this time, and I was under the very distinct impression that this British general was unaccustomed to having junior officers ask him to relocate their seating at a formal event. But he did and required an autograph from Niven for the inconvenience.

Arthur Harris was there on my opposite side, and we had been talking about something which escapes me at present, and Niven interrupted us, which was very impolite, brash, and un-British, to say the least. "General Doolittle, if I may ask, beg your pardon, Air Marshal Harris, but I must know, have you any plans after the war to return to California? I would like to go with you and do more films. You should consider getting into the business yourself. There are many pretty ladies in Hollywood, as you know, I am sure."

I was rather shocked by the comment, not sure how Joe would take it should I accept the offer. And Harris had this look on his face that told me he would have not been more surprised if Hitler had joined the table. I told Niven, "Well, I am going to return home at some point, but I have absolutely no desire to enter into the film business."

Harris was less than congenial, and he said, "Mr. Niven, your manners leave much to be desired. I would have expected more from an officer with your education and background. You should perhaps learn something about common courtesy and public decorum, and I am not amused." That almost made me laugh in front of both of them. I never saw Niven again after that, but I was a fan of his films.[44]

I then made another appointment to see Harris regarding some war business, and after the dinner, we talked for a few minutes. He said I was welcome to visit him whenever I wished. I will say this: Harris was a true warrior, and he would take no nonsense from anyone. We got along together very well. Once, he called me for a meeting in London with other generals, and he was discussing the possibility of having our bomber forces join the RAF in his night bombing campaign. I was against it for a variety of reasons, but I needed to be diplomatic.

I disagreed with their "bombs away and then pray" method of hitting targets. I understood him: he had a nation damned near bombed out of existence, and, for him, it was nothing more than payback on a larger scale. My argument was that we needed daylight precision bombing to ensure that strategic targets were hit; that we were less interested in "dehousing" and more concerned with "demilitarizing" the Germans through attrition and reduction of their war-making capabilities. He once said that "if German civilians do not want to be killed, they need to force their government to give up, or flee for their lives. I will not relent." Yes, he was committed, to be sure. Like LeMay in many ways.

On Churchill: I knew him well, and we had many long chats, and I always thought that he was one of the most informed and knowledgeable men I ever met. He was just what the British needed, and I admired him. He was a true leader, and I do not mean just a political leader; I mean he was a spiritual leader, and a common man's leader, and despite his noble background, he always remained connected with the average Briton. That was what set him apart from all before him and most who came after him.

By April 1945 there was nothing of any great value left to bomb, and most of Germany was occupied. We switched to operating in a tactical role. When the war was over, I gave authorization for about thirty thousand Eighth Air Force ground personnel to fly over Germany to see what we had done. I wanted every man to take the image home and see for himself what the effort was all about. I then returned home and saw my wife, Joe, and we had a well-deserved vacation. Later, Joe and I visited Patton and his wife, Beatrice, for a West Coast speaking tour, which was a real good time. I finally got to the Pacific theater and landed at Kadena, Okinawa, on July 17, 1945, after a wild ride that saw us abandon our B-29 and finish the excursion in a B-17.

I found out firsthand about the atomic bombs when Chuck Sweeney, who dropped the Nagasaki bomb, landed at my base due to a fuel shortage after hitting Nagasaki on August 9, and I did not even know about the Hiroshima bomb being dropped three days earlier. I did meet with and speak to Paul Tibbets, who dropped the first bomb, a couple of times, as he was stationed in England, and I liked him very much. I was very happy when the Japanese decided to surrender.

On the Surrender of Japan Aboard the USS Missouri *on September 2, 1945:* It was a very somber and moving experience—almost surreal.

As soon as the formalities were over, a mass formation of bombers and fighters flew overhead. It was truly a glorious moment, and I was blessed that I was able to be there. The best news I received was that my men from the 1942 raid who were still alive after being captured were in hospitals and being treated, and they would be fine. That really made me actually cry, which I did privately. I wanted to see them. I wondered if they would blame me for their years of torture and hardship. I learned that they held no grudge against me; they accepted the risk, and they were just happy to be alive and that we had launched the first strike for freedom in winning that terrible war.

Chase Nielsen probably had the worst time of them all. He had been roughed up a lot, and he looked it, not to mention the malnutrition. "General," he said to me, "I only regret that we did not have the atom bomb when we hit those bastards in '42. Hell, I would do it again, just not get caught the next time." That told me all I needed to know.

I retired in 1946 and went to work for Shell Oil Company. I did a lot of traveling again, but no one was shooting at me. Then I worked for TRW Aerospace Corporation. I took up hunting again late in life and enjoyed it immensely. I stayed with Joe a lot when I retired.

Opinions on What Makes a Great Leader: Well, I would not even begin to say that I was a great leader. I was adequate and accomplished the mission. But to answer your question, I would say the following are critical and nonnegotiable: integrity, morality, understanding, accepting responsibility for your actions, and providing encouragement and praise when necessary. Let the men know they can trust you and that you have their best interest at heart, and they will follow you anywhere. Live by the same rules you enforce, and never waver from a sound, well-thought-out decision, even in the face of stiff criticism. These are the traits that define a great leader, as well as a great man.

I made my mistakes; I was not perfect. However, I never placed blame upon anyone else for anything that occurred under my command. That is the first trait of a bad leader. Plus, to be a good leader, you have to follow orders as well, and not just the ones you like. Men will follow you if they have faith in you, no doubt. But they will fight and even die for you if they respect you and you have their loyalty. That is earned, not given.

THE ULTIMATE WARRIOR

★

Robin Olds

F ighter pilots are a different breed. That being said, Robin Olds was a different breed of fighter pilot. In fact, he was a different breed of man in general; a true American warrior. Olds was never a strictly-by-the-book officer: if it worked, he did it. His career was tumultuous, to say the least. As Colonel Francis S. Gabreski put it, Olds was "a combination of John Wayne and Errol Flynn, with a touch of Machiavelli."[1] Or, to quote Colonel Hubert "Hub" Zemke, he was "the one guy you wanted to go to the bar with, and the one you stayed closest to if the shit hit the fan."[2]

My first in-person interview with Robin Olds took place in 1989, and, later, another along with Colonel Buddy Haydon in Steamboat Springs, Colorado. Per Buddy's advice, I brought along a bottle of single-malt scotch. The atmosphere was very comfortable, and Olds seemed both excited and relaxed. Our interview lasted for two days, with lunches at the Steamboat Springs ski lodge restaurant. Subsequent interviews were conducted by phone between 1990 and 2003. Robin's face lit up when he spoke of specific events in combat or recounted anecdotes about certain people he'd worked with.

Olds fought many battles in the sky, but some of his greatest conflicts took place on the ground against the armchair commanders and politicians whom he felt were betraying the country. You were never unclear where Brigadier General Robin Olds stood on any subject. He did not mince his words: his language was colorful, his delivery solid and deliberate, his words definitive. His candor was often his undoing where higher rank within the military meant higher political implications. Yet his talents and daring still continued to amaze, for he continually managed to step over or around anything put in his way.

I'll always remember a comment about Olds that General Curtis LeMay made to me during one of our telephone interviews in 1989: "I was stunned that they made Olds a flag officer. I just assumed they would force him into retirement. He pissed a lot of people off. We had that in common, so as Robin would say, 'Fuck them in the ass sideways.'"[3]

I wish to thank Christina Olds for the memoir she wrote about her father, *Fighter Pilot: The Memoirs of Legendary Ace Robin Olds*, which filled a lot of gaps regarding the full names and ranks of persons Robin mentioned to me in passing. I also thank Christina for her friendship and assistance, including providing unpublished photographs from the Olds family collection. Breathing life into his words, her personal touch was of tremendous help and added a valuable layer of perspective to the interviews.

ROBIN OLDS

I was born on July 14, 1922, in Honolulu, Hawaii, when my father was stationed at Hickam Field, which is at Pearl Harbor. My childhood was really magical in many ways. I idolized my father, Robert. To me, he was the greatest guy in the world. With him being a US Army Air Corps pilot, I learned all I could from him. I knew every type of aircraft there was. I read everything I could on aviation. The stories of the First World War pilots intrigued me. I thought about Rene Fonck, Manfred von Richthofen, Max Immelmann,[4] Raoul Lufbery,[5] Billy Bishop,[6] and, of course, Edward Rickenbacker. Their stories were what I wanted to live. They were my heroes.

When I was growing up, the barnstorming age was in high gear. Pilots from all over the goddamned world would show up at these events, many would offer rides, some gave flight lessons. It really was the golden age of aviation. I was hooked like a drug addict, and my dad saw that. He was great. He took me flying; taught me things that would later prove to be invaluable. I knew that when I grew up, I was going to be a fighter pilot or a football star—I was indecisive at about ten years old. But in the end, both won out.

My mother, Eloise, was by all accounts a great lady, and I mean lady to the tenth degree. She was a noble-looking woman, poised, elegant in every way. She was the perfect career officer's wife, and I could not have asked for a better mother, but she died when I was a child. I was really blessed to have such great parents, and I learned a lot about life, loyalty, friendship, and discipline from them, especially my dad.[7] His circle of friends would later come to influence my military career as well.

Dad remarried afterward, and I had two younger half brothers. Dad was tough on discipline, but he was also a caring man; the punishment always fit the crime, but I tried not to be a habitual offender. I was still a precocious boy, but not too mischievous. I loved sports, and my dad really fostered that aspect of my life. He used to say things to me like:

"If you commit to something, stay with it until you succeed."

"Never give your word easily, and if you do, you keep it. Your word is your honor, and that is your legacy."

"Be your own man, not what people want, or even expect, of you, and never compromise if you know you are right."

"Losing is sometimes a part of life, but if you accept losing, then you will never be a winner. Screw losers; they are a dime a dozen."

"Sports are like life. Competition is what drives us forward, it separates winners from losers, and the best always rise to the top."

My father was aide to General Billy Mitchell, who, as you know, really pissed off a lot of high-ranking people in the military with his insistence that air power, in particular bombers, was the key to winning future wars. The navy sure as shit didn't take that very well, as the leadership of the Department of the Navy were all old battleship officers. They firmly believed that the battleship was still, at that time, the weapon to win future wars. I guess the aircraft carrier was not yet on their radar, because aviation on ships was also what Mitchell was talking about.

My dad knew that this myopic bullshit was narrow-minded thinking, and Mitchell saw the future. Mitchell was a visionary, an analyst. Dad was like Mitchell: they both saw the future like few men could, like a military Nostradamus. Dad was an intellectual pilot, so it seemed natural that I would follow in his footsteps. My dad was with Mitchell during his court-martial, and that was a real fucked-up travesty of military justice, all because one officer had proven a theory that destroyed the long-held beliefs of narrow-minded fools. I would learn that there were more of these fools than there were visionaries, let me tell you.

One point of interest was that my father hobnobbed with a lot of celebrities: actors and other people, many of them high-ranking military personalities. There is not a name you can mention that I was not familiar with, including many pilots from the First World War. I had read about them. I remember meeting Rickenbacker, as he was God in my eyes, and I was not alone. I was stunned and virtually unable to communicate with him. I also met Ernst Udet, who was the highest-scoring German ace of the war. He spent a lot of time in the United States, barnstorming, and I think he did more than any other German to repair the ill will we Americans had toward the Germans after that terrible war. I was in the company of greatness.[8]

Udet was a very gallant gentleman indeed. Later, when I was fighting the Germans, I would think of Udet, wondering if he was on board with Hitler and that collective clown show. After the war, I learned of his suicide and the reason for it. After the war, our friend Adolf Galland told me firsthand of the circumstances. Udet's death really sent a wave of depression throughout the Luftwaffe. I think that may have been the start of the Luftwaffe pilots' dislike of Hermann Göring [World War I ace who flew with Richthofen, and was the Luftwaffe commander in chief in World War II]. Galland and most of the others admitted to hating him. Hell, Göring even threatened to have some of them shot once for treason. That is a great story also.[9]

I grew up in the company of the greats in aviation, such as General Carl "Tooey" Spaatz and Lieutenant General Ira Eaker, both of whom became commanders of the Eighth Air Force in Europe, along with [General] James Doolittle, whom I met a few times. Dad had parties in the house—nothing raucous, but just good times. All of these legends who were my father's friends would come to help me later in my life and career. Eaker started out in the infantry and then took to flying. He was a great leader and a damned good human being. Spaatz became something of a mentor to me as well.

Eaker was also involved with a tour through South America that involved my dad. [See LeMay interview for details.] They were flying Loening OA-1 float planes of the Pan American Goodwill Flight on the trip that covered over twenty-two thousand miles. Dad flew bombers and was something of a celebrity as well, being one of the first B-17 pilots. He took the flight to South America on the goodwill tour, which was really a propaganda mission. We all knew [later] that Germany and Japan were becoming aggressive. I guess the tour was as much a presentation to the rest of the world as it was a mission to cultivate relationships. That was amazing back then.

Eaker got along pretty well with the British, although he decided that daylight precision bombing was preferable to the British method of night bombing. History shows that the results of strategic bombing were less than we would have hoped, but Eaker wanted to prove his theory, and we were far more accurate than the British. He firmly believed in the "round-the-clock bombing" theory, and you have to admit that it made sense on several levels. I would argue that the greatest impact was our getting fighters into the escort business, which we called Ramrods, as well as search and destroy missions: tactical ground attacks on German airfields, bridges, railways, that kind of shit. When Doolittle came on board as Eighth Air Force commander, he wanted the fighter pilots to engage the German fighters, taking them on. The Mustang made that happen—ask any German.

The British thought he was fucking nuts, and they pretty much said so, as they firmly believed daylight bombing in large numbers was nothing less than mass suicide. They had horrific losses from flak and German night fighters.* I think they lost as many if not more crews as the entire American Air Forces combined, but I could be wrong.†

But then again, they had been fighting since 1939, and after they had their ass handed to them in daylight raids, Churchill adopted the night bombing campaign. Hell, they even bombed Switzerland by accident a couple of times, believe that shit. Eaker officially took command of the Eighth Air Force in December 1942, which was only four months into operational status, mainly hitting coastal targets in France and Belgium.

Now, you have to understand that Eaker was not a bomber pilot, he started out in what was then called "pursuit" aviation, which we call fighters today. However, he was also a visionary and his ideas often crossed wires with Hap Arnold, his boss. Eaker really pushed hard to get B-17s and B-24s into the theater in large numbers, and he stressed the need to get more fighters with drop tanks and longer-range fighters into the fight. There was some kickback, as some of the senior bomber leaders felt that the bombers could defend themselves without fighters. Well, that line of thought went right out the damned window a few times.

Before the war and even during the early days there were still

---

* Bomber Command combat losses were 55,500 killed in action, with a total of 73,741 total casualties, including 9,838 airmen captured as prisoners of war. Colin D. Heaton and Anne-Marie Lewis. *Night Fighters: Luftwaffe and RAF Air Combat over Europe, 1939–1945* (Annapolis, MD: Naval Institute Press, 2008), 153.

† During World War II, one in three airmen survived the air battle over Europe. The losses were extraordinary. The casualties suffered by the Eighth Air Force were about half of the US Army Air Force's casualties (47,483 out of 115,332), including more than 26,000 dead. 389th Bomb Group newsletter and Eighth Air Force Loss Records, http://personal.psu.edu/kbf107/Losses.html.

those in the senior military roles who believed that airplanes were only good for reconnaissance, observation, and bombing to support ground operations. Basically, airborne artillery. Strategic bombing was new, innovative, and not well understood, and fighters were still relegated as forward eyes for the ground commanders. World War I taught us something important: whoever controls the air controls the battlefield below. Later, Jimmy Doolittle took over, and Eaker was placed in command of the Mediterranean Theater to include North Africa, Sicily, and Italy, that area. He had the Twelfth and Fifteenth Air Forces, as well as the British air contingent under his command.

My dad was especially pleased when his team managed to get the B-17 design approved, and that was in 1935. Boeing got the contract, and that was the genesis of the great South America tour. Those guys became world famous as a result. My dad helped change history.

Backing up a bit, I was always into sports, as I said, and I was a six-foot-two-inch stocky guy, and I was also fast and could take hits. Hell, I was about two hundred pounds, but all muscle. I was at Hampton High School in Virginia, played varsity ball and became the team captain, and in 1937 we won the state championship. Virginia Military Institute wanted me, and, after talking with Dad, I enrolled in a prep school to study and prepare to take the entrance exam.

Now, I knew that a lot of our guys had joined the Canadians and the British to go fight the Germans. Well, being the kind of young man that I was, I thought about doing the same thing, like Buddy [Colonel Edward R.] Haydon did. I took the paperwork back home, and my dad looked at me as if I were wearing a hula skirt and said, "You've lost your mind! No way!" So I went back to the school; that was Millard Prep. I have to say they did a good job of getting me ready, and I exercised and ran a lot of miles, and did push-ups and sit-ups to ensure I was in top physical shape before I got there. I wanted to be ready.

I had a congressman willing to endorse my application to West Point, but this guy was in Pennsylvania, and we were not in his constituency. I relocated to Uniontown to establish residency; worked a few part-time jobs. That was a coal mining town—hard workers and hard living—and I was paying to stay at the YMCA. I hated it, but it was a necessary evil.

I finally got the endorsement, and my father told me that I had passed the entrance exam, so I headed to Penn Station, and my dad saw me off.

When I hit West Point, the abuse started, but I was ready for it. I raised my right hand and took the oath. I knew in my soul I was not going to wash out, and that was where I met the man who would be my best friend in my life from that day forward. Ben Cassiday was a fellow plebe (new cadet), so we shared the misery together.[10] Our parents also knew each other from back in Hawaii, and that was great. We had actually been thrown together as kids many years before, so, in an abstract way, we grew up apart but together. Ben Cassiday has always been there for me. If you ever met him, you would see what a great guy he is.

Ben and I were in the minority: our fathers were career officers, and we grew up in that environment, so we knew what to expect. We were similar that way but also different. Ben was the scholar and academic superman, and I was the athlete. We both made our marks on the school as cadets. He was also the good boy, while I had a reputation of doing things a little askew to good order and discipline. I played practical jokes all my life, but West Point was not the best environment to hone those skills I had learned.

I will give you an example. Once when I had been in England for a while, we had a new West Pointer, a young lieutenant who had flown over a dozen missions and had damaged a few Germans, but no kills. He was seething to get into the air, and he said nothing was going to keep him from flying and getting his first kill. Well, me being the practical joker, I walked out one morning right before a Ramrod. This lieutenant was jumping up and down; he just could not wait to get into the air. I waited until his back was turned and poured an entire cup of coffee just under his cowling. I walked away as if nothing had happened. Then I walked up to him and said, "Ready to get going?"

"Yes sir, I am ready!" he said smiling. Then I pointed to the ground under his number one engine.

"Damn, bad luck, I guess; no flying for you today!" And I shook my head and patted him on the back.

"Holy shit! What is that?" he asked.

"Looks like oil. Or coolant. Can't go up like that," another pilot said, trying not to laugh because he saw me do it.

"Damn!" He began yelling at his own crew chief. Well, before that sergeant got into trouble, I pulled him back and told him it was a joke.

"That was a dirty trick, sir."

"Yes, it was," I said to him, smiling the whole time, while all the others laughed at him. "Welcome to the unit."

Getting back to the main story: I wanted to play football, and West Point had a terrible record, especially against Navy. The commandant was Major General Robert L. Eichelberger, and he was sick of the bad record, so he brought a coach in from Dartmouth College. His name was Red Blaik, and he was a legend in college football back then. Well, our fortunes changed, and we began winning games against teams that would have been considered impossible, and I played tackle for both teams. In essence, I was both defense and offense, which is rare, and I made all-American, which made me proud, but my dad was ecstatic.

Then when Japan attacked Pearl Harbor, I knew that the world had changed. Ironically, my brother Stevan was at the academy, and we heard that pilots were being sent to Europe in a few months. Our pace was accelerated so that we could graduate in 1943, but that did not mean that the academic standard was lowered. They just pushed more work on us, and Ben thrived in it. Upon graduation, I think almost half the graduating class chose aviation over infantry and artillery. That may have been a record.

The next phase of life was flight school—several of them, in fact. Ben and I both went to Tulsa, Oklahoma, for primary flight school at Spartan College of Aeronautics and Technology and there we met many of the men who would become our friends. And many became legends of aviation. Ben knew some people there, which was why we decided to go. Our training consisted of ground school and basic flight instruction. We studied aerodynamics, weather, emergency procedures, engineering, regulations, first aid—everything.

I took to flying naturally, but many did not. Several washed out for various reasons, and disciplinary issues would also get you thrown out. I had to temper my natural lighthearted nature, not screw up, and stay the course. One day, not long after I had arrived, my instructor told me to take it up and deliver four good landings. Well, of course I was nervous, as this was my first solo. I knew that failure was not an option.

I did the landings, was approved, and completed my final check ride, and was passed on from primary training to basic. Now, in flight school, what they do not tell you until it happens is that the flight instructor at some point will kill the engine. This is when you go through the emergency procedures. But if you were diligent and did not panic, it was not a big deal, and they knew that. What they were looking for in a student pilot was cognitive and spatial skill: always know where you are and have an emergency landing location somewhere in your brain housing group [military term for the intellectual thought process], just in case of a real-life emergency.

After graduating that first phase, we had a ten-day pass before returning to West Point for the next semester. You see, we had summers off to attend various military schools between spring and fall semesters, so, during your summers, you were still in some school somewhere. My dad sent a B-24 Liberator to take me to Spokane, Washington, where he commanded the Second Bomb Wing, and he had been promoted to major general. I was proud of him also. I spent a few days with him and my stepmother before I was flown back in a B-24 to Washington, DC, and then return to West Point.

The next course of study on top of academics and playing football was more flight instruction at Stewart Field nearby. You have to remember that they shortened the four-year curriculum to three years, but that just increased the academic workload. Basically, with all that going on, there was not a personal life. Study, play football, train, catch the bus to go fly, get back, eat chow, and sleep when you could. I think I averaged four hours' sleep a night for that last year, so I was always tired mentally and physically. But that only prepared me for being a leader in wartime; exhaustion overtakes any man at some point. It is being able to withstand those pressures far beyond what even you think you can handle that makes you more effective.

Then things got really intense when we started night flying training, instrumentation, and I had to do this after a hard afternoon of football practice. We were all exhausted. It got even worse when I had my front teeth knocked out by a sucker punch, nose busted. I had my gum and lip sewn up, but I got back in the game. That motherfucker who did it to me got to feel some medieval payback; I broke two of his ribs, and he did not come back into the game. That game against Navy, even though we lost, earned me all-American.

After the game, my buddy Dick McChord said, "Robin, you look really bad," and I said, "How about a kiss?" We laughed, and still I chuckled even though I was in a lot of pain. I was always able to handle pain. I had played with a dislocated shoulder, bruised ribs—all the knocks you would expect. Remember that we did not play with modern pads or helmets, and many times after a game, my head was thumping from the impact.

That game was great, but I also wished that I had my teeth. With football season over, I could focus upon the academics that Ben excelled at. I spoke to my roommate Scat about all of this. Scat Davis was a great guy, but he washed out of flight training because he was color blind. I was amazed they even kept him in the military at all. Scat was a great guy, and I felt terrible for him. People wonder where the name Scat came from on every fighter I flew—well, now you have the answer.

Scat and Ben, along with many other fellow cadets, supported me when I was caught after having a drink in town. A senior cadet, a real asshole who few liked, and he really did not like me, asked me if I had had alcohol, and I told the truth. The board of cadets reduced me in rank, so I went from a senior cadet down to private and given all sorts of extra duty and shit.

Well, my fighter pilot career was almost cut short by this prick instructor who did not like me for some reason, so he wrote me up for bomber training after finishing single-engine training. I was pretty pissed off, but I knew that there was only so much I could control in life, and the military priority always took precedent over an individual's wishes. I thought my dream died right there. Not having football practice also meant more time for pranks and shit like that. We were always pulling practical jokes. If it was possible, we did it; you name it, we probably did it. When I say "we," I have to admit that I also did a few things, but there was always payback.

I started my twin-engine training in New York in the Beechcraft AT-10 Wichita, a steady twin trainer. My instructor was a great guy, and he felt my pain. He was suffering from the same problem: he wanted to fly fighters in combat as well. Well, my instructor and I broke all the rules, flying to have fun, under bridges, buzzing roads—the kind of shit that would get you grounded if not court-martialed. He was so impressed with my flying, he wrote a recommendation that I be sent to fighters, so the previous prick's recommendation was overruled. I was happier than a pimp on payday.

———

I was getting ready for final exams at West Point when my brother and I were notified that my father was ill. He'd had a heart attack. Steve and I flew to see him, that was permitted. My father was well known to the cadre, and when a major general asks to see his sons, no one was going to say no under those circumstances. We were with him, as well as my stepmother. I told him that I got my wish: I was going to be a fighter pilot. He smiled weakly and told me to never think I know everything. He died soon afterward. I was devastated. I knew that I was going to accomplish great things to honor my dad as much as for myself. My dad's mother came to visit me as my guest. I received my diploma and commission, and Hap Arnold had pinned my wings on me the day before. He told me, "Your father would be proud, Robin." I felt like crying but held it back.

Later, I completed advanced fighter pilot training with the 329th Fighter Group at Grand Central Air Terminal in Glendale, California. Twin-engine training for bombers started at Williams Field, near Chandler, Arizona, in the Curtiss-Wright AT-9, followed by transition training to the P-38 Lightning. The hours of grinding paperwork were supplemented by insults hurled at us from the instructors. These clowns were fucking amateurs, because after the bullshit at West Point, I had to try not to laugh. The biggest way to fuck up was to announce you were a West Pointer. That would bring a world of verbal hurt and even extra duty. Keep quiet, slide along, get through, and get the hell out. That was my plan, anyway.

Our training started in the Curtiss AT-9, which would be my plane for some time before I even got near a P-38. Then after all that, we were sent to fly the Lockheed P-322, which had the props spinning in the same direction. The P-38 had opposite-rotating propellers, so totally different animals. The P-322 also had a few idiosyncrasies that made the British refuse to accept them on Lend-Lease. [The Lend-Lease Act was the American wartime loan agreement to the Allies.] Well, in traditional military wisdom, this garbage was sent to the training school instead.

I guess some congressman made a nice pork barrel project to get his constituents to build them, and now we had to live with them. In essence, the P-322 was a dangerous, unreliable plane. I guess they figured if you could fly that piece of shit and survive, you could handle the Lightning. The P-322 also did not have turbochargers, and you had to keep your eyes on the gauges, or bad shit could happen. I called it "doing the voodoo you do so not to get screwed." I guess you can tell I really did not like that aircraft. It killed a buddy of mine in training, Bob Orr; the engines just died. Sometimes students or instructors would have to land with an engine problem. It was as if the gods of aviation took a squat and shit that plane out. I could not wait to be rid of it.

But it was not all doom and gloom, although a few of us got into trouble when we were in a loose formation, when we decided to bounce a stray P-322. We swooped in from behind and below, harassing the hell out of the guy, and I know he could see us laughing at him. Well, when we landed, we were ordered to the CO's office. Unknown to us, it was him whom we had pissed off. He asked whose idea it was, and I stepped forward with another pilot. I do not think the major was expecting that, but we followed the honor code and admitted it. I thought my career was over, but he just told us not to do anything like that again. That feeling that my career was over after either a stupid or even well-thought-out stunt would become all too familiar during my career.

We then went for gunnery training at Matagorda, Texas, in August 1943, a humid piece of hell that was as barren as the surface of the moon. The water was undrinkable; Coca-Cola was used for everything except bathing. No one wanted to drink the brown water. The last thing anyone wanted was dysentery. But this was a great time for flying and shooting, as we were in the AT-6 Texan, a great, fun plane to fly.

The Texan had a 16-millimeter camera to record our gunnery, and it was armed with a cowling-mounted .30-caliber machine gun, synchronized to fire through the prop, just like all modern single-engine fighters. We shot at these towed target sleeves and were evaluated on the film footage and what the target streamer looked like. That was not a big deal for me; I was pretty good at the shooting. We had classes in all the math and science of shooting, but all of that came naturally. I understood g-forces, platform and target speeds, declination, angle of fire, target lead, drop and angle off deflection shooting. It pretty much just took a pilot knowing his weapons and how to use them.

I then went into P-38 training at Muroc Army Airfield in California. This was called Muroc Dry Lake [today known as Rogers Dry Lake], and for good reason. This was where we had fun—no bullshit. We ended up near Barstow, and this place made our previous station look like a fucking paradise. No shit, I tell you, this was a place that as soon as we set foot on it, depression set in. I looked around at this train station, such as it was, and saw a phone on the wall. Since no one else was there except us new arrivals, I picked it up, and a voice asked me, "How many?" and I said, "Seven." We were told to wait; a truck would come get us. I was just hoping we would not have to push the damned truck when it got there.

Our quarters were wood-framed tents, basically; no amenities at all. The P-38s were a battered bunch of old worn-out warbirds, but we were still eager to fly them. Some were older C and D models, with a few E models in the mix. The controls were very different from anything I had previously flown, as was the power in the twin Allison engines.

There were training deaths: one guy came in for a landing and rolled over right into the ground. Explosion, fire, and certain death. Then not much later that day, another P-38 was taking off but never made it: the nose gear collapsed, and he just slid into the desert, though he was fine. That same day, coming back from lunch in the truck, we saw two more birds nose up, and then two pilots bailed out. Then, the same damned day, I remind you, another pilot tried landing with one engine, and his effort was less than stellar. He touched, bounced, and ended up in the dry lake with his nose gear collapsed under him. Last but not least, two pilots died when they collided. Nine accidents and two deaths in one day may not have been a record, but it sure as hell was a great preparation for combat. We came to the same conclusion we'd had at our previous duty station: if the training aircraft does not kill us, we were definitely immortal.

Well, they bounced us around to various bases, waiting for combat orders which never came, and eventually cooled our heels in Glendale. The common consensus was that this was a much better assignment than Texas. At least there was booze and even a few broads. When December came, we were all promoted to first lieutenant, and we were proud. That meant a pay increase on top of our flight pay, and we got per diem also.

Then another setback happened when another pilot and I were called in to the flight commander's office, and he yelled at us and told us we were grounded. We were charged with misallocating assets, unauthorized use of the P-38s—that kind of bullshit. The new rule from Fourth Air Force was that there were to be no transfers to combat units except for pilots designated as flight commanders; but only pilots with a combat tour could be flight commanders.

I told him that I wanted leave to go to Washington, DC, and he asked why. I told him that I wanted to see General Hap Arnold, and he seemed to get even angrier. I was double fucked, stuck, and there was not a damned thing I could do about it.

My partner in crime and I decided to drive to HQ in Los Angeles and see if we could speak to someone. We came across this crusty old sergeant, and after a light discussion, he was typing up orders. I told him of the other five poor souls stuck there with us who wanted to go into combat, and he typed his ass off. That old grunt became my best friend really quick, I can tell you. Leave it to the NCOs [noncommissioned officers] to get shit done, I always said.

Well, I managed to be assigned to the 434th Fighter Squadron of the 479th Fighter Group, based at Lomita, California. I had logged around 650 hours of flying time during training, including 250 hours or more in the P-38 Lightning, as the 479th was being built up as a combat group. I knew that if I racked up any more hours, I would never leave the States. They would have made me an instructor pilot until the war was over.

The night before we left, we had a unit party. We were raring to get the hell out of there, for sure, and I woke up the next morning in a bad way. Let's just say I was really torn up from the floor up, and when I opened my eyes, I saw this room basically destroyed. I thought I had missed the movement to the train station, as we were going to the East Coast to get ready to embark on a ship to Europe. If I missed movement, I was a dead man.

I staggered to my feet, grabbed my bag and pistol belt, made sure the .45 was still there, and walked out to see the entire formation already lined up, and most of them were doing well just to stay straight and vertical, like me. I wanted to puke. We boarded the train and tried to get comfortable. We were bored like hell, but we did pass the time shooting our pistols and shit like that, until the CO came and confiscated our guns. Not our best moment.

After a few days we arrived at Fort Dix, New Jersey, collected our bags, and were assigned to our barracks. This was time for us to get briefed on what we could expect—basically, an intel brief. We watched a lot of aerial combat footage, studied enemy and friendly aircraft silhouettes and nomenclatures, did ship evacuation drills, mass exits, poison gas drills, rifle drills—you name it. I was confused as shit. Was I going to fly or go to the infantry or navy?

We then boarded another train and rode until we hit the dock, and then we all shipped out aboard the USS *Argentina* for Europe on May 3. I remember seeing the Statue of Liberty as we passed, going east, knowing that so many new Americans first saw that statue as they came from the opposite direction to start a new life. The next day, we were part of a massive convoy. Everyone was quietly wondering if we would get hit by torpedoes, and we were one of the largest ships. If I were a sub commander, I would be looking at my big-ass ship through a periscope also.

Then one day we heard—no, we *felt*—this big *thump* against the hull. Then another. We all thought it was a U-boat, but we were told that it was a destroyer laying depth charges, and we were feeling the concussion effect. I thought that if we felt it that strong, those poor bastards under the water would really hate life. I was then really glad I was an airman and not a sailor.

We arrived in Scotland on May 14, 1944. Then took the train to the RAF base at Wattisham, England. I was amazed at the difference between the British trains and ours; we were a primitive culture when it came to rail comfort. We rolled through the darkest night I ever experienced. The British practiced the total blackout, unlike us. Then our train stopped, and we were told to get out. This was amusing, as you could not see anything in front of you—pitch damned black. You had to walk with your arms out to feel your way forward.

Next we were told to climb into a truck bed and then we were off—minus my bag. We drove for about an hour until we stopped at a building. We got out, walked in, and entered a room with blackout curtains. Our squadron intelligence officers were there to greet us. This half-assed makeshift hotel was a really nice place, and we had nice rooms, and our bags were already there waiting for us. They even had a bar.

The next day, we took a tour of the new base. It had taken a few hits by the German bombers but overall was one hell of an upgrade from the deep shit holes we had been placed in back home. Then we saw an entire line of new P-38Js—beautiful—but we were told we had to attend classes on them before we flew anything.

The next day, we had an inventory issue, new gear, everything we would need in case we were shot down. We were issued a parachute, dinghy, Mae West,* flare pistol, leather jackets, gloves, boots, signal mirror—that sort of stuff. I remember one of the guys asked, "Where are the rubbers?" He meant condoms, and everyone laughed. He didn't laugh; this guy was serious! Another guy asked about shark repellent, and he was told that the water was too cold for sharks, so we did not get any. "Do not worry, you will die of hypothermia before anything could eat you anyway."

I have to admit that our classes were a bit of a culture shock. Figuring out British money was not easy, but the beer was all right. I was looking for the good stuff: single-malt scotch. We were in the

---

* An inflatable life jacket named for the buxom film star.

bar when Lord Haw-Haw was on.[11] He was talking about us, welcoming us to Wattisham, and he mentioned that we would be paid a visit very soon. Then a German bomber dropped a few bombs across the base, so it looked like we must have made an impression. I just wanted to start flying. I always wondered how the damned Germans knew so much.

I have to say this: there were two types of Brits where we were concerned. There were those who were happy as all hell that we were there helping out in the war. Then there were those who wished we had never arrived; most of these were some of the RAF boys and all the male civilians. You have to understand, we were well-paid, dashing young officers, fighter pilots, and we were like exotic creatures in a very small zoo. The women loved us, and that caused a few problems on occasion.

It was May 22, 1944, and I was assigned to the 479th Fighter Group at this particular time, with the job of flying P-38 Lightings, and we soon joined many other groups on Ramrod missions. We had been doing ground attack, strafing and dropping bombs in a tactical support role, but those were not the missions that made you excited to get up and strap in. I remember in one briefing that we were told to expect something like 50 percent losses per mission. Guys began shaking. Some could not eat breakfast before a mission; others who did eat threw up before starting the mission.

Over the next few weeks, we practiced and flew a lot, getting used to the new P-38s. It was like an entirely different aircraft from the birds in California. They were smooth and sweet, and the power in conjunction with the intercoolers and super turbochargers gave us a climb rate that was incredible. We were briefed on the dangers of a high-speed dive. It had been recorded that compression lockup had been experienced on the yoke once you passed six hundred knots. I recorded that data for future reference. I knew we could outclimb and outdive, but it would be a bad day if you could not pull out of a dive.

In fact, I compared our training back home to what we were doing at Wattisham, and there was no comparison. We were poorly prepared for what we were expected to do, and this refresher training turned out to be the best training we had overall. We also had some losses in training there, aircraft and pilots, but that is part of the program that you have to accept. Besides, you always knew that it would only happen to the other guys, never you.

When I got my own P-38J, I was the happiest I had ever been in my life up to that point. My crew chief was a great guy, Glen Wold, and I can tell you that the best relationship in the world is between a pilot and his chief mechanic.[12] That is no bullshit, either. Wold painted "SCAT II" on the nose. I was going to keep my promise to my friend Scat Davis. I remember that I had a photo taken not long afterward and mailed it to him.

We also learned the procedures for a combat flight briefing on weather, altitudes, rendezvous points, target identification, time on target, the best intelligence available on antiaircraft and fighter defenses, radio channels, both primary and emergency. Then we began the ritual that would precede every mission after breakfast: we hit the latrines, collected maps, parachutes, Mae Wests, took all of our personal items and placed them in the locker with exception to dog tags and a wristwatch. Nothing to be taken into the air that could give the enemy any intelligence on us should we be shot down.

I always felt that was kind of horseshit, since Lord Haw-Haw had greeted us on the radio when we arrived and knew exactly who we were. On top of that, my suspicions were proven correct. Those guys who I knew, like Gabreski and Zemke, were captured and interrogated, and that interrogator knew everything about them.[13] He knew where they were from, their parents' names, siblings—even the names of their wives and kids, if they had any. This guy knew their unit. Hell, this fucking German even knew their call signs. Talk about effective intelligence.

After all the crap that we had to endure, I managed to go on my first combat mission, and it was a no joy, really [no enemy activity], but I did suffer from lack of oxygen for a bit. We were at twenty thousand feet doing a sweep over northern France, and I think the problem was that the open lever just did not open all the way. I was getting some O_2 but not enough, but I managed. We all knew that at some point there would be a cross-channel invasion. I expected all of us to be pulling air cover for the naval and ground forces when that day arrived.

The next few missions were bomber escorts, which was a double-edged sword. First, you knew that the Germans would come up to get the bombers, which meant the chance to engage and get kills. But we also had orders to stick close to the bombers as protection, and that severely handicapped fighters. One thing I liked about Zemke was that he threw that bullshit aside and still followed his orders. He sent out three waves, the last staying with the bombers, while the first two groups would engage and whittle the enemy down, keep them busy.

I knew that Curtis LeMay was promoted to general and was a bomber group commander. He had been flying since the first days the Eighth Air Force had been assigned to Britain. I wanted to look him up if I could, as he had been an aide and worked for my father. LeMay was another guy who was an ultimate no-bullshit warrior, and I will quote him: "Get the fucking job done, kill as many as you can, then get home and plan the next mission." We all loved that guy for his warrior ethos, but he had problems also with his superiors, and he had a tendency to be totally inflexible and hardheaded. But the Brits pretty much loved him. He picked up a second star and was sent to the Pacific, so I did not have the chance to get together with him until after the war.

Our first few missions were really uneventful. Watching the flak explode around you was enchanting, but you really did not want one of those to hit your bird. As I saw all that flak over Germany, I again went through my bailout procedures in my head. I had yet to see an enemy fighter—it was as if they had packed up and gone home. The bombers just kept pounding the hell out of the French coast; we were just along for the ride, I guess.

Then we were given a very long, in-depth briefing on ground attack missions, targets of significance, and targets of opportunity. Railways, road traffic, petroleum locations, and airfields were the top priorities. The theory was that if you shot up trains and destroyed railways, no supplies. Same with road traffic. Hitting airfields was self-explanatory: destroy aircraft on the ground, hit aerodromes, crater runways if you carried five-hundred-pounders. Hitting fuel and oil supply depots was a bonus. Mechanical shit needs fuel and lubricants. The problem with hitting airfields and railyards was that they all had defensive ground fire to nail you when you arrived or when you tried to leave the target area.

These were the least-favored missions, I can tell you. It never really bothered me too much. I felt comfortable knowing that I could dive down, scream in at over four hundred knots, shoot shit up, then pull away unscathed. But I also knew that there were graves and prison camps full of guys who thought the same thing. That was how they got Haydon and Gabreski.

Later, as ground attack missions intensified, they said some bullshit like 80 percent or even 90 percent losses could be expected by us fighter pilots doing ground support. Well, I knew right then and there that was not a statistic I wanted to be a part of. That kind of information makes you look around the room and wonder who in the hell was not going to be there for a debriefing when it was all over. I was frustrated that we were not allowed to drop down and shoot up the shit we saw. There were many targets of opportunity, but unless we were unleashed, we had our orders. We could not understand why we were not being allowed to attack ground targets at will, but quite a few of the guys were happy about it.

We were getting the combat reports from all the other fighter wings. The Fourth, 352nd, 357th, and Fifty-Sixth Fighter Groups were chewing up Germans at a rate that made us wonder if there would be any enemy left for us. I was pissed, and I was not alone. So, one day I was flying along and saw another train. I did not ask permission to attack, I just radioed that I was going in. Now, there were several things that could result from that action. I could get a medal, I could get killed, or I could get court-martialed for disobeying a direct order. Hell, knowing the army, they would probably dig up my corpse and sit me in the courtroom just to hear the charges. I said to myself, "Screw this, I am going in," and I did.

Well, I started a shallow dive, lined it up, and aimed for the engine, not the cab. We all knew that the French were normally pressed into service by the Germans, so I did not want to be the "ugly American" and have bad PR by killing some locals. I saw them jump from the target, and I fired. I then pulled up and then came back around, running it from rear to front. I was disappointed that I did not get a big explosion. We saw all those in the combat footage from gun camera films, and I wondered why mine did not blow up. But after I pulled up and turned for a third pass, I saw that bastard on fire. Then, no shit, every other pilot came down to pump some rounds into an already dead-ass train. There was no way they were not going to fire their weapons into a target.

I felt very satisfied with myself, and I was shocked that there was no radio chatter about the event either before, during, or after. Just silence. That was until our flight leader came over the radio, then nothing. We were climbing to head back to escort the bombers headed home after their mission. The flak was pretty heavy, and I saw a B-17 catch a flak shell. It blew up and disintegrated; it became a great ball of fire. I watched it as it seemed to slowly float down to the ground. There were no parachutes, just large fluttering confetti. I then felt really bad for those guys, and I would see more of that. To this day, I have nothing but admiration for the bomber crews and especially officers like LeMay. He led these missions, not just sat on his ass in an office waiting for bomb damage assessments and posting results. That is a true leader in my book.

I was always scanning the sky for the enemy on the way back home. The greatest thing any fighter pilot wants is to tangle in air combat with the enemy. If you are a fighter pilot, that is in your blood; it is why you live. I breathed air combat, and I flew as many missions as I could. I wanted to be an ace, I'll admit it, but then again, every fighter pilot feels the same way. It's sort of like being a race car driver: if you do not want that checkered flag, why fucking bother to even get behind the wheel?

Well, that radio silence was not a good omen. Even after we were over the English Channel, and even over England, no one spoke—not even the CO, which was not a good sign. I knew I was in trouble. I was not sure if it would be just me or the entire flight. After landing, we caught a ride back to the operations building, did our debriefing, and then it happened. I was called in to see the major. I was right.

He came up to me in front of the entire squadron, public humiliation. He read me the riot act, listed all the violations I had committed, and asked me to give him a reason not to put me in Leavenworth. I have to admit that I felt about as low as a rattlesnake with a bull standing over him ready to drop. That was my chance. I told him that I had radioed the target, my intent, his voice said, "Roger," so I thought that was permission to attack. I had him, and he knew it.

I enjoyed the Ramrod missions. Keeping the Germans off the bombers was the main priority, and Hub Zemke's Fifty-Sixth Fighter Group were the go-to guys. Hub's methods taught me a lot; he made up his own rules, and, as a result, his pilots were the hottest in the European theater. I would follow his example twenty years later, but we will get to that. His Zemke's Wolfpack had the best guys, like Bob Johnson, Frank Gabreski, Bud Mahurin, and even Hub himself. They were just slapping the living hillbilly hell out of the Luftwaffe.

Johnson was the first to break Edward Rickenbacker's score of twenty-six kills, along with Major Dick Bong in the Pacific. They made Johnson go back stateside on a war bond tour, so for him the war was over. We spoke about that after the war, and he was pissed off about it. I would have been too, because they let Bong go back to become our top ace of the war.

Hub thought up a plan to take his P-47s into three waves; a Pathfinder group fanned out wide to stir up trouble and bring the Germans up, a second wave to then engage the enemy after the first wave whacked them, and the third wave to stay with the bombers and pick off any Germans who got through the first two waves. It was a very effective method, and it was adopted pretty much by everyone not long afterward. It was a sound tactic, and Doolittle made it a standard mission practice.

Our group worked very well with Zemke and the other groups. One of the greatest problems was communications. Radio silence was sacred, in order to not alert the Germans to our presence, but we knew that they would pick us up on radar and be waiting. They had the advantage of flying over friendly terrain. If a German bailed out safely, he was back in the air soon. If we went over the side, it was into a prison camp, unless you pulled off a Yeager or Mahurin and managed to get friendlies on the ground to get you out.

Previously our fighters, especially the P-47s, had limited range, and by the time they hit Belgium, they had to turn back, until they got the drop tanks. The P-38s had a greater range, especially with the drop tanks, but it was the P-51 Mustang that really took the war to the enemy. The Rolls-Royce Merlin engine replaced the earlier Allison, and with the two-speed, two-stage supercharger, lighter airframe weight and wing design, the Mustang could fly to Russia. In fact, the first shuttle mission was flown by Colonel Don Blakeslee around June 1944, I think. That shows you the range of that wonderful aircraft.

The six .50s [.50-caliber machine guns] delivered less lead on target than the P-47 with eight guns, but we could climb faster and had a better roll rate and turn radius. But we could never take the amount of damage a Thunderbolt could. Those big-ass birds would come in shot up so bad you had to scratch your head as to how they still flew. Plus, the P-47 had a great advantage on the damage factor, being an air-cooled radial Pratt & Whitney, whereas we were liquid cooled, like the Me 109. If you took a hit in the radiator, you had to make quick decisions in short order.

The P-38 was great for several reasons: being a twin engine, if you lost one engine, you could still get back, and it gave you a great power-to-weight ratio. The Allisons were liquid cooled, like all nonradial fighters, but the superchargers were great. You really had to keep an eye on your RPMs and trim, and maintain vigilance on the throttle control, so you were kept busy. The best part about the aircraft was the nose-mounted weapons: .50s and a 20-millimeter cannon, depending upon the variant you flew. There was no need to harmonize the guns, as they were not wing mounted. You had a lovely line of sight to line of impact, and the firepower was devastating.

The Lightning was perhaps the most versatile aircraft in the war, next to the de Havilland [DH 98] Mosquito. It was a fighter, fighter-bomber, photo reconnaissance, night fighter—it was suited to everything. Really, the only major change in the Lightning during production cycle was in the P-38J. They placed the intakes under the engines, making them bigger to accommodate the core-type inter-coolers, and the standard curved windscreen was replaced by a flat panel. It also had larger boom-mounted radiators. The two engines were 1,425 horsepower, and with drop tanks, its range was over two thousand miles.

The bail-out procedure was one that none of us Lightning pilots wanted to experience. Unlike the single-engine fighters, you had to exit the cockpit and slide down the ass-end, dropping between the twin-boom section. The thought of hitting the horizontal stabilizer was enough to make you not want to take to a parachute, but it was what it was. I used to go through the bail-out sequence in my head should I ever have to get out. I thought about a sharp climb to bleed off airspeed, dump the canopy, and slightly invert the aircraft at the apex of the stall, then push out with my legs. Amazing the thoughts that you have as a pilot.

Well, one day we walked out to our aircraft to see that black and white stripes had been painted on our booms and wings. These were to help easily identify our planes from the enemy so that our own pilots and ground gunners did not shoot us down. That morning of June 5, 1944, we were briefed. The invasion was on for the next day, and we were going to join other P-38 units on the first support operations that day, since our planes were easily distinguishable even at high altitude to the naval gunners. I really did not want to get killed by my own people—that was not acceptable to me—but it did happen on occasion. Perhaps the best example was P-51 ace Major George Preddy. He got nailed by American ground fire chasing a German. Shit happens, I guess.[14]

We took off and crossed the channel and could see the Normandy coast ahead. We saw hundreds of ships. I had never seen as many in one place before or since—it was incredible. I wondered about those poor soldiers going to hit those beaches. We knew the navy had been shelling inland and the bombers had been saturating the countryside to destroy structures and kill as many Germans as they could to soften up the area. I just hoped that they had done enough, because the weather was supposed to be terrible for them. I knew that I was probably having a front seat to the greatest show on earth, one that would never be repeated. Well, we then turned back having not seen any Germans, which I thought was odd. Maybe the other fighter groups had killed them all, or they had been sent to Russia. Who knew?

The morning of June 6, we all wondered what it would be like. Would the Germans come up in force to attack the landing beaches? Would the German navy crawl out to engage the Allied warships? What about our troops hitting those beaches, what would they face? I suddenly felt very sorry for those ground troops, because I was safe high overhead. Well, I guess the word "safe" is a relative term. My day started out fine, but I could not find my lucky socks, and that pissed me off. I always flew with them.

Let me tell you, despite the amount of education and experience any fighter pilot has, there is one universal truth: we are all superstitious creatures to some degree. For me, it was my lucky socks. I always flew my missions in those socks. I had to wear another pair until I could find them, and that made me nervous. I finally found them later, and I wore those old things even during Vietnam.

We took off and saw what had been happening. It appeared that the Germans were not quite bombed out of their positions, as shore batteries had hit a few ships, which were smoking. I could see our men, probably mostly boys, in the water, some disappeared, others on the beach, most were not moving; those who did move stopped suddenly. It was hell down there. I did pray as I saw it. One of my West Point classmates was down there; "We played football together," I thought about him.

Our orders were clear. We were not to engage ground targets lest we hit our own troops, but we could easily distinguish between the Germans on the cliffs and our men catching hell below, and I wanted to roll over and just strafe the shit out of them, but I knew I risked a court-martial if I violated my orders. I had already dodged a couple of those in the past. Pushing my luck was not part of the program, and I felt guilty as hell about it. We cruised up and down those beaches for hours, and I never saw a German aircraft.

After a couple of weeks, we were reassigned to interdiction missions: that meant ground support. Those old statistics were brought up again, as if we needed reminding. We were to carry bombs as tactical bombers to knock out bridges, hit marshaling yards, troops in the open, airfields, trains—whatever we could find. Our job was to be the tactical scalpel supplementing the heavy- and medium-bomber chain saws. "Interdiction" is a nice, fancy word for just fucking things up for the enemy, and I liked it. But I wanted air combat.

We were not naïve. We knew that there were Germans out there with many years of combat experience and dozens of aerial kills. Some of the Germans were known to us. We had heard of Adolf Galland, Josef Priller, and the like. The Brits were very familiar with them. We knew a few of these guys had over a hundred kills. That was a sobering thought. These were not guys to take lightly. As we did these ground attack missions, those damned statistics were proving accurate. We lost a lot of pilots, and we kept getting in replacements. They must have thought we were old men, just like we thought of the cadre when we arrived. It seemed like every mission meant another pilot lost, if not more. We had to believe that the damage we were doing warranted those losses.

One day a B-17 came in low and bellied in near the base. We all heard it, stepped outside, and saw the big bitch plow up the field with the props. It came to a smoking rest, and the crew began to exit the plane. The crash crews rolled the truck out to pump water on it. One of the guys was yelling that they had a gunner still on board. Later, we found out it was a tail gunner. Then another guy running away yelled "Bombs on board!" and we all headed for shelter. I ran into the officers' club and took a dive over a table, and then it happened. The explosion rocked every building, blew out windows, and rattled my remaining teeth. My ears rang for a long time. Incredible, really.

Our drought finally ended on July 5, when one of our pilots shot down an Fw 200 Condor taking off from his airfield, our first kill.[15] That was followed the next day by a Messerschmitt Me 109 being taken down. A few days later, we hit an ammo dump, and I guess we got a little close and nursed some damaged Lightnings home. My crew chief took a photo of the bird when I stopped. It looked like someone had just gone to town with a shotgun and peppered the damned thing, but nothing vital was hit.

In July I was promoted to captain and made a flight leader, and I was prouder than a kid in school losing his virginity. But we were pissed off in general, and I was really upset in particular, as I had not scored a single air victory. I knew that the S-2 [military intelligence] had the info, or at least I believed he did. I wanted to know where the Germans were. The photo recon pilots took the pictures, and the intel goons made the maps and marked the targets. Sometimes we would get orders to hit an airfield, but many times they were empty—no planes on the ground. Where the hell were the fighters that were stationed there? Why could we not find them? It made no sense to me. What really pissed me off was that we rarely got intel on the defenses of a target, their locations, and estimated caliber. That would be good shit to know.

Well, I offered our S-2 a chance to take a ride with me in a two-seater P-38, as we had a couple of them. Sometimes these types were converted to night fighters with an airborne radar on board; the backseater was the radar operator and navigator. What my S-2 captain did not know was that I had the four .50s and the .20-millimeter loaded. I was going hunting with him on board. I decided to fuck with him, and I flew over to Holland. He thought we were still over England when I called out a train. I took the bird down, lined up the attack, and pumped a mega million rounds into the locomotive.

My S-2 lost his fucking mind. He thought I had just blown up a British train. Then we started receiving ground fire. Big-ass tracers flew right by the Plexiglas cockpit and under the wings. He was screaming in panic. I then decided to take it to the deck and zoomed across to the coast. He never spoke a word, even after we landed and took a jeep back to the office.

I think he was scared shitless. I had wanted to make a point. I asked him the same kinds of questions about how many targets, where was the flak—all the silly questions asked by someone who was not a pilot. I wanted him to understand that when you are up there, you are just too fucking busy to take notes and write a goddamned essay. He got the point. By the way, that was not an authorized mission, I got no credit for the flight or the destroyed train. I just did not need that kind of heat. But it was fun as hell. Sometimes you just have to do what you gotta do, you know?

Well, one of my more memorable missions was flying this Ramrod, and we all had drop tanks. We used up the fuel in those until they were dry, or we engaged the enemy, then we dropped them—hence the term. That really gave us better range. That above all else was what killed the Luftwaffe. They could produce fighters, although not as many as we could, but killing their pilots was our great advantage. Galland admitted that. That was Doolittle's mantra.

We encountered what must have been around a hundred enemy fighters in three waves: Me 109s and Fw 190s. I saw about fifty of the bastards in front of me, slightly below, and I tell my wingman we are going in. It's only the two of us, and we had all those lovely targets. Later on, it dawned on me that two Lightnings engaging fifty Germans without calling in support was not such a bright idea, but what the hell. I guess you take what you can get. I managed a kill and a damaged, and everyone felt some kind of love on that mission.

Regarding being out and about with the locals, my first pass I took was to London, where I gained valuable intel on customs, courtesies, and such. It was there when I saw my first V-1 flying bomb. I saw it go over, heard the noise, then silence, and then it must have landed not far away. The dull *thump* was followed by an explosion. While there, I met some great people, but most interesting I ran into an old classmate and fellow teammate, Dick McChord, who was flying B-17s. He was stationed right near me. Go figure! We caught up on things and counted the numbers of V-1s that we had both experienced that same day.

We spoke at length about his missions, my little ones, and I told him how much I admired what his guys did. I just could not fathom flying a bomber into the clouds of flak, enduring German fighter attacks, knowing that I had several tons of fuel and high explosives under my ass. Those guys were real heroes. Then I thought about my dad and his efforts to get the B-17 into production. I often wondered what he would have thought about the way things worked out. I think he would have been proud.

Well, August was an eye-opener, and after three months, half of my squadron was gone: killed or languishing in POW camps somewhere. Most of the time, we would get word about one of our guys through the Red Cross, so we knew they were alive, at least. I cannot imagine what their families went through. I really hoped my family did not get one of those, or, even worse, a Western Union delivery.

This was when I met Colonel Hubert "Hub" Zemke. His Fifty-Sixth Fighter Group had produced the highest aces in the theater to date; they were aggressive and effective as hell. We admired them, and he was like a god, just like Don Blakeslee, who commanded the Fourth Fighter Group. Zemke came to us with a shitload of experience. He was a longtime fighter pilot, flew everything, had trained the Russians on the P-40 Warhawk, and his ingenious tactics brought results.

Here is a fucked-up example of how strange the world is. You mentioned a few names, Germans I met, and Gunther Rall was one of them. He is a great guy, and I like the hell out of him. He and Zemke's boys tangled a few times. Shorty Rankin shot off his thumb and shot him down, but they became great friends.[16] Go figure. Gunther was one of those guys you feared, with years of experience he shot down over two hundred planes.

Well, Hub was our new commander as we had been informed that we were going into Mustangs in the near future, and he wanted to fly them. He gave us a wealth of information on German fighters, their abilities, tactics, and methods, and compared their aircraft strengths and limitations with our own fighters.

Zemke drew diagrams, had models made, and taught us what we needed to know about dogfighting. He gave us a lecture that he said he gave to his old unit: "Think several maneuvers ahead of what you plan to execute, know your aircraft, remember the capabilities and limitations of your fighter and that of your opponent, and never go into the fight alone. Radio your intentions, location, call out bandits, and do not leave your wingman. Anything else is a fucked-up operation."

Well, we got our orders. We were to bomb and knock out the bridges to block the German army's retreat, slowing them down as our ground forces tried to encircle them. Sounded easy enough. We could not understand why we were given these tactical bombing missions, still being based in England, while the Ninth Air Force was now stationed in France. They were the tactical fighter-bombers in the theater. I guess Zemke had some pull somewhere.

That morning, we had to take off early, and it was still pitch-black outside. I was commanding my own flight on this one. The takeoff that morning was a massive cluster fuck of unparalleled proportions, and I almost collided with a P-38 that was half off the runway. I managed to have enough speed to pull back and lift the gear, totally expecting to belly in when I stalled out. That would have been great, loaded with fuel and bombs. I could see it now: that Western Union telegram, informing those back home that "Captain Robin Olds died in the service of his country by pancaking on his own fucking runway. His sacrifice and the resulting explosion and column of fire lit the runway so the rest of his unit could take off without incident."

I radioed back to the field to illuminate the P-38 blocking part of the runway, so that we did not lose a plane or pilot on takeoff. I was pissed and already drenched in sweat. The radio headset was full of panic and static, as all the pilots had something to add to the confusion. I just wondered what Zemke would make of this circus sideshow. If there was to be any heat, we flight leaders and our squadron leaders would get the bulk of it. I just prayed the damned mission went well. That morning did not provide me with much confidence starting out.

Well, I was alone in a two-ship formation hoping to group up with the rest, and not long after crossing the Normandy coast, I had a few tracers fly up past me. As it was still dark, I just assumed it was blind fire from the ground. I then heard that the other element was headed south, as we were headed northeast. I thought, "What the fuck now?" I was going to my target: a bridge over the Saône River. I saw it and started my shallow approach and waited until the right moment to drop my two one-thousand-pounders. I wanted to strike dead center to bring it down. Once the bombs were away, I kept low and banked hard left to avoid the blast and try to avoid getting hit by ground fire. Once again, those bail-out procedures went through my head. Then I realized I was too low to even accomplish that bullshit. If I went in, it was a hard landing or a fireball. Death or captivity.

I saw the flash behind me and knew the bombs exploded; just not sure if I hit the bridge or not. Well, I was not going back to check it out. I was not going to give any gunners a second chance to nail me. That would be like putting your dick in a doorway, knowing that it will get kicked shut. I just stayed low and began looking for targets. Why not? I was all alone and no one to bitch at me. Then I saw shapes. I was just off the ground less than a hundred feet, and I confirmed two aircraft, just not sure whose they were.

I saw they were Fw 190s, and then I saw the black cross in my rear three-quarter-view angle. I fired, and he spun into the ground. I knew that I had to get the second quickly or run for it, because I could not outturn that fighter. This guy made a hard break left, and I was far enough away to pull lead on him, and I fired. He pulled up and jumped out of his seat, and we were less than fifty feet off the deck, but he got a good parachute and landed near his burning plane. I turned around and flew back over him, and he stopped running and hit the deck. I waved and did victory rolls. I was proud as shit.

Then I thought, "Damn, you're an idiot! No wingman to confirm the kills." But then I wanted to slap myself because I remembered that I had a gun camera, and then I hoped it worked. I also had to worry that I had not joined up with the rest of my flight, so I headed home alone. I told the S-2 and the others what had happened, and there was some skepticism, but Zemke walked in and said that pilots from the 355th Fighter Group were above me and saw the action, so the kills were confirmed. My camera also confirmed the action. That made me feel better. I hit the bridge, by the way; the others striking other bridges were less lucky. So, I was the golden boy: a bridge and two kills.

———

Just over a week after that momentous mission, we had orders to do a forward sweep ahead of a Ramrod. This was the Zemke method, and I liked it. Our morning briefing showed that we were to fly between the two large bomber formations, far ahead as pathfinders, and hopefully interdict enemy fighters sent up after the bombers. Zemke briefed us on where we would go, what we were expected to do, what not to do—all that stuff. His word was law, he was the lawgiver, and we were his disciples.

We took off for Holland on August 25 and climbed for altitude. We would reach twenty-eight thousand feet and push far out. If there was any bad shit out there, we wanted to find it first before the bombers had to feel any of it. At that moment, I thought of LeMay, McChord, my dad, and all the other bomber guys again. It was our job to keep them alive. There can be no greater responsibility on earth, and I took that shit seriously. Each bomber carried ten men. Ten lives, people with wives, families, maybe children. Failure was not an option.

The entire flight over Holland was uneventful, minus a few flak bursts far below us. As we crossed into Germany, we became very alert. We knew we were on their radar. Then I saw them: a shitload of black specks getting bigger as they flew across from three to nine o'clock. Then we had confirmation: about fifty Me 109s. Man, now we were in it. Full throttle, full rich mixture, gun sight on, pipper [glowing reticle] active, game on. I dropped my external tanks to have more speed and maneuverability.

Then I heard Zemke, the "Big Bison," ask my position. To be honest I had no fucking idea where the hell I was, but I did see a lake. I called out the lake, my altitude, and that I was going after about fifty bandits headed north of the lake. I figured that any ass-chewing for not knowing my exact position could be mitigated by finding the entire Luftwaffe. After that transmission, my radio headset exploded—everybody wanted to join my party. I really did not have the time to send out formal invitations.

I went after the tail end section on the left at my three o'clock, and as I closed in on their seven o'clock, my engines started sputtering, then they stopped. I had failed to switch my fuel tanks over after dumping the auxiliaries. I became a damned glider, and vulnerable, but as I slowed, it drifted me into a perfect firing solution. I pressed the trigger, and pieces flew off the closest 109, and as he burned and fell, I pulled right and managed to get my engines restarted. Feeling that power return was better than sex, let me tell you.

The Germans realized they were not alone, but I was going after another one. My wingman was in the perfect firing solution, and he knocked two out with great shooting. Three down for us so far. I then pushed the throttle and closed on another, fired, and he began to fall apart. You have to appreciate four .50-caliber machine guns and a 20-millimeter cannon. Like shoving raw meat into a grinder. That fourth 109 passed under me, going down.

But then I saw a 109 being chased by a P-51, and another 109 on that Mustang's tail. The P-51 was alone, no wingman, so he would not have known of the threat. I rolled over, nose down, to help him out and get the other 109. I soon realized that I had a problem: we had been warned about compressibility, that issue that arises when you have too much g-force and speed rendering your yoke, elevators, and ailerons worthless. They are frozen. We knew that few pilots ever recovered from this event, especially in the P-38. Now I was scared.

I threw the throttles into idle and adjusted everything to slow down and reduce my vertical speed, and finally I managed to recover at twelve thousand feet. There was a massive bang. I had fallen sixteen thousand feet—over three miles. If I had done that at a lower altitude, I would not be here talking with you right now. I learned later that what must have happened was I broke the sound barrier in a vertical, and then when I decelerated, the reverse pressure caused me to almost black out. I recovered about thirty or so feet above a plowed field. I was alive. I do not know if that was divine intervention or just simple luck, but by all measures, I should not have survived. That experience always stayed with me.

I gathered my senses and did an evaluation. I lost the left side of my canopy after the g-forces blew it out, and as I looked around, I saw a 109 firing at me, closing the distance from behind me. This guy must have followed me down. I pushed hard left rudder and aileron and pulled up, standing on the port wing turning into him, throwing him off. He averted collision and flew past me, so I then threw the plane right and put my gun sight on him as he grew smaller. I pulled the triggers, all weapons fired and blew his ass apart, and he impacted into the ground, and I passed over the wreckage.

I then had the time to take in all that had happened as I flew over the German border and into Holland. I had some flak and ground fire try to hit me, but I was not at a high enough altitude for the big guns to be effective. I had more of the bastards shooting at me as I crossed the coast, I could see geysers of water rise ahead of me as they missed. When I reached the North Sea, I really wanted a cigarette, but the wind blowing in from my fucked-up canopy prevented that small pleasure. I just leaned back and tried to enjoy being alive.

When I arrived at base, I hoped all was well with the aircraft, in particular the landing gear. I had no idea if those were damaged by gunfire or the g-forces. When the lock light came on and I heard the *thump,* I breathed a lot easier. When I came to a stop, my chief walked out, looked at the bird, and just shook his head. He was getting used to me bringing back a lot of garbage to be fixed. Wold asked me why I was so late; the rest of the unit came back a long time ago.

I explained what had happened and held up three fingers. "Get the gun camera; I hope it is still in one piece." He confirmed that the unit had not lost a single bird or pilot. Now I had to see what Zemke had to say. Thinking about that, I really needed a cigarette. Wold walked around the P-38, made some sounds of astonishment, and said, "By the way, Captain, that makes you the first ace in the 479th." I had not even thought about that. Well, if true, then perhaps Zemke would show me some mercy. I was in fighter pilot nirvana.

Zemke did want to have a word, and he had this look on his face that would make a woman go into premature menopause. I walked in, saluted, reported, and he said, "Stand at attention, shut the fuck up, and listen to what I have to say . . ." Well, he chastised me for not giving my exact position, for not joining the rest of the flight after they gave a heading correction, and then he congratulated me on the three kills and for not losing my wingman or my aircraft. "I may consider putting you in for a medal, but right now, go get a shower and get some chow. Debrief can wait." That was a real leader.

———————

On September 7 Zemke informed us we were, in fact, getting the P-51s. We were to replace the ageing P-38s, and we were all excited. We knew that, while the P-38 was faster than anything the Germans had except for their new jets, and we could outclimb and outdive them, we could not really dogfight. Everything the Germans had could out-turn and outroll a Lightning. I was wondering if we would go through the torture of transition training like we did back in the States, with a shitload of downtime, classroom instruction, and check rides. I just wanted to get the manual, get the ground check, a good familiarization ride, and get back into combat.

Now, there were some misgivings among my comrades, as they had come to love and were totally familiar with the P-38. Change was, in their opinions, not always a good thing. For me personally, and I told them this, we would have a fighter that was just as fast, more maneuverable, greater range, removing compressibility—which I had experienced—better firepower, and better roll rate. We could match the 109s and 190s on their terms. I had spoken with a lot of Mustang drivers; a few aces who confirmed what Zemke told us.

We were going to transition slowly, a squadron at a time, incrementally, flying both fighters together until we were all in Mustangs. The next day, our first four new P-51s arrived: lovely aircraft, smooth approach and landings, and precision taxi and braking. Outstanding piloting. That was not the surprise. What shocked us were that the pilots were women ferry pilots. They were known as WASPs [Women Airforce Service Pilots, also called Women's Army Service Pilots or Women's Auxiliary Service Pilots]. I looked at my wingman, he winked at me, and all the men walked over to the women. I was the oddball. I walked over to a new Mustang, admiring it. I knew that I would get kills in that beautiful bird.

The P-51 had more leg- and headroom than a P-38, and at over six feet, I needed all of it. There was plenty of shoulder room to move around. You know what I was thinking: more room to maneuver in case I had to bail out. It also had a traditional joystick, and all the gauges were easily readable, all the switches were right there—no fumbling around. I felt like an idiot. I had to get instruction on how to start the damned thing and gather as much intel on the operational methods as possible, and as quickly as possible.

Well, I had the cockpit check, they fueled her up, and I started that thing up. The roar and vibration were quite different from the twin-engine P-38. It was more of a throaty roar: you could feel the Merlin grumbling, so I took off, familiarized myself with the need to maintain trim at varying speeds, and, despite that one small issue, I liked the hell out of that. I was having a great time, but I knew that I had to land so others could get their shot at flying it.

We received more Mustangs over the next few weeks, and the transition was going smoothly. The big event was when bandleader Glenn Miller brought his band to the base.[17] They traveled around entertaining the troops, and it was a great morale boost, and we loved it. Big band and swing music were our Top 40 in those days, not like a lot of the garbage kids listen to now. Not long after, we were sad to hear of Miller's disappearance over the channel; rumor had it that perhaps a German shot down his transport. Who knows? [Miller disappeared on December 15, 1944.]

I have to tell you that in my second flight, I had a slight landing mishap. I approached at the wrong angle and had to compensate for the high torque of the prop, so I managed to go off the runway and dip the left wing where it made ground contact, bending a few feet of it skyward and sending me headed straight for the band. They all scattered as I came in, but I cut power and slowed to a quick stop. I had learned a valuable lesson on this bird—a completely different animal than the Lightning—and I almost died in the process. I would never take the Mustang for granted again.

The day I said good-bye to my P-38J SCAT III and said hello to my new P-51D SCAT IV was bittersweet for me. I felt like I had lost a child in a custody hearing but adopted a new stepchild, if that makes any sense. I loved it. Our next missions were all bomber escorts. I liked the Ramrod missions, especially being a pathfinder—farthest out, looking for the enemy—when my flight was assigned that duty. I wanted to get good at it to continue getting those assignments.

We had some R & R coming, and we decided to go take a look at Paris. The city was liberated on August 25, 1944, and we were surprised that after four years of occupation by the Germans and the fight to take it, it was in better physical shape than all of London. I did the typical tourist shit: Notre-Dame, Louvre—although there was a story that the Germans had looted all the great artworks. The French ladies were marvelous to me.

September was really busy on that note. We had some engagements, and we had some losses. We lost a pilot during a takeoff, and a few were shot down. This was during the period of Operation Market Garden, when our paratroopers jumped into Holland, supported by the British, to take the main bridge at Arnhem. We flew overwatch, one element hoping to draw ground fire so the rest could spot them and blow the shit out of them. That did not work out too well.

The plan was to drive into northwest Germany and end the war by Christmas. Somehow I had my doubts that would work. Call me a skeptic, despite seeing the daylight parachute drop, which was massive, and impressive, to say the least. On that day, we were in a real fight with the Germans; they came from everywhere. When it was all over, we had scored eighteen kills with only two losses. We were feeling good with ourselves, and we had reason to feel that way. The rest of that month was fairly mild; not a lot of contact.

October was a different month, and on the sixth, we were on another Ramrod mission with B-24s and B-17s heading to Berlin. All the way in, we never saw a single enemy fighter, which I thought was strange as hell. It would not be until a couple of decades later that I learned why, when I spoke with Galland: he said that he had organized the fighter defense to remain close to targets, saving time and fuel, until we were picked up on radar.

The Luftwaffe would then attack in waves. The first wave would attack, land, and refuel while the next wave attacked and did the same. By the time the first wave was back in the air, the bombers would have been hit by three or four waves of fighters. Our job was to fuck that plan up without even knowing about it. We flew alongside the bomber boxes, trying to identify those squadrons that we were assigned to protect, and that was not easy at all.

Far ahead, we saw action, and we dropped external tanks and burned in to see waves of 109s and 190s tearing into the bombers, and when we saw a few smoking bombers and a couple going down, I prayed to see parachutes. Those Germans were good, hitting fast, pulling up and away, P-51s chasing them, more Germans coming to their brothers' aid. I jumped right into it. I saw the 190s pull a collective split-S as they attacked to dive away. I followed one down and tried to close, but I couldn't get him right away, so I adjusted the gun sight and nailed him. I saw the canopy fly off as he lost speed, I fired again and ripped the cockpit up. He flipped over and went straight in. I did not see a parachute or a pilot.

But what I did see shook me to the marrow of my bones. It was one of the most haunting things I remember from any combat experience I ever had: the separated tail section of a B-17 falling toward me. I slipped to avoid it, as it would have killed me if I had collided with it, and I saw that a crewman's parachute lines were tangled in it. He was trying to get free, and we looked into each other's eyes briefly, and he was still attached to that spinning tail section. I pulled up and rolled slightly left to get a look, and it looked like a damned snowstorm, parachutes all over the sky.

I was not sure if it was the same B-17, but large pieces of a bomber, or more than one, I am certain, drifted down like confetti. Then I saw tracers fly by my canopy and right wing. I screamed at my wingman to get this guy off my ass, and when I looked, it was my own goddamned wingman who had been shooting at me! I ordered him to stop shooting. On the return trip, I tried to mentally calculate how many fellow Americans were lost.

We herded our remaining bombers, most of them trailing smoke and full of holes. I looked over this one: I could see through it, all the way through the fuselage from the left waist gunner's position to the sky on the right side. The hole had to be about two feet wide. There was a dead gunner slumped over his .50-caliber machine gun. There was a blood stream frozen on the side; a trail of red that showed where the flak shell had hit him. I am sure that he died instantly.

Then I looked at the cockpit as I slowed down. I could see the left seat was empty; that was where the pilot sat. Then I looked closer. The pilot was there, but there was no head. The front of the bomber looked like it had been smashed with a hammer. The bombardier's nose section was gone, and I saw the copilot. He looked over at me as I was on his left. He looked like he was ten years old; his eyes locked on to me. I saw fear, and he was bleeding from a head wound.

I was still passing by when I came across another bomber in much better structural shape but with both left engine props feathered. The number four engine on the far right was smoking like a chimney. I saw the propeller stop. He was on one engine at that time. He was slowing down and falling behind the rest. That meant death or capture if the Germans caught up to him. There was little we could do. I said a prayer for them.

Seeing all of that was depressing. I still have those images in my mind after all these years. I recorded the tail numbers of both aircraft hoping to find out if they ever made it back. Neither one did. To this day, I do not know if they were captured or died. The only thing I could think of was, unlike a fighter pilot, at least they would not die alone. They were with their brothers. I think I actually cried when I saw that. It is a human emotion that, if you do not possess it, you have to be a fucking soulless animal. I will stop there. [Authors' note: Robin Olds cried while relating this event, and we took a break, poured some scotch, and chatted about other things. He needed a break, and I felt intense empathy for him. At that time, our friend

Nelda Haydon, Buddy Haydon's wife, suggested we have lunch. Olds and the Haydons had been great friends for many years.]

That flight back was the most depressing feeling I had ever had, even when fearing a court-martial for doing some dumb shit. These were dead men, dying men, and I felt that we had failed them. That is a heavy burden for a twenty-two-year-old pilot to carry around, and I was not alone. Following our debriefing, I understood that at least fifteen B-17s went down. Others arrived damaged and scrapped. And those bombers came back with wounded and dead, you have to remember that. All total, I think over twenty B-17s and B-24s were lost, with the majority over Germany. That was at least 150 or more men gone. Our hearts sank at that thought.

Once the debriefing was over by the S-2, we were informed that higher authority wanted an in-person explanation how everything got so fucked up. I forgot about my air victory; it meant nothing. I volunteered to go, since I was the first to spot the enemy fighters, and Major John G. Glover from the 435th Squadron joined me. We took a trainer to Cambridge to stand before this general who wanted answers.

After it was all figured out, the general realized that his flight leader had sent his bombers farther north of the rendezvous, which we were at looking for them. That was the force I saw getting hammered to the north by the swarm of Germans. It was their fault, and his men paid a heavy price for it. Galland's method had proven to be near perfection. As we left, his aide walked with us back to the flight line. He told us the reason the general was so upset was that the Second Bomb Division had lost forty-two aircraft, not the nearly two dozen we thought. That was 420 men gone. Then I really felt bad, regardless.

On the flight back, I really felt bad because I was dead-dick tired and fell asleep. I woke up and looked at my watch, and we should have landed back at Wattisham by now and been in the rack. I punched the radio and asked the major, how much longer? I never heard a response. I was looking at the instrument panel and saw that we were headed northeast, not south back home. Then I looked out, and I was sure we were over the North Sea. "What the fuck has happened?" I thought. Well, we finally took corrective action and finally landed.

Thoughts went through my head about the day's mission. What if we had applied more airspeed? Then we would have been with the bombers sooner, even if they were in the wrong place. That way, we could have been more effective in protecting them. I spoke with Glover about that, and he said forget about it. Nothing we could have done, so no reason to think about it. We ate that night, although few of us had appetites. It was the most silent meal I ever had during my career. Not a word was spoken.

Soon after that, I was given a cold-water awakening. My crew chief told me, and then showed me, where a window had been placed into the fuselage for a camera. I was then told by our intel guru that the target was to be a big marshaling yard in Stuttgart. I was to fly low and slow before the bombing, then fly back through during the bombing, and then fly back through again after the bomb run, taking pictures for the bomb damage assessment. Basically, I was to fly an armed photo recon mission during every phase of the attack.

Well, in not so uncertain terms, I told him that he was clown-fucking crazy. No one flew low over a target like that because of all the defensive firepower, let alone three times. And most important, who in holy hell would fly through and under a bomb run? I asked him about every damned thing imaginable. I wanted to see detailed photos on where the flak guns were located, did he have a weather report over the target area, what were expected fighter defenses like, was there going to be anything resembling air cover for me being down dickhead level to the enemy—that kind of shit. I reminded him that "precision bombing" was at best an oxymoron and at worst a wasteful delivery of ordnance that would hopefully hit something of value. From over twenty thousand feet, it was anybody's guess how effective it would be. I just did not want to be a part of that BDA.

Well, I can tell you that when I thought about strapping in and taking off, that bail-out procedure went through my head again. But then I thought, "What the hell good would that do at just a few hundred feet above a bomb run?" Here I was on this top-secret bullshit mission, and I wondered if the German spies were as good as we were told they were, because if they knew about this job, I was one dead guy. I was really more worried about the heavy bombers being scattered by flak or fighters, or even getting hit with a hard crosswind, throwing their aim off.

The main briefing went in one ear and out the other. I had my orders, and no one else in the room except the CO, XO [executive officer], and the S-2 even knew about it. But it was the standard briefing, only this time we were given special attention about the German jets that had really started hitting the bombers. All of us wanted a crack at those fast bastards. We had been through several briefings, and a few RAF and American pilots went on a lecture tour explaining how to fight them.

The briefing continued, with all the rendezvous locations, altitudes, compass headings, time on target, flight schedules, formations—all the regular shit. Then at the end, the room was told that I would leave the flight early and my second in command would take over. They all looked at me with this "What the fuck?" look on their faces. I was asked why, and I just said that I could not say; they had to go to higher up. After the S-2 gave his briefing the CO gave his. More of the same shit.

We collected our flight gear, including chutes, Mae Wests, charts, et cetera. We then walked out to the jeeps to go to the flight line and did our preflight check. My chief, Wold, was spending a lot of extra time with me, and he mentioned the details of the camera and all that shit. I realized that he knew something was up; he was no fool. He looked at me in a strange, unusual way and said, "Good luck, Robin." Now, that was unusual: he did not call me "Captain" or "Sir," which was customary, and we had never shaken hands before a mission, only after I scored a kill. That morning, the handshake lasted a lot longer than any other, and I looked into his eyes.

"You know, don't you, Chief?" I asked him. He looked around and said that when the guys came by and installed the camera, he knew what was up right away. He did not know the target or the specific mission, but he knew that what I was carrying was a low-level high-speed camera.

"Yes sir, I have an idea. Just try to bring it home in decent shape. When you don't, I get very little time in the enlisted club."

We laughed at that—almost gallows humor—and I told him I would do my best. I climbed in, strapped in, and did the functions and preflight checks, then cranked the beast to life. I looked over the left side to see Wold give me the V sign for "victory," and his signature hand gesture for "smooth sailing." I smiled and gave a thumbs-up. I did not know if I would ever see him or Wattisham again.

I taxied out to the runway, waiting for the flare to go up, and when it did, I slid my canopy forward and released the brakes and rolled forward. I picked up speed and then I gently pulled back on the stick. Knowing my ass was going to be under all that shit would have made my breakfast come up, if I had bothered to eat anything. I lit a cigarette after the gear locked in place. I thought it may be my last one, so why not enjoy it?

The flight to Holland was enjoyable, but I had this bad feeling about my personal mission. Stuttgart was one of the most heavily defended areas of Germany, as was the route to get there. I knew that personally. The rendezvous location was not too far from a flak battery that probably had a personal ax to grind with us. Once again, I was going through those bail-out procedures; it was easier in a Mustang than in a Lightning, but if I were hit, I would have to climb at full power and hopefully get to at least a couple of thousand feet to safely open the chute. Then it dawned on me that if I were hit, there would be so many guns on me, I would probably just blow up. Even if I did get altitude to jump, there would be so many shells flying around, I would probably get shredded under the canopy. I prayed.

I broke off and headed to my target, and as I approached, I confirmed my location by landmarks, compass heading, and then I saw the marshaling yard. The bombers were not far away, and I expected the flak to go up real soon. I nosed down, cut the camera on, and then zoomed by. I will admit that I was always great at controlling fear. Fear is a natural condition; it is how you handle it that often determines the outcome of a situation, and I was scared. But then I switched into game mode and focused upon the job at hand.

I did not get much of a reaction as I banked left and rolled around out of the impact zone. I was on the outer perimeter of the impact zone, or so I hoped, so that I could switch the camera on and get some good strike photos. I could look up and see the bombers coming in, a few smokers, and the flak puffs. I kept waiting for the *thump* of impact on my Mustang once the gunners became aroused by my presence, and there were a few tracers aimed at me, but nothing hit me.

I was still in a hard-right turn when off my right wing I saw the first explosions. The sad part was that the bombs were falling off to the right, but my focus and camera angle were looking to the left, and the bombs were not falling there. The fucking bombs were hitting over a half mile away from the main target area that I was supposed to be filming. I remember thinking that if I got killed or captured for this shit, I was going to be really pissed off. Well, I still rolled what I thought was going to be worthless footage and burned at high speed maybe fifty feet off the deck to get the hell out of there. I made the channel and landed back at Wattisham, happy as hell to be alive.

My postmission debriefing was one for the record. They wanted to know if I got the pictures, and I told them that I had no idea, but I turned the thing on and off. I also informed them that I did get through the first two passes, but there was not a third flyby for a BDA. They were pissed and wanted to know why. I told them, "Because they never hit the damned marshaling yard, so why risk getting shot down as an uninvited tourist?"

October was pretty busy, and we had some losses, but Zemke's was the biggest blow to us. He failed to return and ended up in a POW camp, I later learned.

Then sometime in November, I was called in and told that I had reached my tour limit, and I was going to get sent home. I was not really happy about that, as I had just over fifty missions or some shit, but I knew guys who were flying over a hundred missions and allowed to stay. Even Yeager in the 357th Fighter Group was allowed to continue flying, and he had been shot down and evacuated by the French Resistance, while Bud Mahurin in the Fifty-Sixth Fighter Group under Zemke had the same experience, and he was forced to go home.

The rationale was that if you were rescued, you had valuable intelligence on how the Resistance network operated, personnel, and routes into Spain through the Pyrenees Mountains—hence Mahurin gone. But Yeager and a few others were allowed to stay and extend their tours. I wanted that same consideration. And I knew I had the high-ranking contacts to push that issue if it came to that.

Then I was given an option: extend on the spot for another twenty-five missions or go home for a two-month leave and come back for a full tour of duty. I thought about that, and it just did not seem right, because some of these guys, like Zemke, Gabreski, Blakeslee, and those clowns, were never sent home. It happened to Bob Johnson. Once he hit twenty-six kills, his ass was out of there at the speed of light. Well, in fairness to Gabby and Hub, they did become POWs. But I knew that they had been there since even before the USAAF arrived in full force, so why could I not get the same consideration? Well, after my last few missions, I was headed home.

I caught a transport back to the States. After landing in New York, I took a trip to see my brother, who was still a cadet at West Point. While I was there, I managed to log some more flight time, as they had a few Mustangs, trainers, and even a few Thunderbolts. I had a good time; it was nice to be back in the air without being shot at. Then I ran into one of my old flight instructors, the pissant prick who never liked me and wanted me placed into bombers.

He looked at me, and he must have felt like whale shit. I had the Silver Star, American and British Distinguished Flying Crosses, and Air Medal with Oak Leaves. He was one of those career officers who basked in the comfort zone of a noncombat assignment. And let me tell you something, those are the worst guys in the world who achieve high rank and then try to dictate terms to those of us who have our asses on the line. He was one of those types: career safety assignment.

While I was in DC, my brother came down, and we went to a few gatherings—nice, really—as we were well known due to my dad having been there for so long. I realized that I had absolutely nothing in common with any of these people who were my age—not even with my brother—but Stevan was a different case. He was still a cadet and in that military-oriented mind-set.

Then I reported for transport back to England. I was booked with others on the *Queen Elizabeth*. The liner had been pressed into military service as a transport, along with her sister ship, the *Queen Mary*, among other ships. I had expectations of a luxurious cabin, room service, and shit like that. Man, was I off the mark.

My group was billeted at the Biltmore Hotel, awaiting our orders to board the ship. The girl I met before came to stay with me, and that was a good time for many reasons. [Authors' note: Robin smiled at this statement and laughed.] Then one morning I had the call that I was to join the rest of the men and report to the ship. I was informed that, as an officer, I was in charge of the troops in the forward section, and this was a ship with a division of infantry. How in the hell was that going to work? I was just a captain anyway.

Well, for the second time, I saw the Statue of Liberty pass by while I was on a ship to Europe. During our trip, we had an army full bird [nickname for a colonel, referring to the O-6, the eagle insignia of rank] with us; he was our transfer group leader, and a great guy. Here I was on this former luxury liner, with almost twenty thousand personnel on board, and I was supposed to do checks on about half of them. When we docked, I took a train to London and then got back to Wattisham. It felt good to be there, back with the men.

I found out a few weeks later that I was being promoted to major, and with that came additional responsibilities, because we also had a few transition pilots. These were guys who were given the opportunity to fly fighters after doing their tour in bombers, and we always needed pilots.* That may sound easy, but it was not. Going from a slow, lumbering bomber into a high-performance fighter like the

---

* Many bomber pilots who had flown their required twenty-five missions were allowed to transition to fighters, allowing experienced pilots to stay in combat. Some of these pilots suffered from post-traumatic stress disorder.

Mustang was a major transition. Most pilots who fly one type of bird develop habits—sometimes bad habits.

The reality is that you have to ditch that old shit and learn all over again, and that is sometimes hard. I learned that when going from the P-38 into the P-51; they have different dynamics entirely. Sometimes you were better off with a new pilot, fresh out of training aircraft, who had no bad habits. In fact, one of our new converts tried to have a one-man air show over his base, and he snapped into the ground, costing us a pilot and a valuable fighter. Shit happens.

I was back in the air on Ramrods, and we were enjoying ourselves, or as much as you could in a shooting war. I was thinking about those German jets. I really wanted to bag one of those bastards, and I was always on the lookout for the telltale smoke trails, or contrails, they left behind them in the cold air. We still followed the Zemke method, and I was leading my element out front, hoping to get into some shit. Well, we got our wish.

This was around February 9, 1945, I think. I dropped my tanks and called it in, so we barreled right after the Germans—a bunch of them. They were going for the bombers, but they saw us and broke off. I nailed one Me 109 and then focused on another one. My fighter felt that it was being beaten to death, but I stayed on that guy. Then he pulled up, and we were in a thick cloud. We were on total instrument flying from that point forward. [They then returned to base.]

On February 14 I got three kills, I was having a great time—until I was informed that there was an arrest warrant for me.[18] I asked what the hell for, and I was told it was for desertion. I knew they had to be fucking with me; then they said it was because I had not cleared the ship properly when I returned, and I was considered a deserter. They got me, and I had to admit it was a good one. I remembered that, and I later pulled that joke on one of my guys in Thailand once just to jerk his chain and see what the reaction was. I'll you about that later, but it was a classic.

My greatest wet dream came true when we had our first encounter with the Me 262 jets. [Authors' note: this was the first operational jet aircraft, seeing first combat in July 1944.] I saw bandits, but no identification yet; they were coming almost head-on and faster than shit. I had one blowing by at my two o'clock just fifty yards on my wing, and I turned to get on him, but he and his buddies were already too far down range. I knew that with their speed, the only way to bag one was to catch one in a turn with a long-range deflection shot, or if they pulled up close enough. Even when they climbed, we could not catch them. They were wonderful to watch.

We ran into the jets several times after that, but we always had intense discussions about those jets. One of the major bitches was why we were not hitting their air bases, and why we did not have good intelligence on what we were facing. That would have been good shit to know, I can tell you. We had been briefed on the 109s and 190s when we first arrived, but on the 262s, there was a fucking media blackout. And that bothered us to no end.

What we learned from our encounters was that they were fast in the climb and dive but had no turn radius or roll rate. Unfortunately, I never got to nail one hard, but I did damage one once, on April 7, 1945, and we called them "blow jobs" as a pun. If a pilot had an encounter with one, he would be asked publicly, "Well, did you get a blow job?" You had to look around to be careful of the company you were with before saying that.[19]

We had a lot of missions where we encountered more Germans on a large scale. I got two more kills in a big swirling melee: a 109 and a 190. In March I was the squadron commander, and it felt great; I was not even twenty-three years old, but I was the "old man." Soon we were running out of aerial targets, so we started back on ground attack missions, hitting trains, airfields—that kind of shit. This was not prime duty for a fighter pilot, and those old statistics went through my head again. I had a lot of ground aircraft destroyed, but they were not air victories. Still, it helped the war effort and probably saved American lives, so it was worth it.

April had some action, and I did get a couple of scalps. In May the Germans surrendered, and I had thirteen kills in the war.[20] I felt great that the war was over, but in the same thought process, I sort of felt sad that my job was over. I met many fighter pilots who felt that way, and we seemed to be the only guys who felt that way. I never met an infantryman or other ground soldier who said, "Damn, I wish I still had a job to do," or "I really do not want to get back home," if that makes any sense.

Our British friends were of an entirely different mind-set. I spoke with some of the RAF fighter pilots, and they were all glad the war was over. They had been in it a lot longer than we had. Many had served in North Africa or the Pacific theater and had seen a hell of a lot more combat than any of us had. Come to think of it, I never heard any bomber boys complain that they did not have a job either, but that was understandable. They were flying targets, at the mercy of the gods.

I also met some of the RAF Bomber Command guys. They were a lot like our bomber boys, only if you saw a guy with a couple of years of action behind him, you were looking at a ghost. Those men flew at night, through flak and night fighters, and they lost something like half of their entire aircraft and personnel force during the war, if not more. I heard stories from these guys, and you could tell they were not bullshitting. I saw what our guys went through on day missions. I could only imagine what those poor Bomber Command boys endured.

I saw these Bomber Command guys, some about twenty years old with white hair; they were old men already, with blank stares. A few had hands that shook so badly they would have to order a half beer so as to not spill it before they drank it. I felt sorry for them. Their youth was gone forever. That was when I really hated Hitler and his Nazi fuckers.

I received orders to Paris, where I met with Tooey Spaatz. He was commander of all Allied Air Forces in Europe, and an old friend of my dad's. I had not seen him in years, but he had been keeping tabs on me, following my career. I got dressed and flew a Mustang to Paris and landed, wondering what the hell was going on. Well, a car took me to the HQ, a lovely chalet, and I was placed in a holding pattern.

Then the room began to fill up, and everyone who was anyone walked in. I saw some old familiar faces, and a few new ones, but all of them wore eagles or stars. The biggest celebrity fish was Jimmy Doolittle. With exception to Doolittle, who was always a polite and charming man, the rest ignored me, the lowly major. I guess they must have thought I was the fucking butler.

Then General Spaatz came in, and everyone was greeting him, fawning over him like a Greek god. He seemed to ignore all of them and waved at me and said, "Hello, Robin, I see you made it; thanks for coming." Then they all turned to me as if they had been bitch slapped. At that point in time, I would have been more comfortable flying low over that railyard in Stuttgart again than being in that room. He ignored all of them and walked over, put his arm around me, and took me into his private parlor. All I could think of was that I still had an empty glass of really good scotch and had not refilled it.

Spaatz made me feel comfortable. He wanted to have a serious conversation with me. He knew that I planned on staying in the service, so he gave me what was perhaps the most important talk of my career. He warned me about the various types of people I would encounter as I rose in rank, who to avoid, who to search out, and what to beware of. He explained the difference between the career armchair leader and the get-shit-done leader.

He also warned me about roadblocks: senior officers, jealous types who would try and put obstacles in my way. Then he said something that was the same advice my father gave me: "Always be yourself, and not what you think you should be to others." Basically, he gave me a method of assessing character, and how do deal with them. Then he gave me a fistful of francs and told me to get lost.

Let me say my few days in Paris were great for a good-looking single American guy with money. I was never an angel, but during this holiday, I think I broke most of the acceptable social mores. One morning I woke up, and these girls were gone. They had stolen my wristwatch and wallet with my remaining money. I was pissed, but then I thought about what they must have endured during the war and did not push the issue. The only major problem was that my two-day visit to Spaatz lasted a week, and when I returned, I was wondering who would be waiting to chat with me about being AWOL.

We had to undergo classes on fighting in the Pacific, because that war was far from over. Lectures on jungle diseases like beriberi and malaria, mosquitoes, sharks, snakes, fucking crocodiles, of all things, dangers of contaminated water, identification of Jap planes, ships—all that stuff. We were all pretty sure that we were going to end up going to that theater of the war, and that was fine with me.

But the best part was the return of our guys who had been in the German prison camps. Zemke and many others stopped over to say hello and good-bye before they went home. That was the best part of the war in Europe being over, seeing these guys again. Yes, you can imagine we got totally fucked up and drank everything in sight. That was when we learned that we would not be leaving for a few months. My mind was turning at that idea.

We had some new P-47s arrive that we were supposed to transition into. We also ferried some older planes to be disposed of. Most were scrapped, and that pissed me off; such beautiful birds should have been preserved. But no, some political cocksuckers thought they were worth more as scrap metal. Bastards, I called them. Just so you know, I generally hate politicians; some are worth the air they breathe, but not too damned many, from my experience. I had more respect for the Germans—at least they put their ass on the line.

We were still awaiting transfer orders when we got the news that the two atomic bombs had been dropped on Japan. Later, I was impressed to learn that LeMay was involved in that operation. Well, then I was handed my orders, cryptic and confusing, but they emanated from the Pentagon. I was going home—DC, from the look of it—so my curiosity was piqued.

The flight back stateside was boring, and I began to experience what we call combat decompression: that feeling of all the adrenaline running out of your body; a depression that falls over you because you feel that your entire purpose for living is over. Finally, after a stop in Iceland, we landed in New York. Then we had a lecture on our behavior while back in civilization before we got off the transport.

That next morning's breakfast, I will always remember: real eggs, bacon, everything. I was a glutton, and I am not ashamed to admit it. Then we had medical inspection, shots, just as if we were going back overseas. We then had a dickhead lieutenant walk in and shout, "Orders!" We were supposed to hand over our orders to complete processing. I had my telegram and showed it to him. He said it was unacceptable. I explained to him this was what I was given, but he was not interested. He was a real prick. Well, I got into a bitch session with him until this light colonel walked in and wanted to know why I was upset. I educated him really quick.

In the end, the senior officer said that I could name the place I wanted to go, and he would cut the orders, so I told him Los Angeles, and he said fine. I would get forty-five days' leave. I was happy as horseshit about that. I just wanted out of that place. I ended up with my aunt and uncle, and my stepmother was there. I went to a few parties, since she knew everyone, and I met many celebrities, including Judy Garland. Thing was, I did not know who the hell she was at the time. I guess I had been gone awhile. Well, I ran into a senior officer I knew as a cadet at West Point, handed him my "orders," such as they were, and he gave me wisdom and a destination. Of all things, I was headed back to West Point.

I had bought this Buick and drove cross-country to report. I was told that I had been requested to work for my old football coach as an assistant. I arrived and took a verbal beating for my appearance from this colonel. He must have thought I was a senior cadet in a shabby uniform from flight training or some shit. I had walked into a world far different from the more relaxed environment of combat, if that was even possible. Well, I was disillusioned at the thought of spending four more years at West Point. I wanted a flying assignment, so I drove down to Washington and got one. I was going back to California.

I arrived at my new duty station and met Colonel David Lee "Tex" Hill, a real legendary pilot. He was the top ace killing Japs with the AVG [American Volunteer Group]—most people know them as the Flying Tigers.[21] He was impressive, to say the least; a real combat pilot. We all heard of him and the Tigers. Hill commanded the P-80 unit, our new jet fighter. His problem was that he was overstaffed, and I was just another round in the magazine. I cooled my heels until they could justify my existence.

I took a desk and wondered what hell I was going to do at March Field if not flying? I wandered over to the Ninety-Fourth Squadron office and tried to get on the check-ride list for the new jet. It was an openly hostile environment: a bunch of alpha males pissing all over the place to mark their territory, and I was the new guy. I was told I would get notification if and when a slot came open. Then I had a thought: no one knew me, and I was a ghost, so why not take advantage of it?

I went to the ready room, got a flight suit, parachute—all the trappings—walking in and out as if I owned the place. Your demeanor can either help you or betray you, so I walked as if I were the top dog in the outfit. I went to the flight line, spotted the jet, and spoke to the crew chief.

After a short chat, he bought my bullshit and gave me the instrument and cockpit check procedure. I was amazed that this shit was actually working. It had tricycle landing gear and on taxi handled a lot like a P-38. Most of the instruments were similar as well; the new stuff I absorbed rapidly. Seemed easy enough. I recalled that I would probably have some answering to do when I landed despite the control tower giving me permission to take off. Regardless of how it ended, this was going to be a very interesting day.

Well, to my surprise, when I landed—and the flight was wonderful—I was told that the bird I flew did not even belong to the Ninety-Fourth. I had basically stolen an aircraft. I just rolled forward and played it off as if I were doing an official test flight or some shit. Believe this or not, they bought that bullshit hook, line, and damned sinker. Soon I was called in to meet Lieutenant Colonel John Herbst, who was better known as "Pappy," as he was the top ace of the Fourteenth Air Force.[22] He wanted me to join him in a mock dogfight against the new navy planes, and I was all in.

We took off and won the mock battle, and I learned a few things about flying fast jets: the days of dogfighting may not have been dead, but they were severely limited. Hit-and-run, speed, and altitude advantage were the way to win. We were also the first pilots to fly the Lockheed P-80 Shooting Star at night totally on instruments. At high altitude, the night sky is like magic.

Speaking of hit-and-run operations, being stationed there was what made me meet my first wife, actress Ella Raines. She had been in some John Wayne films which I saw, so I knew who she was, and I owed my friend "Ace" Hastings a thanks for facilitating the meeting.[23] Well, Herbst wanted to create a flying exhibition team—really a forerunner of what we have today, like the Air Force Thunderbirds and the navy's Blue Angels. But back then, it was new, and stunning to the civilians on the ground. One of the new technologies was the creation of the g-suit. I can only imagine how many pilots' lives would have been saved from blackouts during the war if we had these.

I was still trying to get more flight time when an old acquaintance walked in: Colonel Leon Gray, whom I knew in England.[24] He asked if I wanted to join his squadron. After an uneasy reacquaintance, I accepted. We turned out to be great friends for the rest of his life. This turned out to be a good move because this photo reconnaissance unit flew more hours than anybody, even the fighter units.

We also flew higher altitudes, over forty-two thousand feet. Our scientists learned a lot, and the technology was great. Pressurized cockpits had been developed late in the war, but I had not experienced this until the P-80 Shooting Star. The sad part was that we lost Pappy during one of these flights. That was a bad day, as he had just been married. Even worse, his second wife was there as I taxied in, alone. That was a bad feeling. We lost others in training, including two in one day in a collision, and I saw it happen. That is the kind of shit that reminds you that life is a very fragile thing, and you go through all the mental gymnastics on making sure you do not fuck up like that.

After I married Ella, I got to meet a lot more of the big movie stars of that day. John Wayne was a really cool guy. I knew David Niven, who had been a British soldier in the war. He told me a story that was very similar to the one Jimmy Doolittle told me about some dinner party in England that had issues, and I did not press him for the details. He also had a habit of pissing off all the right people, so we had something in common. I got to know Jimmy Stewart, and he was a superior officer. He had flown B-24 Liberators during the war, so he was a legitimate hero to our country. Clark Gable, whom I'd met before, was also a volunteer in the war.

I was not surprised at how many of our movie stars enlisted after we were at war. Just as amazing was how many of our troops later became movie stars, like Lee Marvin, Tony Curtis, James Arness, and guys like that. That just goes to show how great a nation we were. During Vietnam, you never saw a single fucking celebrity of military age join up to do shit, except Jane Fonda, and do not even get me started on that bitch.

Ella and I transferred to Florida, where I was to be a selection officer near Panama City. Good duty, although temporary. After a while, I went back to California and was able to get a one-year assignment as an exchange officer with the RAF in England. After Ella finished her new film, she would hop over. I was really looking forward to that assignment. The Brits were flying their new jets, the Vampire and Meteor. My station would be with Number One Squadron at Tangmere.

Well, my first flight in a Meteor was something to remember, as I was more confused by the cockpit instruction than you would expect. There was little in the language that I could understand despite its being in English, and it seemed as if they just wanted to see how I would react or perhaps survive my first ride. They gave me no call sign, no assigned frequency—hell, I could not even find the runway for takeoff! But I said to hell with it and rolled out. It looked like the Brits might accomplish what the Germans couldn't, and that was kill me. It was rather uneventful but memorable.

These pilots were almost to a man combat veterans, some with more combat time than I had, and I respected that. The fact that I respected that earned me their respect, so it worked out. I really had a great time with those guys. There is a camaraderie that pilots have. Even when you meet former enemies, that feeling of fellowship exists, and most people will never understand that. I wondered what would follow this period in my life, and in 1949 I had new orders. There was a new jet fighter rolling out, and I was going to fly that thing.

I went to the First Fighter Group back at March Air Force Base, glad to be back in California where there was little rain and good flying weather, unlike England. My new job was operations officer for the Ninety-Fourth Fighter Squadron, where I had met Tex Hill a few years earlier. They had the F-86 Sabre, replacing the P-80. We did a lot of flying and gunnery practice, and on one flight, I had a wingman crunch down on my vertical stabilizer in an unanticipated tight turn following our flight leader, but we did not lose anyone or any planes. Then shit changed.

We heard that North Korea had invaded its southern neighbor, and we had troops trapped in their path. All of us expected to be sent to Japan or South Korea to fight. The North Koreans were supported by the Communist Chinese, who took the country over in 1949 with backing from old Uncle Joe Stalin. Instead, our entire unit was transferred to New York in case Canada decided to attack New England, I guess.

I was made the base commander while we were interned in Pittsburgh, a rather grim place that I never wanted to return to. My pilots were getting siphoned out to fight the new war, and despite my putting my name at the top of every list, I was getting smacked down. I was not sure if they were trying to punish me or protect me, but I didn't like it. Basically, I was flying a desk, handling airfield improvements, dealing with manifests, architects, and engineers—the kind of thing that we fighter pilots called hell on earth.

I can tell you that Ella was great about dealing with all the moving around, because she still had a contract with Universal film studios, and then she did these television shows once that was a major technological development. During this period, which I called the "Dark Ages," I hooked up with Eddie Rickenbacker again, and I was honored to see that he remembered me from all those years ago, as he always liked my father. He had followed my combat career and even offered me a job at his company, Eastern Airlines.

It was through Rickenbacker that I met Larry Rockefeller,[25] son of the famous John D. Rockefeller Jr., and that started a lifelong friendship. Unknown to me, after introducing him to my wife, the trajectory of my life was going to change drastically. We would spend much of our free time in Wyoming with Larry and his wife and their family, as they had a ranch. I liked horseback riding, fishing, and the outdoor life. It was good for the girls too, but that was much later.

Sadly, Ella had a miscarriage while I was stuck in Pittsburgh and she was in New York, and I never knew she was pregnant, and neither did she. It was just one of those moments that saddens you and brings all of your other miseries into clear, unobstructed focus. During all of this, I was still trying to get to Korea, and I always thought my CO was the reason. I was stuck training pilots to go over and fight, and I was smoking pissed about that.

It was just a couple of years ago, in 1998, that I learned from an old Pentagon officer that my wife had used her considerable influence, and her Hollywood and TV contacts with Larry Rockefeller, to convince him to wink and nod to his high-ranking military and political friends. The powers that be were killing my combat service because producers wanted to keep a star happy. In retrospect, I can understand that, but what pissed me off was the lack of transparency. The Machiavellian bullshit was what got my fucking goat.

Later on, my anger was increased when the guys I knew, like

Gabreski and Mahurin, among others, were racking up kills and making history while I sat on my ass. I felt like I was the kind of pilot I used to loathe: an instructor happy to be out of the conflict, safely teaching others to fly and fight at no risk to himself. I just hoped to God none of my students thought that way of me. After we heard Mahurin was shot down and missing in action, I began to reflect upon how luck plays a part in life, good or bad. I really hoped he was okay because Bud is a great guy. I can tell you in those days I had a short temper due to not being sent into combat. Putting me on desk duty was like nailing a vampire to a crucifix; it was just not a natural damned thing to do.

The great news was that Ella gave birth to our first child, Christina Eloise Olds, on January 5, 1952. She was named for my mother, and as she grew up, Chris was like her old man: took no shit, gave no quarter, and did things her own way. But she was an Olds, so I guess being intelligent and headstrong was in her genes. I commuted as often as I could, flying back and forth to see them both. Chris was probably the first reason that made feel happy to be alive. I just wish she would have known her grandfather.

Having me as a father was probably a challenge, but I think I did a pretty good job. She took more after me than her mother, I think, but despite that detriment, she is a lovely lady, and I am proud of her. Her sister, Susan Bird Olds, was born and named after Ella's mother on March 12, 1953. They grew up together only just over a year part, so that made them a handful, for sure. I am pretty sure having me as a father was probably not too great for their dating relationships. I tend to come across as a hard-ass sometimes. Our friend Nelda Haydon, Buddy Haydon's wife, calls me a gentle bear. Maybe so. I guess getting older mellowed me out.

I was offered a job as a test pilot at North American, and, given my distaste for the politics of military life and the fact that test flight pay was better, I submitted my resignation. But my CO, Major General Freddy Smith, convinced me to trash it and take a position as a senior staff officer. The only reason that was not a totally disastrous decision was it kept me on active duty; otherwise my only experience in Vietnam would have been watching Walter Cronkite moan about it.

I finally ended up in West Germany at Landstuhl, and I was informed that I was to be more of a dorm mother than a group commander in the Eighty-Sixth Operations Group. Pilot behavior apparently left much to be desired, and the new boss was a senior colonel, the wing commander, and he was less than enthusiastic about my arrival. I was just a new colonel, lowest on the tally sheet, so I now had to adjust to this new role.

During this time, Ella and the girls were staying in England again, and we would all see each other when we could, but the military way of life was killing her career and making her unhappy as hell, and I knew it. I also had surgery due to flying: high g-forces, and all that. Flying takes a toll on a human body, and I spent over a month on my back with a sporadic fever and constant pain.

It was while in that bed I that was informed that when I got out, I would take over the training center at our base in Libya. Ella was like "No way in hell" was she taking the family to North Africa, and that was that. I was given medical leave to go back to stay with her and the girls in England until I recovered, despite more surgeries. She took great care of me and lost a part in a film because of it. After I recovered, she and the girls returned to California. Later, she did come to Libya with the girls, and that made me happy, but it took a while.

I arrived in Libya, and we had a base called Wheelus, which was the most remote, desolate, and godforsaken place I had ever seen. It was not a base, just a bombing range in the Sahara Desert. It made the Mojave look like Broadway, although the weather was very similar. I remember speaking to one of the junior officers who had been there awhile. I told him, "Well, at least we will not have rattlesnakes to deal with." He said, "You're right, sir, none of that. Just look out for the scorpions and cobras." Well, that made me think.

This was also the first time that I got to meet and know Ben Davis [General Benjamin O. Davis, then chief of staff of the Twelfth Air Force, leader of his famous Tuskegee Airmen].[26] I always liked Ben; he was a great, down-to-earth guy. We often had discussions about World War II, and our two experiences could not have been more different. He explained how the prejudice and discrimination were always present, and how his men had to be better than the white pilots just to be tolerated, but that was his mission. He succeeded.

Once President Harry Truman integrated the armed forces, eliminating the segregated military, I think that was perhaps his greatest legacy. It should have been done a long time ago. I never understood the need to be an asshole to people because they were different. I was never a racial bigot, but I sure as hell knew a few who were. I called them assholes, too. I know that there were some old-timers who fell into that social Darwinism bullshit; they did not know any better. I just thought it was foolish.

While I was there, I was on a sort of fact-finding mission to see what was needed, make the calls and get the contracts approved, and basically just get shit done. We needed adequate quarters, so structures began to get built—trailers and such, some small houses—and we really needed a real modernized and unfucked runway with an operations tower, none of which existed when I arrived. I remained there until 1958, when I was assigned to the Pentagon.

That Pentagon job was flying another desk. I hated the thought of it and tried to get out of it, so no joy on that one, I can tell you. At least my wife was happy about it, she would be back in civilized society. I would be in political living hell, and I knew it. The words Spaatz said to me all those years ago came back to me like a tidal wave. I remembered.

Well, Ella set up shop in New York while I navigated the hallowed halls of the five-sided puzzle palace, knowing that I was a ring fighter thrown into a room of crooked bookies fixing the fights. That tour of duty cemented every single prejudice I had of senior officers with no combat experience playing their political games just to get along, get promoted, and get the hell out with a nice retirement, and maybe a postmilitary consulting job, making big bucks. It made me ill.

LeMay and I spoke about that because we crossed paths again after several years. He hated that horseshit as much as I did. Difference was he had the stars on his shoulders to say what he thought without going to trial for insubordination. They just retired recalcitrant flag officers. If people think I am irreverent and vile, they just need to sit back and let Curtis roll out his diatribe; it is an educational experience, as you know. But LeMay was really part of the overall problem, at least where SAC [Strategic Air Command] was concerned. He and others were all about the nuclear weapons programs and cared little for the continued R & D [research and development] for conventional warfare.

I was now in the cesspool: where flag officers offered everything short of blow jobs to members of Congress to get pork passed for petty-ass projects. Generals fought admirals for every allotted dollar, lobbyists spread money around like sailors at Mardi Gras, and no one seemed to give a real hoedown shit about what the average soldier, sailor, airman, or marine needed. As long as they made their footprint, that was all they cared about. There was more backstabbing than at a Macedonian wedding, I can tell you.

The Pentagon is a rank-heavy zoo full of exotic creatures who thrive in their natural bureaucratic habitat. The higher the rank, the more they loved it, unless they were warriors. The warriors hated it, and you could see them a mile away. That was why I stood out, I guess. Again, I remembered Spaatz's words of wisdom. I could clearly see what he was talking about just by going down the hallways. Colonels made coffee for generals, junior officers swept floors or some shit, but that was the way it seemed to be. Enlisted personnel typed and filed, hidden away like laboratory rats.

The air force had replaced the F-86 with the F-100 Super Sabre, and then that was obsolete, so we then had the F-101 Voodoo and F-102 Delta Dagger, all of which had short shelf lives. The next great projects were the F-104 Starfighter, which was a fast interceptor, and the F-105 Thunderchief, a supersonic fighter-bomber, not worth a shit in a dogfight but a really fast bomber that could shoot shit down if it were engaged, and then it would have to light the afterburner to get the hell out of Dodge.

Then we had what I called the "R & D Wars" that had every four-star and their prostitute congressmen slashing at each other to get money for their pet projects. Part of my job was to look at proposals, analyze their value, and then pass my recommendation up the chain of command. I took that shit very seriously. This was why I had contact with LeMay again, as he was in essence the father of Strategic Air Command. There could not have been a better overseer, in my humble opinion, when it came to waging a war, but in peacetime, with all due respect to Curtis, I think he fucked things up for the next decade.

The great problem was that the primary head-shed people were always thinking about the "big picture," and I am talking nuclear war, missiles, and all that shit. That was where LeMay was. I always knew that we were more likely to get involved in some conventional combat situations where the nuclear idea would not even be part of the frag order. Then after weeks of looking at all the reports, garbage statistics, and such, I realized we were in no way prepared for another conventional conflict.

Financially, we spent billions on missiles that would never fly and ignored aircraft and men who would always be the first to get the orders into a hot spot. Then we were given the task of reorganizing the entire Air Defense Command, from TAC [Tactical Air Command] to [CONAC (Continental Air Command)]—everything—and do it rapidly. We got this assignment on a Friday, and they wanted it done in a few months. We were told in no uncertain terms that we were not to even dream of getting budgets for fighters, bullets, training, bombs, or anything related to a conventional war. Something told me we were fucking up badly.

I spent another three years in DC and attended the National War College as well as having to work in the Joint Chiefs of Staff. Working through the Eisenhower era and into the Kennedy period's debut was an interesting time, especially when we had the 1962 Cuban missile crisis. This was where LeMay was either perceived as a genius or a madman. I could see both arguments. In either case, he was dedicated.

The greatest tragedy was that while the air force had neutered our fighter combat commands, the navy had really increased their budgets and their capabilities. They were on top of their game, for sure. I envied them and saw what they were doing. Later, when I came back from Thailand and was commandant at the academy, I would steal away and get some flying time with the navy at Miramar [this is the former Miramar Naval Air Station, San Diego, now Marine Corps Air Station Miramar]. They had the best program, sorry to say. They really took it to the edge; they trained like it was war. The navy did it right.

Then, in 1963, I had orders to go back to England to command and fly. I was all about that shit. Leaving the Pentagon for me was like being paroled from prison. Ella was less than enthused, but I thought the girls would make the transition rather easily. I hated the English weather, but if it meant flying again, I would endure anything. At least I could get good scotch.

When I arrived as a new wing commander, my deputy commander was Colonel Daniel "Chappie" James, a really sharp guy and a good man, by all measures. Like Ben Davis, he was a Tuskegee man and a fighter pilot. He first flew combat in Korea and later became the first black officer to reach four-star rank, and he earned every damned star. We later flew together in combat out of Thailand over Vietnam. I liked his ass a lot, great man, although we had different leadership styles, to be sure. [Authors' note: James and Olds were well known and nicknamed "Blackman and Robin."]

This unit was the Eighty-First Tactical Fighter Wing at Bentwaters, and they were flying the F-101 Voodoo. The neighboring base at Woodbridge was great, as that gave us all a larger sense of family. The mission was simple: fly fast at supersonic speeds and drop tactical nuclear weapons on prime Warsaw Pact targets and try to get the hell out.[27] All of us knew that the likelihood of surviving, let alone returning from, such a mission was somewhere in the 3 percent category. So as a result, we ran escape and evasion training for the pilots, should they ever get that mission and bail out. I was not really sure about the clowns that thought that was viable, because, despite my limited knowledge of nuclear weapons systems, parachuting down into enemy territory under a fucking mushroom cloud pretty much ruled out a successful opportunity to get home. Well, we did our job and trained pilots for this low-level tactical delivery of Armageddon.

I was at my desk on November 22, 1963, when my phone rang. I was told that President Kennedy was dead, and Vice President Lyndon Johnson had assumed the presidency. I was stunned, to be honest, because after what I had seen and been through, it took a lot to shake me. I spent a couple of years there back in the United Kingdom, and when I got word of a place called Vietnam, I was already plotting my moves.

One day I had a call from a friend still trapped in the Pentagon, and he gave me the quiet word that I was on the promotion list for brigadier general. That was a problem for me, because I knew generals did not get cockpit time in a combat zone. Then a light went off in my head: I had to do something that would have my superior remove me from the list but not get me retired or, even worse, court-martialed. Then it came to me: I would get a few pilots together and do an aerobatic show over the base without permission. That would do it. Hell, he might be pissed off enough to send me to Vietnam as punishment. That would be like putting a drug addict in the pharmacy. I was going for it.

I had my pilots, and although the Voodoo was the last aircraft in the world to consider doing aerobatics in, it was worth the shot, I thought. We did a dry run before that over Mildenhall, and I got the call because I had violated safety regulations. My two-star was pissed, yelling at me on the phone, he said he saw that show. I could only assume he had not yet heard about the stunt we pulled that day on my base [the low-level supersonic fly by]. When the call was over, I had to catch a train to London for my formal ass-chewing. I think it was perhaps the only ass-chewing I actually looked forward to.

Well, I could not even fucking believe what happened in his office. He shouted and showed me my fitness report, saying I was basically garbage, that I would never get promoted, tore up my Legion of Merit recommendation, and told me that I would be sent to Southeast Asia. I guess he thought that was punishment. As sure as hound shit, I was later sent to Shaw Air Force Base in South Carolina and prepared to go overseas. The plan worked like a charm.

This meant I could get more flying time, and, even better, my next transfer was into another war. I did not get the promotion, but I knew I would get something a lot better: a combat command and time in the cockpit killing Communist bastards who were trying to fuck the world up. I was going to war again, and I liked it. Ella was far less enthused.

I then had a major problem. Well, perhaps not "major," but it was an issue. I told you that the navy was on its game well ahead of us air force types in money, training, and R & D, and the McDonnell Douglas F-4 Phantom was the new fighter-bomber in the inventory. It was a navy project started in 1958 that came online in 1960. By 1961, it was on carriers, and they were carrying the war to North Vietnam from ships in the South China Sea, which was called Yankee Station. We got them in 1963, and I can imagine how much political bullshit flew around on that transaction. The navy boys were in it thick by 1965, just as the first major troop deployments hit the South, with the marines landing in force at Da Nang.

We all knew about it, and in its usual fucked-up wisdom, the air force turned the damned thing down, because it was considered a carrier-based bird. What the hell? I said, "Just take the fucking tail hook off, and it can be anybody's aircraft." I was met with strange looks. I guess the air force did not like picking up something that the navy developed. One thing I never understood were the idiotic civilians and politicians who always screwed up a good thing. We all got the Phantom; they just did not put guns on the damned thing. We were a missile-firing military now, so who needed guns on a jet? I always hated when pride got in the way of prudent decision-making. Again Spaatz's words came back to me.

My orders came in to go to Ubon, Thailand, and I was still not a qualified F-4 pilot. I knew that Chappie James was at Davis-Monthan Air Force Base in Arizona, so I called him up. He was really a great contact, and another good guy was Major Bill Kirk; he was an instructor pilot on the Phantom. So, I shipped my gear to Thailand, the girls were all staying in DC, and I was getting ready to qualify in the new bird.

I arrived in Arizona and began my check rides, and I had about a week to become a qualified F-4 pilot, which is record time for any aircraft, to be honest. I was excited to fly it, and, at over Mach 2, it had some get up and go. Well, I had a come-to-Jesus moment on my second check flight when I experimented with reverse yaw and lost both engines, which created a flat spin. Let's just say for a pilot, this is one of the worst conditions to be in and still have a pulse rate. Bill was in the backseat as we dropped from over fifty thousand feet to almost twelve thousand feet. I had the nose down, adjusted trim and ailerons, and regained control. We regained engines at below ten thousand, which was good. I had just learned a great lesson that would be invaluable in combat.

It is often said, and I believe it, that a pilot learns something from every flight. If he does not, he has a really short career and an even shorter funeral. We pulled so many positive and negative gs that the needles were stuck. I was excited as hell, my adrenaline pumping like hydraulic fluid. But poor Bill had had enough; I know I scared the living hell out of him. I am sure the ground controllers were in a state of apoplexy upon hearing all that bullshit. Chappie came to me and asked, "Well, how did it go?" as if he did not already know. I just told him that it was exciting.

"I'll bet, sir. Kirk is shaking—looks like he just punched out into a beehive."

I just laughed.

I had to clear the base so I could get on a flight to Thailand. The process was agonizingly slow; pathetic, to be honest. Dozens of men waiting to out-process were all being held up due to idiocy and bureaucratic bullshit, but I straightened that shit out in a fucking hurry. Incompetence is one thing that I could never stand; it pissed me off more than anything else. Perhaps laziness is another close second on that list.

I then had to weapons qualify on the AIM-7 Sparrow and AIM-9 Sidewinder pod-launched missile systems. That training was at Point Mugu, so I went back to California. After that, I ended up at Travis Air Force Base in Sacramento, and then flew out with a bunch of others to a war I knew little about. But I was fast learner. After stops in Hawaii, Guam, and the Philippines, we landed in South Vietnam. I was ready to get the hell out of that civilian bird for good.

There were military personnel and dependents on the flight, and we were told that it would be at least an hour to get off, but the heat was unbearable, so I took the initiative and managed to get us all the hell off that thing. Everyone got off and managed to get some liquid in them, and later we reboarded and continued on to Bangkok. After initial in-processing, I jumped on a C-130 Hercules transport, which is a loud-as-shit bird to begin with, and, after several hops around the country, finally ended up at Ubon.

The heat hit me like a tidal wave; even worse than at Tan Son Nhut in Saigon. The heat came in waves, and your sweating never ended. Well, I sat there with the enlisted guys, wondering where in the hell our transport was. We had some light conversation, and I guess my eagles of rank made them a little nervous, so I tried to keep it a little relaxed and off the record, but I was pissed that we had to wait. Hell, I was the new commanding officer, and they had to know I was there. Well, I was wrong.

A captain finally drove up in his truck to give us a lift, and he dropped us all off at the wing HQ. I realized that my arrival was something of a surprise to all of them. Typical snafu ["situation normal all fucked up" or "fouled up," depending upon the delivery] as usual, I thought. I was greeted by "Pappy" Colonel Vermont Garrison, whom I always liked, and we worked well together. Great guy.[28] He was shocked that I was not given a briefing before my arrival, which meant that he did not get word that I was coming. Pappy caught me up to speed on what had been going on, and now that I was the CO, I was going to change a whole lot of shit at that base.

There was so much wrong with the way that base operated, so I had my work cut out for me. What I did like was the base commander being my subordinate. That meant I was in charge, and tough shit if they did not like it. I also learned that we were just "guests" of the Royal Thai Government, and that my alter ego was a Royal Thai Air Force light colonel who had to give approval for anything resembling construction, changes, et cetera. No big deal to me.

———

I had not even changed clothes when I issued my first orders. There would be a reception NCO in Bangkok to help the incoming newbies twenty-four seven. There would be a centralized in-processing location for one-stop processing upon arrival. Every department would be there and get that done immediately. Then I issued an order to have all pilots in the ready room for a briefing the next morning. The look I got was one of a stunned blank stare, as it would be the first time any of the pilots and GIBs [guys in the back] had a simultaneous briefing. They always got their mission data at the squadron level, never from the wing commander. Talk about a life-changing moment.

I wanted to take control—that's natural. I wanted to place my individual footprint on this unit but do so in a way that elevated morale and the fighting spirit, not lower and demoralize it. I had seen that happen also. I had a lot of experience to draw from. My senior predecessors as well as my father taught me a lot of what I called the spirit of command. Being an authority figure works due to your rank and position. Being a good leader requires more.

Getting to know the people, what makes them tick, and who the clowns and the determined were—that was the secret. Making men feel at ease without having them think that you are a pushover is critical. Leading from the front, taking the same risks, hanging your ass out with them in combat was a novelty to these guys. Their previous wing commanders had hardly ever flown with them. They soon learned I was there to fly, not just administrate.

On the administrative level, I knew that I had to clean house; almost everybody had to go except Pappy. I needed dedicated, intelligent, and diligent officers who got shit done, and done the way I wanted. I managed to coral Chappie into agreeing to come, and later he did. I had a few more people I wanted to lasso into my fiefdom, and I began cutting orders and issuing requests at a furious pace.

One thing I learned from the S-2 guys and the younger pilots who had been there was that their orders never changed, except for designated targets. They always flew the same pattern, same formations, same altitudes, same routes, and always the same manner of delivery. No fucking wonder they had lost almost a third of their pilots and planes. That meant the enemy knew the playbook. Insertion points and methods were not hard to figure the hell out, and I never assumed the North Vietnamese were stupid. I could not say the same about some of my superiors in DC.

It seemed that no one had any creativity or sense of urgency, and I blame the previous commanders for that one. I was not having any of that horseshit. Innovation in aircraft and weapons had to be harnessed with innovations and in out-of-the-box tactical thinking. Look at what worked and improve upon it. Look at what was totally fucked up and change it until it worked. I was really good at that.

They had lost men and machines due to laziness and incomprehensible incompetence. Those days were over.

I was looking at the various unit loss reports. The Thud [F-105 Thunderchief] units had been hammered; those damned SAMs [surface-to-air missiles] had been taking a toll on them, and a few had been bagged by North Vietnamese MiGs. Our losses prior to my arrival seemed extraordinarily high, and when I reviewed the mission debriefs, especially on targeting, I saw what was glaring. We had been wasting time, ordnance, fuel, and men on dropping napalm and frags on bullshit targets and wiping out low-value bullshit.

Very few missions included anything resembling true air support for ground forces. That was some shit I knew a lot about. Air-to-air combat was not even on the register. MiGs did not come up for fighters, they wanted the Thuds and B-52s if they could get them, and I am quite certain some SAM site gooks were just sitting there waiting for a nice gaggle of incoming Americans to lock their radar on. The North Vietnamese had the strongest air defense network I ever saw. It made Germany in the war look like a state fair.

What also changed for the F-105s was the introduction of the ECM [QRC-160 electronic countermeasure] pods that reduced the effectiveness of the radar-guided SAM sites by scrambling their signals. Well, that meant that the enemy aircraft had to take the fight to us to offset that disadvantage. That made life worse for the Thuds, but it gave me a brainstorm.

The primary antagonist was the MiG-17, which also carried wing-mounted air-to-air heat seekers. But unlike us, it also carried two 23-millimeter and one 37-millimeter cannon for close fighting. That's a shitload of firepower. Then we had the MiG-21 to look forward to, and this was a real interceptor with one 23-millimeter cannon, but it carried air-to-air and air-to-ground rockets, and it was supersonic, although not as maneuverable as the MiG-17.

These "Rapid Roger" missions were bullshit.[29] They were intended to keep the sortie ratio up to justify congressional spending, but they wanted fewer fighters in the air to lower the operational costs for fuel, weapons, and parts replacement. That meant a small number of aircraft flew round the clock until their operational overhaul periods. That cost time and efficiency. I was sick of it. Some dickhead with a slide rule in one hand and a martini in the other whose only experience in aircraft was flying first class was determining how we should fly combat missions. The entire organizational structure was a complete butt fuck. And by the way, I was not the only one who noticed; I was simply the only one willing to rock the boat or who had the rank and command presence to fix that shit. That was my primary mission.

Another thing I noticed when I flew in support of the bomber missions was that the Thuds would go in waves to a target, along the same flight path, the same route, altitude, and speed. That was just about the dumbest shit I ever saw. The reason was, after the gooks had you on radar, and they threw up flak, they tracked the initial F-105s with radar and then would fire a few SAMs if there was enough altitude. By the time the next wave and beyond came in, the enemy had already vectored the bad shit they had and just waited. Like shooting a bunch of ducks following the previous gaggle through birdshot. To make matters worse, our fighters were supposed to follow the same flight path, giving them cover from enemy jets. Why? I could not understand it.

I decided that the missions as flown by the Thuds were erratic and dangerous. Even more to the point, I was not going to have my fighters harnessed to a suicide run on heavily defended targets. Our advantage was altitude and air-to-air radar for air superiority. Dropping low to watch a 105 make a bomb run was about as stupid as a blind man driving race cars. No more of that shit for us.

Then we were getting shit for not covering the bombers. Well, I hated to have to educate the Ivy League assholes like Robert McNamara and company, but telling me how to fly a mission was not fucking working. They could fire me—hell, they could even retire me—but not before I took major corrective action. Screw them. I was doing things my way. I told my men that. They seemed shocked that I was going to change a long-standing tradition of fucked-up missions. I assured them that there was a new sheriff in town, and regulations were only as good as the men executing them. Well, I was apparently pissing off all the right people, and I would hear about it real soon.

One thing I instituted was a complete radio chat ban: no more idle chatter and discussion. Radio silence, or your ass was mine. They did not have to comment on every bank and turn or explosion below. The enemy was listening. Even if we were not on radar, they were picking up radio chat and knew someone was coming soon. I stopped that shit hard. And it was hard. Trying to shut up fighter pilots in combat was tougher than jump-starting a dead battery with a hose pipe.

Another problem all the units shared was that we were not getting real-time and important intelligence from S-2. That was something I could not fucking understand. The more we knew, the better prepared we were. The justification of the assholes higher up was that, if we acted upon real-time intel, the enemy would know that they had been compromised and change their methods and tactics. My response? So fucking what? Then we adapt and alter our methods accordingly. It really did not seem that damned difficult to me. But who was I? Just a damned colonel with more time in the cockpit than some of those idiots had on planet earth, that's all.

One thing I did was inform my men of everything—no secrets, no bullshit. It was their lives on the line. I kept a big map where I pinned every mission, every target, and every critical item from every mission, and I studied it. I then came to a few additional conclusions, and I worked with my own intel guys, and we were developing some really good shit. I told them that it was not the fastest or strongest boxer in the ring who won the fight, it was the smartest; a man could read his opponent and predict the punches and counterattack or defend accordingly. Intelligent fighting was better than brute force—be a scalpel, not a chain saw.

———

Every mission debriefing that I had was meant to be a learning session, not just a recap of what we did. I wanted mistakes to become lessons on what not to do. I wanted them to come home alive, and they knew that I cared. I was in the air with them on almost every mission, not sitting behind a desk. You lead by example, and the men will follow you if they trust you. But that was a two-way street. I asked them to evaluate me, correct me if I made mistakes. We all had to learn from each other. I told them I would be damned if I was going to write a letter to a man's wife or parents that started with "I am sorry to inform you that your son died because I fucked up or he fucked up."

I then made the decision to have all the other wing pilots from around the country attend regular head-shed sessions, talk about and figure shit out. This became a regular event at various bases, and it began to reap big rewards. First of all, and most important, it fostered trust and allowed us all to get to know each other. It was a lot easier to risk your neck for a man with whom you had just had a beer than for some obscure unknown pilot in an aircraft from a different unit. It fostered brotherhood and trust. That was what I wanted.

All the fighter pilots wanted to get the MiGs up and tangle, but we knew that they only came up after the bombers. If we were in escort, they would rarely take off. They knew better than that shit. Then we came up with a plan. Chappie had arrived, and he was all on board. He said, "Robin, you know it may get you into trouble?" My response was typical: "So what else is new?"

Now, understand something. In the military, we get our frag orders. That prepares us for the basic mission planning. Once we get the operations order, that is when we go into full five-paragraph mode on steroids. We pilots were given missions and targets that emanated from Washington, to theater, then filtered through typewriters and teletypes and underworked bullshit artists down to the wing commanders like me. I always found it fascinating that some clown sitting twelve thousand miles away thought he knew what needed to be hit, and more important, how it needed to be hit, more than we did. It was the same as backseat driving a New York cabbie; he knew more about the terrain than you did, and you were just going to piss him off. And rightly so.

Well, I met with my commanding general, Lieutenant General William Wallace Momyer,[30] in Saigon, and he wanted to hear my plan on getting at the MiGs defending the so-called high-value targets.[31] After I gave him my plan, he told me to go speak with Brigadier General Don Smith.[32] After we chatted, he would speak to both of us. For the next couple of weeks, we planned out our mission, right down to the smallest detail. From takeoff, to refueling in the air from a tanker, to rally points and target headings and escape routes.

My plan was pretty simple: make the damned gooks think we were F-105s and send the MiGs up after us; then we would give them a fight from hell. I wanted to give Ho Chi Minh a stroke.[33] We knew from previous pilot reports and our now very accommodating intel types that the MiGs would be in the air waiting for the 105s. They would have them on radar, and they also monitored radio chat. As soon as they heard radio chat, they knew something was coming, and they were ready. On this occasion, I was hoping they did not change their modus operandi.

The plan was as simple as it was ingenious, if I say so myself. We would emulate Thuds: call signs, formation, routes, altitudes, even radio chatter, which I would allow to stimulate the Commies' more innate interests. Like a gourmet meal, it was all about the presentation, and the meal would be served hot. However, unlike Thuds, with their bombs, we would carry air-to-air missiles for fighter combat.

My plan had four components: we would lure them into the air and fight, another group of F-4s would cover the approaches to their base to bag any trying to land and refuel or survive. Another group would fly the pattern blocking any escape to China, effectively eliminating any chance at sanctuary there and basically building a wall for them to run into. The last part would be a high-altitude orbiting echelon to catch any stragglers that may get away and provide high-perch observation and confirmations. We were going to lure them into putting their dick in the doorjamb, then we were going to kick it shut.

There was a lot that we did not know that we had to get up to speed on. First, we did not know what the air combat time was for the MiG-17 and 21, as they were interceptors. I could only imagine they were not long-range fighters. We got the info we needed, finally, from the spook services who were usually loath to give us any damned information. I guess someone liked my idea, which I called Operation Bolo, and very few people even knew it existed.

Once we had that knowledge, the rest of the planning came together. First, the gooks did not have air-to-air refueling capability. Second, they were severely restricted with regard to hang time, from what we knew—maybe fifteen minutes of airtime and perhaps five minutes in combat—which meant we had the advantage on fuel. They also had several airfields they could land on, but we had them plotted. I figured just placing a flight of four Phantoms over each would render those sanctuaries worthless, except for the airfield defenses. That was a problem, and working around that was a challenge. I assumed that they would not fire upon their own aircraft coming in to land. I would be proven wrong. Those crazy bastards shot at anything.

We also considered the overlapping and different approach paths for the support aircraft. Obviously, the ground radar operators would need time to digest all of this information, then send that information along to the clown who could make a launch decision. What I wanted was to instill complete sensory overload: confuse them long enough to hit the MiGs and then roll out before they even knew we were not bombers. It was a delicate and precise operation; every moving part had to be in complete harmony with every other.

I knew we could do it. We had great guys. If it did not work, after all the bullshit I put my superiors through, my career was over. Then we had our ECM F-105s working to jam their radar with support fighters covering our egress points. One element would come in from the east and hopefully catch the MiGs already waiting for the bombers, and another would cover their escape routes. I was really hoping those ECM boys had their gear working. If not, this was going to be the biggest air disaster for the air force since Schweinfurt in '43, and my name would be attached to it. I could just imagine if only one F-4 loaded with fuel and ordnance blew a tire on takeoff. That would be twenty-five tons of debris and fireballs ruining the entire runway and possibly damaging other aircraft, thus aborting the mission.

Okay, with all that planning laid out, I had to worry about something that I had zero control over: the intel guys monitoring enemy traffic had to share this with us. My plan was to have all of the targeted airfields, which we were never allowed to hit, for some fucked-up reason, according to the McNamara Doctrine, given names of cities back home. This way the intel types who were sensitive about the enemy realizing we had compromised their communications would not know what and where we were talking about. Our radio guys just had to tell us what activity was going on over "Los Angeles," "Seattle," "Frisco," and the like. That would let us know what to expect.

With plan in hand, I went to Saigon and secured the assets I needed, from tankers to ECM birds, ground relays, search and rescue, in case we lost anyone, support fighters—everything. I left nothing to chance. However, as we all know, any great military plan works until you launch it. I then went to Da Nang and gave a couple of briefings, to get everyone on board. One of the saving graces was the fact that we were to be given ECM pods, just like the 105s carried. That would really help the masquerade because F-4s did not carry them at that time.

The rub in this was that the 105s still had to use them for their missions and then have them sent to us in a couple of days. We had a limited number of those at the time in all of Asia, so we had to retrofit these bastards on and get them working to ensure the ruse worked. We would have two days to have all F-4s operational to appear to be F-105s, as well as ensuring that all of the ground and air assets were coordinated to the second.

This had never been done before in Vietnam, and I know for sure that there were a few higher-ups scratching their heads, wondering if I would perform a miracle or career suicide. I know that there were a few who hoped for the latter even if it meant losing young American boys, so fuck them too, I said. What really pissed me off more than anything was the fact that our early F-4s did not have guns.

Some inbred genius decided that the days of dogfighting and the need for guns was long over, a Dark Age scenario, long in the past, whereas the missile was the weapon of the future. Well, I never got the chance to meet that dickhead, but I wish I could have pulled an LBJ on him in the latrine and given him a little close-up and personal attention.[34] Having cannon or even a Gatling gun on the Phantom would have really been an asset, especially in close-quarters engagements where the missiles would be ineffective.

You ask any of those damned navy pilots if they feel differently, and I will wager a month's pay that they agree with me. Later models of the F-4 did get guns, and all other fighters that came into the inventory afterward were also armed with guns. I guess someone woke the hell up and decided it was just a sound concept.

I cannot stress the technical difficulty we had with mounting these larger ECM pods under the F-4s. We carried external fuel tanks and missiles, but the mounting configuration was totally different from what we needed as opposed to the 105s. The machine shop had to bust all-out ass to rework these things in order to give us the mounting brackets we needed, and then we had a wiring issue. Then we had to order adapter kits from the States and hope like hell we could get enough pods and jammers. Then, at the end of December 1966, we got thirty jammers, and I canceled all leaves and passes. No one was going anywhere; I had a total base shutdown. No one in or out without my permission, no matter who it was. Mail going back home was stopped from going out.

Then we got the word: the authorization to launch [January 2, 1967]. We had been held up by a myriad of things, but weather, or "WX," as we called it, was the primary reason. Well, my selected crews were on the way to the flight line. We took off knowing we were doing something new. After taking off, we headed north and topped off from the KC-135 Stratotankers.[35] Once we were nearing the target area, I gave the order to "hit it," and we formed up and began acting like a Thud formation.

I was primary flight leader, and Chappie had my ass covered, which was a great comfort, as well as for the other guys. We had our backseaters running air radar to see if we could pick up anything flying that was less than friendly, and we had nothing on visual reported in the headsets. Then I heard Chappie call out "MiGs," and I looked and saw them, and I fired two missiles. Nothing. I was pissed.

Chappie's flight engaged, and his wingman, Ev Raspberry, bagged the first one, and, at that time, I had another one in sight, good tone in the headset, and I fired. I got his ass, a MiG-21. Then my wingman, Ralph Wetterhahn, fired and got one. Then another confirmation of a kill came over the headset. More calls of kills came in. By the time we got back, it seemed as if the entire world knew about us and the mission. We had shot down seven MiG-21s and had no losses. I was inundated for weeks by media parasites and others who just wanted to be involved in the postmission glory.

It was not long after that I grew my famous moustache; the one that adorned the photos so many people think of when they hear my name. I had never worn one before, but it sort of grew on me, I guess. Things really got heated for us when we were informed that the Communists had placed a $25,000 bounty on my head. I thought that was kind of cheap. I had cost them a hundred times that much in planes and trained pilots up to that time. I at least thought they should have made it a million dollars. Sometimes, like Rodney Dangerfield always says, you "don't get no respect."

Then I sort of became a victim of my own success. I was informed that I was being groomed for a desk job as assistant division commander, which might involve a belated promotion. Despite the possibility of a star, I was not jumping at it, I can tell you. I had a good thing going on, and it was a wild ride, and I did not want to get off.

I managed to stay in theater and fly more missions, and I was always amazed at just how heavy the antiaircraft defenses were over North Vietnam. Uncle Ho spent a lot of money on that, and I always wondered why we were never allowed to strike the damned source of all that shit. I guess "Strange" and his boys were too busy trying to make more money in the defense industry.* He was another prick I hoped to meet in the back of a very dark bar in a shitty part of town one night. And I was not alone.

Instead of hitting the source of our misery, like airfields and factories, we were given targets like ammo and fuel depots, hitting the Ho Chi Minh Trail for vehicle traffic, and dropping ordnance on a monkey fuckfest somewhere. I was not alone in my disdain for our idiots in charge back in Washington. All of us knew where the high-value targets were and what they were. All of us burned in frustration, especially when you saw an American aircraft blow up from a SAM hit, knowing that we could have neutralized the fucking thing long ago if people just got their heads out of their asses.

One of our postmission requirements once we went through SAM and flak hell was to have another pilot do a look over: flying under and around your bird to check you out and ensure that you did not have any damage that you were unaware of. Holes, leaking fluid, or undropped ordnance would be a red flag, requiring decision-making from that point forward. We all did that to make it safer upon return to base. Sometimes you could have damage that your instruments did not reflect, because sometimes the avionics got shaken up.

On top of all that bullshit from the morons in three-piece suits, I had to deal with a bunch of replacement pilots. Hardly any of them were fighter pilots, and very few had any combat experience or were even trained in the F-4 when it was a fully loaded warbird. I could not believe the guys they were sending. Nothing against them, it was just that I was in a hot war, and I needed guys ready to go. I would lose

---

* Olds was referring to Robert Strange McNamara, who served as secretary of defense under Presidents Kennedy and Johnson. McNamara was one of the least respected men from both administrations, especially among the men fighting the war in Southeast Asia.

valuable combat time and more wear and tear on my already weary fighters having to run a training school. But I got lucky: these boys learned fast and were dedicated to the task, so my initial disdain was unwarranted.

Then, adding to all that mountain of bullshit, I had a really pissed-off wife who wanted a divorce. Ella had had enough of the military wife way of life and felt that she had killed her career to be a wife and mother, while I got to go and do what I wanted to do. I knew she had a point, and we met in Bangkok. Well, I knew when I left, that relationship was over, and I felt terrible, especially for the girls. I went back to Ubon to an entirely new fucking problem.

One of the most famous incidents of the entire Vietnam War was what became known as "Pardo's Push." It is a legendary tale in air force circles—hell, even in worldwide aviation circles. I arrived to learn that Captain Robert Pardo had used the nose of his F-4 to push a damaged F-4 that was hit by ground fire.[36] That Phantom, flown by Bob Aman, was torn up, losing fuel, and not going to make it out of North Vietnamese airspace. Pardo's bird was also hit, but he was in much better shape. Pardo knew that if he could get his squadron mate over the border into Laos, they would be able to eject and have a good chance of the Jolly Greens [Sikorsky H-3 US rescue and heavy-lift helicopters] getting to them.

Well, Pardo decided that if they maintained a shallow descent, he could put his nose up the ass of the other bird and push them into relatively safe airspace. But after they crossed the border, Pardo lost an engine, so both crews had to punch out. The good thing was that the US Air Force Air Rescue teams were on station. Chappie had been getting hell for the action; higher brass wanted a highly publicized court-martial to make an example out of Pardo.

Okay, so we lost two F-4s while one pilot risked his ass to save another crew, big fucking deal! My argument was how many airplanes had we lost to date hitting the same bullshit targets mandated from the wizards in Washington who never saw a shot fired in anger? How many men sitting in the Hanoi Hilton would have loved to have someone like Pardo try to save them from death or captivity?[37] The damned thing made me so mad, Chappie asked if I needed a sedative. He brought me a scotch instead, single-malt, straight.

The entire event was unfolding in Saigon, and I flew there to have a meeting with General Momyer, who was sympathetic to Pardo and really felt for his cause. But it was explained to me that the request for punishment came from way above his pay grade, and I wanted to know who. He just said, "Pentagon," and that was it. It may have been possible that not even he knew who came up with the idea. I made my argument, as he was the convening authority, and the case was dropped. Pardo got a Silver Star, as opposed to a few years in Leavenworth.

Then, not long afterward, shit changed. In 1967 we were allowed to start hitting targets that justified the risk. The navy began it by bombing Haiphong and Hanoi, previously off-the-grid targets, but areas where we knew there were great targets we needed to be slapping around. But with these missions came increased risk. If you thought Uncle Ho defended his airfields, you should have seen the shit he threw up around Hanoi.

On one of these missions, my wingman and I went a few rounds with seven MiGs, and we lost a pilot, Fred Crow, to a SAM.[38] We had quite a few close calls with the MiGs, and I knew they wanted my old ass bigger than shit. I was really happy to see all of the air contingents were working as a team. We had managed to streamline the communications systems, so navy and marine pilots could enter the net, and we had great interservice cooperation over targets. This is critical in mission planning, as well as in operations. You did not want to start hitting a target that already had friendlies attacking. Bad shit tended to happen when you crowded the airspace.

Col. Robin Olds at his base in Udorn, Thailand, in 1967

(Robin Olds)

(*left to right*) Madame Chiang Kai-shek, Lt. Col. James Doolittle, Maj. (later Brig. Gen.) John A. Hilger, and Lt. (later Lt. Col.) Richard E. Cole as they receive medals following the raid *(Carroll V. Glines)*

Edward R. "Buddy" Haydon and
his wife, Nelda *(Colin D. Heaton)*

Newly commissioned 2nd Lt. Curtis LeMay
(USAF Museum via Barrett Tillman)

Gen. LeMay during an address
(USAF Museum via Barrett Tillman)

Gen. LeMay takes the oath of office as air force chief of staff from Secretary of the Air Force Eugene Zuckert on June 30, 1961. In attendance are President John F. Kennedy and Vice President Lyndon B. Johnson. *(USAF Museum via Barrett Tillman)*

Haydon describing the Nowotny encounter *(Colin D. Heaton)*

LeMay as a brigadier general in late 1943 *(USAF Museum via Barrett Tillman)*

First Lt. Haydon in his P-51D *Lady Nelda,* named for his wife. It was this aircraft in which he killed Maj. Walter Nowotny and was later shot down. *(Edward R. Haydon)*

Olds and Chappie James
(Robin Olds)

Lt. Col. Hans Philipp (March 17, 1917–October 8, 1943). He flew combat during the invasion of Poland, the Battle of France, and the Battle of Britain, and was awarded the Knight's Cross with Oak Leaves and Swords, flying with JG-54 on the Eastern Front. He was the fourth pilot to score 100 kills, and his final score was 206, with 29 scored in the west and 178 against the Soviets. He was promoted to lieutenant colonel and made *geschwaderkommodore* (wing commander) of JG-1 *Oesau*, the post he held when he was killed by Robert S. Johnson, after scoring his last victory. His wingman Hans-Günther Reinhardt was wounded after colliding with a P-47, but landed his damaged Me-109 G-6. Reinhardt witnessed Philipp's death, as the pilot bailed out only to have his parachute fail to open. *(Raymond F. Toliver)*

Lt. Gen. Doolittle with RAF airmen who have just received the US Distinguished Flying Cross *(Col. Carroll V. Glines)*

Robin Olds *(Christina Olds)*

Maj. Olds in his P-51D
(Robin Olds)

Capt. Olds and his P-38J
(Robin Olds)

Second Lt. LeMay as a flight
student *(Curtis LeMay)*

LeMay and Lyndon B.
Johnson, 1966 *(Curtis LeMay)*

John F. Kennedy with LeMay
in 1962 *(Curtis LeMay)*

LeMay in Japan, 1945
(Curtis LeMay)

Robert S. Johnson with his P-47D
(Robert S. Johnson)

(left to right) Fifty-sixth FG aces Francis S. Gabreski, Walter Cook, Robert Johnson, Dave Schilling, Walker Mahurin, and Tom Landry
(Robert S. Johnson)

Capt. Johnson in his cockpit, April 13, 1944, showing 25 kills
(Robert S. Johnson)

Johnson and crew chief Staff Sgt. J. C. Penrod with his P-47D
(Robert S. Johnson)

June 1944 (*left to right*), Gen. Dwight D. Eisenhower, Lt. Gen. Carl "Tooey" Spaatz, Lt. Gen. James H. Doolittle, and Maj. Gen. William Kepner

(James H. Doolittle)

Lt. Col. Egon Mayer, who encountered Robert Johnson over France, received the Knight's Cross with Oak Leaves and Swords and scored 102 victories before being killed in action.

(Raymond F. Toliver)

Lt. Gen. James H. Doolittle, Gen. Henry "Hap" Arnold, and Capt. Robert S. Johnson after Johnson scored his 28th victory *(Robert S. Johnson)*

Press conference with Robert S. Johnson, Hap Arnold, and Richard I. Bong after both surpassed Capt. Edward Rickenbacker's WWI score of 26 victories *(Robert S. Johnson)*

Johnson and the squadron mascot *(Robert S. Johnson)*

(*left to right*) Lt. Gen. Adolf Galland, Maj. Walther Dahl, and Capt. Karl Rammelt upon Dahl's assuming command of III. JG-3 *Udet* in 1943. Dahl worked with Egon Mayer and Georg-Peter Eder in developing the head-on attack technique of shooting down heavy bombers. Karl Rammelt (June 10, 1914–May 13, 2009) scored 11 four-engine-bomber victories flying with JG-51, earning him the Knight's Cross, with a total of 450 missions. On October 14, 1943, at 14:20, II. JG-51 engaged the bomber formations headed for Schweinfurt north of Frankfurt and succeeded in destroying nine USAAF B-17 four-engine bombers. Hauptmann Rammelt was able to bring down a B-17 to record his 30th victory. However, his fighter was heavily shot up by return fire from the bombers and he was forced to bail out. *(Kurt Schulze)*

(left to right) Kurt Bühligen, Georg-Peter "Schorsch" Eder (without hat), and Erich Rudorffer (far right). This photo was a tactics meeting in 1943, regarding the school for shooting down bombers. *(Erich Rudorffer)*

First Lt. (later Maj.) Georg-Peter "Schorsch" Eder with a model of a B-17 during the classes he taught along with Egon Mayer. They used models and a captured B-17 restored to flying status to train fighter pilots in how to defeat the LeMay box formation after the October 14, 1943, mission, by attacking from the front, where the defensive fire was weakest. *(Georg-Peter Eder)*

The king and queen pay a visit to Doolittle. He was later made a Knight of the Bath. *(James Doolittle)*

Capt. (later Maj., at age twenty-three) Walter Nowotny meeting Adolf Hitler to receive the Diamonds to the Oak Leaves and Swords on October 19, 1943, for reaching 250 victories. He was the eighth recipient. Only 27 Diamonds would be awarded during the war. *(Rudolf Nowotny)*

Robin Olds *(Christina Olds)*

Robin Olds and Lyndon B. Johnson *(Christina Olds)*

Robin Olds and the Ubon crew from Operation Bolo *(Christina Olds)*

One mission really stands out. On March 29, 1967, we were assigned to strike the Thai Nguyen Steel Works the next day, which was another F-105 escort mission. That meant possible MiGs. Well, around midnight, I was informed that the Thud mission was scrapped, and my unit would do the low-level bomb run instead. I was stunned. That made little damned sense to me. They wanted me to hit the blast furnaces, a worthless target in an area that had been visited by us so often, I could have collected my mail there. They had the best defenses in Asia: flak and SAMs, not to mention their airfields for interceptor flights. Three of us would do the mission.

The mission planning was flawed, the method of operations was screwed, and the route to the target was an unfamiliar one that was clearly marked "relief unknown" on the maps. That meant the mapmakers did not even have the elevation for any of the mountains we were to fly through to get to the target, and the weather was bad. Rain and low-hanging clouds gave us a low ceiling. On the way, we barely missed flying into a mountain that was not marked on the map—hence the term "relief unknown," I guess. The only good thing about the weather was that it was so bad it would probably ground the enemy fighters. But we knew from experience it did not do shit to stop flak and SAMs.

The point was made when I saw that I had been lit up by ground radar, so there was no surprise in our approach. After we crossed the river, we went to the deck, just twenty-five feet above the valley floor. That was great to prevent SAMs being launched, but anything else would have an easy shot if they gave proper lead. We screamed in at nearly six hundred knots, blowing shit up with our forty thousand pounds of thrust behind us. I know we had to have pissed off a lot of poor farmers. I would not want to land in their backyard after what we had just done. There was little doubt that those natives would be a little more than restless.

I thought that we might just get away with hitting the target unscathed when that fantasy went right out the window. The ridge ahead of us opened up. All their flak weapons of every caliber must have been leveled right at us. The ground churned up from the heavy-caliber shells that missed us, but I could feel strikes on my bird, and there was nothing we could do about it. I thought about those bomber guys in World War II who just had to fly through this kind of shit, and they could do nothing about it, either.

We were in a flat run for our lives, low and fast. I recall seeing the gunners having to depress their weapons to shoot at us, and I took some hits in my wing. Normally, when you feel hits, you instinctively look at your instruments. Is there anything glowing that should not be? Are your gauges all reading within the normal range? Well, I will tell you that I had no time to glance at anything, just hang on for the ride. When I pulled up coming in on the target, I had a bang in my right wing.

Then I was notified that I had a fire, but it went out. I then lined up the target, released the bombs, and pulled hard to get away from what was going to happen next. All three of us then scooted back toward a valley that I hoped would provide something resembling sanctuary from SAMs. We were then in the murky fog, but, luckily, I saw the mountain in front of us, and we pulled up to twenty thousand and headed for the KC-135. We were almost dry after that run and had to top off. But I had a problem because I was losing fuel out of my right-wing tank. I was very grateful for that tanker crew to stick with us to make sure I got back. All three of us made it safely, and I was exhausted.

We had more missions that involved working with the F-105s. They were still going down in large numbers. The SAMs were deadly, but the MiGs were back at it again. I thought it was about time to smack them down once more. The marines and air force in Da Nang and the navy guys on Yankee Station joined us, and we overlapped on MiG caps, and the 105 losses halted. We had new F-4Ds joining our worn-out F-4Cs, and the newer jets were equipped with the right pods and shit, so that meant we could also project and disrupt as well as engage enemy jets and bomb targets. This was the way it should have been all along, and the Thuds were given more protection. But we still did not have guns.

Well, then there was that one mission where we were really low on fuel after a MiG encounter, and all of us needed to top off or eject. I had the tanker on call, vectored, and I took some fuel and backed off so the rest could get some. Then I reengaged the boom to complete refueling, when the fool pilot radioed that he was "bingo" on fuel and headed home. I knew damned well that he was within his limits to land at any number of friendly bases. I was in the process of taking on JP [jet petroleum, or jet fuel; there are different grades, such as JP4 and JP8] when the boom detached before I completed top-off. I got into a pissing contest with that pilot, who was not interested in helping me get home. I can tell you now that if I ever thought about skull fucking somebody, that guy was on my list. I was going to scare the shit out of him.

I told him that if I did not top off, we would have to punch out, but before that happened, I would fire my remaining Sidewinders at him as a polite gesture before I pulled the ejection handle. Well, I imagined that there must have been some level of consternation in that cockpit, because the boom came back down, and they completed my refueling. It dawned on me that my transmission on that channel was probably monitored by someone, somewhere, who would take offense at my thinly veiled threat. I did not give a shit, to be honest. When I landed, I called the CO of that tanker unit and told him what had happened. He understood my situation, and I believe he was genuine in his apology. I was assured that it would never happen again.

Then it happened, as I knew it would: I was ordered to stand down. I could lead no more missions. I was still in command but not leading combat missions over enemy territory. It was a collective belief that, because the enemy knew who I was and there was a bounty on my head, that my death or capture would be a PR nightmare for the air force and the United States. I guess the thought of televised images of me being paraded through the streets of Hanoi like some of the others who were shot down was not what Washington wanted the American public to see. I understood that concern, but I had another plan. I *always* had another plan.

There was always a way to make even the most annoying situation work to your advantage. They stated that I "could not lead" anymore. But the order did not say that I "could not fly" anymore. So, I interpreted that as saying I had to pass combat lead over to my XO, which I did. I also knew that the powers that be were watching that mission board. Once any pilot reached the magic one hundred missions, it was a ticket back home. I removed myself from the mission boards to keep the actual number a secret. They would eventually order me home at my end of tour anyway; I would just get shipped out sooner if I hit the hundred-mission mark.

When we began to get the F-4Ds in larger numbers, we had to have transition classes on the new plane, learning the minor differences between the C and D models. The F-104 pilots would also transition to the newer Phantom. One thing they did was arm it with the AIM-4 Falcon heat seeker—like the Sidewinder in application, but a different item altogether. We had the tech briefing on it. When that briefing was over, I was sure that someone had his head so far up his ass that he had died of colitis.

One might think that before they put a new missile in production to replace a great working model, they would perhaps ask for some input from those actually using the weapons in actual combat. Perhaps it was just me, but I would think that, before I sank a shitload of money into R & D and even more in production, I would do something resembling a necessity check, to see if we even needed it. And, if so, was it worth even putting into production? But hell no.

The problem was that the new Falcon had a cooling-off period, where the infrared-heat-seeking component had to cool down before firing—about a minute—which had to occur between firings. Even worse, it had a contact fuse, unlike a Sidewinder, which had a battle-proven proximity fuse—like a grenade blowing up near the target as opposed to a bullet that had to make direct contact. It was not even a new missile; just an upgrade from shit that had been developed a decade earlier. It had a radar-guided mode also, but it was still a point target weapon as opposed to a fragmentation projectile. I was not a fan. I decided that we would exhaust our supply of Sidewinders and shit before we even thought about using these.

And besides, the activity was steadily increasing, and this was just when the action was really getting hot. April had been busy, and May was looking great. On May 4, I believe, we were on a Thud escort when we had four MiGs grow some balls and rise up to greet us. The MiG-21s wanted the F-105s, and I told them to break. I locked on to one MiG and fired a Sidewinder and hit his wing, but then I had to break when I had MiGs on my tail. I rolled out and pulled hard, but my wingman confirmed the kill. That was my second kill in this war, but I was far from being finished.

We concluded the escort to Hanoi and covered the F-105s as they completed their bombing mission. They fired some SAMs at us, but they were not a problem. That was when the call came that there were bandits below. They were MiG-17s going to land. We dropped and ended up right over their airfield. I was wondering when I would get hit by antiaircraft fire and hoping they would not shoot for fear of hitting their own guys. I was out of missiles, and not having a gun on the F-4C pissed us off because we could have had more kills.

As I said, May was busy, and we did get an entire new squadron of F-4Ds and new pilots. We also had a shitload of the new Falcons, and as far as I was concerned, those things could remain in the ordnance depot. My judgment seemed to be sound on May 20, when we did another maximum effort with fighters covering the bombers. Our route was to enter from the Gulf of Tonkin and then head into Hanoi. We knew that there was a good chance the MiGs would come up for the Thuds, and that was what we wanted. While the 105 drivers dropped their ordnance and lit afterburners, we would be in perfect position to bounce the bandits from altitude. We also had a good spread of fighters: an overlapping escort staggered to be most effective. I wanted the Commies to know that we owned that airspace.

Then suddenly the word hit the headsets: MiGs, over a dozen of them climbing onto our six. I hauled hard left and pulled back to roll and get a look. There they were. One thing about the F-4 was our long, black smoke trail; there was no way to hide the fact that we were there. Then the sky was full of bandits and friendlies, twisting all over the sky. I will give those gook pilots credit: they were good, and they had home field advantage.

I no sooner saw a MiG go down in flames than I saw my wingman and his GIB [guy in back] get hit and eject from their Phantom—which became a fireball and then exploded. They were alive but not going home, and my heart sank, but I was still in a fierce fight.[39] The MiG that may have nailed them was in my sights, and once I had growl [the sound in the headset when target was acquired], I fired a Sparrow. It blew up near him, but no kill. So I switched to the Sidewinder, but I was still too close for that missile. At that time, I was really wishing I had guns on this aircraft, because one came at me almost head-on, and it would have been a lovely kill.

On top of all of this, I guess our MiG's buddies on the ground decided to get involved anyway, because a SAM flew right up into all of us. (Nationality was unimportant, I guess.) Then we had radio calls that the Thuds were done and heading back, but we were still involved with this group. The MiGs resorted to what the British used in World War II: a half-assed Lufbery, or wagon wheel, where they flew in a circle to protect the asses of the one in front and behind. After fourteen minutes, the fuel warning told me that this show was over.

But there was this one MiG down below, just circling a few thousand feet under all of us. I wondered if he was a flight controller, as he would have had the best view overhead and been able to direct his men in their attacks against us. I called to the formation to get back, but I was going after that one guy. I rolled over and returned to the scene of the crime, and there he was. He was heading to his base, and he must have been warned because he took evasive action. He streaked right over the ground, with me closing in on him, maybe fifty feet or less off the deck.

I backed off the thrust so I would not overshoot, which would have then given him a shot on me, and that was unacceptable. As I chased him, I saw that he was going to have to clear a ridge in front of him, so I got ready, and waited. Sure as hell, he pulled up and I fired. A Sidewinder blew off part of his tail section, from what I could see. He rapidly decelerated, and I passed by him by less than a hundred feet, and, as I had to pull up, I could not observe the crash for us to confirm the kill. I then went to rendezvous with the tanker. My other two planes were good to go.

Perhaps the bright spot was that we bagged MiGs. My solo attack was credited and confirmed as well.[40] One problem that I had to stress to new pilots coming in was that, yes, the F-4 was the best all-around combat bird in the air over Vietnam, but it was inferior to the MiG-17. They would have this stunned look on their faces when I said that. They were coming in from training facilities all pumped up about how we were bagging MiGs left and right, hence we had a better fighter.

I corrected that shit right away, and I told them why. Forget what you were taught in advanced training. We have no guns, they do. They do not take off with fifty thousand pounds of fighter, fuel, bombs, and missiles. They were strictly interceptors, and they were smaller, lighter, and more maneuverable. I told them not to try and turn inside a MiG; they would only get screwed. Hit-and-run and use teamwork—that was how you beat them. Any thought they had of a classic dogfight did not exist in this world. I also told them that we were screwed using the Falcon missiles—do not rely upon them—and I was proven correct many times, as were the other pilots. I began doing requisitions for the old faithful Sidewinders.

I had a chance in June to fire a Falcon with a good lock tone on a MiG-17, and just when it looked like it was going to work, that bastard lost lock and fell away. Well, that enemy pilot knew I was there, so my fly was open, and I was now at a disadvantage. I was about to head us back home when I saw another loner down below. Well, hell, you know what I was thinking.

But my wingman called him out, so I told him to go for it, and I had his cover. He dropped down and fired a Sidewinder and splashed it. I saw the pilot eject, but he was really too low for that to work. Below him was a bright fireball when the MiG impacted. Good kill, and I was happy to confirm it. I was pissed about that damned missile, though. When I landed, I told the chief to get rid of them—take them off every F-4 and replace them with Sidewinders. I never wanted to see another one, and I was not alone.

However, I was informed that there was a slight problem with that request. Apparently, the D model was not configured to use mounted rails for the Sidewinder and carry outboard bombs simultaneously. I was informed that everything I wanted to do violated not only the McDonnell Douglas technical manuals and flight configuration, but it also altered a military aircraft without regulations, which was a fast way to end a career. I said, "Do it," and I would fly the first test bird to see if it would work. I also wanted the C models to be so retrofitted if it worked.

Following my field-expedient method of altering the Ds for Sidewinders, it then became doctrine, and the AIM-4 was done away with. Now this was a strange period, because I had four MiG kills, and there was no American ace in the war yet. Washington was all up in arms over the propaganda press value of whoever became the first ace, and, of course, the air force, navy, and marines were equally eager to claim the first "ace" in their ranks. I was told that McNamara was behind hyping up the first ace shit and mentioning me in press releases.

Problem was, the Communists already knew who I was, had a bounty on me, and McNamara and Secretary of the Air Force Harold Brown wanted me to be their golden boy.[41] I knew that once I got a fifth kill, my ass was going home forever—maybe a promotion, but definitely a desk job somewhere. I guess I broke a few hearts when I told them that if getting another kill meant going back to the Pentagon and leaving my men, then I would just not shoot another one down. I would let my wingmen take the shots.

For the next three months, I had plenty of chances to bag more MiGs—about ten or so, I think—but I didn't. Then we had an incident where another wing hit the off-limits zone, strafed a Russian ship, and killed a sailor. The hook was out because of the international

223

backlash. I was interrogated, and I had no clue what they were talking about. I reminded them that my fighters did not carry guns, so we could not strafe even if we wanted to.

Turned out there was a big cover-up, and Colonel Jack Broughton's career was ended after a couple of his pilots decided to destroy the camera footage.[42] I was then told that I would be a juror in the court-martial, so I flew there and reported, but I had stated that, as I knew facts about the case, it would be improper to sit as a member. Fucking waste, if you ask me. It was a war, and if the damned Russians did not want to be casualties, then stay the hell out of it.

I just kept wondering what I could have done if I had been allowed to fight in Korea, where the stories from "MiG Alley" were entertaining, and I had to read reports and listen to the stories from the guys who flew in that war. I really felt cheated, in a way, but as I said before, if I had flown in that one, I may not have been able to fly in Vietnam. Maybe things work out for some strange reason—I don't know. I had scored four kills in this war. I learned later that my wingman in the previous mission had chased two MiGs off me when he was hit. He did his job and paid for it. That was the first time in two wars I ever lost a wingman, and I felt like whale shit. Those two would not return from Hanoi until 1973.[43]

We always had mission debriefings, but this one was rather solemn, given our loss of two great guys. As usual, we discussed the tactics, the methods, always trying to improve upon things so the next missions would be better. That's what combat pilots do: we analyze. After a couple of weeks with no real enemy fighter threats, June 1967 became another busy time with MiGs; they really seemed to want to get even with us. We had kicked them in the balls on every mission, and they must have had some really interesting postmission debriefings themselves.

Remember when I said that fighter pilots are a superstitious group?

I had a really bad encounter with Chappie when I learned that he had cleaned out my drawer and threw away my stinking socks. They could not have smelled that bad, because I washed them on occasion. Well, I told him to go get them, and they were in the trash heap. He dug around until he found them. I told him I'd had those suckers since World War II, and I always flew with them on.

Okay, I will tell you the story of the monkey. I met a young F-105 jockey named Karl Richter, great guy, and he had the most missions in theater of anyone. He was also, I think, the youngest pilot to get a MiG kill, and he did it in a Thunderchief.[44] He was killed in action bombing a bridge, ejecting after ground fire took him out. He was recovered but died from his injuries. He was only twenty-three years old. His squadron mates in Korat, Thailand, knew we had a father-and-son kind of bond, and they gave me his pet monkey.

I thought that was a nice gesture, until that little prick destroyed my living quarters. I called it "Stokely Carmichael," and that got me a few side-eyed looks, I can tell you. He became the unit mascot.[45] I learned that the reason they gave me the damned monkey was because the little shit was uncontrollable and destroyed everything.

August 11 was a great day because one of our primary wish list targets was given the green light: the Paul Doumer Bridge in Hanoi, over the Red River. This was where they received most of the rail traffic from China to supply Hanoi and the rest of the country with Chicom aid, and now we could hit it. Well, we were told to expect massive ground defenses. Jamming aircraft and Thuds went to work, and we had the cap [overhead aerial support]. On the way, everything you could expect was thrown into the air at us: bullets, shells, and SAMs. And then we saw MiGs. The bridge was dropped, and we went home, but the enemy fighters never engaged, which was strange to all of us.

Two days later, we targeted another bridge, which the 105s went after, and my flight was bombing the main marshaling yard northeast of Hanoi. Then we saw one MiG-17, and I said I would go after him. I chased him down, and then two SAMs came up, and I rolled away from one, but the second hit their own plane, taking him out. I guess karma is a bitch after all.

When I rejoined the flight, one of my F-4s was in a vertical climb with a damaged engine, and he had three MiGs on him. I told him to get to the deck, and I chased. My wingman and I fired a couple of Sparrows that had no hope of hitting them, but they did break off and head home, and so did we. We had to top off, and I was worried about the damaged Phantom.[46]

The pilot said he and his GIB would punch out over Laos due to smoke in the cockpit and damage. He was losing fuel at a high rate as well. The tanker pilot apparently heard the chat and vectored to our position and nursed that bird all the way to base. This more than made up for the pricks who were going to let me run dry and bail out. Once the damaged bird made it back, it lost both engines due to damage. Close call, but a good day in my book.

Well, that bridge we blasted had been rebuilt, so we had to go hit it again. The mission on August 23 was of interest—also because I was almost at the point of going home, whether I liked it or not. We escorted the 105s to strike the bridge, and we had MiGs come up after us. The two bandits shot down two of my planes on one pass with missiles, so we turned to engage as the Thuds continued to their bomb drop. Then we lost another F-4 just as I heard the 105s call "Out!" as they dropped and then lit afterburners to go home. We had MiG-17s all over us, and we were three fighters down in the count.

In the midst of all this, I saw a 105 running like mad with a MiG on him and another 105 screaming in behind him, firing him up. It was a wild show. The MiG burned in, and the 105 driver had managed to pull up just above the grass and continue his egress. That was some shit to watch, I tell you. When I landed, I called the 105s' CO to confirm the kill.[47] The result of that mission for me was six lost men: one confirmed dead, three guys bailed out, and the other two listed as MIA until they were released after the 1973 agreement.

I was pissed off at the losses, and I knew there had to be answers, and there were. Come to find out the S-2 knew that the gooks were starting to take off well in advance of our arrival and hang around at greater altitude rather than just take off in response to our arrival. I told them that it would have been nice to know that, and I laid the loss of six great men at their feet. I was not polite about it, believe me. If memory serves, I think my hand was instinctively on my personal sidearm. Not sure if I would have used it on them or not.

I was waiting for my orders, which had to be coming in soon. My departure was three weeks or less, and then I found out that I was requested to take over at the Air Force Academy, which was created following the creation of the air force as a separate branch of service from the army in 1947. I was not really sure if that was something I would want to do. I could have just put in for retirement. I tried to extend for another tour, but the powers that be in the Pentagon were not going for it. I spoke to my old friend Ben Cassiday, as he had pulled a tour there, and he assured me it would be a good gig. I had to report in October, and I hated the thought because things were getting even more heavy in the air.

My last flight was a free-for-all, and I took three birds crewed by good friends since my second England tour. We had no action but dropped some bombs and upon returning pulled a low-level air show right over the airfield, which did not amuse my new replacement. I changed out of my flight suit and headed for the officers' club. The men all grabbed me and lifted me like a gladiator. I knew I was going to miss them. This was their way of saying they were going to miss me. Despite the problems and our losses, those were some of the best days of my life.

I went to Hickam Air Force Base in Hawaii and dealt with the press, and then I went to DC to see the girls, as I had been gone over a year. They met me at the airport, but I had to report to the Pentagon, where I was greeted by General John P. McConnell, US Air Force chief of staff.[48] First thing he did was order me to remove my moustache. Then he told me I had to go to the White House the next day to meet President Johnson. Well, that meeting was interesting. LBJ asked me about the family, what it was like to be home, and I told him that I was fairly stunned at how much had changed, and I mentioned the hippies I saw along the route.

I also told him that I was surprised at how little people knew about what was really going on in Vietnam. Johnson said something about how the public would be educated by the returning veterans, and I had to ask him, "Well, what do I say to people who ask me what we are doing there?" Without flinching, he said:

"You just tell them that we are protecting the South Vietnamese so they can live in a free democracy."

Well, to me, that was my open door, and I told him that I could not do that. I also told him that the war was winnable, but we had to remove all the off-limits targets: bomb the railways connected to China, bomb and mine Haiphong to prevent Soviet ships from resupplying the North. This was crucial because they had no real industrial capacity. Choke off their hardware, bomb Hanoi's seats of power, and wipe out their sanctuaries in Cambodia, and basically stop letting damned politicians dictate the war and select our targets. They were not there, we were. That would do it, and we could probably do it in a year.

Well, old LBJ looked at me for a while and told me to "come back tomorrow and give a briefing to Walt Rostow." I had no idea who that was.[49] My escort, Colonel James Cross, educated me: Rostow was the president's national security advisor. Then, upon leaving, I was ambushed by the White House press corps. After a bunch of straightforward and even a few stupid questions, I was asked by one, "How should we end it?" and I said, "Win it." Pretty simple to me. Not long afterward, a cartoon ran in a newspaper of me with Johnson using my response in the caption.

The day was not over, and I was called to the Pentagon to answer to a three-star who was less than enamored with how I'd handled the press, and then I was on Capitol Hill to meet some congressmen, but nothing really earth shattering. They just wanted to talk to a high-ranking combat officer who had just come back. I did manage to get home but much later than planned. One problem I had was that I could not hide my shaking hands. It was a nervous tic, and very noticeable.

It was great seeing my daughters. They had grown a lot in the year I had been gone, and they were always a joy after a tour. They always had questions, and they always seemed interested in everything I did and what I did. I never discussed the more painful and traumatic events; that would have made no sense to them and been cruel. Let's just say that my homecoming was far less than I had wished for but probably what I almost expected.

I went back to the White House and met Rostow, and he seemed as perplexed as I was as to why we were even having this meeting. Well, we chatted for little while, and I told him what I thought, how to win the war, what targets to hit, and, more important, how to eliminate their ability to fight—the same shit I'd told Johnson. He seemed to understand what I was saying, but I did not leave with the impression that it was going to change any course of action in the war.

During the transition, I had more Pentagon meetings and briefed the Joint Chiefs of Staff, as well as more press corps shit that I had to deal with. I was finally packed up and had my gear shipped out, and then I drove my car. The family would follow later. When I arrived at the academy, I was introduced to the cadets, and I gave a short speech and gave them all the bird. Yes, that's right, the bird, and it really livened things up.

I settled into my job and saw that some things needed to be changed. Morale seemed to be lacking, but I used my personal tough methods to handle a few indiscretions. Having been a master prankster myself, I understood the need for discipline and punishment for infractions, but I also understood that you had to measure out punishment to teach and deter, as well as punish. Being humane in such a situation never hurts, and you still get your point across.

Once I was well established, I had Chappie James fly in, and we gave the cadets a great air show in our F-4s, and that was great for morale. But then we had a F-104 dedication, and a flight flew by, and then one broke from their formation, came in low and supersonic, and the shock wave blew all the glass out of the windows, inside and out. It was all gone in every building, just about. The resulting furor was almost immediate, and the offending pilot was grounded but then allowed to return to duty. Well, at least I was not blamed for that one.

I was promoted to brigadier general while commandant of cadets, and, of course, with that was a standing order that I was not allowed to fly. I was not even forty-eight years old. Yeah, right. I still got some joystick time, even going out to see the navy guys at Miramar on occasion. Flying with those guys was as good as it got, and they helped me keep my secret. They respected a fellow fighter pilot, and I respected and liked those guys a lot.

I was commandant of cadets at the United States Air Force Academy in Colorado Springs from 1967 to 1971. And I will say that professionally it was very educational, although it was just the last nail in my marital coffin. The girls were basically grown up, starting their own lives. Ella and I were too broken to fix. I knew it years ago, but sometimes you cling to hope. I really loved Vail and Steamboat Springs, which is how Buddy Haydon and I became great friends, and Nelda, too.

After that, I served as chief of aerospace safety in San Bernardino at Norton Air Force Base until 1973, when I retired. The move from Colorado back to California was great news for Ella, and she wanted to move back to Los Angeles. The job was very interesting: everything related to aircraft and pilot safety and longevity you could think of was involved, so, on that note, I was very intrigued. On the other side, I learned a lot of what I called the dark side of air force and government bureaucratic bullshit and politics.

I ended up reading all the reports and was basically in charge of Strategic Air Command from that part of the business. The legacy of LeMay and others was that they created an institutionalized fear of retribution for failing at any level. That is a bad environment when you expect people to think freely and take chances to improve the collective condition. It was a cesspool. Their maintenance records were appalling, the loss rates to aircraft inexcusable, and the record keeping and lack of anyone taking personal responsibility were frightening. All of this with a hot war going. As a nation, and air force, we were fucked, and I told them that.

What I thought about Vietnam? We should never have gone in unless we were prepared to win it—total war, like World War II. Even Korea was a fuckup, but Vietnam was an epic American tragedy that could have been avoided. That war proved that politicians dictating military actions, far removed from the theater, is an unworkable condition.

I flew 107 or so missions in World War II, but I got shut out of Korea, and that really pissed me off. However, once that impediment was removed, and Vietnam broke out, I got lucky, and I took command of the F-4 unit in Thailand. I flew about 152 combat missions, of which an official 100 were documented, and I use the word "documented" for a reason: they wanted me grounded, those assholes in Washington.

I was once at a party of sorts when I came back from Thailand. I was in Washington, at a function with Ella, and some of the old usual suspects were there, including LeMay. Understand, I respect the guy for being a great pilot and taking all the chances he did. He was my dad's protégé, and he was a strict leader, but I think that somewhere along the way, Curtis lost himself. I mean his true self; that part of a person that allows you to be human, relaxed, and accept that not everyone is perfect.

As a general in World War II, he flew those dangerous missions; Christ, he was a part of Black Thursday [the second raid on October 14, 1943, against Schweinfurt-Regensburg]. He wrote hundreds of letters to the families of the men who never returned. But what he did when he became head of SAC and chief of staff was scare the shit out of people, and SAC was never going to be the same. His legacy of punishment for anything and everything was the running theme for survival, which was hide, duck, run, cover, and for God's sake, never accept responsibility for anything fucked up, or your career will be over.

My retirement in 1973 could not have come at a better time, and we moved to Steamboat Springs, where we bought a house. I knew that I was where I wanted to be, but Ella wanted to be back in LA, where her youth and career had started. We were divorced in 1976, and it was not really on the best of terms, but the girls were okay, and that was all that mattered to me. Ella died in 1988, and I know it was hard on the girls. I also lost my brother. Tough year.

I remarried in 1978 to Morgan [Sellers Barnett], but, sadly, I lost

Chappie to heart failure. Even though he outranked me, he still called me boss. We had our differences, and different styles of operating, but he was a great man in my eyes. He had his flaws: I think he became more political as he gained rank, which affected his leadership, and that disappointed me.

As a pilot, a warrior, people assume that you get used to death. You don't. You just get used to dealing with it, and we all deal with that shit in our own unique way.[50]

With regard to my former enemies, I have never come face to face with any of the North Vietnamese airmen I fought, probably because they were dead. I did become friends with Gunther Rall. I liked him from the moment we first met, and we still talk on occasion. I was with Rall and Hub Zemke once, and Hub was making fun of his missing thumb, the one Shorty Rankin shot off. I met a few others along the way, like Galland and Hartmann, and a fellow named Dietrich Hrabak. It was a real shame that we were enemies.[51]

Here's a story you will like about LeMay. I was at this cocktail party, and there was the usual small talk. I just had a scotch poured, and then, out of the blue, I heard LeMay say, "Well, I do know one goddamned thing: if coffins could fly, Robin Olds will have a fucking joystick in it."

Now, I have to admit that I liked that. I was not sure how or even why my name came up, but I really hope there is a heaven. I would like to see those friends I lost long ago again. I would like to see my parents again, especially my dad and family. I do not know if they have airplanes in heaven, but if they do, then I will be right at home. Hey, are we out of scotch?

COWBOY ON A THOROUGHBRED

★

Edward Ross "Buddy" Haydon

visited Buddy Haydon several times, sitting down with him at his home near Robin Olds's house in Steamboat Springs, Colorado. One day after breakfast, he took me out on his property, a rolling terrain on a small plateau. It was November, snowy and cold, and he paced his land with a divining rod, a Y-shaped instrument used to find groundwater. After we walked around awhile, his stick bent down toward the earth. "I should dig a well here," he said. "Never hurts to have more water."

Buddy Haydon was a short, slim man who walked with a deliberate step, always sure of himself. He hailed from the Wild West country of San Angelo, Texas. As a young pilot during World War II, flying his P-51D Mustang—which he called *Lady Nelda*, after his wife—Buddy was truly a cowboy on a thoroughbred.

Sometimes the future may be altered by a seemingly insignificant event, the result of an action whose importance becomes apparent only much later. Such was the case when Buddy encountered a Messerschmitt Me 262, the first jet-powered fighter plane, low in the sky over Achmer, Germany, on November 8, 1944. The pilot who lost his life that day was twenty-three-year-old Major Walter Nowotny, a 258-victory ace and Diamonds holder, and a personal favorite of Adolf Hitler's. Nowotny's death so rattled the Führer that he nearly terminated the Me 262 jet fighter program altogether.

Buddy and his wife, Nelda, were both gracious and friendly. They had married before he shipped out to Europe, and, during the war, they exchanged letters often. Nelda was lovely and graceful, and one of the kindest people I have ever known. Her most frequent question to me was "Are you hungry?"

Over the years, Buddy and I passed many enjoyable hours over the telephone. He always became greatly animated when discussing his experiences during the war, and he provided information on many subjects related to my research, clarifying and adding details. I cherished those talks, especially if Nelda was in earshot, because you just never knew what the two of them would come up with on any given topic.

In their twilight years, the Haydons moved from Colorado back to Buddy's hometown of San Angelo. After Nelda passed away on February 7, 2009, Buddy went to live in Bozeman, Montana, with his daughter, Claire (known as Cis), and son-in-law, Charles Hager, where I had the privilege to have many more conversations with him by telephone.

On November 20, 2012, Buddy Haydon died at age ninety-two and had his headstone along with Nelda's in Fairmount Cemetery in San Angelo, Texas. His grandson, Brian Ross Hager, scattered his ashes in the mountains as a fitting tribute. Buddy and Nelda are survived by their children, Christopher Gunn Haydon, Frank Armstrong Haydon, and Claire Gibbs Haydon Hager, and their grandchildren, Brian and Alexa Augusta Hager Benner.

Rest in peace, cowboy. You and Nelda are both very much missed.

BUDDY HAYDON

I was born on April 24, 1920, in San Angelo, Texas. My father's family came from Kentucky. His father was a German immigrant who had escaped conscription in the Prussian Army in about 1880. Since he spoke German, he was placed in charge of German prisoners of war who were working as farm laborers here during World War I. My parents divorced at the beginning of the Great Depression, and I have a younger brother, Christopher. When our parents separated, we went to live with our grandparents. We went to work in the fields right beside the migrant workers, which was, in my opinion, instrumental in my developing a sense of responsibility, not to mention a solid work ethic. I also learned that you have to use finesse in interacting with people, especially bootleggers, whom I dealt with on occasion.

After high school, I attended Texas A&M University, but was unable to finish my year in 1938, so I went to college in San Angelo for a couple of years. I then took off cowboying for a couple of years in West Texas, which was still a wild frontier back in those days. They even still had very rare, yet almost expected, gunfights, where frontier justice was alive and well. I came across all types, but the bootleggers were the most interesting and also the most dangerous group if you ran afoul of them. Otherwise, they were reliable guys. I never had a lot to do with them, and they never bothered me.

When I returned from cattle roping and all that stuff, the airplane was in vogue. As a young boy, I had taken lessons from our neighbors, who owned an airfield, so that was where all my money went. I fell in love with flying. I really took to it in the ROTC [Reserve Officers' Training Corps] program, and from then on, I made all As in school. I soon had my private and commercial pilot's licenses and training certificate. I logged many hours at military airfields, and I qualified as a check flight instructor to work for the army as a contracted civilian. I went to Bullard, Texas, and took instruction from Cloyd Clevenger, an old-time pilot who beat out Ernst Udet and others in aerobatic championships.[1] He certified me. I knew that I wanted to fly military unless I could get a really nice civilian flying contract.

But then things changed. On December 7, 1941, when the Japanese attacked Pearl Harbor, I was in a movie theater with my then fiancée, Nelda. The red tape to apply for flying duty was incredible, so I went to Canada, wanting to fly fighters, as I thought the US Army would make me an instructor. I wanted combat, not a flight line job. Well, the Canadians wanted the same thing. Since I had all this training, they wanted a permanent instructor, but I found it a little too uncomfortable. It was too British this, too British that, too British everything, so I went home, where they were finally accepting pilots.

Instrument flying was very new and experimental, to some degree, but by the end of the war, we were turning out some great pilots. However, there were no promotions in this field, and after two years, I made first lieutenant. I trained in the P-39 Airacobra and P-40 Warhawk, but then I was transferred to fighters and into the North American P-51 Mustang training course. These were B and C models, of course, with the Allison engines. This was the best and most fun airplane with a propeller ever built; I really enjoyed it. But it got even better later when we had the D model, and the Rolls Merlin engine—the same used in British fighters. Then it was a real monster. It's a shame I did not get right into combat with my thousands of hours as an instructor. That kind of pissed me off.

I immediately became a flight commander, not because of my seniority or academic qualifications, only because I was competent. The integrity of the flight was the most important thing to remember. It was, after all, a team effort, and getting my pilots and planes back after a mission was the most important thing next to the mission itself.

Then we were assigned to groups. Our unit, the 357th Fighter Group [known as the Yoxford Boys], of which my 364th Squadron was a part, arrived in England as a well-trained Bell P-39 squadron. It was usually reserved as a ground attack fighter, and it was best suited for that. We received the Mustangs, which we flew for the rest of the war. By November 1944, we'd shot down more than five hundred planes, and now we were getting ground attack missions. We flew many missions in succession as ground attack fighter-bombers, where we were briefed to expect 80 percent losses from ground fire as we strafed and bombed stationary targets.

This new mission statement was not very well received. Guys who had flown many bomber escort missions, or Ramrods, who mixed it up on occasion and had nerves of steel, suddenly started trembling. Many of them would get up in the morning, go to the briefing, and then go outside behind the planes and throw up from nerves. A lot stopped eating breakfast because it would not stay down. We climbed into our fighters, and without saying anything, we would look at each other, as if to say, "Hope you make it," or "Better you than me."

The announcement that we could expect eight out of ten planes and pilots not to make it back unnerved many pilots. It affected us on the ground and in the air. You must understand that all fighter pilots just don't *think* they are immortal, they *know* they are immortal, that nothing will touch them. It's always the other guy. It comes as a shock to realize that you're not. I think that we were the most cautious flight because we never flew anyone into the ground or left them uncovered or alone. We took extra precautions and tried to make sure that we always brought everyone back, even when they were badly shot up.

I spoke with quite a few British fighter pilots, and all of them were happy that the RAF had Hawker Tempest and Typhoon squadrons for the ground attack role. I met one of these Typhoon pilots: a sergeant who had two air kills and over a hundred ground attack missions. He said that more than half the time, he had to change into a different aircraft due to the damage he received from ground fire.

He was a good-natured guy. "Yank," he told me, "just be sure your parachute harness is tight, and after going in to strafe or dropping your eggs, you push the throttle to the firewall and weave out of the target area. Those bloody Jerries are good at shooting up our aeroplanes. I had three scrapped in a month coming back from that type of work."

Well, that did not make me feel any better. We had a few guys get shot down, of course—not as many as expected, but so many Mustangs came back shot up that they were mostly cannibalized for spare parts or scrapped.

I met this other guy once. He was also a Typhoon pilot, specializing in hitting German tanks, guns, and other shit. He also told me that had he been in any other British fighter-bomber, he would have never made it back. They fired rockets from underwing racks and sometimes dropped a couple of bombs, depending upon the mission. He said that one man in his squadron was going to hit a suspected fuel dump, and when he dropped his bomb, the explosion was so massive that his fighter disappeared in the bright flash. They never saw him or the plane again. He just vaporized. This pilot I was speaking with was perhaps a thousand yards behind him, and he pulled up after the explosion. There was nothing left. I thought that was incredible and very unnerving.

The Ninth Air Force was really heavily tasked with tactical close air support and interdiction. They were probably responsible for more ground losses by the Germans than any other outfit. They were damned good at it, and used mostly P-47 Thunderbolts, which was a much better fighter for that kind of work anyway. It was just more rugged and carried eight .50s, compared to our six, and although they had a shorter range even with drop tanks, they could carry heavier external payloads. It was a big son of a bitch, too.

We were tasked with hitting airfields in northern France, Holland, Belgium, and sometimes in Germany. Most of the targets were railyards and trains if we caught them. Troops in the open were rare targets, and I never saw any. We did dominate the roads during daylight hours. Hundreds of vehicles were wiped out due to strafing attacks. I know we hurt the living hell out of the German military transport system.

We had some interesting missions besides ground attack, such as the much-preferred bomber escort. My P-51 was named *Lady Nelda,* for my girl, and we married before I shipped out. Nelda always had faith in me. When I told her not to worry, I would be coming back, she knew it.

I had quite a few experiences that I will never forget. I remember once on a mission near Peenemünde on the Baltic Sea, I encountered something for the very first time. I was cruising at about twelve thousand feet when, off my left wing, I saw a V-2 rocket shooting up through the light clouds.[2]

It was a clear day, and I was thinking that since I was so close, I could put a few rounds into it, but then it slowed down and started listing, and I was so fascinated I just watched, never taking the shot. I could have had a V-2 kill, but it turned over and went straight down on its own contrail back to where it came from. All I could think about was how bad those Germans on the ground were going to feel real soon. There was too much cloud cover at lower altitude, so I could not see it hit, but I felt the explosion, which rocked my Mustang. We continued hitting ground targets, shooting up anything worthwhile and generally making life miserable for the enemy.

Well, we had just finished a bad skirmish with a lot of German fighters, up in the middle part of Germany, and it was time to go home. I was at around thirty thousand feet with the rest of the flight, watching for enemy fighters, which came up regularly, especially during a bomber mission. Since they were concentrating on the bombers, we were not expecting any trouble, and I was just daydreaming, thinking about what a bad day it had been. I was just glancing over the left side when I saw a Messerschmitt Me 262 below me at about ten thousand feet.

Since there were not a lot of German planes around, I broke the loose formation after calling him out. I dropped the nose and slipped a bit, and I watched the jet as I descended, never taking my eyes off him. My aircraft was faster than that of my leader, Captain Merle Allen, so I closed faster. I made almost no adjustments and got squarely on his tail, and he took no evasive action whatsoever, but stayed on that vector. I noticed that the 262 was not going as fast as it should have been; that there was a problem. I should not have been able to close on him so quickly.

Well, he dropped to the deck on that same heading and leveled off, making no corrections, with me closing in with an altitude advantage. I was almost ready to fire, waiting to close in and shoot this sitting duck. Suddenly, off my right wing at great altitude, I saw two Mustangs from the Twentieth Fighter Group that had arrived late but were diving, converting their altitude into speed. They were way out of range, over two thousand yards, when the lead P-51 fired. I saw the tracers fall short as much as 60 percent to the target, and there was no way he could have hit it. That pilot was Captain Ernest Fiebelkorn, as I later discovered.[3]

The Germans were alerted, so the element of surprise was down the shitter. I knew what was coming, so I called to the flight to break hard right and away to avoid the flak while I went hard left down to the deck, which was safe to some degree because the larger guns could not depress elevation to hit you. They could only shoot below the horizon with small arms, which could still knock you down, but I slipped in anyways. Suddenly I flew into everything they had.

I have to say the jet pilot was good. He knew what he was doing. In case he had anyone on his tail, he would lure them into the flak zone, so he could drop below into the flak-free zone and land. No one would have voluntarily flown through that to get down to the jet. But see, I was already below this height at his level, below two hundred feet, and made the turn. I was worried about trees—there were many ringing the airfield. I was still turning around this small forest. I still had plenty of speed, and I thought for sure that I would never see that jet again. I turned no more than 20 degrees to 50 degrees, because I was receiving no fire, and rolled level.

I weighed my options, knowing that I was the only American in this unfriendly area. I was just trying to scoot across the field and either find a place to hide or rejoin the group. Well, as I came around the tree line, directly in front of me was this 262 again, so I slowed down as if on a downward leg, 180 degrees from his previous position, and he did not see me, not at that time. I chopped the throttle, cutting power, sliding back to the right a bit. I could not believe how damned lucky I was and how unfortunate he was going to be.

Remember that when you cut power on a propeller-driven plane, you lose speed quickly. I ended up in the perfect position and let her drift right into him, just like shooting a student out of the traffic pattern. I was below two hundred yards behind him and closing quickly, since he was slowing down. I was going faster, probably three hundred knots or less and falling about a hundred feet or so right behind him. I was still going fast, so I lowered my flaps a bit to avoid a collision.

We both slowed down, and I was on his left side, and I saw what I thought was smoke from his right engine. I was on his seven o'clock until we were almost side by side, and that was when he saw me.

He looked over, I could see into his cockpit, and he looked right at me. I could see his face clearly; we were easily less than fifty feet apart. Well, the moment he saw me, he got a startled look on his face, and we were about a hundred feet off the deck. It was totally animated, as if he thought, "I have really screwed up." He thrashed around in the cockpit as the jet appeared to stall. He looked at me again, and then he snapped right in, falling no more than half a rotation to the left, and I was so enchanted with what was happening, I never fired a shot, which would have given me the kill by myself.

I thought about that a lot later, knowing that if I had fired, the gun camera would have recorded it, but Merle was watching us from higher altitude, so he was a witness. He saw what happened: the jet snap rolled right in with me following close behind—perhaps too close—and I pulled up as he crashed into the ground. I felt the explosion, which lifted my plane up in the air, and as I pulled up, I saw the cloud of smoke where he landed.[4]

I thought that I had sufficiently stated [in my report] that I had run him into the ground without firing a shot, but I ended up sharing the kill with Fiebelkorn, who had earlier pulled up and away. He was nowhere near the action, and Merle knew it. But Fiebelkorn saw the jet crash and got credit for a half kill. I don't think he claimed it, but others saw the action and reported it. He was not even in the neighborhood. I am perfectly convinced that had I not arrived on the scene, Nowotny would have landed the jet. Even if he lost hydraulics, or all power, he could have landed on the nacelles [the two engine housings, one on each wing], and the plane would have probably flown the next day. Once, in the late 1940s, someone handed me a *Stars and Stripes* or *Air Force Times* where someone had written that

I had shot down the sixth 262 in the war, which I don't think is correct. That was the first time it ever came up.

That was not my only encounter with the jets. January 1945 was
interesting. On January 14 I shot up a couple of planes on the ground,
with no damage. On January 20 we ran into some 262s near Munich,
and we got busted up pretty good trying to catch them. My flight
included, I think, Dale Carter, who was in a Lufbery Circle with a 262.
The jet had higher speed, but the Mustang had a tighter turning radius. Each plane was trying to gain on the other without success.

I winged over and entered the chase, but from the opposite direction, head-on. I passed within inches of the 262, canopy to canopy,
and this happened twice. Neither of us could get a shot. I thought that
it was crazy, that I might hit him, bringing him down by guns or
ramming him, and I might be able to bail out afterward. It was a
stupid thought, and I woke up smartly after the second pass, but there
was nothing I could do. I saw another 262, probably heading for
home, so I decided that he was not going to get away. I firewalled the
throttle and dropped altitude; there was no flak at all at first. I closed
with him, using altitude for speed, and opened fire. I was getting
good strikes as he went in for a landing, with me screaming down on
him at about five hundred knots. He was touching down, and I had
to pull up or crash.[5]

I never got the chance to file a report; the best I could do was to
have claimed a damaged or probable anyway. As I pulled up from the
airfield, something shook my aircraft, like something had punched
it. Instantly I had fire in the cockpit, and smoke was pouring in, so I
pulled straight up, using the high airspeed to gain altitude, and rolled
the canopy back. I was still pulling good power even though the
smoke was heavy and a fire had broken out in the cockpit, so I unstrapped, slightly rolled the bird over, as it was still almost vertical,
and just as it slowed down in a stall, I went over the right side.

Now I had another problem: my shoulder straps had become entangled around my waist somehow, pinning me to the plane, which was still trimmed for 450 to 500 miles per hour. It nosed over and headed straight for the ground, and here I was stuck to the side, but I was still not feeling panic.

I was discussing this mentally, and I figured that due to the slipstream and pressure, there was no way I was going to get loose unless I broke loose from the stress. In fact, I decided at that time to go ahead and accept death. It was the most serene, inviting, and calm decision or feeling I have ever had in my life. I felt the war was over, and there was absolute peace, and there would be no more problems. All this time, the plane was winding up, gathering speed and headed for the ground.

Suddenly I was able to sit up sufficiently against the force of the wind, and I broke free. I smacked the tail of the airplane with my back—a glancing blow as I flew by—which put me in a spin. Without thinking, I pulled the rip cord on the parachute. I was thinking that I would have a nice, gentle trip down, when I realized I had not pulled the rip cord out far enough, and that I was tumbling. The parachute was still in the container.

Realizing I had screwed up, I found the wire, and I can tell you that I pulled that sucker out by the root. I had not slowed down from the great speed imparted to me by the aircraft. The opening was violent, which stopped my tumble. However, I was thrown into a swing, like a pendulum, and placed my body parallel to the ground, and I saw a telephone pole with two wires under me. Then I smacked face-first right into the snow. I was stunned and not sure if I could move, but, in minutes, some Germans were there, very excited. I think they were amazed that I was alive.

They helped me up and wanted to know where my pistol was. The shoulder holster was empty, as was the sheath for my boot knife. I am sure that they were ripped away during the adventure. Anyway, I was taken into the commander's office by two German officers. They treated me as a gentleman warrior who was not a combatant but their prisoner. They did not interrogate me; they were just concerned as to how I felt. They gave me medical treatment, since I had burns on my face, eyes, hands, and so forth. When this was all over, after a discussion in German about me, they handed me over to a very young SS trooper. It was his job to get me to the main interrogation camp, which I think was Oberursel.

———

We went to the *Bahnhof* to begin this trip of several days. The train was packed with people, but I was placed into a private area with my guard. He had this Schmeisser machine pistol, magazine in, and I was pretty sure that he would have shot me if I tried to escape. But if I had escaped, I knew that I would not get too far wearing an American flight suit, bandaged up, and not speaking German. We finally pulled into Stuttgart, which had only hours before been heavily bombed.

The civilians were angry, and so were the troops from the front who were there. They had me backed up against the wall, and, being a good old southern boy, I saw a lynching coming. There was no way out, either. I figured that if this was it, I would stand my ground. Well, that fourteen- or fifteen-year-old SS soldier lifted his Schmeisser and fired over the heads of the crowd, which consisted of not only soldiers but old men, women, and children. They all stopped their angry chants.

Here I was, an American airman, the reason for their misery. Well, that SS trooper saved my life. He had orders to follow, and despite his personal feelings, whatever those may have been, he carried out those orders. That was discipline. He finally delivered me to Stalag IIIB after a long trip from Nuremberg. Hundreds of us Americans were thrown together, along with a few British and Commonwealth airmen. We were all pretty much aircrew and pilots, with a few exceptions. The city of Nuremberg was wiped off the map from bombings by the Eighth Air Force from England and the Fifteenth Air Force based in Italy, with the British bombing by night. It was hit pretty regularly. In a few weeks, we had been moved farther east, and the weather was warming up a bit. Before that, we had been freezing, it was so damned cold.

Then I was moved with a lot of other guys to another prison camp farther to the east, which we then had to again evacuate because the Russians were coming. One day the German guards became very excited; they were jabbering about something. One of the guys with us spoke German and was translating what he overheard. "The Russians are almost here, it seems, and they need to get the hell out of here. They are taking us with them." I wondered, why would they bother? They could have just left us for our allies to scoop up. I never learned the answer to that question.

The German guards then began force-marching us to the west again to evade the advancing Russians. We crossed the Danube at a bridge that Waffen SS troops were rigging for detonation with what looked to be five-hundred-pound bombs. We had to walk across, but before that, we milled around while they decided our fate. The Volkssturm leader in charge convinced the SS men to let us cross.[6]

This was a nervous time for me. Now, let me tell you, those SS soldiers were tough, hardened veterans. They were different from the rest. They had a mission to destroy that bridge, and it must have been important, as there were many senior officers present. The situation got serious. Our guards began throwing their weapons over into the river while we and they both were standing on tons of explosives, and the SS troops were watching! I knew we were done for. The SS would have been justified in dropping the plunger on us, and I don't know why they didn't. Well, after a couple of more days, our guards abandoned us, and we were left to ourselves. We continued walking west, not really knowing where the hell we were going. This lasted for a couple of weeks. I remember being hungry as hell; we had not really had a meal in over a week.

Later, we saw General George S. Patton riding by on his tank at the head of a column. He liberated us. He dismounted and was walking around talking to us, asking how we had been treated, along with an entourage of other officers. He came to me and asked, "Who are you?" I saluted and stated my name and rank, and he said, "Glad you made it." I looked at him and pointed to a guy—one of our fellow prisoners sitting in the mud, who was quite sick. I said, "Sir, that guy there is a general!" Patton immediately placed him in a vehicle. That was on April 20, 1945.

I later learned something interesting: when I was shot down, the other members of my flight saw the plane crash but did not see a parachute. The Germans who captured me returned my dog tags via the Red Cross, and I was labeled missing in action until the tags were received. I did have a Red Cross POW card filled out, and they also took my photograph and fingerprints, but I guess they never made it back to our people. Then the War Department classified me as killed in action. The word was that I had died of my wounds. I was awarded a posthumous Purple Heart, and they informed my wife that I was dead. They stopped all allotments and pay and were going to pay her my serviceman's life insurance.

However, she knew that I was alive, since she received a letter from me—actually, just a card—from first the POW camp. After that, I had dropped off the radar. We still have that card today. She took it to the base and told them she was sure I was still alive, since I talked in it about other people in the camp who were known to be POWs as well. After an investigation, they decided that I was, in fact, still alive, although the governor was not informed, and he issued a death certificate in my honor.

———————

After the war, I had the opportunity to acquire a large ranch from a friend of mine in Montana, but I decided to stay in the army until the US Air Force was created and get a regular commission. I went to military schools for tactics and strategy, then to the War College. I later flew F-86 Sabres in Germany, and I had a great experience. I once came in for a landing, and there was a malfunction with the canopy, and, for some reason, the damned thing blew off. So, I landed this jet and rolled right past a massive formal ceremony without my canopy. That drew some attention.

I later took command of an F-102 squadron based in Goose Bay, Labrador, in Canada, and that was interesting duty. I am still good friends with many of the old pilots: Clarence Emil "Bud" Anderson,[7] of course, who flew with us; Chuck Yeager was also in the group.[8] Robin Olds and I are still good friends, and I was friends with the late General John C. Meyer, who was my boss for a while.[9] Olds and Meyer—those were two guys with completely different personalities.

Meyer was able to become an administrative type, and he was apparently good at it. Olds barely survived peacetime, and we always worried about him. He just needed a war—that is the way he is wired. From our discussions, I guess I was pretty lucky if that jet pilot I went head-to-head with was Theodor Weissenberger.[10] I wonder who it was I was shooting at when they nailed me. I would like to know the name of that flak battery commander and the officer who interrogated me.[11]

MASTER OF
THE BOMBERS

★

Curtis Emerson LeMay

had just completed interviewing Colonel Gregory "Pappy" Boyington at his home in Fresno, California, in 1986, when I received word
that General Curtis LeMay was available for an interview as well.
This had been facilitated by General James H. Doolittle, who knew I
wanted to add LeMay to the collection I had been working on. LeMay
and I had previously spoken on the phone, and this time when I
called, his wife, Helen (Estelle Maitland), answered. When I identified
myself, she remembered my name and called out, "It's that boy who
wants to interview you!" and then LeMay was on the phone.

"How the hell are you, Mr. Heaton?"

I told him that I had finished a lengthy interview with Boyington.
I will never forget his response:

"Boyington should have been a good one—he's a real bastard, too!
Come see me, and I'll tell you some real stories. Are you a liberal?"

"No sir, I am apolitical; just a former soldier doing interviews with great heroes from the war."

"Doolittle said you were a stand-up guy, so here's my address. See you here."

Then he hung up, and that was how it started.

When I arrived at their modest home in Newport Beach, California, LeMay and Helen proved to be gracious hosts. For the many hours during that first sit-down, Helen excused herself and left us alone. LeMay said she was really good about welcoming historians to "meet and greet," but did not like hearing about the war.

My interview with Curtis LeMay that day was the liveliest and most energizing I ever conducted, with the possible exception of Boyington's. LeMay had no qualms about discussing the history he had lived through and helped to make. His unapologetic defense of what he called "command morality" was clear and unambiguous, as were his impressions of notable persons. Helen served a light lunch, and by midafternoon, we'd had a few drinks. Unlike LeMay, I was never a whiskey drinker, so I declined his initial offer. So, he pulled out the scotch, and a good one, too, a single-malt, and we continued the interview.

With LeMay, there was no gray area—he was as black and white as a human being can be. My interview with him was a historian's dream: it had all those qualities that bring a man's story to life and allow us to know his mind and the rationale for his decisions. Both in person and during follow-up calls, he was always gracious, yet very blunt, becoming verbose only if asked a detailed operational question, when he went into extreme detail and made sure you absorbed every bit. Like Robin Olds, he was very good, too, at answering questions directly and recounting his life story in a fairly smooth and chronological manner.

There was no hesitation when it came to his feelings about

circumstances or people. He was colorful in his language and descriptions, and his method of delivery was not the most politically correct compared to many others. Whether discussing fellow officers, senior statesmen, celebrities, or his former enemies, he held nothing back: "If I labeled them a coward or a fool, trust me, they earned it." A historian could ask for nothing more.

Many people thought LeMay was a bastard, but he at least had the friendship, if not outright admiration, of many of the military's and Hollywood's elite.

General Curtis LeMay was honored by many countries for his military service. The United States presented him with the Distinguished Service Cross, the Distinguished Service Medal with two Oak Leaf clusters, the Silver Star, the Distinguished Flying Cross with two Oak Leaf clusters, and the Air Medal with three Oak Leaf clusters. In 1977 he was inducted into the International Air & Space Hall of Fame at the San Diego Air & Space Museum. He was also a recipient of the French Légion d' honneur.[1]

In a strange twist of what can only be called complete irony, the Japanese government conferred upon him the First Order of Merit with the Grand Cordon of the Order of the Rising Sun, on December 7, 1964. In another strange irony, LeMay had been awarded medals for his service in Europe during World War II from the Soviet Union—the greatest moral enemy of his long and distinguished career. He was elected to the Alfalfa Club [an exclusive club that meets once per year at a black-tie event] in 1957 and served as a general officer. In all, he received thirty-two decorations from thirteen nations, and spent twenty-one years as a flag officer. He died on October 1, 1990, and is buried at the United States Air Force Academy cemetery in Colorado Springs, Colorado.

I personally believe that inherent genius often lies undetected until prompted to rise by circumstance. Like Doolittle, LeMay was just such a genius. Whether you liked him or hated him, you could not deny that he was always true to his nature. As he stated: "I may have been called an arrogant, prima donna bastard by some people and a hero to others, but you can bet your sweet ass that I am the bastard they would all want in their corner when the shit hits the fan. I bet the same silly hippie fuckers who protested the war in Vietnam and wanted all that free-love shit and hated me in the sixties would have been begging for me to bomb any bastard threatening their damned marijuana supply." Such was Curtis LeMay.

CURTIS LEMAY

I was born on November 15, 1906, in Columbus, Ohio, and we were a real working-class family. My family was not the usual story of wealth and privilege seen in the backgrounds of most of the general grade officers, especially from World War II. My father, Erving, worked hard, and my mother, Arizona Carpenter, did her best as they raised a family that moved around. Dad was a steelworker, and we moved the family, which included my brothers, Leonard and Lloyd, and sisters Methyl, Patricia, and Velma, all over the damned country, wherever he could find work.[2]

We grew up poor as hell. We never had much of anything—few people did—and after I got a bike, I became a paperboy. I did anything I could to make money; that was how I bought the bike. I cut grass, washed cars if I could, painted fences and houses—I did anything I could to make money because I was also helping the family out. I liked guns and radios, which explains my interest in communications many years later. I saved my money, too. I was also a Boy Scout for several years, and I learned a lot from these experiences.

Self-reliance was big in my family, and that concept was expanded in the Scouts.

My father was a hardworking man who had little time to be a family man. He was always looking for more work; hard work in iron and steel. He worked double shifts at foundries when he could, and he was also a major believer in saving money. One thing about my father was that he never trusted banks. When I was in school and getting ready to start flight training, the stock market crash hit. The banks closed, and almost everyone lost their money. My dad would just say, "See, I told you never to trust the banks."

I was a reader. I loved books. I read everything by Sir Walter Scott, Edgar Rice Burroughs, Jules Verne, Alexandre Dumas, especially *The Count of Monte Cristo,* a few of the Dickens books, especially *A Tale of Two Cities*, and Robert Louis Stevenson's *Kidnapped*, and Daniel Defoe's *Robinson Crusoe,* which I liked a lot. I also liked history and stories about warriors. I admired men like George Washington, Julius Caesar, and Alexander the Great. I read Robert Baden-Powell's work *Scouting for Boys*. I also read about him. I liked guys who were willing to fight, risk it all for something that was a lot bigger than themselves.

I loved any books and stories about Daniel Boone, Davy Crockett, Sam Houston, John Paul Jones—those guys who did not seem to fear anything and were ready to fight in a second. I was also like that. I did get into fights growing up—all kids do—but I was of the belief that if you throw a punch, you should not ask for mercy when I come down on you. You asked for it, so don't bitch about it. I applied that concept during the war. I believed in Teddy Roosevelt's "Walk softly and carry a big stick" theory. I always wanted to have the biggest stick.

I also read all I could about flying. I loved airplanes and read about pilots. World War I raged when I was a kid, and I read the papers trying to learn all I could about what was going on. After the war, we began to get a lot of those pilots from all over the place touring the country, giving people rides and doing air shows. I read all the publications available. The air aces were the big heroes from the war.

We all knew about guys like Rickenbacker and Frank Luke.[3] I actually came to know Rickenbacker many years later. You do know he created Eastern Airlines? I read the stories about Captain Edward "Mick" Mannock,[4] Albert Ball,[5] Ernst Udet,[6] Manfred von Richthofen,[7] Oswald Boelcke,[8] Rene Fonck,[9] and Douglas Campbell.[10] Those were my air war heroes. Then Charles Lindbergh did his transatlantic flight and made history.

I studied maps and charts when I could. I wanted to know about the world, beyond the stuff I learned in school. I was a big reader of *National Geographic*. Back in those days, the world was still carved up into empires by the European nations. We still had territories that would not become states for several years. You could say I was probably more self-educated than formally learned anything. I also did really well in mathematics and geography. When I learned about the American involvement in Haiti and Nicaragua, I knew where they were on a map. I also got really good at orienteering [navigating with map and compass], and could read a map by age twelve and orient a compass. Those skills would come in handy later also when I became a navigator.

I liked watching movies, especially history and military-type films. I really liked the old cowboy movies. I grew up in the time of the silent films, you know: Charlie Chaplin, Buster Keaton, Fatty Arbuckle, Gloria Swanson, and those types of movies. Then the sound films came into vogue, and I went to see them when I could. I never spent my money on much, but I did go to the cinemas when I could.

I started Ohio State University's ROTC in the fall term in 1924, but it was tough to meet the tuition requirements. I still had to work jobs, mostly at the steel mill. We were all just simple working-class people, and we did not have political connections, so going to a West Point or Annapolis was out of the question for me. I had to drop out of school, but I joined the National Guard. I knew I wanted to fly, but beyond that, I had no idea where my ambition would take me. Just the idea of going to a college or university was almost insane for people like us, unless there was an athletic scholarship involved or, even more rare, an academic scholarship. I decided to be an exception.

This turned out to be a good move. I was accepted for flight training in 1928 and sent to Riverside, California. We flew the Consolidated PT-3 two-seat open-cockpit trainer, which was a nice plane. I was given good reviews by instructors and made great grades in all areas. After basic flight school, I went to Kelly Field in Texas. That was a period of flying that was pretty grueling, as we had pretty good weather and zero distractions. I managed to log a lot of airtime and get very good at dead-reckoning navigation [assessing one's location using terrain, sun position, or stars without use of navigational aids] and working out maneuvers and stall recovery techniques. When not flying, I read papers; I tried to keep up to date on what was happening in the world.

I was finally commissioned as a second lieutenant in October 1929, which was made official the following month. The bullshit of it was that I was a butter bar second "lewie"—slang for lieutenant—on three different occasions because of the bureaucracy. I had an Ohio State National Guard and then Army Reserve commission, and then was commissioned as a second lieutenant as a flight cadet, but then I was made a regular commissioned officer from a reservist in 1930.

Then the Great Depression hit, and there were so many people out of work, you could see dozens of them showing up at the air bases, hoping for any kind of work that they could get. Cutting grass, filling potholes, whatever. I spoke to my dad on the telephone, and I asked how the family was doing. He said that he still had work, fortunately, but he also still had his money, because he never trusted banks. He was proud of me, I knew that, and I wanted to make them proud.

———

I qualified on single- and twin-engine aircraft and flew fighters in Selfridge Field, Michigan. This was the Twenty-Seventh Pursuit Squadron, as all fighter units and planes were called "pursuit" back then. It was not until the war that this was changed to "fighter." I also studied celestial navigation and took extra courses in advanced instruments and such. I wanted to know everything about the business from the ground up. I always reflected back to Billy Mitchell and his strong belief in air power, and I believed like he did that bombers would win any future war. My perseverance paid off, and in 1933 I went to Langley Field [later Langley Air Force Base, today called Joint Base Langley-Eustis in Hampton, Virginia], where navigation was the primary focus.[11] I think that was when I decided that I would fly bombers. It just sat well with me.

This included celestial and dead-reckoning navigational methods, which was a far more detailed and intense method than just visual observation. I knew, as did anyone with a brain, that if you had bad visibility, visual navigation was worthless, and then you could be in a world of shit. Later, I would go to Wilbur Wright Field, Ohio [later Wright-Patterson Air Force Base], for blind flying training. The previous Douglas O-2 model was nothing compared to the Martin B-10, which was twin-engine and faster—with all of the accompanying complications that came with a newer and more advanced flying platform. I liked it, actually.

Probably the best part of all of that was when I met my future wife there. I knew Helen was going to marry me, I tell her that many times, and she just laughs and says, "What makes you think you had anything to do with the decision?"

I read the papers to keep up to date on what was going on in America, but also the rest of the world. I also read about the stock market and the jobless problems, companies going out of business, all of that. I also knew that Europe was in a worse state than we were. This was when I first started taking an interest in what was happening in Germany—I would say around 1932 and afterward. I did not pay much attention to that guy Hitler when he came on the scene. To me, it was just another politician working to jerk his way into office. But in time, my opinion would change.

Now, you have to understand. The Great Depression that smacked the shit out of us in 1929 really put the hurt on military spending. The army and navy were fighting like winos over muscatel to get congressional funding. The navy wanted their battleships and also to expand naval aviation, and the marines were involved. One thing I will say about all of that bullshit: of all the branches, I will give the Marine Corps credit. They really created, or at least refined, their close air support doctrine. The navy was having a civil war among themselves, battleship guys against carrier guys.

But money allocated to the Marine Corps was whatever the navy gave them after they carved up the congressionally approved pie, so to speak. With battleships, new aircraft carrier development, and the accompanying fighters, dive bombers, and torpedo bombers they would require, as well as the growing submarine force, the marines were basically getting screwed. It has always been that way. Then there was the Army Air Corps, and, of course, we wanted our share of the pie. We knew that the navy would focus upon fighters, but we would be able to push our interest in long-range bombers.

I was wondering what I was going to do, because my opportunities depended upon forces well beyond my control. Then, in 1934, the army got the mail contracts, so we would take over the Air Mail Service. I started flying in the winter, doing the Virginia and North Carolina routes. We had some losses, so that work ended pretty quickly.[12] We just did not have the collective training or proper aircraft. That type of flying needed better avionics, which we did not have. Bad weather accounted for most of the aircraft and pilot losses, because the airplanes were all open-cockpit types, many of them worn the hell out and just not maintained to the proper mechanical standards.

I was married to Helen in Cleveland in 1934, and then I was assigned to Wheeler Field in Honolulu, Hawaii, a place Robin Olds knows all too well. This was the Sixth Pursuit Squadron. When I finally arrived, I saw that the unit was somewhere around 30 percent to 40 percent short on personnel, so I had a bunch of responsibilities. I was the unit engineer, navigation officer, mess officer, assistant operations officer, maintenance—I had it all. But where most people would squirm at the multitude of jobs, I saw this as a learning opportunity. I would gain more knowledge, and that would mean greater proficiency.

I really liked that assignment, because the weather was warm, and we had a lot of great clear sky to fly in. Hawaii back then was a distant paradise, one of those places you read about and hoped to visit one day. Not like today, I guess. Back then, it was not heavily populated, and the military earned the best wages when compared to most of the locals. The single guys had a blast, I can tell you.

I had the great opportunity to spend some time with Amelia Earhart when she flew into the area. That was one ballsy lady, I can tell you. She commanded a lot of respect from all the men fliers. She was nicknamed the "Lady Lindbergh" for good reason. She was probably a female version of me. She was pretty confident and steadfast, and she would not take any shit from anyone. She became world famous after she soloed across the Atlantic. She was the first woman to do so. She was also talking about being the first woman to solo around the world. You have to remember that it was a much different time back then—almost unheard of for women to be flying at all.

I remember when she went missing, the entire world was on alert, and FDR organized the greatest single maritime search and rescue in history just for her and her navigator. That fact that they have never been found is not that surprising; the Pacific is a big place to get lost in. I have heard all the rumors about her spying for the government, getting caught by the Japs, all that shit. I do not believe any of it, really. I think that she had navigation problems, missed her touchdown, and ran out of gas, simple as that.

While I was at Wheeler, I was responsible for teaching navigation, and we had all the pilots rotating through the classes. We turned out a lot of very proficient open-water pilots. As there are no landmarks, you had to use the instruments, especially the clock and compass, and have your navigator writing down all the coordinates. The pilot, co-pilot, and navigator had to be in sync. When that happened, things went well.[13] Most of these were very sharp guys, and they caught on quickly. This was really important when flying over a big-ass ocean.

I was promoted to first lieutenant and assigned to the Second Bomb Group in Virginia around December 1936. I decided that I wanted to fly strategic aircraft, take the war to the enemy. I believed in General Giulio Douhet and Mitchell, that the bomber would be the weapon to win future wars. Well, if I thought I was going to fly, I was mistaken. They made me a navigator and expected me to run their school for navigators, which I could do, but I wanted to fly. I reported for duty at the Forty-Ninth Squadron as the assistant operations officer. This was really a great job because I handled all the flying assignments and mission planning. These skills would be honed to perfection in Europe, I can tell you, and I could still get cockpit time.

———

The best thing about being at Langley was the delivery of the new Boeing B-17 heavy bombers: long range and very impressive to look at. We were to evaluate them and document any anomalies—issues with the electrical or avionics systems and especially the engines. These were meant to be high-altitude long-range bombers, so we had to make sure that government money was being well spent.

Perhaps even better than learning to fly the B-17 was meeting a man whom I always thought highly of. He was the group CO, Lieutenant Colonel Robert Olds. I always thought he was impressive. He was confident, self-assured, but not arrogant. He was like his boss, Billy Mitchell, a thinker. I wanted to be like him, someone who could write up a proposal and have the big brass do backflips to implement it. I came to know him and his family rather well over the years.

Olds was pretty much the sole reason that the B-17 even existed. I cannot explain to you how much military and political resistance there was to that damned project. It was always an uphill battle, and it was about several things. First and foremost, the navy did not want the army to have any air capability at all, because that would reduce their ability to secure government funding for their own carrier aviation program. But that was also hypocrisy, because the navy had infighting between the surface fleet guys—mainly the battleship officers—and the newly anointed aircraft-carrier-minded types.

The surface guys did not want the money Congress allotted from giving them priority on building more, newer, and even bigger battleships. They then had issues with the aircraft-carrier-minded boys. Why? No big damned surprise: carriers require aircraft. Mitchell proved his point, and that, more than anything, pissed off the battleship guys and the aircraft-carrier types. Mitchell was the only guy who could have brought those two warring factions together in a common cause, and that was a plan to nail his ass to the wall.

Robert Olds was not impressed or intimidated by the navy, despite the high ranks involved. He did have a lot of army support, and that was critical. It was not uncommon for him to just make a telephone call and state his position with a congressman or senator, especially if he knew that their state would benefit from the jobs that would be created by the building program. He had that much clout with the upper echelons, both military and political. Robert also had a lot of friends in Hollywood, and these people carried a lot of weight in the court of public opinion, and flag officers are, by our nature, political creatures. I tried to learn all I could from him—not just technical things but also his leadership style. You could meet a hundred military leaders and have a hundred different leadership styles. Olds was the guy who mastered all of those skills. Not easy to do.

There was another name worth mentioning, and that was General Frank Andrews. He was like Mitchell, and, like him, he pissed off all the right people and was persona non grata until he was rescued by General George C. Marshall. Andrews was another one of those leaders I wanted to learn from.[14] He said it like it was, spoke his mind, and screw the results if he felt he was right. I suppose I adopted that trait fully.

I wanted to be the kind of leader who knew that my orders were followed without much question, but I also wanted my subordinates to know that I was going to be there with them, sharing the load. I had experienced several types of leadership styles. I wanted to be effective and respected; and being feared did not hurt. But being firm and fair at the same time while leading from the front is the best type of leadership, I thought.

In August 1937 we had this joint Army Air Corps and navy exercise, and since I was considered the best open-water navigator, our task was to locate the USS *Utah*, which was basically a target ship out in the Pacific. The navy moved the goalposts on us because we failed twice to find the ship, although we were over our coordinates. Later, the navy had to admit they had moved it away from their scheduled location just to make us fail. They basically fucking cheated, but we proved that we could find a ship in the great expanse of an ocean, and Mitchell had proven that planes could sink them.[15] The navy got caught red-handed, but we were in our element. We had a great bomber that was pretty much good to go upon delivery and, with a good crew, could reach, locate, and sink a ship anywhere within flight range. No matter how well things go, there are always things that can be improved on any aircraft design.

In February 1938, we started the Friendship Tour down to South America with the airplanes, such as the B-17 which Robert Olds had advocated. This was really a show-of-force operation, while we displayed strength, hopefully as a deterrent, I think, as other nations were being aggressive. I was given the job as lead navigator. Robert was a firm believer in the Mitchell Doctrine, as was I, that air power was crucial to any future conflict. This flight would show our reach and growing power to the rest of the world.

All of us read the newspapers. We could all see what was happening in Europe and Asia. Olds was no fool when it came to reading tea leaves. He told us in no uncertain terms, "Be ready for war. It will come, even if America is not prepared. We have to be the point of the sword while the politicians ignore reality." I knew he was correct. He and I often discussed the events of the day, talking about what was happening in Europe and Asia. The Japanese were the main point of interest because they started their shit so early on in China. We carried papers with us on the flight to South America. It would be one long flight.

We landed six planes in Argentina, and later we were awarded the Mackay Trophy. That is awarded annually by the air force for the best flight performance every year. We had made our mark, and navigating over the Andes was something else. It was also cold as hell at altitude, I can tell you, and the winds were also unpredictable. We did another flight down there in 1939 in another formation tour. Right after we got back, I was promoted to captain. I actually wrote an evaluation of both of those flights, laying out what we could have done better, what was done well, and trying to analyze the missions.

I later applied that method to all of my bomber missions during the war. Recognize what can be done more effectively, from both an individual and collective perspective. One method I adopted and stuck with all the way though my career was asking questions of the men. I wanted their observations and recommendations. It is amazing what you learn from a junior officer or enlisted man after a mission. As a commander, you cannot be in every bomber. You cannot be at every position, gunner, copilot, pilot, navigator, engineer—whatever. A bomber had ten men, so that gives you ten different perspectives on just one airplane. Multiply that by a few dozen, and you begin to get a really big picture of how shit is or is not working.

Our success at long-range navigation brought us international attention. We were informed in May 1938 that Ira Eaker had a mission for us to fly long range over the Atlantic and locate the Italian ocean liner *Rex*, in the Atlantic Ocean. Eaker and Olds were old friends, and it was no great surprise that we got this assignment. She [the SS *Rex*] was headed to New York, so if we could locate and intercept her, it would be a massive public relations coup for us. Even more important, it would take the wind out of the sails of those in Washington who wanted to kill our program. This was a really big press event, too: there were reporters and photographers all over the place and on the aircraft. We took off from Mitchell Field on May 12, and that mission was a damned nightmare.

The weather was horrible, near zero visibility, all instruments for the pilots. We had to try and climb above the thunder bumpers, and the winds were variable and high, sometimes gusting with crosswinds that totally fucked up accurate calculations. So here I was navigating, where I had to have the aircraft airspeed, direction of travel, altitude, compare air with ground speed, and take headwinds into account, which meant the pilots had to increase power to maintain a constant airspeed. If they did not, then the calculations had to be started all over again, starting with your last known position.

That's a lot of stuff to figure out, but I was good at it. By the way, I reflected upon this experience later, when I was stationed in England. The RAF got some grief from us for their lack of accurate bombing, but they flew at night and had bad weather like this a lot of the time. I always gave those Bomber Command guys slack because I understood their problems. However, there was no way that they applied the same rigorous navigation methods that I employed; they couldn't have. They had one guy, the pathfinder, who would navigate to the target using dead reckoning, often using the river system to navigate comparing them to their maps.

Anyway, we had three B-17s in a vic [V] formation, which was the standard until World War II, and we climbed to about six thousand feet or so. We were bounced up and down like a roller coaster. I had to spin the whiz-wheel [navigational "wheel" that has degrees and assists in calculating airspeed] and recalculate position and watch the clock and my compass, adjusting my navigation the best I could under the conditions. Then, twelve hours later, we found her as we broke through the storm and into great weather. Down below, the liner was steaming along, big as shit. We radioed the contact, and I could only imagine the navy types, hoping we would fuck it up, squirming as they got that damned message. I was sure that our allies in Washington felt better about their defense of our position. All of us were vindicated.

We dropped down for a low-level pass to give our civilian photographers a really good view so they could take pictures, and we had this radio clown reporting on our mission. If we failed, the whole world would know it. Luckily, the world knew that we could do our job. Our problem now was flying back west into the same stormy shit we had just fought through, and our fuel level was on everyone's mind. Flying into headwinds tends to make you use fuel at a much higher rate. The headwinds and crosswinds were even worse than the first time, and I was not feeling all that well as a result.

But we made history, and the major newspapers printed that US Army pilots had done what most thought could not be done: locate a specific target in the great expanse of the ocean. When we landed, we were heroes, and Hap Arnold and Ira Eaker knew that we had just driven the final nail in the coffin of the navy bastards who said that we did not need or even deserve long-range bombers, since, according to them, they would not be effective. Screw them, I said. Olds agreed. I knew at that time that I had just cemented my career as an air force officer. Nothing was going to stop me from that point forward.

———————

Olds was right, and I knew it, when he said that we would probably be in a war sooner rather than later. He was not alone in that belief, either. The Japs and Germans had been getting really active in their respective spheres of influence: Japan was fighting the Chinese and the Russians, and the Germans [backed the Nationalists under Franco, the Soviets backed the Republicans, who were Communists]. The Brits and Prime Minister Neville Chamberlain had caved in to Hitler with that damned Munich Agreement, which really just emboldened that bastard to start taking Europe piece by piece.[16] Well, that turned out to be a real great event in world history.

I always found it amazing that it was politicians who started the damned wars and left it to the military to fight them, but then the same damned assholes who started the shit wanted to dictate how we fought them. In my lifetime, it would become worse with every damned war we fought. I considered World War II the last "good" war, because our objectives were crystal clear, despite having several restrictions placed upon us. Invade shit, bomb shit, kill shit, and end that shit. Pure and simple, which was about as black and white as anything can be.

We could all see that the shit in Europe and also in Asia was getting crazy. That was the August we took another flight of B-17s to South America, this time to Colombia, as a tactical training mission. The crews were really learning to use all of the required accoutrements, getting used to high-altitude operations. Almost weekly, there was more crazy news in the world's papers. I think Olds and I both knew that war was coming sooner than we thought. We did not know when, but we knew that it was now inevitable.

I kept thinking about Hitler, and I figured that bastard out. He was wanting nothing more than to conquer territory that Germany had lost after the First World War, and perhaps even more. He had his ass kicked in the 1936 Olympics in Berlin. Jesse Owens broke it off in his ass.[17] Then you had Joe Louis come back and beat Max Schmeling [1936 Schmeling victory, and 1938 Louis victory, respectively].[18] I followed boxing, and have always been a fan, like baseball. I later heard that Schmeling had a tough time with the Nazis. I guess he was probably a good guy then. Schmeling was as famous as Muhammad Ali in his day, one of the best-known people on the planet. Same with Joe Louis.

Hell, Hitler was even *Time* magazine's Man of the Year in 1938. Then Hitler took Austria, and then Czechoslovakia, and I knew that he was not going to be satisfied with those. I studied history, and I read about Hitler, and saw that his plan was to reoccupy all of the lands in Europe that had once been under the old German Empire. The fact that the Allies were not going back into Germany even after all that shit told me that Hitler was emboldened. I was right.

Just a couple of years before, Hitler openly bragged about his new military, including fighter and bomber aircraft, and all of that had been banned by the Treaty of Versailles. Under Hitler, that treaty meant nothing, and he was basically telling the world, especially France and Britain, "Fuck you, what are you going to do about it?" We all knew that there was no way militarily or financially the Western powers were going to be able to go to war against Germany. In America, people like Charles Lindbergh were of the position that nothing that happened in Europe was worth our getting involved.[19] For the most part, I agreed with him—screw the Europeans. But the problem with that thinking is that anything that happens there always spills out onto our backyard.

Now, I met Lindbergh, and he seemed like a nice enough guy, but he took a very friendly position with Hitler's gang. I am not sure if it was out of sympathy for their bullshit or because he had so many friends in Germany who were fellow pilots. I knew some of them, or at least met them. I know that he was a pacifist, and I have no problem with that. I wish there were no wars. But sometimes you have to pull your head out of your ass and be ready for when the bad shit comes around, you know?

However, despite how erratic Hitler was—or I guess I should say calculating—none of that really made me think as much as what the Japs were doing. I knew sure as shit that there was going to be a war between Japan and the Europeans because of their colonies in Asia. Japan was not a nation with abundant natural resources. We supplied them with iron and oil, and the Dutch also supplied them with oil, manganese, and rubber. Well, it did not take an Ivy League dickhead to figure out that if those supplies stopped coming in, Japan would have to go take them. And I knew that the only two nations in the world capable of putting those plans on hold were the United States and Great Britain, at least from a naval standpoint.

Something else I knew in my bones was that we were going to

need long-range bombers stationed around the world at various installations, along with the navy's ships in their bases and patrolling the seas. The navy would have great striking power with their carriers, but they would have to be augmented by our bombers. They just could not get there fast enough, and their planes would not have the range or the load capacity to be as effective as we could be. That is real large-scale strategic thinking. Yes, we had Hawaii, Guam, and the Philippines, as well as other areas in the Pacific region. That was our strategic advantage should the need arise, and I was sure Japan was going to poke the hornet's nest at some point.

Many things were happening in 1938, and I became a father that year also when Janie [Patricia Jane] was born that February. I was pretty excited, as was Helen. I remember looking at her, being so small, and thinking, "She is the future," and that I would do all I could to make sure that she had a good one. Then my thoughts went back to Hitler when I saw that *Time* magazine. All because of that damned Munich Agreement, I guess. I noticed that Chamberlain did not get much press here.

Talk about cowardice and incompetence. I guess Hitler and Ribbentrop had Chamberlain's balls in their hands and squeezed them like shit to get that fool to sign that damned document. Churchill was a very different kind of leader, and, yes, he was controversial, and I knew him. He was a real leader, and he took no shit from anyone. He was the definition of a statesman. Chamberlain simply sowed the seeds of his own destruction when Hitler pushed that expansion issue in 1938.

The world was just starting to burn at that time. The Italians had invaded Africa years earlier in Benito Mussolini's half-assed idea to rebuild the fucking Roman Empire, and, if memory serves, they sort of had their asses handed to them by a bunch of illiterate camel jockeys. Libya and Ethiopia had been active for a few years as Mussolini sent his ground and air forces to conquer some of the most worthless real estate on the planet. What a fucking idiot. What is even more fascinating is that Hitler admired that shit. And then we had the Bolshevik bullshit still going on in Russia. Who would have thought they would become such a pain in the ass a few decades later? At least their crazy shit later after the war kept me employed for a long time.

Hitler invaded Poland on September 1, 1939, and then, a few days later, France and Britain declared war on Germany. The shit had hit the fan, and I spoke to Olds about these events. He told me, "Anyone who thinks we will not be at war in a couple of years is living in a cave. See what is happening and prepare to react correctly when the time comes." He was absolutely right. As I said, he was like Mitchell: a visionary who read the tea leaves.

There was another long-range flight in December 1939, and once again I was the lead navigator to Brazil. I do not like using the word "propaganda," but that was what these flights were all about. High profile, in your face, we are here, so take notice of us. It was also a warning to others about our industrial capabilities.[20] I have no doubt that this was a signal to Hitler and Japan: fuck with us at your own risk.

However, all we could do was read about the Brits getting bombed, then in 1940 the French were defeated, and the British were trapped against the English Channel at Dunkirk. That May we were stunned that Churchill had rescued three hundred thousand men from those beaches. What an operation. Then that summer, the air war really kicked into gear with the Battle of Britain. Hitler was sitting his ass in every country in Europe, damned near. Poland, France, Belgium, Norway, Denmark, Austria and Czechoslovakia, and Hungary, Romania, and Bulgaria were his allies along with Italy.

Quite a few guys I knew and had trained with went to Canada to join the RAF. Some went to Burma and China, like [Brigadier General] Robert Scott,[21] who joined [Colonel Gregory] Boyington,[22] [Richard]

Rossi,[23] [Brigadier General David Lee] "Tex" Hill, and those guys with the AVG [American Volunteer Group].[24] Francis Gabreski was actually sent to England to work with the Free Polish pilots flying in the RAF, since he spoke Polish. That is a great story also.[25]

Those Eagle Squadron guys and the AVG were where the action was, and I wanted sure as hell to get into it somehow. The only way was to resign my commission and then sign on to a mercenary contract, but that was problematic. I did not want to terminate my active duty service, since getting back in uniform might not be possible. I spoke to Olds about this, and he said, "Be patient; your time will come soon enough." He was right.

I still followed what was going on with those guys in Burma and England. They were really getting some fighter kills. I was a bomber pilot, but I also knew they hired transport pilots. They were getting their supplies out of India for the most part, flying "the Hump," which I would become very familiar with a few years later. But the AVG guys had a great advantage, since they were getting a high salary plus kill bonuses, which the European guys did not get. I heard from General Claire Chennault later about his innovation to keep the men entertained.

I followed the air war there in Burma, China, and over England with great interest, especially from the creation of the RAF Bomber Command. The Brits were taking the war to Germany in night operations. I read all I could and tried to study their methods, aircraft—all that shit. About that time, I was getting more involved in every aspect of the bomber: its equipment, every small detail right down to the electrical system. I wanted to know everything. I even worked with the ordnance crews, refuelers, and crew chiefs on engine maintenance. For over a year, I trained on the Norden bombsight, which, at the time, was the most advanced bombsight in the world.

———

The Norden sight basically consisted of a gyroscopic stabilizing tele-scopic sight with an electrically operated mechanical computer. The bombardier input the data for altitude, crosswinds, atmospheric con-ditions, airspeed, ground speed, and drift. During the bomb run, when the bombardier controlled the aircraft as the pilot released con-trol, the sight was connected to the automatic pilot. This allowed the bombardier to guide the aircraft to the exact release point. When in a large formation, the lead bomber carried the leading bombardier. It was on his release that all the bombers would, in turn, release their ordnance over the target. The average anticipated altitude for mis-sions in the B-17 was to be between twenty thousand to twenty-five thousand feet, sometimes higher.

All of our bombers, heavy and medium, carried the Norden. Now, this equipment was top secret; few people had access to it, even on a bomber crew. It was dismounted and taken into lockup under guard. Our orders were, should the bomber be abandoned, the sight had to be destroyed.

One factor that was problematic was that only navigators and pi-lots were to have access to the sight. You had to sign for it, and God help you if you lost possession of it. I could only imagine the problems such an unfortunate soul would have if such a situation occurred. I once spoke with [Brigadier General] Jimmy Stewart, and he told me of a navigator who slipped on some ice dismounting after a mission and dropped the sight, damaging it. From what I learned, he was a terminal lieutenant from that point forward. "Poor bastard," I thought.

I was promoted to major in 1941 and was assigned as a squadron commander in the Thirty-Fourth Bomb Group. This was in Massa-chusetts at Westover Field in February 1941.[26] This was the time when

I was contacted about the new North Atlantic Ferry Command, sending aircraft over to Britain.[27] The problem was, there were not a lot of aircraft, and getting crews seemed to be an issue.

This was also about the time when the Army Air Corps started the WASP program,[28] where the women were trained as pilots and navigators to ferry aircraft around the world, freeing the men up to fight the war, and still deliver badly needed planes. We also had ferry routes from Brazil to Africa, dropping bombers off in Egypt, and then, after Operation Torch, aircraft were flown to Algeria and Morocco. These were the backbone for air operations from North Africa into southern Europe.

Early in the war, the British did not have any long-range heavy bombers to hit back with, as all they had were twin-engine medium bombers. They mainly used the Vickers Wellington, Short Sunderland Stirling, and Handley Page Halifax and Hampden. Soon they began building the Avro Manchester and later the Lancaster, which was the best British heavy bomber of the war, no doubt. That big bastard carried fourteen thousand pounds of bombs, almost twice a maximum load for a B-17 or B-24. It was a wonderful weapon.

I was able to qualify in the Consolidated B-24, which we called the Liberator, of course. It had greater range if not fully loaded with ordnance and a faster speed than the B-17 with the later variants. The B-17 weighed in at fifty-four thousand pounds of bird gross weight, with a max takeoff weight of about sixty-four thousand pounds fully loaded. It could carry up to about eight thousand pounds of bombs on a short run, but longer missions were normally a load of about four thousand to six thousand pounds. It had a max speed of around 200 miles per hour. The average cruising speed would be about 140 to 160 miles an hour.

With a full bomb load, the B-17 had about a two-thousand-mile range, which was good, but in operational planning, we had to compensate for fuel, bomb load, et cetera. Operational altitude also depended upon the bomb load: the more weight, the lower your operational ceiling. The Fortress could hit about thirty-five thousand feet when light, but, fully loaded, we flew no higher than twenty-five thousand.

The B-24 weighed in at fifty-five thousand pounds and maxed out at sixty thousand on a full load, and it could also carry an eight-thousand full-capacity bomb load. It could fly lean about thirty-seven hundred miles but less than the B-17 when fully loaded—maybe fifteen hundred miles. Its ceiling operationally was less than thirty thousand [actually twenty-eight thousand feet]. Senator George McGovern told me his stories of flying that bird; good stories, too.[29] That was what [Brigadier General James] Stewart flew also.[30]

When we heard that Pearl Harbor had been hit by the Japs, I knew what that meant. My entire life had been geared for this moment. The great problem was that due to that event, most of our assets were shifted to the West Coast for deployment to the Pacific theater, which was the only theater of operations for us at that time. We took Liberators to Oregon, but I was soon transferred to Wendover, Utah, to join the 306th Bomb Group. I could think of no place on earth as desolate and inhospitable as that damned place.

I looked at the other unfortunate souls there. It seemed as if the life force had been drained from everyone. I really had to figure out a way to get another transfer, or I feared I would go nuts in that place. I was the new executive officer, and I brought the family down—I suppose to either share the misery or relieve me of mine. Finally, I was sort of reprieved when I was sent to command the 305th Bomb Group, which was a position normally reserved for a higher rank, but I had the experience.

In January 1942 I became a lieutenant colonel, and by May, I was "officially" in temporary command of the 305th Bomb Group, which had all of three B-17s—that was it. We needed everything and had nothing. It consisted of four squadrons on paper, but, in reality, it did not exist, so I had a ton of work to do. The first thing you do in a situation like that is locate and procure the best people you can find. You need people who are experts in every facet of operations, from tactics, logistics, and intelligence, right down to fuel and chow.

It all had to come together, and then you had to get pilots and crews. "Welcome to the land of fucking Oz," I thought. That comes down to proper leadership: being an authority figure but also someone who can get the best out of your personnel. I always believed that a leader learned from every success, and every failure, in order to do better in the future. Whether mission planning or personnel handling, you have to balance discipline with pragmatism.

One major factor in leadership that I should mention: every leader has doubts, about his unit, his men, and even himself. That is a natural human condition. Any man who does not have doubts about his performance or self-awareness—let alone has no self-analysis—is a damned fool. There will always be doubts that eventually go away as you gain even more experience. The secret to successful combat leadership is to never openly display or allow your subordinates to know that you have those doubts. That should be the best-kept secret you have.

Your men need to have complete confidence in your leadership abilities and be comfortable knowing that you are with them, not just issuing orders, and the more competence you exhibit with the technology and tactical proficiency, the more confidence they will have in you. Following those points, leadership by example is the most critical factor.

Well, I did start receiving pilots from basic flight school after completing primary, and even a few from advanced training, but very few had any time in the B-17. I had the same problem with qualified navigators and maintenance crews. I had my work cut out for me, I can tell you. I held very long orientation sessions on flying the B-17 and even longer hours on navigation.

I brought my experience to bear, and I brought it down hard. I was less worried about pilots fucking up than I was about navigators. I told them, "You can fly this thing on two engines on a good day, and three engines will get you home, but if you can't figure out where you are and get to where you are going, four engines will do you no damned good."

———

We had our orders and shipped out for Britain in September of '42. We ferried those things across the Atlantic following the standard ferry routes to join the Eighth Air Force, which began doing milk runs to coastal France with fighter escorts earlier, but we did not start our missions until November. The first B-17Fs for our use began arriving that June, but we had already stationed personnel there a month before, long before I arrived.

I became commander of the Fourth Bomb Wing and was promoted to colonel on June 17, 1942, and we were still technically part of the Eighth Air Force headquartered overseas in England. I held that position until the next year, and I was thirty-six years old, just short of my thirty-seventh birthday.

We were still in the process of organization and getting bombers, as well as getting the logistical issues ironed out, and that took two months. We did not fly our first mission as an organized group until November 17, which was the twentieth mission in total for the Eighth. We were to be a decoy party to draw German interest away from the main strike force that actually carried bombs as they hit Saint-Nazaire, France. I understood the necessity of these missions, but I wanted to be the main strike force and rip some ass. But as an officer, I had to follow my orders, and I did.

One of the primary operations for any bombardment group besides dropping bombs on targets was the bomb damage assessment, or BDA, as we called it. This was when we compared prestrike photographs of a target with the poststrike photos, examined the results, and then higher authority assessed the extent of the damage and determined if a target needed to be revisited. Both pre- and postoperational images were collected by photo recon aircraft. The Brits had one such unit, and then we did also. I can tell you that upon seeing the postmission results, we were less than impressed with the bombing accuracy. You had to weigh the effort of the strikes with the damage and losses you expected to receive. The air war was all about risk assessments and bombing results.

I decided that I was going to try and effect a few changes on the way we operated. I went on missions with a notepad, took down notes, observed everything I could, and tried to come up with realistic changes that would enhance not only our bombing accuracy but also provide better protection for the bombers and their crews. I can tell you I noticed a few problems with our methods. I continued my policy of asking my men for their impressions of the events after each mission. I wanted their insights.

The conventional wisdom that "the bomber will always get through" died on the vine of idiocy some time ago. That was buried because we knew unescorted bombers were just big, fat targets for German fighters. Even if you took flak out of the equation, every mission over German-held territory was fraught with danger. However, another issue that was affecting our bombing accuracy was the tendency for the pilots to jink the bombers around whenever they encountered fighters or flak. I knew from my own experience that you will never compensate in time to have dead-dick accuracy if you were skidding a bomber around trying to dodge danger.

I made it a steadfast rule punishable with a court-martial in my unit that once we hit the IP [initial point], until the bombs were dropped, there would be no evasive maneuvers. Once we hit the IP and the bombardier had control, it was a straight and level operation; otherwise you might as well just hurl the fucking Norden bombsight out with the ordnance. That was one change that I saw had to be made.

My men bitched and grumbled about that order, but I was unyielding. My logic was that we stay the course and accept the losses to get maximum bombing results. Otherwise, we risked even more losses coming back to bomb the same target again because we fucked up. I did not like paying for the same real estate twice. I could do math, and I knew that Washington was looking at three things: BDA results, aircraft losses, and casualties. There was a possibility that I could make each of these better, reduce losses, or at least justify those losses with good bomb runs, and I was going to do it or die trying. I earned the nickname "Old Iron Ass" from my men, and I liked it. The grumbling stopped when I was leading these strikes, and all bombers were in the same danger. I was usually lead bomber with the lead navigator.

One of my observations was that the German fighters were very effective in attacking bomber formations that were spread out. They could pretty much choose the time of their attack without having to worry about the other bombers' defensive fire. Again, basic geometry came into play, and I had an idea. I created the box formation concept, which we practiced, and then I ran it up the flagpole.

Another issue I had but could do nothing about was the lack of escort fighters. We had P-38s that could just about reach Berlin, but if they entered combat, that range was reduced. The early P-51s and P-47s, as well as Spitfires and Hurricanes, could not reach beyond the German border with Belgium and Holland. Now, this was critical. The damned Germans in northern France would engage the bombers and often the escort fighters in waves. I knew even then that these were JG-2 and JG-26 fighter wings. Later in the war, we would engage other units. Those Germans were good. Many times, the Germans would just orbit outside the bomber formation and wait for our escorts to peel off due to fuel concerns, and then they would hit us.

One thing I wanted to learn, and I wanted my men to learn, was what we were up against. We brought in American and British fighter pilots, some with two years of air combat against the Germans. I wanted them to explain to us what we were looking at, and the information was about damned sobering, I can tell you. The Brits had a shitload of intelligence on these German units. They even knew the names of many of the pilots, especially the squadron, group, and wing leaders. What I was hearing was staggering. Some of these guys had flown in Spain and in this war since 1939; a few had over a hundred kills. I do not think there was a sound to be heard during one of these familiarization classes. One of these instructors was Pete Townsend.[31]

Townsend was very lively and animated as he discussed the German fighter pilots. He had spoken with a few who had been shot down over England, and it was the RAF that actually adopted the "finger four" flying formation which the Germans created. Townsend said that as a fighter pilot, he felt comfortable going against the Germans in their Messerschmitts. The Focke-Wulf 190s were another matter. He warned us that "those buggers have great firepower and can take a lot of damage."

We also had a chance to meet another ace, one of the best: [James Harry] "Ginger" Lacey.[32] Lacey had scored a lot of his kills during the Battle of Britain, and he gave a lot of good information. These men had the combat experience to be taken seriously, and they gave us great information. They also spoke to the fighter units. All of this was very educational for us. We learned about the enemy fighters, the different types, their abilities, limitations, and deficiencies. We were educated on the weapons they carried, speeds, operational altitudes, methods of attack. We even had some biographical information on a few of the better-known enemy pilots.

As I sat through these briefings on enemy fighters, wheels were spinning in my head. I doodled, did math, drew diagrams, and worked my brain into oatmeal trying to devise ways to protect our bombers. One thing we learned from previous experience was that if there were any stragglers—bombers that were damaged and unable to keep up—they were easy prey for the fighters.

Pretty much as soon as you saw a B-17 falling back, often smoking, which was a dead giveaway to the enemy, you just recorded their tail numbers, said a prayer, and hoped they got lucky. The sad part was that you often knew that crew very well from a personal standpoint. Like watching a friend drown, and you cannot do one damned thing about it. It was even worse if you saw the Me 109s and Fw 190s descend upon a lone bomber, carving it up.

I remember more than once hearing the screams of wounded men over the headset; as flight leader, I would try to assess the condition of each bomber and the crew. I would usually be in radio contact with the radio operator, pilot, or copilot. Over the transmission, you could sometimes hear the panic and the surviving crew begging for help as shells slammed into their aircraft. Then a wing would fold, and it would roll over and spin toward earth. Sometimes they would just blow up and disappear with no chutes. Many times, the pilots just tried to hold level long enough to get the crew out and then jump themselves, to parachute down into captivity.

———

I need to explain another aspect of combat leadership, and this is perhaps the most important—and the most fragile, in many respects. That is the mental health of crews. There was a reason why we flew twenty-five missions and then rotated. The human being, in particular the mind, can absorb only a certain amount of trauma, exhaustion, and fear. I once saw some of the RAF boys from Bomber Command, and I spoke to a few of them. They explained their method, which I totally disagreed with, but I openly stated that I admired their bravery.

I spent the best part of half an hour talking to this one middle-aged-looking pilot. He was on his second tour and had flown from 1940 until 1941, flying Wellingtons, and then rotated out into training duties. Now he was back, flying Lancasters. I assumed he was about my age, but he was only the equivalent of a captain. Well, come to find out this "old man" was twenty-three years old. He went to light a cigarette, and both of his hands were shaking so badly that I steadied them for him. I asked him how long he had been suffering from that problem. He said since the day his Wellington took flak that killed four of his crew, including his pilot. He flew the rest of the carnage back to his base, wounded himself.

He also had to help take the remains of his friends out of that wreck, then go to the hospital. It was his twenty-second mission of the war. I was fucking stunned into silence. This guy was still going back, but I could see he was done, and probably more of a danger to himself and his crew than an asset. He was a walking ruin. I then thought about the request the Brits had of us joining them in the night bombing campaign. I knew that we were proficient enough to do it, but I also knew that bombing accuracy would suffer tremendously, and I was happy that we never followed that program.

I often thought about that young "old" man, and I thought about what my crews would endure. I realized that, at some point, there would be mental issues, and they could manifest in any number of ways. I would learn to identify them all. One thing never really discussed in air war documentaries and books is the base shrink. We had one, a psychiatrist who was to evaluate people if requested by a commanding officer. I never did.

Something that really amazed me, which I learned after the war, was that there were many German fighter pilots who flew well over a thousand missions. Bomber pilots also. I think that was probably a double-edged sword for the Germans. Sure, they gained a lot of experience, but, then again, that pressure also made them exhausted. They did not usually rotate their pilots out of combat, making them instructors and giving them a break. The only long-term rest they had was if they were wounded to the point that they could not fly.

Now, one thing I will say up front is that I never placed any high value on shrinks, civilian or military. In my opinion, they were voodoo witch doctors with an opinion. However, they carried a lot of power, like a flight surgeon. They could pull a ticket in a damned heartbeat, but I stood my ground. I ran more than one out of my office in my career, although I understood the need to be cognizant of the mental condition of the men. We are all just human, and all of us have a breaking point, depending upon our experience.

The one thing that the crews did was to calculate their odds of making twenty-five missions alive. At the rate we were going, those numbers were abysmal, and they knew it. It is one thing to send men on missions to do a very dangerous job. It is another thing altogether when those men see no chance of survival during their tours. I think this was the main reason that drove me to fly all those missions, share that risk, and be there for them. If you are not in the thick of the shit, then you are worthless as a combat leader. If you expect men to risk injury or death, then, as a leader, you have to motivate them, encourage them, and share that risk.

I may not have been able to stave off depression and panic in every case, but I could sure as hell let my men know that they were not alone.

Morale, like bitching, goes from the top down; leaders are responsible for maintaining it. For example, when I saw a pilot in particular who had several rough missions that were beyond comprehension, I would transfer him to another duty. Same with the aircrews: give them some downtime, rotate a few of the ground personnel who wanted flight time, put them on the waist guns if they were qualified, et cetera.

I spoke with the unit shrink about a few of the men, and I was given a rare education into the mind of people. Now, I liked this guy. He was not the usual soft-handed clown; he believed in the war effort and knew that men had to be prepared to fly and, if necessary, die. His main ambition was to ensure that no one man was a danger to the others, either due to a death wish or some form of mental collapse, being unable to do his job.

The shrink told me that he had identified five pilots and crew who were at the breaking point—nervous breakdowns—and were almost worthless due to mental exhaustion. But there were differences. Four of these men needed a break; they had to have time off from the missions, having pulled almost the limit for rotation. I agreed with the psychiatrist and gave them some downtime. I think a couple were placed into instructor slots for new pilots, as we were getting more fresh pilots in who needed airtime.

However, there was one very specific case that the doctor warned me about. There was this one particular pilot who was up for promotion to captain, and he flew every damned mission possible. Even when his own aircraft was down for maintenance, and his crew could get some well-deserved rest, this guy volunteered to fly other birds, every time. And he was not alone. I apparently had a ball turret gunner doing the same thing.

I asked the shrink why this was a problem. They were obviously motivated, wanting to get the mission requirements in and get home, and I liked that fighting spirit. The shrink said that these two were fatalistically driven—either a death wish or adrenaline junkies—and that was also a problem regarding flight integrity. Well, on this note, I disagreed with the doctor, but in his capacity, although I was a light colonel and he was a major, he could still pull medical rank on me. All he had to do was write a report, and the situation was out of my hands.

I told him that I wanted to talk to both men individually, and he could be there. I wanted to hear what they had to say for myself. I always believed that I was a good judge of character. I could also smell a bullshit artist from twenty thousand feet. I would know if there was anything fishy about these guys. Well, Doctor Shrink set it up. I spoke to both men, first the lieutenant. After thirty minutes, I saw what I needed to see. What I saw was a man who was driven to fight, driven to kill, and was willing to continue taking those risks. What struck me the most was when I asked him, "What are your plans after you rotate out? You have about eight missions to go." His response took me back a bit:

"Rotate? Sir, with all due respect, I want to extend or go kill Japs. I do not plan on going home until the war is over. Besides, sir, who wants to go back to the farm with all this action going on?"

I liked that guy. He was like me, and I could see the shrink sitting there, writing his notes, probably trying to figure out which nut hospital to place him into. I dismissed him and told the shrink, "You find me a hundred more like him, and I can win this damned war."

Well, then we met with the enlisted man: a sergeant ball turret gunner. He had flown about eighteen missions; three of his B-17s were so shot up they were scrapped. On one mission, there were only four living crewmen: the pilot, flight engineer, a waist gunner, and himself. He was the only one unhurt. In fact, in all these missions where they came back with casualties, he never had a scratch. His only motivation was the flight pay. I kept him also.

Getting back to my ideas, I knew in my gut that I could improve upon the three problems Washington, DC, was concerned about. My box formation idea would provide greater defensive fire, as the bombers would be staggered in formations of nine, eighteen, or thirty-six ships—each at a different altitude but able to cover their neighbors with more concentrated and effective defensive fire. It also concentrated the aircraft and assisted in bombing the target as one collective, making it more effective, as the aircraft were closer together, reducing the risk of scattered ordnance. This produced much better results. Then I put that plan into effect on the mission of November 23, 1942.

What I was not privy to, but suspected and later learned, was that some of the asshole politicians in DC were just looking for a reason to terminate our daylight bombing program. Some wanted us to join the British night bombing campaign; others wanted it eliminated altogether. They saw it was a wasteful expense of taxpayer dollars for negligible gains. After I submitted my plan, provided the after-mission reports, and the BDA came in looking good—as well as my lack of great losses against the enemy—this method became bombing doctrine throughout the Air Corps [Air Force by this time].

This method improved results, and we started flying missions in earnest in 1943. I was praised by Eaker for my developments, and I was promoted to full bird colonel. Soon we heard about FDR and Churchill meeting in Casablanca, Morocco, where a few things happened. Apparently, Old Rosie [Roosevelt] had stated that nothing short of unconditional surrender would be accepted from the Axis powers. I heard it from several sources firsthand that Churchill, uninformed of this coming declaration, almost had a fucking stroke when FDR said it. Talk about getting ambushed.

Churchill, unlike Rosie, knew about war. He had been captured in the Second Anglo Boer War, had seen some of the fiercest fighting in that conflict, escaped captivity, been First Lord of the Admiralty in World War I, and was now prime minister in World War II. He knew that if you give an enemy no room to maneuver on terms of surrender, no negotiation, then that gives your enemy few options and reinforces a fighting spirit that was soon to be proven incredibly lethal. It is like placing a price tag on a car and not being willing to haggle over the price. The owner may be stuck with it if he remains inflexible, and still paying the property tax and maintenance.

The other thing we received was that there was a new edict for us called the Operation Pointblank [also known as part of the Casablanca Directive], which dictated and prioritized our targets in Europe. The target list made sense.[33] I looked at it, and we knew where the vast majority of those targets were. Unfortunately for us, most were deeper into Germany than our fighter escorts could go, and they were heavily defended with antiaircraft batteries.

Then you could look at the various entry and egress routes to and from those targets on a map, and just know that Adolf Galland had his damned fighters ready and waiting to greet us once we crossed over land. We had to deal with the fighters on the way to and then again out of the target areas. That was a long six-to-eight-hour round-trip to be picked off by Germans.

The end result was that my group had better BDA [bomb damage assessment] and fewer operational losses up to that time than any other bomb group—serious shit. I can only assume that the Germans recognized tail markings of each individual group, and since we laid down heavy volumes of fire, they may have avoided *us* as a whole. The BDA was improved by designating specific crews to lead missions, and soon Eaker adopted all of my innovations as policy across the board. I fully believed that my box formation concept was the best innovation for the Eighth Air Force. I even spoke to a few Germans after the war, and they told me that my idea forced them to reconsider their attack methods, adjust their tactics. Sure, they still shot bombers down, but not as many, and it cost them a lot more fighters to get the job done.

Nineteen forty-three was becoming very busy for us. We earned a Distinguished Unit Citation after a few highly successful missions. The 305th Bombardment Group made the news, and Eaker said that we had saved daylight bombing. Well, that theory was soon put to the test. Eaker and the Eighth Air Force prioritized the German fighter aircraft industry, engine factories, and oil and ball bearing manufacturers. I knew sure as shit that these would be the most heavily defended areas on the planet. I did not withhold the S-2 material from my crews, either. I wanted them to know exactly what we were headed into. I also wanted them to know that I was going to be there with them.

In every ready room, we had a large map of Europe. Pins indicated primary, alternate, and supplemental targets. Red twine stretched from our base to the target of the day, and, as we saw, that twine was often getting longer by the week. About that time, I learned that Robert Olds had died. I knew that two of his boys were at West Point. I had met Robin, the oldest, before. I knew that he had an interest in aviation like his dad. I figured the boys would be in the war soon enough. I was hoping we could end the damned thing before that happened.

But we were going to have many more losses that year. At this time, we were losing upward of 8 percent bombers, with an average of about 4 percent. While these were within the acceptable range of 10 percent, it was still too damned high for me. My box formation reduced our losses to fighters, at least for a while, since we did not have long-range escorts. Well, the Germans were not completely stupid. They figured out that our weakest point on the bombers was the front. On average, the other bomber units were suffering well above 10 percent losses. Most were from fighters, I was told.

If the German fighters attacked from the flanks, they had a top turret, ball, and waist gunner focused on them. If they attacked from below, their rate of climb was slower and gave the tail and ball turret gunners time to aim on them. The B-17F did not have any frontal forward-firing .50s. The only protection was the top turret gunner firing forward. If a fighter came level or from dead ahead and slightly below nose level, he had a single .50 trained on him from the bombardier's position.

The Germans perfected that head-on attack method. I wrote reports and made suggestions, as did other leaders, and the result was the development of the B-17G with the chin turret. This was mounted below the nose, with twin .50-caliber guns. That helped, but it was not perfect. You could see the 109s and 190s as they came in from the front, their guns would sparkle, then you would feel the impact of the bullets and cannon shells. The Germans would attack, fire, and then roll away into a dive, get out of the defensive fire zone. I always thought those were some gutsy bastards. I once saw a 109 do this, and when he rolled out of the attack to dive, he collided with a B-17, and both went down.

I was reassigned to the Fourth Bombardment Wing, and this would be a transition presenting me with many unique challenges. We were following the Pointblank Directive, and our biggest mission to date was to become one of the two most expensive missions of the war. The next mission would almost break the Air Force and we would get a Distinguished Unit Citation, which seemed a consolation prize, in retrospect. It was a nightmare, to be honest, although my boys came through really well.

I was the flight leader on the August 17, 1942, Schweinfurt-Regensburg mission, and I led the Regensburg section to hit the production plant. Brigadier General Robert Williams led the Schwein-furt group. Our mission [LeMay flew with the Ninety-Sixth Bomb Group] was to hit the factory building fighters and then fly on to North Africa. Two hundred ninety-one bombers took off for Schwein-furt's ball bearing industry, and I believe about one hundred eighty-three reached the target. I think about a hundred forty-six of the bombers took off, but only one hundred twenty-six bombers reached Regensburg.

I then learned that the First Bomb Division under Williams had not yet taken off. This revelation came to me as I crossed into Bel-gium, and as our P-47 escorts turned back, the Focke-Wulfs and Messerschmitts came in at us. This was putting us into the stiffest air defense we had yet experienced in the war, and not just flak. German fighters were effective as hell. Since we were the only group in that air-space, that just allowed the fighters to focus on us, but my unit flew the box, held tight, and defended well. When we reached the target, despite a lot of damage, we dropped about three hundred tons of ordnance and had about 50 percent of that facility destroyed.

But then we had to get the hell out of that area and get to Africa, but as soon as we banked, we had Me 110s coming in at us, and they took out a few of our bombers. We breathed a little easier after we crossed the Alps and saw the blue Mediterranean Sea under us. The rest of the trip to Algeria was uneventful, but I took note of the known losses. I always did. Upon landing, despite my group not having lost anyone, the other losses began coming in.

The 100th Bomb Group suffered heavily again; this was how they earned the name "Bloody Hundredth," due to the continued losses. Schweinfurt's strike force had lost 35 bombers on the mission; the total number of destroyed aircraft was 60 bombers. Unlike us, they had to fly back to England through that nest of fighters that we had stirred up. Later, they calculated the additional aircraft that were scrapped and cannibalized due to too much damage to be repaired. I believe that 120 aircraft came back with some degree of damage.

I learned later that Galland had 300 fighters scattered at strategic locations in an overlapping defensive operation—three waves at various stages, to keep us busy. Then there was the flak, which was just something you could not control. The lack of long-range fighter escorts really cost us on that one. We did cost the Germans 38 fighters, but most of those pilots were probably back in the air by the next day. Our guys not killed were captured. All counted, I think if you include the men dead upon return to base, we lost 650 men that day and many more wounded.

I wanted my bombers repaired and rearmed, so that I could do a strike on the way back to England, and Eaker finally agreed to the plan. At first, he did not want to subject my boys to more combat than necessary, but I told him that we would have the element of surprise, and we could make the trip count. Eaker relented. Why wouldn't he? It was a great plan! The following month, I was promoted to brigadier general.

October 14, 1943, was the famous Black Thursday, when we lost seventy-seven bombers on the mission, more than on the August mission. Again, Galland had his fighters staged at various locations around logical targets and en route to those targets. They had all pretty much adopted the head-on attack method to shoot down heavy bombers. The first group of Germans would go up once a scout plane, ground observer, or radar picked us up coming in over the North Sea. They also had radio listening posts waiting to pick up our transmissions. They could hear us over England as we formed up. That was why radio silence was absolutely critical.

Unfortunately, while my boys maintained their radio chatter to the absolute minimum, the fighter pilots seemed to be pretty chatty, and that pissed me off. They would usually hang around until the escort fighters had to turn back. Galland's boys were not stupid, they were smart, brave, and dedicated. A few Germans would sometimes probe into the fighter escorts, keeping them busy or try to draw them away from us. Then after they saw the escorts head back, they hit the bombers like a pack of wolves.[34]

That group of Germans did the same thing as in August. They would attack in waves, from different directions, until they had to land, refuel, and rearm. Then the second wave would hit us in more concentrated numbers until they had to land. Then the third group would be in the air, hit us, and land. By that time, the first bunch of fighters we'd already encountered would be refueled, rearmed, and airborne, waiting for us as we exited the target area. They would not normally fly through their own flak, just orbit outside the flak zone, then attack once we cleared the area. We lost 176 bombers that month alone. That was over 1,700 men.

Doolittle preferred the B-17s, for a variety of reasons, and many of the pilots did also. They considered it to be easier to fly than the B-24, better to fly with engine damage, and, of course, ease of maintenance. There was a lot of publicity over the B-17; far more coverage than given to the Liberator. Once Captain (later Colonel) Robert K. "Bob" Morgan's crew completed their twenty-fifth mission, they became celebrities.[35]

After I was promoted, I was sent home on a damned war bond tour with Hub Zemke and many others—high-profile types, names and faces people would recognize. We sailed on the *Queen Elizabeth* to New York. I was ordered to jump onto the lecture circuit, to impart my wisdom, such as it was. It was great to see the girls again, but I did not get much time with them, as duty still called. I really remembered that I wished that I could sleep—just sleep for about two straight days without being disturbed. Like that was going to happen.

After that dog and pony show was over, I returned to England, only to be greeted by a stand-down order. I was no longer allowed to fly missions. I thought I'd read it wrong, so I called Eaker. He said, "Doolittle will take charge in a few weeks. You will need to talk to him about it. I am going where it is warm and sunny." I was stunned. Then, no shit, Doolittle took over Eighth Air Force operations, Eaker went to the Mediterranean theater as commander, and I was nailed to a desk. I was not going to let that shit fly if I could help it.

Big Week was the last week of February 1944, which also launched the third raid against Schweinfurt for the ball bearings, and Regensburg and other locations where the fighters were built. By this time, we had the P-51D Mustangs *and* the P-47D Thunderbolts with drop tanks to help escort the bombers to and from the targets. This really reduced our losses and increased losses to the Luftwaffe. Now, there were some heavy losses [for example, February 22 saw forty-one bombers lost], but nothing like before we had those fighter escorts.[36]

Even Galland admitted that this method we used started the eventual destruction of his fighter force. Even though they produced even more aircraft in 1944 than at any time in the war, they could not replace those damned pilots. That was what Doolittle wanted. Planes are worthless without men to fly them. Galland knew it, too. I learned that the Germans had a few captured B-17s and B-24s that had been shot down. They repaired them and used them as training aids.[37]

That explained their proficiency at knocking them down. However, I felt great vindication when I was told that my creation of the box formation caused the Luftwaffe a lot of headaches. That was when they began working on the frontal attack method, which was a hell of a lot more difficult to achieve. I knew that they had a complete unit of captured Allied fighters that they remarked and used to train their pilots. Hell, we had enemy aircraft also. The Germans really feared the bomber formations. I credit them with having the guts to go in the way they did.

Believe it or not, in the 1950s we had several B-17s being used by the CIA for special missions. These aircraft dropped agents into China, flying from Taiwan, with Taiwanese crews. During these missions, I believe we lost four B-17s—shot down. We still flew them throughout Asia doing spook shit.

On March 3, 1944, I was promoted to major general, making me the youngest at that rank in the entire army, because I was only thirty-seven, so I guess someone thought I had been doing a good job. I was then given my orders: I was going home to take over the Boeing B-29 Superfortress transition into the Air Force. I knew about it, but I wanted to experience it myself. I was excited as all hell, I can assure you. It was the most expensive military expenditure of the entire war [$3.2 billion in 1944 dollars]—even more costly than the Manhattan Project, and that created the damned atomic bombs.

I was relieved of my command in preparation for my departure, and I had some downtime. I called [Major General William] Bill Kepner, and we flew a pair of P-47s over the beaches after D-day. We landed and were met by [Brigadier General James] "Big Jim" McCauley, who commanded a bomber wing in the Ninth Air Force, and we took a car. Kepner found this abandoned car, and we towed it back. McCauley wanted to take it back home with him later after the war. Not sure if he ever did.

In reflecting upon my time in England, I will tell you my thoughts about the many people I knew and worked with. First of all, I admired Churchill and Sir Arthur Harris. They thought like I did. They were fighters, no bullshit, kill-shit-get-it-done kind of men, and that was what I understood. However, I will say that I sensed a certain degree of what most people would call arrogance in Harris. But I just took it as self-assurance. He knew what he was doing, and fuck anyone who did not like it.

Churchill was dedicated to his cause, and he was the right man at the right time after Sniveling Neville Chamberlain was gone. The Brits needed him. Hell, the world needed him. I liked him a lot. I also met [Sir, Lord Avon] Anthony Eden, who was anti-Communist as hell, and although he was not 100 percent with Churchill on every decision, he did the right thing and supported his prime minister.

Hell, Eden became prime minister after Churchill. Eden once told me something that I never forgot: "When dealing with a Russian, remember that they will always smile, agree to anything and every-thing, but in their mind, they have already violated any agreement and buggered you to their satisfaction." Point taken. Hell, he knew Stalin, after all, so I figured his opinion carried some weight. I would develop my own opinion of the Russians later.

Now, about this situation between Ike [General Dwight David] Eisenhower and [General James H.] Doolittle. I can only tell you what I know. Ike was, and this is only my opinion, a little perturbed at all the media adoration and sensationalism around Jimmy. Ike was never a combat leader, and that was not why he was chosen to be the supreme Allied commander. He was a diplomat, and his job was making the right calls to keep the Allied cause together.

I can tell you, having to deal with the likes of Montgomery, George Patton, and fucking de Gaulle, he had a full plate.[38] With all the shit he had to deal with, he really did not get much recognition, and I suppose that was why he felt Jimmy Doolittle was a glory hound. But to be honest, Doolittle never sought the limelight, it just naturally followed him. He is perhaps the humblest person I have ever known, next to Omar Bradley. I think Ike was jealous, pure and simple, and I think that Medal of Honor that FDR gave Doolittle only made things worse. Anyway, that's my opinion.

George Patton was a pure killer, no shit, and if he had access to a bomber, he would have probably started World War III, or at least shifted the balance of power to continue World War II. No one hated the fucking Russians more than Patton, and I mean no one, and I will compare him to some Germans I knew. Ike really saw Patton as a major problem in the alliance factor, but not because he was combat ineffective.

Patton was very effective, and he was the exact opposite of Ike in personality—and most other generals, to be honest. Many of his peers were also killers, but they just hid it better. He was direct, blunt, in your face, and ready to bitch slap you in a moment if he felt the inclination. Some have compared me to him, but I never slapped a soldier or airman like he did. I can tell you there were quite a few times I sure as shit felt like it.

Omar Bradley was a fantastic man, and he really was the soldiers' general. He had no pretense; nothing about him would indicate genius or an outward appearance of command authority. He was just the humble guy who had a lot of rank and responsibility, and he was a very levelheaded man. I liked him a lot. In fact, unlike most people, I cannot think of anyone I ever met who knew him who did not like him. Even Ike liked him, and Ike really never liked a lot of people, he just tolerated them.

[Lieutenant General James Maurice] Jim Gavin was another really good guy, and I understood him completely. That guy was a steroid-pumped leader of real fighting men. He made every jump with the Eighty-Second Airborne in the war. We had a good chat once, and he said, "You know, if I had it to do all over again, I can't really think of anything I would change, except perhaps some of the tactical decisions that were made above my pay grade." Gavin was one of the real heroes, a fighting general, and his men loved him.

The same could be said of [General] Maxwell [Davenport] Taylor, who was another warrior type. I knew him briefly during the war, but I really came to know him better after he became the chairman of the Joint Chiefs of Staff. He was very cordial, serious, and thoughtful, and he was willing to listen to anyone, regardless of rank, if he thought there might be a good idea in it. He had his own conflicts with the politicians making life tough for us, but unlike me, he was very diplomatic in his approach when dealing with shitheads. I disagreed with him regarding some policy issues, but I never lost my respect for him.

However, he openly disagreed with Eisenhower—and his former boss was now president—on many new policies when he was chairman. I think it was the combination of Ike's falling into the JCS paradigm of reducing the infantry and airborne forces in favor of supporting the nuclear options, which I was a sponsor of, that made him retire. Although Taylor and I disagreed on various strategic ideas, there was a mutual respect. After all, he was an infantry officer, and I was an air officer, so we fought and thought in different ways.

Funny thing is that after the Cuban shit hit the fan—you know, that Bay of Pigs debacle—JFK convinced Taylor to come back and lead the intelligence section for the Joint Chiefs, which I thought was a good call. Kennedy knew that the CIA dickheads had failed him, and he wanted someone he could count on to give him good intel. I always said that the intelligence failure was because the CIA kept recruiting pricks from the Ivy League schools. Letting a social pedigree dictate someone's ability to work in that field was insane. But Kennedy had to shoulder most of the blame. It was he who was in charge. He had access to all the information and wisdom available, and still he approved that stupid mission.

You might be a great mathematician or a great writer, but that does not mean I want you repairing my airplane, if that makes any sense. Most of those guys were out of their intellectual depth. I once got into what became a heated argument with one of LBJ's people, some undersecretary of some shit. Somehow the subject of recruiting the Yale, Harvard, and Princeton guys to work in government, even intelligence, came up. This clown said that we always needed the best and brightest.

I reminded him that I was not an Ivy League asshole, and if I had to choose between a Harvard man with an expensive degree or an enlisted man who barely survived high school but became a top-notch aircraft mechanic, I would take the enlisted man. The reason being, I know that guy not only knew his job but also he probably had a better work ethic, and he will never lie to you about the work he did. His ass depends upon me getting back safely. Your Ivy League prick has no skin in the damned game, so what the hell would he care? He still gets a paycheck.

Bay of Pigs. That was some of the dumbest damned shit I ever saw. And you know what was really interesting to me, and probably necessary, was that Kennedy made Taylor his personal military advisor and cut the JCS right the hell out of the loop. Kennedy always feared that the Joint Chiefs were more concerned about appeasing the politicians on Capitol Hill than in really doing the hard work required. They wanted funding, so why rock the boat?

Taylor and I did have one major point of contention: he was able to work with [Secretary of Defense Robert] Strange McNamara, on a level I could not understand at all. [Authors' note: LeMay kept calling McNamara Strange or sometimes using his last name. He detested the man, apparently.] I hated that Ivy League prima donna prick, and he never liked me, either. He was a pure politician, with his hands in almost every sector of the defense industry. Strange never did shit unless it benefited him. His dumb ass cost a lot of lives in Vietnam as a result, and Robin Olds will tell you, those dozing bastards should have never had their hands in the war-fighting policy. If they had been in charge during World War II, I could only imagine the fucking tragedy that would have been the result.

Matt [General Matthew] Ridgeway was another guy who was

interesting. He was also a chairman of the Joint Chiefs, and great résumé, too. After Truman fired MacArthur, he made Ridgeway the supreme Allied commander of the United Nations Forces in Korea. That was a really good call, in my opinion. One thing Ridgeway did: he carried the fight to the Chinese after they entered the war. Those Communist bastards did not adhere to anything resembling the Geneva Convention, and Ridgeway gave his division commanders a shitload of latitude to conduct operations.

Ridgeway was later sent back to Europe as Supreme Allied Commander Europe to oversee NATO [North Atlantic Treaty Organization] and put together a coordinated air and ground defense plan for Western Europe.[39] I spoke with him about that a few years after the fact. I was perplexed but came to understand his position on German commanders who were in prison. Most of these guys had been tried for war crimes on the Eastern Front, and after he reviewed many of their actions and policies, he saw that many of them had not really violated Geneva or Hague.[40] I read a few of their files. We had brought a lot of Germans over to work for us who would have qualified for prosecution according to the criteria I read. [General Walter] Dornberger,[41] [Dr. Wernher] von Braun, and others could have been hanged for using slave labor or some shit, but they got a pass.[42]

Taylor made written recommendations that, on a case-by-case basis, these Germans should be released, and their experience in Soviet military methods should be brought into the collective. Ridgeway and Eisenhower also differed on policies, and he was totally against any reduction in ground forces in favor of the nuclear options then available. I was a nuclear proponent, but I never thought I was qualified to tell a ground commander how to do his job. I did not expect them to tell me how to do mine.

I have to say that Ridgeway made a valid point: you can bomb it, even nuke it, but someone has to take the ground and control it when the dust settles. He also believed that the Soviets would never launch a first atomic strike in their desire to take all of Europe, and they would sure as hell rethink that plan if they saw that NATO had overwhelming numerical superiority in ground forces and nukes.

Another thing worth mentioning is that during this time, the French were in the process of having their asses handed to them in Vietnam. It was called Indochina back then. Well, the French wanted American help, such as dropping a few nukes on the Communists to rid them of the problem and providing ground support to help secure their colony. Eisenhower thought about it, and Tricky Dick [Vice President Richard M. Nixon] and [Secretary of State John Foster] Dulles all thought it was a great idea. But not Ridgeway. He argued that doing anything of the kind would bring the Chinese in, maybe the Soviets, and divert attention and resources from Europe, making it vulnerable to a Warsaw Pact attack and then get America bogged down in another Asian war that had no strategic value to us.

Ridgeway and I got to know each other a lot better in the 1960s during Vietnam, as he was on the president's council. They called it "the Wise Men," and these were people who, with their education and experience, held court with LBJ. These head sessions were meant to give Johnson sage advice on what should be done during Vietnam, apart from the Joint Chiefs and the elected officials who had no sons in the war, and most had never served in the military themselves.

Basically, Ridgeway, Gavin, and others opposed the bombing of North Vietnam, and they stated that South Vietnam was not worth the pain and suffering. Now, Omar Bradley and a few others were of the opposite mind-set, and they supported escalating the campaign, but then again, they also wanted the targeting restrictions lifted.

Having specific locations marked as off-limits to our bombers was a completely stupid thing.

I know from my talks with all of them that their opposition was not against bombing the North Vietnamese entirely; they were opposed to the fucking restrictions placed upon the military on what targets they could bomb. The great fear of the Chinese and Soviets getting involved was bullshit. They were already involved. They both gave sanctuaries to North Vietnamese soldiers and pilots, and the Chinese let them fly from their airfields in complete safety, as we could never bomb them.

And the Russians? Those backward borscht-eating bastards had so many ships in Haiphong Harbor it looked like fucking Fleet Week. They were already involved; the only thing they did not have were ground divisions fighting our troops. I know that Ridgeway and Gavin carried a lot of sway with [Secretary of Defense] Clark Clifford, and that made a huge difference. I think that if Congress kept its damned hands out of the shit, things would have gone a lot better, we could have won that thing in a few years, and had the Vietnamese begging for food stamps.

[On General] Douglas MacArthur, well, that is another story. I can only give my personal opinion on him from my observations when I reached the Pacific. Mac was really a lot like Patton. He had an ego that would fill a room, and he was always the smartest guy in it, or at least he thought so. I know some people give him shit for leaving the Philippines in 1942, but you have to remember he was ordered to evacuate by FDR. What most people never forgave was the abandonment of our troops to fall into Japanese hands, and we all know how that shit played out.

[Getting back to the war] I looked forward to getting into the war against the Japs. After I got back from my distractions, I qualified in the B-29 in preparation for going to that theater, and I had studied it and written up a detailed evaluation of it. The plane had great promise, but it had a shitload of bugs to be worked out. That is not unusual for any new aircraft. In fact, it is expected. The engines rated twice the power of the B-27. Both used the Wright Cyclone design after the B-17s, but the newer Duplex-Cyclone cranked out 2,200 horsepower to the previous version, which produced 1,200.

That was a lot of power for one engine, and it carried four of them. The B-29 was designed for extremely high altitude, to fly above the antiaircraft expected and also to operate above the ceiling of enemy fighters. It was expected that we would get them into the European theater, but that plan changed. The main reason was that the Pacific was much larger, with greater distances to be flown, and the Superfortress had much greater range. The problem with the B-29 was that it was developed and built in wartime without the benefit of a thorough peacetime evaluation process.

The greatest innovation was that the B-29 had separate pressurized compartments and electrically operated guns for defense. I crawled through those birds from head to ass, checking out everything. Preflights were like church service, and postflight debriefings were often a maintenance chief's worst nightmare. While I was doing all of this, we had B-29s flying operations from China, and the results were less than impressive. I made my recommendations, and expected results from the powers that be, and then I went overseas again.

In August 1944 I took command of the Twentieth Bomber Command in Kharagpur, India, and China on a trip that allowed me to see India, which was a lovely country from the air. It was only when you landed you realized that you were in a tropical shithole, but I would see worse real soon. We had birds in India and China both assigned to my unit, all flying missions, but there really was not much in the way of high-octane gas or even spare parts. Training missions did not exist, only limited operations, and those from crews often with less time in the plane than I had.

One tragedy that could have been avoided was when I arrived and reacquainted with my old friend [Brigadier General LaVerne G.] "Blondie" Saunders. He survived a B-25 crash that cost him his leg and ended his career. That was a tragedy, but at least he was alive.[43] Well, to sum up my new assignment, nothing was good. I did have some very experienced pilots and crews, which was good, but their experience was in B-17s and B-24s, for the most part. As I said, we lacked fuel and parts—even ammunition was not available. Looking for bombs was like searching for leprechaun gold. Our deliveries were not that regular. The food was appalling. For one thing, we had logistics problems, as the C-47s and C-54s had to cross the Himalaya Mountains, which we called the Hump, and it was dangerous business.

Hap Arnold offered to send me more B-29s, but I told him it would not help me. I could barely operate with what I had at that time. They would have just sat on the apron collecting dust. My bases in China were over a thousand miles away [in Szechuan], and I saw problems, and I started my program similar to what I did in England: tight box formations, that sort of thing, including navigation training.

Remember, I was still on a flight ban. I guess they figured it would not be a good thing for a two-star general to land in a Jap prison, and I tended to agree, but then, I also always wanted to lead my men. I had permission to fly one mission. Well, I decided to make it count, so we located a nice target in Manchuria that supplied steel for the Japanese military. There were also fighters located there. However, one of my greatest problems was that we did not have any really accurate maps. Some regions had no maps at all; you had to use aerial photos to assume some knowledge of the terrain. Flying over high mountains requires a few ingredients, like knowing how fucking high all those mountains were and where they all were, in case of limited visibility—it would have been a great help.

Well, choosing a target and plotting the course was the easy part. I had to wait for what seemed an eternity to get the fuel flights in. I had finally acquired the fuel and bombs, and we took off. We flew at high altitude, and the fighters came up, but these guys did not impress me. My bombers took some hits—no problem, really—and I thought I had a couple of wounded on board, but those were false alarms.

I learned quite a bit about the unit, and I entered into a massive training program. Missions were canceled, all leaves and passes canceled, life as all of my men knew it ceased to exist. I was not impressed, and I would not relieve the pressure until I was satisfied that the men were up to my standard. Luckily, I did have a lot of support for my methods, and Hap Arnold was still in my corner, even from Washington. He knew what I could do to get a unit combat ready.

———————

One problem that we had to contend with was the political bullshit in China. You had the occupying Japanese in Manchuria and along the coast in major cities. Then you had Chiang Kai-shek's Nationalist Chinese Government in the southern part of the country. Then, as if that shit was not a bag of balls, Mao Tse-tung and his Communist pricks up north ran another part of the country. Chiang's government was always deemed as unreliable, and when it came to fighting the Japs, the Commies were far more effective in that venture. The senior Nationalist ground commander in the theater was corrupt and incompetent, the Japs were ruthless, and the Commies just killed everybody.

Then I had to deal with the British because India was their crown jewel within their empire, so that meant that this theater [China-Burma-India, or CBI] was controlled by [Lord Louis] Mountbatten. I met him—nice fellow and seemed to know his business—but he answered to the king. And then there was [General Joseph W., nicknamed "Vinegar Joe"] Stillwell, and that was a rather acerbic relationship. Great allies to have altogether if you could call them that. Basically, Stillwell was an arrogant Anglophile asshole who should have never had any fucking say as to air operations. He just had no damned idea about what was required and what was possible.

Now, I got to know Claire Chennault pretty well, as he was the most experienced air commander in theater. He had commanded the AVG before they were absorbed into the air force. If you think Strange and I had an abrasive relationship, Stillwell and Chennault fucking hated each other, and the big thing was they never tried to hide that from anyone. It became so bad that MacArthur had to intervene, and I can tell you he sided with Stillwell, but Washington, in its rare display of wisdom, sided with Chennault.

The problem was that Stillwell wanted control of all of Chennault's air assets to support his campaign in Burma and into China and also cover the land supply routes from India, such as they were. Chennault felt that his force was better suited to attacking Japanese forces over Burma and China, especially the air assets, maintaining air superiority. He also wanted to plan and execute bombing and strafing missions against Jap airfields, destroying them on the ground. His argument was that if he got to the enemy fighters and bombers first, Stillwell would not have the problem he was always bitching about.

Stillwell pulled rank, using Mountbatten, but Chennault was not one to let a little thing like rank interrupt his plans. Chennault said that he would petition Washington and present his plans, but Stillwell knew that it would take a long time for Chennault to get that done.

He knew such requests eventually made their way through the military pipeline from theater, through various offices and then into the Pentagon, through various politicians, et cetera. In essence, the war could be over before Chennault ever got a response, either "yes" or "no" to his plan.

Stillwell kept ordering Chennault's fighter pilots to do low-level clearance runs into empty jungle, clearing a path ahead for his ground troops. Chennault, in true fashion, then went through Madame Chiang, who then went through her diplomatic contacts, bypassing all the bullshit and straight to President Roosevelt. That was what prompted MacArthur to pay them both a visit, along with Mountbatten. Chennault broke it off in Vinegar Joe's ass, and there was not a damned thing that prick could do about it. Not even MacArthur the megalomaniac could do shit about it then.

Well, during all of this bullshit, I was still planning my missions and trying to organize everything. Stillwell was also putting his hands into my shit, which was not going to fly worth a damn, in my book. I contacted Hap Arnold and told him that I was not a tactical bomber commander, I was strategic, and hitting heavy industry and infrastructure was my job, not bombing monkeys out of the fucking trees. Well, MacArthur made another visit on that note, and I could tell he did not like me very much, but then again, I did not give a shit. Hap Arnold wore five fucking stars also, and I answered to him. I always thought MacArthur was one of those assholes who would never bother leading from the front unless there was a camera crew waiting for him.

In the end, Chennault got his wish to keep hitting targets in China, which left me able to focus upon other parts of China and primarily Japan. But then we had more shit hit the fan because Admiral Chester Nimitz decided *he* had to pay a damned visit, and I could only imagine what the hell that was going to be about, so I waited. Hap told me not to worry, but I had my doubts.

Then I had another fucking problem. Washington, in its wisdom, decided that I needed to have a number cruncher to evaluate my methods. Enter one [Lieutenant Colonel Robert] Strange McNamara. I still have no damned idea why the politicos cling to this dead-fuck belief that Harvard graduates, or any Ivy League prick, always know so much more than the rest of us do.

Well, although we did not hit it off, he was at least able to report that my operational methods and effectiveness exceeded any other B-29 unit in theater.

My operations to Japan were always contentious due to the weather. Our mission was to fly above the defensive threats, but then we could not see a lot of shit if there was a lot of cloud cover. On top of that, after I started firebombing, you could go a few days and not see shit over the target area because the smoke was so thick. The fires were still burning to the point that navigation was not necessary; just follow the smoke clouds and fires below if the same target was going to be hit again.

Then we had extremely high winds due to the jet stream, which was another factor that was new to us at that time, and we had to consider that when planning missions. You could often get a great tailwind heading into the target zone, but then you had to contend with crosswinds or headwinds on the way out, and that would eat the fuel up at a high rate. I had to plan missions around the bomb loads and fuel supplies, fuel being hardest to get. That did limit missions, and I knew that some asshole in Washington was wanting to crunch the numbers and bitch about the expensive B-29s that were hardly flying to justify the cost per plane [$600,000 per unit, or about $8,500,000 in 2020 dollars].

This was where I had to learn and expand my diplomatic skills. Sometimes we would have bombers low on fuel or damaged that had to land, but doing so in Japanese-occupied territory was not an option. I managed to establish direct contact with Mao, and, after some mutual understandings, his people prepared airfields for distressed "Superforts" and C-47 transports to deliver fuel or bring in medical personnel and supplies, as well as fly injured aircrews out. I have to say that the Communists were very effective, and I think they appreciated our efforts. Mao was a much more manageable leader than Stalin ever was.

My targeting profile was changed by higher-ups, and I was ordered to hit Chinese targets to interrupt Jap supplies. That meant Stillwell got fucked, I won, and so did Chennault. I spoke with Claire about coordinating our units—working the same targets that were within reach of his fighters. Having them supplement as escorts made me feel better. But they would also go on fighter sweeps, hoping to engage the enemy in the air. That was what Zemke did in Europe: send out a squadron well ahead of the main fighter force, prompt the enemy to come up and fight, and whatever was still alive had to deal with the second wave of fighters.

———

The primary target was the enemy depot at Hankow, and after that strike [LeMay sent eighty-four B-29s; Fourteenth Air Force sent two hundred more bombers of various types], the sucker burned for several days. This result also told me something that I learned from Arthur Harris: incendiaries were good bombs to drop. As I said before, I tried to learn from every mission. What went well, what did not go so well, but what really needed to be addressed. I did this all the time, and we were narrowing down the fuck-ups to the point where we really had nothing within our control that we could not fix. The jet stream was what it was. I have to admit that if you got a tailwind in the fast lane, you were really cruising.

I decided to use incendiaries on damned near every mission, because the Japs were like the Chinese: most of their structures were made of wood, not steel. A lot of the buildings were brick and stone, but those could be blown out with a firestorm, like Harris created in Hamburg, Cologne, and other German cities. I would burn those bastards into submission, and it was all perfectly legal, too.

I later took over command of Twenty-First Bomber Command, based in the Marianas, where I was stationed again with Paul Tibbets. As you know, he flew the B-29 *Enola Gay* and dropped the first atomic bomb—"Little Boy," we called it—on Hiroshima. His partner in crime Chuck [Charles W.] Sweeney dropped "Fat Man," the plutonium bomb dropped on Nagasaki.[44] This was a wonderful location when compared to India or China, because we had a steady supply stream, and we could get everything we needed as we needed it. The only problem was that I was still on a stand-down order. I had just been read into the fact that we had the atomic bombs—not exact details, just that we had them. I found it fascinating that when FDR died, Vice President Truman had to be read into it. He didn't have a damned clue about it.

The island-hopping campaign was paying off big-time. Every time we kicked the Japs out of a nice location with a good airstrip, that put my men that much closer to Japan; it reduced flight time and exposure to enemy threats. It also meant less time over open water. And this was another thing that I kept stressing: navigation was the most important thing, especially in the Pacific, where you had no landmarks. You had to be precise in your plotting and maintain position awareness at all times.

I surrendered Twentieth Bomber Command to my successor, [Brigadier General] Roger Ramey, then I was basically in charge of all bombing operations against Japan, and I decided to fall back upon something that Arthur Harris told me: "If you bomb the enemy industry, you create a depressed economy and limit their war-making ability. But if you bomb them into homelessness, you deflate morale. That forces the population to reconsider their leadership."

I thought about his words, but then Britain had been bombed like hell for three years, and their spirit never broke, and it did not break the Germans, from what I could see. The only thing it did was create large streams of refugees in Germany. But, I thought, that may be just enough. I knew we had a plan to invade Japan, so it made sense to reduce morale as much as possible, flatten out and burn the shit out of their cities, which also meant there was little cover for the enemy ground forces to hide in an entrenched urban warfare scenario.

When the decision was made to transfer all China-based bomber units to the Pacific, I was happy as hell. As soon as the army and marines took an island, if it did not have an airfield, the Navy Seabees went in and damned well built one. Often times it was a matter of improving an existing Jap airfield or lengthening a runway for B-29 operations. Some islands were just too small for us to use, but they were great for the fighter groups.

One day McNamara the Wise walked in with the S-2. He was doing another one of his postmission calculations, looking over the BDA [bomb damage assessment] and then asking the intel man a bunch of stupid damned questions. The S-2 looked at me as if begging for a rescue, so I felt sorry for him. So, I called Strange over, and I told him that I might be able to answer any questions he might have.

He wanted to know the following: how many bombs and what types, what load each bomber carried, how much fuel per bomber, how many rounds per .50-caliber machine gun, typical things. Those were routine, and in that, I knew he was just doing his job. But he was going about it the wrong way. I told him that if he wanted the actual data, he would save us both a lot of time and anguish if he went to the ammo depot and asked the armorers questions about bullets. He should then talk to the ordnance chief, who had the record of all bombs and types loaded, and the fuel depot had all the gallons loaded onto the fuel trucks, and those were kept as a dispensation record. So, if he did not mind, would he get the hell out of my CP [command post]?

McNamara also wanted all the postmission data and BDA from each target we hit. He wanted to see the aerial postdrop photographs to assess damage. What he was doing was sending back information for the idiots in cheap suits on Capitol Hill who were still bitching about the cost of the bombing offensive. If they did not see tangible results, they wanted to pull the proverbial plug. Well, after I started using incendiaries, all that shit stopped, and then we had another problem.

Apparently, some bastard in Washington was concerned that I was burning out civilians as opposed to hitting legitimate targets. Hap Arnold gave me the warning order on that one, and he told me in no uncertain terms to make sure that whatever I hit had some form of military or industrial value. I responded back that I was doing just that. I outlined every target, its value to the Japanese war effort, whether it made planes, bombs, ships, or rice wine, as well as troop barracks and training centers. I think I said something to the effect that "Well, if the Jap soldiers move their families on post, then I guess they are responsible for their safety, not me."

Then there was an issue with my fighter cover. I did not blame [General George Churchill] Kenney—it was out of his control—but someone with more rank or political power than brains decided that the majority of the fighters should be sent on close-support fighter-bomber missions, attacking tactical targets.[45] Now, I saw the value in that, hitting trains, roads with traffic, and airfields—okay, all good there. But I smelled the hand of Stillwell in all of this. He wanted my bombers to saturate an entire country to allow him to push into Japanese-controlled territory, but I argued that it was a tactical mission. Well, I guess he turned his attention to the fighter commands to get his support at the expense of my fighter escorts. That pissed me off because he was working very closely with Mountbatten, and they had RAF fighter and bomber assets available. I really wanted to piss in his eye.

I always liked having fighter cover. Every island we took meant we got that much closer to Japan, but that meant greater threats from flak and fighters. The Japs simply pulled their air defense in tighter and closer, like Germany did, and that concentration of antiaircraft guns and fighters meant even more dangerous missions. The only saving grace was that we had far less distance to travel to a safe zone after we engaged.

We could not do too much about flak, but I knew that losses to fighters had been higher than I liked to see. I did establish a good relationship with General Nathan Twining in command of Twentieth Air Force. The fighter units, both our air forces, marines, naval assets, and even the British did a great job, in my opinion. However, I was still not getting the results I wanted due to the wind and weather conditions. Twining was just about as fucking done with Stillwell's shit as I was, although he had a decent relationship with him.

I will give MacArthur and Nimitz credit for the plan on hitting the islands that were crucial and bypassing the real estate that was essentially worthless for us. Many of the islands bypassed that had Japs on them were either too small for a naval and air base or were just in the chain of islands that placed them in a lower priority. Why waste men and materiel on a few islands, when bigger and better islands lay farther north that served our purposes better?

These locations in the Marianas were excellent, as we had the range to hit China and Burma if required, Japan as a necessity, Taiwan (which was Formosa then), and all the other smaller islands where the Japs still were. But we were far too distant from the Japanese home islands to be comfortable. Getting those island bases closer to Japan would make me breathe a lot easier, and we were taking them. I looked at Japan first, then our current location, and all the islands in between that would be great for establishing air bases. I cannot tell you how many hours I spent looking at the BFM on my wall. That means Big Fucking Map, by the way.

I always wanted to be in the loop on the operational planning, so I would know which islands were going to be hit next. This allowed me to start my planning. I knew the range of the fighters and the bombers when fully loaded, their range when payload free, and had calculated all of those high winds and their typical direction. I knew that if I flew straight to most of the targets, I would get a good crosswind. If I hooked left, I might get a good tailwind that would increase the range with the increased wind speed, and since I was dropping firebombs, I was less worried about precision as much as area saturation. We would sometimes fly saturation missions and soften those places up before naval gunfire would drop big-ass shells on them, preparing for the seaborne invasions.

———————

Taking over the Twenty-First and being in the Marianas also relieved me of the burden of politics. I did not have to deal with the British or anyone else; the only concern I had was working with the navy and coordinating our missions. It was also great because I was reunited with a lot of old friends—guys I had worked with in the past and could trust. That trust factor is the most important, and they were proficient.

Now, just because I was the commander, I still had my orders coming from Washington. It was not as if I could just dream up a mission and launch it to my heart's content. If that were the case, I would have been in damned utopia. I had the division G-2 [intelligence] in my back pocket. We got along, and he kept me up to date with the latest aerial photographs and industrial locations, what was going on, and which targets seemed to be of greater tactical and also strategic value. The great thing about the G-2 was he always knew when Strange was coming back for another one of his assessments. He was also sometimes privy to what McNamara's reports said before he sent them off. Good G-2, he was my spy.

Like a good commander, I listened to him—he knew his shit—and I then compared his analysis of targets with the orders and target instructions I was getting from Washington. I was curious to see if they were on the same page. I had my maps on the wall: the greater central Pacific with all the islands tagged, and a separate BFM of Japan. I had over a hundred pins in selected targets, color coded for aircraft manufacturing, engines, explosives factories, airfields, shipyards, naval bases, and the commercial ports, of course. Regardless of what Washington thought, I knew what I wanted to hit.

I saw that Imperial Palace, and I only imagined the hoot and holler if I dumped a few hundred tons of incendiary on the Hirohito Hilton. Now, MacArthur, he was of a different mind-set than I was, and he was, of course, not just my superior officer, he was the Supreme Allied Commander in the Pacific Theater. I once had a discussion with him about my idea: hit the Imperial Palace, kill the top brass and the emperor, shut that shit down, end the war.

He just could not bring himself to consider hitting the palace. His arguments were that even with the emperor dead, the military would still be in charge under Tōjō, that nothing would change. I disagreed. After all, it was a legitimate target. The emperor was the legitimate traditional leader of the Japanese military, and even though he was a head of state, I said, "Fuck him—let him surrender or burn the hell up." MacArthur just told me that I would never be in danger of becoming a diplomat. By the way, Kenney and Chennault loved my idea, as did Hap Arnold.

Besides, MacArthur apparently had long-range plans where Japan and Hirohito were concerned. The greater political landscape had been decided for Europe at the Yalta Conference. Our leadership was very concerned about the Russians wanting to creep into Japan and establish a Communist government. That shit would be easy to do if Stalin invaded Japan after we destroyed their military capabilities.

I had several discussions about that possible scenario, both during and after the war. Where we were willing to drop two atomic bombs to not have to invade Japan, the consensus was that Stalin would have no qualms about wasting another million lives of his men to invade and take the brunt of that shit. I was also thinking that maybe that would not be such a bad thing: let them die in big numbers in Japan, and that would weaken their grip on Europe, and we could follow Patton's advice and take all that shit they occupied. I'll bet that if I had voiced that opinion publicly, they would have probably had a shrink send me off to a rubber Ramada Inn.

At the very least, since we had the bombs, we could bluff their asses into falling back and honoring the agreement Stalin signed, which he later reneged on. He promised free elections in Eastern Europe, but everyone except Rosie did not believe that he would honor it. My position on this and other matters labeled me a madman to some and a visionary to others, I guess. I remembered what Anthony Eden told me back in England about dealing with Russians. I never forgot it.

I had gone over all the previous BDA from my predecessor and saw that there had not been a lot of activity, and what had been done showed miserable results. There were reasons, but it was still unacceptable. The greatest problem was the winds, some recorded between four hundred and six hundred miles per hour—tough to fly in and impossible to accurately bomb in. Calculating with navigation and the Norden bombsight was almost as tough as just relying upon a crystal ball.

I still had some issues with logistics, because once the ships arrived, they would have to off-load and send ammo or fuel to their respective depots. Then you would have to have that shit sent to the airfield depots, and then fuel or load up, which wasted time. I just had all my stuff sent straight to the flight line and had the birds readied up, saving time and energy. Now, my methods did piss off a few people, as I never asked permission or submitted the proper paperwork requesting shit through official channels.

We did have radar-guided bombing capability, which was good, but you still had to identify the targets and use good navigation. In February 1945 we began to target big cities, Tokyo in particular. Again, every time I thought about that city, the Imperial Palace came to mind. I even had the thought "What if it was wiped out by accident?" I knew that shit would fly like a lead weight. The problem I still faced were high winds at thirty-five thousand feet or even slightly lower. If we dropped lower in daylight, we had to contend with enemy fighters and heavy flak, and if we bombed at night, we still had the flak defense that could reach us at altitude, since they had radar-guided antiaircraft as well.

I had the idea to fly even lower than expected and do it at night. Going in at high speed below ten thousand feet at night was the best way to go. I figured that it would be more difficult for the Japs to track the bombers at night, and they would have to take more time to adjust their guns. My bombers would be lighter once we removed the guns and ammo, since it was a night mission. The Japs did not even have a night fighter force. But this was a plan I had to run up the chain of command.

I was informed, in no uncertain terms, that while I had almost unrestricted latitude in my command decisions, if my plan failed, I was done—my career was over. But I knew this: my plan was a radical departure from conventional wisdom, but I decided the risk was worth it. But I had to think about my crews; was it worth it to them? I was placing their necks in the noose to try to prove a theory, just like I did in England. The difference was, unlike here, I was flying and leading missions over Europe. Here I was one of those armchair commanders who sat in the comfort of an office while sending his men out to possibly die. Now I knew how Arthur Harris felt and why many of his men called him "Butcher" Harris. He was not allowed to fly, either.

I was situated in Guam with a great air base, good men, and excellent support staff. I had the best bomber in the world and the best logistics ever seen in warfare, and targets within easy reach, and the numbers of aircraft to get the job done. But I still had sleepless nights, uncomfortable with my inability to lead my men when it counted. I finally said to hell with it and sent the message that the mission was on. We had several B-29 airfields scattered around the Marianas, and they would all coordinate takeoff and target approaches to the minute.

Routes to and from the target areas were clear; supplemental airfields were established in case of damage or fuel concerns. Air-Sea Rescue was on standby with a separate emergency channel. The navy was well informed as to my mission, including takeoff times, routes in and out of the target area, and estimated time to target and bomb run, and that allowed their air recovery assets to be ready without having to orbit areas for a few hours, wasting time and fuel.

I made sure my crews were aware of every aspect of the mission in the briefing, to include support and recovery assets should they go down. I also established codes for the various locations, so that if a crew had to bail out or ditch, they could call in the location. I did not want my men floating around in the shark-infested waters any longer than they had to.

———————

March 6, 1945, was a day that I knew would define or terminate my career. Over 300 B-29s took off and headed into a very uncertain night. I returned to the operations building to see what would happen. Later, I had the commentary over the target that it was a complete success for us and a total disaster for the Japs. Afterward, we learned that this one raid had killed as many if not more people than the later Hiroshima bomb.[46] The heat wave bounced the heavy bombers around, and we only lost four bombers [1 percent loss].

Two nights later, we did the same thing to Nagoya, as it was a main producer of aircraft, a great target. Then we hit Osaka, and so on. I bombed those bastards until I was out of bombs, and fuel, but I think I made my point. Even Strange McNamara had to admit that I was effective, and I'll bet he hated to do it. I killed a lot of people, made even more homeless, but the most important factor, which I learned after the war, was that I had cemented into the Jap mind what Doolittle started in 1942. Well, the Japs knew who Doolittle was, and they apparently now knew who I was. I felt flattered, but that was just one more reason to have me grounded. I was a wanted man.

I adopted Harris's method of targeting a city center, knowing that the industrial complexes would be located nearby. Make that your aiming point at night, the lead bomber drops, and the rest follow. Being spread out meant more coverage per bomb load. I could not even begin to imagine the hell on earth I created with that, but I do know that I was making progress and getting results, and results were all that mattered. And getting results with minimal friendly losses was the best-case scenario. Anything below 10 percent was considered acceptable, and I never really had to worry about that—not like in Germany—but there were many reasons for that.

Japan and Germany as targets were as different as night and day. The main reason was that in hitting German targets, you had to fly over hundreds of miles of German-occupied Europe, defended by antiaircraft batteries and fighter units. By the time we even hit the German border, we had often experienced three or more hours of fighter attacks and flak, and that was not even the heavy shit you had to look forward to. After I left, we were able to establish bases in northern Italy, France, and Belgium, which minimized the exposure time, but that also increased the enemy defense concentrations.

Japan was not really any problem getting to, like Germany was. As we took the islands and had bases closer, we still never had to fly over a large, contiguous land mass full of defensive fire and fighters. Also, with our fighter escorts during the day, they ruled the sky. And when I started the night bombing, we did not have the problems that the British did, because unlike the Germans, the Japs never created a night fighter force. Germany's was the most lethal night fighter force in history. Japan was probably wishing they had one after I started hitting them at night.

When Jimmy Doolittle hit them, they knew they were vulnerable. When I hit them, they really knew that their shit was over, done with. It was only a matter of time. Only the morons in Tōjō's entourage could have believed that they would survive this shit.[47] It was my job to prove them wrong. My job was to win a war, kill the enemy, and save American and Allied lives. The only reason I stopped bombing was because I was out of bombs and very low on fuel. I had to wait for the navy to deliver more ordnance.

I have been asked many times how I felt about killing women and children. My response has never changed: under the Geneva

Conventions [Geneva III was signed in 1929, Geneva IV in 1949] a government at war was solely responsible for the safety of its population. They placed war-making industry near populated areas. They failed to evacuate their people to safer areas, if there ever was such a damned thing, and they had the chance to surrender. Their failure to do so cost lives. That was their fucking problem. They started it, and my ass would end it, guaran-damn-teed. My job was to save Americans, not the Germans or the Japanese.[48]

But one thing that has always really pissed me off is that I never get a question like, "Did you feel justified in your bombing Japan the way you did because of what they did to the civilians in China, or Korea, or Burma, or how they treated our POWs?" You will never get that question from a brain-dead liberal. It is as if they cannot even formulate the concept. Ever hear of quid pro quo? Well, I was the deliverer of that message. I have never lost a night's sleep over it, and I am sure I never will. I had a job to do, a family and nation to protect, and I was part of a large mechanism in the process of ridding the world of evil. Simple shit, even to a liberal.

One thing that we did, which also provided a lot of cover with regard to the laws of war, was that we dropped millions of flyers in Japanese telling the people to leave the cities; that they were targets. This was to have three other purposes: one, inform the civilian population they were in danger; two, force them to leave places where they worked to debilitate the war economy; and three, to create frustration with the people toward their own government for not protecting them from destruction. I learned after the war that the Japs actually made it a crime for one of their citizens to be caught with one. They called it propaganda, and having one was punishable with jail or possible death. I am not sure if that was true, but I was informed that at least we gave them a lot of toilet paper.

We were given even more missions, such as mining operations, and these orders came from Washington. Apparently Chester Nimitz thought it was a great idea, and he paid me a visit. Japanese transports were the targets, as well as any of their naval escorts. Their subs were also a problem, and the thought of sinking one of those was comforting. He brought up the concept, and I liked it. Hell, we had the planes and crews, and these were milk runs compared to what these men normally endured. I had no problem doing these missions. If it sank enemy ships and impeded their supply network, I was all for it.

The Japs still had a grip on the Dutch East Indies at that time, as well as Indochina and places like that, so they had access to oil and rubber, and they transported that shit to Japan through their cargo ships. Our medium bombers were good at hitting them, and the navy was great at sinking those things from the air and using subs. But mining the harbors and shipping lanes was another plan of attack. Crippling Japanese acquisition of raw materials was just another tried and proven way of waging war.[49]

That was why Hitler wanted the U-boats to starve out Britain in the war, and the Royal Navy blockaded Germany in the First World War. Cut supplies, starve out the people, reduce war-making potential, create public dissent. It's all part of the program. And we sank a shitload of ships as a result of the mining [averaging 3 ships per day with 670 sunk or damaged, denying Japan 1.25 million tons of material].[50]

I was briefed on the planned invasions of both Saipan, Tinian, and Iwo Jima. Saipan was the key to getting us into Japan by air, as well as the surrounding islands. Tinian was from where we would launch Paul Tibbets and the first atomic bomb. But Iwo Jima was also important. I knew that it would be a critical location for an air base, and it would increase operational effectiveness. If we were going to invade Japan proper, we needed forward air bases much closer, and then next on that list was Okinawa, the crown jewel.

Saipan had been bloody, and I felt for those marines—I saw the casualties—but they had helped win that war. God bless them. I was able to launch missions from where I was because of their sacrifice. I have never said a bad word about a marine since. Incredible men. They really helped me to help our country win the war out there, along with the navy. The marines who landed on Saipan and Iwo Jima helped save the lives of my airmen; they gave us another place of sanctuary returning back damaged. It also meant that we had rescue teams close to our aircraft once they cleared enemy airspace.

Then we had the invasion of Okinawa, Operation Iceberg. The preparation was detailed, but I was a little pissed off that Nimitz wanted to control me and my Twenty-First Bomber Command, which was still subordinated to the Twentieth Air Force, which fell under Nimitz's control for this operation. So, then we had to work as tactical bombers against various targets, mostly on Kyushu. The navy was getting slammed by the kamikazes, and that was where most of their airfields were. I hated to have to educate a five-star admiral, but B-29s were not tactical bombers. Just as I tried to explain before when Stillwell wanted my bombers.

I was finally relieved of those mining duties [May 11, 1945] and allowed to return to my first love: bombing and burning out Japanese cities. I hit Nagoya again in daylight [May 14], and then we went back the next night—just a repeat of our previous missions. Things were going great when I learned that Paul Tibbets was on Tinian. He was a great, reliable pilot with a great service record in Africa and Europe, and now he was here. Tibbets was also on a no-fly order over Japan, because, like me, he was well aware of the bomb.

I really needed him and others like him. I was having some real problems with Nimitz having a choke hold on my supplies and wanting to direct traffic on my missions. I still felt that Stillwell was involved somehow. Luckily, Hap Arnold flew out on his "inspection" tour and had a chat with his opposite number. Before he left, he gave me some news: apparently, McNamara's reports were subject to interpretation, and he had it in for me. He did not lie in his tabulations, because math is math, but how he wrote his reports before submitting them was what mattered to the politicians who were not my biggest fans. Fucking Strange was the biggest pain in my ass, he was unworthy to wear the uniform, and, in my opinion, he was a worthless human damned being. The fact that I had to work for him later pissed me off more than anything else in my life, and even worse, that prick had kids, so his spawn would live on.

I had to go back to Washington and defend my existence and that of the B-29 program. Well, we arrived, I saw Helen and Janie, and then we gave the briefing, and the Joint Chiefs approved an invasion plan for the home islands. I was in there for what seemed forever, asked about the most stupid shit.

I will give you an example: I was asked if the cost of incendiary bombs versus fragmentation bombs was justified by the targets I hit and the resulting damage.

I responded that, yes, it was justified, because fragmentation blew things apart which could be reassembled, such as brick buildings. Fire burns everything, and that has to be completely rebuilt, but it also forces the populations to flee due to the fires that raged around the target areas. It also impeded the enemy's ability to rebuild war industry until the fires were put out. I also added that returning to a target on another night that was still burning enhanced our target visibility.

I reported on the missions and BDA against Japanese cities and industry, showing those industries that were totally destroyed, partially destroyed, and the percentage of damage. I also pointed out what the Japs could not make anymore, what they would not be able to make for a long time, and what was still being made but at a much-reduced rate of production. The subject of civilians came up again, and I was asked if I was targeting civilian population centers.

I said, "Absolutely not. I am targeting industrial sites and the surrounding complexes that support their function." That means I was bombing the living shit out of the workers' homes nearby, following the Harris model, but as they were near the target, and fires tend to spread out, whereas fragmentation is blast specific, shit happened. I could not be accused of bombing civilians if frag was not used. I cannot control fires and high winds.

I was not really sure what Strange had written that could contradict the facts as they were presented, and that meeting seemed to pacify the headhunters. I felt that I had just wasted a week out of my life that I would never get back. After I was done, a user-friendly senator came up to me and said that it was the best damned briefing he had ever seen on the subject. He was certain that the B-29 program would be continued. I was then handed a message from one of the White House aides who was present at that briefing. I put it in my pocket. I was at the house when I reached for my lighter to light a cigar and found that paper. I had forgotten all about it. I took it out and read it.

———

The note told me that as I was getting ready to fly back, I had a request to meet with Major General Leslie Groves.[51] Groves was a stand-up guy, and he was a construction engineer, and we saw eye to eye on everything. He was in charge of the Manhattan Project, which I was sort of aware of, but no great details at that time. Groves informed me of everything that he could. We had a nice talk, and he told me that I would be getting the first bomb around July, courtesy of the navy, and another not much later.

Well, I still did not have all the facts as to what these bombs could do, but I had a pretty good idea. He told me that the bombs would destroy anything within a one-mile radius of the blast zone, and create winds greater than hurricane force, and burn everything manmade and natural to a crisp. Now he had my attention. I was also under orders, should the president dictate, that each bomb was to be used at targets to be determined later. I also learned that we had only two bombs in the inventory.

I then climbed back into the B-29, and we headed back to the Marianas. I knew I was going to drop those bastards if Hirohito did not give up, and I knew in my gut that would not happen. I then thought about the shit we may get if we did drop the bombs. I knew my ass was in the clear if I dropped a couple of atomic bombs: those orders would come from the president himself, down to me. I would just be following orders, and we did warn them before they were dropped. I know in my heart that if we had those bastards before D-day, we would have dropped them on German targets. I know it for a fact. I would have flown the bomber myself if it meant saving Allied lives.

I saw the casualty estimates for the invasion of the Japanese home islands, and I knew sure as pig shit that there was no way in hell Truman was going to absorb a half million killed and another million American—and maybe even more Allied—casualties, when he could just drop a few bombs. If the American public ever knew that we had these weapons, let alone our Allies, and he did not use them to save American lives, there would have been a public lynching. And I am not using a fucking metaphor, either.

And you have to remember: the closer the land and naval forces got to Japan proper, the stiffer the enemy resistance became. Saipan, Iwo Jima, Okinawa—each was worse than the last one. The suicide charges grew more fierce, and fewer Jap soldiers were being taken alive. There was no doubt that these impediments would be increased exponentially once we hit the home islands. Those fanatical bastards were willing to die and take everyone else with them.

I respect the warrior code, and I was willing to kill all of them and assist them with their mission of dying for the emperor. I just did not see any need to join them in the process.

I think Truman realized that if he did not do it, he would never be able to look into the faces of the family of a dead American fighting man who landed in Japan and died. He was also a political animal, and public sentiment would not be on his side if he did not do it. In my opinion, it would have been a criminal act not to have dropped the bombs.

The first bomb arrived on Tinian when the USS *Indianapolis* docked. Very few people on that island knew what was on board, and I was one of them [who knew everything]. They off-loaded the bomb, which was crated, and then they took it to the staging locations. I was told that the fuse was kept separate. What happened later to that ship horrified me, and I always felt a great amount of sorrow for those men. I really did not learn the full details until maybe the 1960s. I do not think it was the navy's best moment.[52]

On August 2, 1945, I flew to Tinian and spoke with Tibbets and briefed his unit, including the target priorities. Priority one was Hiroshima, critical as Japanese army headquarters. Then we had several options, like Yokohama, which was a naval base and critical port; we had Kokura, which had war-making industry, like aircraft and subs or some shit, and other locations. The last target was Nagasaki, which produced ships and engines and such, if memory serves. Their launch date was August 6, weather permitting.

Paul took off, and the rest is history. I saw the postdrop imagery, and I was impressed with the effectiveness. That was the uranium bomb, at fifteen kilotons. But we still did regular bombing missions even beyond August 9, when Chuck Sweeney dropped Fat Man, the plutonium bomb. The next day, we flew conventional bomb missions, hitting Tokyo again. On August 14 I sent a massive [752 bombers] force to hit shit, and they returned to hear the news that the war was over. Truman ordered all of us to stand down. The next day, on the fifteenth, Japan announced its surrender. But the Russians had just declared war on Japan also, and the thought of those bastards running the country probably helped them make that decision.

I flew to Yokohama to attend the formal surrender ceremony. I met Mac [MacArthur] and the other leaders on the USS *Missouri*, and the Japs arrived in formal wear, looking pretty dejected. Once the formalities were over, almost the entire B-29 force in the theater and other aircraft flew overhead. I flew back to Guam after an aerial tour of the major cities we had hit. It was truly a destroyed country. Then I took a B-29 in a three-ship formation back stateside to Washington, DC. I reported to General Carl Spaatz. I received my orders back to Wright Field. I was going back home with the family.

We had just arrived when shit changed again, and I was then reassigned. I was appointed as commander of the Army Air Forces Research and Development program in October 1945. I had to go back to Washington. I liked the idea of that assignment from a technical point of view, but I hated Washington and the bureaucracy like nothing else.

I realized that a major part of my job was speaking to both houses of Congress, getting appropriations, explaining the need for funding, justifying past expenditures, and answering questions on current and planned programs in the future. Then there was the big fight over creating a separate air force, which the navy opposed—all that shit. I was more focused on the future. I knew that nuclear weapons would play a major role in any future defense planning.

Things with the Russians were getting tense, so I was sent back to

Europe. But I had been recommended by Spaatz, who was now chief of the US Air Force, and I was promoted to lieutenant general on January 26, 1948. That day, Doolittle called me to congratulate me, and I received a few boxes of Cuban cigars from several people, as they knew those were my weakness. I had about eleven boxes stacked up in my office, and I placed them in a closet. I had a nice, nearly one-hundred-year-old bottle of Kentucky bourbon that was delivered from Hap Arnold.

I got to meet and know many of the Germans we brought back. My department was in charge of Operation Paperclip, and we managed to get the best and brightest scientists Hitler had—or at least we hoped, because Uncle Joe Stalin had forcibly taken many to Moscow.[53] The result of both our efforts and the Russians' was that we both had space programs. They beat us by putting the first satellite [Sputnik] and man [Yuri Gagarin] in space. We caught up and landed on the moon, the only nation to do so, and many times. Hell, we have a space shuttle now, so screw Russia.

I spoke with Wernher von Braun in 1963 or so, and he gave me a signed copy of his book, and I read it. Later, we chatted and I asked him about the Nazi Party, Hitler, and how he felt about the war. He was very candid, and he said to me, "General, you must understand, that in this country you can openly criticize your president, your government, and have no worries about retaliation. In Germany at that time, just the accusation that you had those thoughts could place you in a concentration camp."

I asked him about using the slave labor, and if he knew it. "Yes, of course we knew. But I was of the belief that if I had men working, they were not being executed, and Albert Speer felt the same way.[54] If we had work for them, they lived, and I did my best for them." Well, maybe so. At least he was working for us now.

We were the most successful, and as we learned, we had a much better safety record. We had astronauts, they had cosmonauts—or "cosmonuts," as I called them. The Russians killed a lot more of their people in their space program than we did. The difference between us and the Russians was that we openly advertised our space program and had the media all prepared to cover each launch, and our astronauts held open press meetings. The Russians never said a word until their mission was over, and they only advertised their successes, never their failures. When we had a disaster, everyone knew about it.

I became intimately involved with the expanding atomic program, and I actually went to the Bikini Atoll tests. I was a strong supporter of further testing and building more bombs, bigger bombs, and better delivery systems as a deterrent. You see, we were the only nuclear power on earth at the time, so we had the upper hand. Then we found out later, long after Stalin detonated his first atomic weapon in August 1949, about the spies within our atomic program.

Those are the bastards, like the fucking [Julius and Ethel] Rosenbergs, who I would really have liked to lock into a dark room and carry a baseball bat in for a little close-up interrogation.[55] We had the upper hand in atomic weapons, we controlled the balance of power, and we could dictate terms to those fucking Communists, and they would have had to sit in shit and swallow it. Then these pricks give up our secrets, let Stalin get the bomb, and destroy the possibility of a true world-peace-through-superior-firepower option that I thought we enjoyed. I am glad they fried their asses.

I proposed that the air force take charge of the atomic weapons program and develop weapons for long-range delivery, and Ira Eaker supported me. At that time, we were still part of the army, but that shit was about to change. When the air force became a separate branch of the military in 1947, that really opened up a lot of doors that would have remained closed for the air services, I can tell you. This allowed me to take over as USAFE [United States Air Forces in Europe] command in October the following year. This was really the genesis of NATO as a visible response or deterrent to the Warsaw Pact.

Another drastic change was that the old War Department was now the Department of Defense, and we now had four branches of the military: Army, Navy, Marine Corps, and Air Force—although, technically, the marines were still under the Department of the Navy. I wondered if the air force would be under the Department of the Army. Truman signed it into action, so we had our own branch. That was critical for expansion and reorganization. It also gave me more operational freedom to do what I needed to get done.

This assignment gave me my first taste of just how much a pain in the ass the Communists were going to be. They had sealed off West Berlin from the rest of West Germany. Remember that they divided the country after the war between East and West. This was because the French, British, and US had our various zones of occupation, while the Russians had the eastern part of the country. I guess they wanted to make the point that they were in charge, but with my position and rank, I decided to show some force myself.

We started the Berlin airlift in June 1948. The population was being starved out. Stalin wanted to make it a fucking point to stick his finger in our eye, just to see how far he could push us. Well, I knew that we had the upper hand at that time, and I thought that we should just Fat Man and Little Boy the shit out of Leningrad, Moscow, Volgograd, and shit like that. What were the Commies going to do? Sure, they had a numerical advantage in ground forces, but we had deployable nukes, and they did not have any at that time.

One thing I learned by being back in Europe, and with my access to the data on the new air force and our assets, one thing was really clear: we were too understrength and too scattered to have any real response to any serious threats anywhere in the world, and Europe was the hot spot. We did not have the aircraft or manpower to fulfill our obligations. This became even more evident when I was later appointed to run Strategic Air Command. I knew at that point we had no choice but to stockpile as many nukes as we could as a deterrent. The Communists had us outnumbered at every turn in the air and on the ground. Hell, even their navy was expanding at a rate we could not believe. I guess having a government that does not have civilian political oversight on military spending was a good thing for them.

I was told by General Lucius Clay that we had to break the Russian road blockade of West Berlin. We had the right of passage to travel through East Germany to West Berlin, but now they were making it impossible to get food and other supplies in. Coal was a big deal because that was how they heated their homes. I developed the transport flights to deliver all the required items listed. We did airdrops and also landed planes at Tempelhof and Gatow Airports, and the Russians did not stop any of that. The airlift was a great success for many reasons, but mainly it showed Stalin that we were not going to back down.

During all of this, I was officially appointed as commander of Strategic Air Command in October 1948, probably as a result of the airlift, which was a great success militarily but even more so politically. It pretty much told the Germans and the rest of free Europe that we were there to help and protect them; that all was forgiven and that we now had a common enemy. Never underestimate the value of good PR. We called it hearts and minds.

We called this Operation Vittles, and because of the enormity of the mission, we had to drag every type of aircraft into the game, from the States and all over Europe, and I did not have the logistics on the ground to support the operation. I gave the order to hire Germans who were out of work. Many were former mechanics anyway, and they could work on the engines. Many more were just laborers hired to load the aircraft. They knew what it was for, and they were more than willing to bust ass to help fellow Germans, especially because they really hated the damned Russians. Over the next year, it really paid off.

I was sent back stateside before the airlift was over, but I kept thinking about what we had done. That massive airlift operation and the rapid need to organize every aspect of it made me think of how to improve our own military transportation system. I can safely say that the operation laid the blueprint for what later became Military Airlift Command, which is the most crucial part of the military, in my opinion. You can't fight if you can't get men and materiel into a theater and then keep them resupplied.

SAC was a new organization created by Spaatz in '46, and General George Kenney was the first commander. Kenney was an older and somewhat revered figure, but he never took to the job. I just do not think that he had the mental acuity or stamina to tackle the job, and we had our confrontations even back when I took over the Twenty-First during the war. Kenny was just a dinosaur living in a space-age world, so I was his replacement. So, basically, there was a new sheriff in town.[56] Well, it was a paper-thin organization, and if the enemy knew it, they might have pushed the issue. I do think that we could have forced them out of Europe with conventional forces, but we will never know. Think about how that would have changed history.

SAC was established at Offutt Air Force Base in Nebraska, and I entered the scene. It was about as fucked up as a military organization could be, and I was not in the mood to listen to excuses. I just rattled a shitload of cages and kicked a lot of ass. I cleaned house and got rid of the dysfunctional dead weight and began getting people I knew who were solid, competent, and trustworthy. I created a new series of training manuals and appointed training officers to enforce these as required reading. One young officer told me the men called them "the LeMay Commandments" and "LeMay's Bibles." They covered everything from administration, to ordnance, logistics, and operational flying—you name it. I also required all officers and aircrews to be cross trained on every aspect of a mission, aircraft, or procedure.

Everything was a wreck, morale was almost nonexistent, and I had to get funding and build everything from the ground up: buildings, runways, and create a table of organization that was workable. Finally, after making the living conditions better, we started having better reenlistment rates. Before that, guys just wanted to get out and take their skills into the civilian market for more money, if they could get jobs. The biggest bitch from the men, which I understood, was the pay rate when compared to the civilian sector.

I also drafted a war plan with the atomic weapons as the basis for a total victory against the Russians. Drop over a hundred bombs on almost a hundred cities, like Japan, and that would adjust their attitude. And let them know what we planned to do if they fucked up. They already saw what I did to Japan. I am quite certain that they would not need a crystal ball to predict their immediate future. But as the years rolled by, they began to increase their own nuclear arsenal, and that forced a different plan of attack: you had to hit their launch sites and airfields first to neutralize their delivery capability.

Now it was a race to have bigger bombs and more of them, but also a varied array of delivery systems to increase lethality and survivability. That included creating a solid and workable air-refueling system, which we did. Boeing came through with the KC-135 [based upon the 707 airframe design], which served the country for many years and was a damned good tanker. That aircraft alone made SAC airborne operations more viable and gave me the ammo to tell Congress to give me the damned money.

I also wanted to test the Russian air defenses—see what they had, get their response time and from what bases they would send any interceptor assets. I sent flights over the Kamchatka peninsula doing photographic reconnaissance, and we did have some intercepts. One of my bombers got hit by a MiG, but they made it back. I was of the opinion that the Russian Bear's bark was far worse than its bite, which meant that we still needed to outspend and outbuild them as a deterrence.

———

It was during this period that my younger brother, Lloyd, came to work for me. He had chosen an air force career, and he was with me when he heard that North Korea had invaded the South, trapping our troops. I knew that this was not going to be a Berlin airlift situation. That became a United Nations mission; basically a World War III with the global implications.

There were not that many countries in the UN at that time [fifty-nine nations], and the majority [forty-eight] assisted against the Communists, and twenty nations supported with logistics or troops. People just do not realize how large in scope that war was. It was much larger than Vietnam and equaled both world wars politically. All these nations telling Stalin and Kim Il Idiot [North Korean dictator Kim Il Sung] "Fuck you."[57]

This was the scenario that really brought me into regular contact with Matt Ridgeway. I was asked to divert my treasured bombers to support the war effort there, but I did not want to relinquish my jet bombers, so I sent the B-29s. That was a tactical war, not a strategic war, and I needed strategic aircraft to be ready and on standby. No one knew if that bullshit in Europe would blow up even bigger. The greatest fear was that China would get involved and that Stalin might use the opportunity to invade the rest of Europe while everyone was distracted in Korea. I had to be ready.

Truman really could not handle MacArthur's hawkish attitude toward fighting the war. Now, MacArthur and I had serious differences of opinion in World War II, but I was on his side in Korea. I know that Truman feared expanding the fight with China and Russia. But they were already involved by supplying the North Koreans and allowing them to use their bases. In November 1950 the Chinese joined the fight. I could see no damned difference, as the Chinese sent thirty divisions [three hundred thousand men] over the border. MacArthur, to his credit, wanted to push beyond the thirty-eighth parallel just after securing Seoul and drive those bastards into the Yalu River on the Chinese border.

Truman said, "No," and he was not alone in his limited-conflict policy. I could not understand any of it, because we had no target or operations restrictions against Japan or Germany, other than cultural sites. I could not think of a single cultural site in North Korea that was worth a single American life. Not even the holiest Temple of Kimchee. In addition, our fighter pilots—and I spoke to Gabreski and [Frederick Corbin "Boots"] Blesse and many others about this—they could not even chase MiGs going into China for sanctuary. I know that a few of the guys did violate that order, but nothing official was ever done about it.

I received my fourth star in October 1951, so I was a full general at that time. I had a lot of experience where the decision-making was concerned. I proposed bombing every major city in North Korea like I did in Japan, but again the Truman response was not to do anything— just basically contain the Communists, not wipe them out. Korea was a wasted opportunity, in my opinion.

I assured Truman that I could hit every target in North Korea, bombing them until their rice bowls glowed and do it all within twenty-four hours. He just looked at me and said, "No, General, we will keep them at bay, just let this thing peter out. It cannot last much longer." Well, after he said that, all the respect I had for him went down the shitter. He was willing to let good men die to save a country that we had little strategic interest in at the time, all because he was afraid of escalation with China and Russia. He was running for re-election soon, after all.

Well, I still had SAC but was keeping an eye on the global picture. Korea was a sideshow for me. Truman and later Eisenhower both negotiated the peace treaty, which I thought was bullshit, because there was no way the North could sustain the pain and suffering that we could inflict from the air. I also doubted that the Russians would go into full war mode over North Korea, even if I vaporized China. Omar Bradley agreed with me, and he said that "Ike is a politician now, not a soldier."

Just like my plan for the Soviet Union, I would have bombed their air bases, industrial sites, ports, and military installations, and after the first few waves did not get the point across, a single tactical atomic drop would have definitely made the point. Sadly, [Major General] Orvil Anderson proposed the same method, and he was fired for his objective yet, in my opinion, very astute opinion.[58]

But after the Chinese came into it, that was what really got Mac-Arthur relieved of his command. He thought like me on that level: just destroy the fuckers and end this stupid shit. Truman was not of that mind-set, and neither was Ike. I think both feared that such a bold move would force the Russians into it. Stalin had just died, and there was a new Soviet leadership. We knew and understood how Stalin thought, but we did not have a lot of intel on the new head honcho, Nikita Khrushchev. He would become a prick, too.

The armistice was signed in June 1953, and the Cold War went back into a dormant stage until Kennedy came into office. In 1957 I was the air force vice chief of staff, and in 1961 I was sworn in as the chief of staff, so I was in charge at that time. Communist revolutions were erupting all over the globe. The biggest problem was Cuba. Fidel Castro overthrew the Fulgencio Batista government and allied himself to the Russians, and that shit was not sitting well with JFK or anyone else with a three-digit IQ, including me. Even Strange [McNamara] agreed that it was an intolerable situation. That was probably the most lucid moment his ass ever had.

Well, the Bay of Pigs situation blew up in our faces—and, no, I was not directly involved. The CIA decided to run that operation, and their intelligence was less than stellar. I was aware of the operation, and it was even considered that the air force provide air support—that was my suggestion—but if that happened, plausible deniability was out the window. This was black-bag shit, but I did let them know that I could nuke Havana in about three hours if necessary. Strange said that would be a bad idea, as we would probably kill Russians, so I did not get a very warm reception with that idea, and then I said, "Hell, I can hit Moscow, too." I think they thought I was joking. Well, as history showed, all of that was for nothing except that the Russians took those missiles out of Cuba.

Once SAC was complemented with missile silos in conjunction with air-deliverable and submarine-launched ICBMs [intercontinental ballistic missiles], I knew we had a solid defense network. The electronics war was an ever-steady, ongoing process. From scrambling, encoding, decoding, detection, jamming, whatever, that still goes on today and always will. During that period, we had a wide variety of aircraft, such as the B-36 Peacemaker, B-47 Stratojet, B-58 Hustler, and the B-52 Stratofortress—the air arsenal was pretty potent.

But the Russians were not sleeping through all of this. They developed their fighter program, such as the MiG-15, 17, 19, and 21 series of fighters, each with their various capabilities and limitations. Their SAM [surface-to-air missile] program was really developing at a pace. They were designed for fast high-altitude interception, and that was what took out Francis Gary Powers's U-2, and a lot of planes in Vietnam.[59] They are still used in many countries today.

I left SAC and reported to duty as air force vice chief of staff, which meant going back to Washington. I dreaded the concept, but I followed my orders.[60] My boss was Thomas D. White, and we knew each other from way back in the early years, even before Pearl Harbor. We were never friends, but we had a mutual respect for each other based upon our situation. We were just different people in the way we handled things. He was a negotiator, and I was a brawler. But he was dedicated to uniformed service. We had differences and discussions, but I never felt it was my place to contradict him publicly and seldom in private. I just gave him my thoughts, and I know that he appreciated that.

You have to understand that much of our global planning and doctrine was started after *Sputnik I* hit orbit [October 4, 1957], and you could feel the entire world shake, and the tremors in Washington and throughout the military were noticeable. When I heard about that, I wondered if we really got the good Germans after all. Then they threw a dog and then Yuri Gagarin into space. The American public thought, "We are screwed," and that our government fell asleep at the switch. I could only assume that our enemies also felt the same way, hence their getting bolder in their global reach.

I was talking to someone a month after *Sputnik*, and I said, "Well, I guess our Ivy League wonder boys fucked up again; the CIA never saw that coming." I did not make many friends with that comment, [Allen] Dulles [CIA director] among them, and I never gave a shit. I always felt that if you were wasting time trying to make friends, you were probably not doing your job. If you do a great job, you will make the friends that count. Dulles was not impressing me. Never did. His brother, John Foster Dulles, was another Ivy League asshole who really needed a day job, and I never really thought much of him, either.

Then when Powers was shot down in 1960, the shit really hit the fan for Dulles and the CIA. I met Powers after the event, and he was a good pilot, and he was flying the U-2 spy plane that Kelly Johnson had designed at his Skunk Works.[61] I think that incident, above all others, finally forced the idiots residing on Capitol Hill to realize that we needed faster strategic bombers and surveillance aircraft to go higher and faster than the SAMs. They had no problem pork-barrel spending for some fucking crayfish farm, or funding some third-world asshole's new swimming pool, but trying to get those shitheads to fund the military was like hoping a chicken laid gold eggs.

I met with and knew every American aircraft designer, and I especially knew and liked Kelly Johnson a lot. That was a genius and a great man all around. I was a supporter of the XB-70 Valkyrie program that North American was working on. It was a Mach 3 six-engine design and was supposed to be a high-speed, high-altitude bomber. It would also have been a great photographic reconnaissance aircraft as well. JFK and his acolytes were not impressed with the cost, and they did not see the need. Well, if their asses were getting trailed by SAMs or MiGs, they would have probably changed their minds. It never entered production.

But Johnson and Lockheed were working on what would later become the SR-71 Blackbird, an upgrade from the bomber version of the XB-70, which was the XB-71 [the original protoytype], and that was a real game changer when it came out. It was the fastest operational jet in history, flew at the highest altitudes—over eighty thousand feet sustained—and there was never one shot down by a SAM or interceptor. It screamed at well over Mach 3. The CIA used the shit out of it, and the intel images it brought back were invaluable. After the U-2 shootdown, the need for a better aircraft was evident. Kelly Johnson delivered it.

But there was a problem: the Blackbird program was expensive, developed from the A-12 program, and when it came out in 1966, it cost over $30 million per aircraft, and I wanted the air force to get a bunch of them.[62] The aircraft was so damned fast that by the time SAM sites had radar lock, it was only maybe a glimpse due to the unique fuselage design; the bird was usually out of range of the SAMs before they could be launched. That was lovely, and it was a dream come true. We never lost one to enemy action.

Thirty-two were built, and I know for a fact that the damned Russians and Chinese had strokes over that aircraft. Most of those missions are still classified, and may always be, and they should be. But there is not a place on planet earth where that aircraft has not saved lives and paid for itself by its valuable service, and it was government funded. Perhaps the best black-bag operation the CIA ever did was to go through several countries, running bogus international front companies, to get our hands on the titanium to build it. The titanium came from Russia—isn't that some shit? We used Russian material, to build an American spy plane, to spy on Russia. You can't make this shit up.

Well, the Ivy League got involved again when Strange McNamara, the bastard, decided we did not need it anymore—no more would be built—and then they destroyed the casts and dies so that none could ever be made again. He was still secretary of defense under Johnson, so he carried a lot of power. Too much power for a number cruncher from Ford Motor Company. He was out of his fucking depth, and he knew it. He deflected his stupidity by making what he thought were sound and earth-shattering decisions. He was a real asshole, and I wish I had been in the position to place his ass on a dangerous mission during World War II. There were always casualties, but he would not have been a loss. Thank God he was not in that office during World War II.

Strange just had to get his hand into more shit, so he was the clown who threw his weight into the F-111 Aardvark program. General Dynamics had the design, and Strange wanted an aircraft that was cost effective, meaning that every branch of service flying fighters and bombers could use it. Well, his royal hindquarters screwed up, because the F-111 could not be carrier based for the navy and Marine Corps. Sure, it was a good basic platform to be a supersonic nuclear bomber. But it had serious limitations where naval service was concerned.

I was in a briefing where the F-111 was going from being a single-seat fighter to the prospect of a longer two-seat fighter-bomber. I knew that it was not going to work for long-range strategic missions. The F-111 had some advantages and some disadvantages, but for the air force, it was fine. But in Strange's world, anything other than a one-service aircraft did not justify the money that could go into other programs. Just this year, 1986, it was the F-111s that gave Gadhafi in Libya a wake-up call, and that was a conventional long-range tactical mission.[63] That was due to the French being typical cowardly bastards and not allowing the overflight from England. Never go to war with the French if you can help it. Relying upon them is about as uncomfortable as having dinner with the Borgias.

Getting back to Cuba, our U-2 flights had proven that the Russians had their latest missiles in Cuba. SS-5s could fly two thousand miles, and Cuba was ninety miles south of Florida. That shit made everyone nervous, and I guess to some, my first-strike concept did not sound so crazy. Well, Ivy Leaguers decided to let the CIA plan one of the most fucked, hillbilly-bullshit black-bag operations in history. Few

plans in history can be labeled failures the moment they are conceived. It usually takes some amount of effort to fuck up, or maybe
just bad luck. But to plan for a failure, know it will be a failure, and
still execute it is beyond my comprehension.

The entire world was watching these events as Khrushchev, bold
as brass, lied to the world, lied to us, then was forced to remove those
missiles even after his famous speech where he banged his shoe on
the podium at the UN and also said, "We will bury you," to the as-
sembly of Western ambassadors in Poland in 1956. I really wanted to
get his address and send him a special package. I would have gladly
pissed in his vodka.

There was a lot of discussion after the reconnaissance photos re-
vealed SAM sites, ballistic missile launchers, and Cuban airfields
with the latest MiGs sitting on them. No matter how you looked at it,
and despite Castro's whining about having to defend himself against
the United States, the placement of Soviet offensive weaponry in our
hemisphere was not going to fly. I sat in on the mission planning, and
I agreed with an invasion of Cuba, followed by a thorough series of
conventional strategic saturation missions, followed up by tactical air
strikes for good measure. We also had the nuclear deterrent as a
backup, even with Russian ships in the region. Well, they agreed to
an invasion, but nothing that I would call textbook or even something sound in application.

I could not believe the amateur-hour shit that was going on with
regard to how JFK and his Ivy League clowns were handling that
bullshit. The Bay of Pigs fiasco was easy to see coming, because there
was to be no overt US air support—that was "too high profile." So, in
their wisdom, they figured that they would use other assets in the
region that were not connected to us. Then they planned on putting
those Cuban exiles on the beach, and with no air support, it was a

suicide mission. I was there when dickhead Dean Rusk [secretary of state] killed the air support. I felt like I was dreaming.

Who were these people? I'll bet you would find that if their son was going to hit that beach, their ass would have had air cover, and I offered it. I offered to bomb the living hell out of Cuba and turn Havana into a pile of rubble. At that point, I could see that there was not a breathing, living organism in that room who knew better, would have the balls to say it. But I did. The official story to cover JFK's ass was that he was fed bad intel and given bad military advice. Bullshit, I was there.

He was told what was needed, but his political career and image were more important than pragmatic military planning and mission execution. Besides, it was a CIA mission in the first place. The great tragedy was that we had naval carrier aircraft in the area that could have been on target in minutes and could have supported the mission. They were too fucking afraid of pissing off the Russians, in case any of them were hit. Jesus H. Christ. In the end, the Russians agreed to remove the missiles if we made concessions in Europe, and the deal was done. Both sides saved face, and there was no escalation of hostilities. Kennedy came out looking like a hero, and it overshadowed the Bay of Pigs issue.

As the air force chief of staff since 1961, I had a lot of say with regard to our policies and methods. I still answered to the civilian authorities, in particular the secretary of the air force, and we both answered to the secretary of defense—yes, once again, Strange. I could not get away from that guy.

I heard from one of my contacts that Strange once called me an arrogant prima donna. My response was, "I can accept that, but at least I earned that right leading men into combat. His ass just went to *Haavaaahd* [emphasizing *Harvard* in the Boston dialect, of course], learned to run a business, do math, and he never heard a shot fired in anger." My disdain for that bastard was well known, and McNamara wanted me gone. I knew it—even the secretary of the air force told me, but the presidents wanted me.

After Kennedy was killed, things changed in the White House. Hell, one of the admirals in the JCS came to me, and we were never friends, but he had similar issues with Strange. He told me one day in strict confidence in 1968: "If we could get McNamara into a car with bad brakes, we would all live easier." That should tell you something.

I found LBJ to be the consummate bastard politician, more wily perhaps than Kennedy, who was pretty black and white on most issues, but LBJ was a hawk in his heart but a dove politically when it suited him. So I played the game. I did my job. But Johnson could change his mind on something that he passionately believed in a split second and adopt the exact opposite position if it meant greater public support. Now, that is hypocrisy. I have been called many things and accused of a lot of shit, and I probably earned most of them, but being a hypocrite was not one of them. No one was confused about where I stood on any subject, which perhaps meant I was never destined for political office, although that opportunity did arise later.

Being a senior officer in a world where politicians can end your career over lunch meant that I was a blind man walking through a minefield. I often spoke to some of my peers about that, and they all agreed that we rarely had the best and brightest in positions of great power where military considerations were concerned. If we did go to war with these same people in positions of power, we were screwed. Well, we did.

I was there in 1964 when LBJ made a comment in passing. Congress had just passed the Anti-Poverty Act, which he signed into law, which was one of three parts of his Great Society program. He said,

"Well, we got it through, so now we will have the nigger vote forever, as long as they get their money." No shit, he said that. His other accomplishments were the Civil Rights Act and the Voting Rights Act—now, those I agreed with. Johnson was a fraud, two-faced, providing one face to the world as this great liberal father of compassion, when in reality he was just another egomaniac with delusions of political grandeur. He flowed with the political wind.

Then we had the Gulf of Tonkin Resolution that led to us getting involved in Vietnam. I was asked my opinion, and I was blunt as hell. I said to Rusk, McNamara, and Johnson, "If you commit us to this, you had better have a plan to win it, and then a plan to get the hell out of it. That Korean War armistice shit will not fly this time." I was met with nods and grunts, as if they understood what I said. Their later actions proved they did not give a shit what I thought.

Not long after, LBJ created his Wise Men council, made up of retired generals and admirals, nearly all of them combat veterans. To his credit, LBJ, like Kennedy, wanted to hear various opinions, and he listened. Unlike Kennedy, LBJ's council of elders was full of flag-rank officers. JFK had almost twenty advisors, and only four wore a uniform. He wanted his Ivy League Praetorian Guard to think for him, regardless of their qualifications.

Well, JFK got us into the shadow war of what would become Vietnam, and LBJ threw our weight into it, but he did it incrementally. I advised against the slow escalation method. I told him, "We need to get in, hit hard, hit often with great local force, and then get the hell out." All we had to do was arm the South Vietnamese military, unfuck their government, and provide them with tactical, strategic, and logistical air support to the ARVN [Army of the Republic of Vietnam]. Well, as if no great surprise, Strange and the others, including some of the Wise Men, decided otherwise.

LBJ then went down a path of mutually assured self-destruction for himself and the country. We had a meeting, and Maxwell Taylor was the chair of JCS, and we had a discussion on Vietnam: plans, procedures, policies, and methods. Nothing was decided that I thought made sense. In general, whenever I walked into a room full of LBJ acolytes, I could probably see my breath—that was how cold my reception was by those assholes. I kind of liked it, because they knew that if I were asked a question, chances were, I would make them very uncomfortable with my responses. I had finally had enough, and I retired in 1965.

I stopped by the White House, where Johnson presented me with the Distinguished Service Medal, and then I went to Andrews Air Force Base for the formal retirement ceremony. The entire LBJ administration was there, except Strange, I was told. Well, not that I cared. I was willing to go home and carry the papers with me and skip the crowd. Helen and I took the family and moved here to California, where I had some job interests. I wanted to keep busy.

I wrote the book *Mission with LeMay: My Story* because I wanted to throw some reality into the history. Later, I wrote the book *America Is in Danger*, which I hoped would be a wake-up call due to what the hell was being done in Vietnam from a political standpoint. I could never understand how you could tell air force pilots not to hit enemy airfields and SAM sites that were responsible for killing Americans. That bullshit pissed me off to no end. I spoke to Olds about it a few times. He was even more pissed off than I was because it was his men flying into harm's way and getting shot down.

Robin Olds is a real warrior, one of those poster boys for air force recruiting. He was a living legend, really, like Gabreski, Yeager, and other fighter pilots. I was stunned that they made him a flag officer, because he was very outspoken and had a tendency to be creative when interpreting his orders. I just assumed they would force him into retirement as a colonel. He pissed a lot of people off. We had that in common, so as Robin would say, "Fuck them in the ass sideways."

General William Westmoreland was a competent leader, in my opinion, but he suffered from political paralysis. He was not going to rock the boat unnecessarily if a request was denied, but he usually got what he wanted. He was handicapped by the politicians. Some of the other flag officers I recall were all interesting people.

Marine general Lewis Walt was one of those guys I could really relate to. He was a killer: just get in there, kill, secure, then get the hell out. He was a no-nonsense ground commander, and I really liked him. Even more important, I respected him. He was a warrior who damned near made Patton look like an ROTC dropout.

He and I had a few drinks one evening in DC, and we were discussing Vietnam, World War II, Korea—that sort of shit. After a few bourbons, I asked him what he would have thought if I had the approval to drop a nuke or two on North Korea to end that shit, like in Japan. He said, "You have always carried your balls in a wheelbarrow, but for that shit, you would have needed a truck. The good thing is, I would have offered to drive the damned thing and been right there with you." What a guy.

I was always fascinated by communications, and I got heavily involved in Ham radio, and I have my own setup. My experience in the military taught me the value of secure and reliable communications. Once I realized that single sideband [SSB] technology was better than our widely used amplitude modulation radio frequencies, which we used for SAC aircraft operating over long distances, I made that the standard in 1957, and I was proud of that. It really expanded our communications capabilities. Of course, we were always concerned about communications security, and the creation of scramblers, coders, and decoders became the standard for all of the military.

I also liked to build things. I built race cars and all kinds of things like that, and that often makes Helen probably want me to take up another hobby. I always wanted to be busy.

Too many politicians fuck up the country with their degrees and pedigrees, and the sad part is that we get a lot of people making life-and-death decisions who have never faced that situation themselves. Even more important, I ask you to name any person sitting in Congress who had a son serve in combat, let alone lost one. One thing that we do have to some degree now are quite a few combat veterans from World War II, Korea, and now some from Vietnam.

Some of these men understand the proportionality required when supporting military funding and the political decisions to be made in times of conflict. They lived it. I do not always agree with these men, but I do respect them, such as Daniel Inouye, Bob Dole, John Glenn, and even Strom Thurmond. As I said, I do not always agree with them, but I do respect the fact that they are vets—hell, Inouye earned the Medal of Honor.

Any Ivy League or military academy asshole can issue orders and take the credit. What matters is when you place your own ass on the line, and your men know that you are not some armchair commander asking them to risk death while you enjoy the good life. Morale is everything, and you do not build it by typing out goddamned reports and having cocktail parties.

Strange, LBJ, and that ilk were like that. Those motherfuckers were whores paid to screw the public, and they really ass fucked the American fighting man in Vietnam. And you know what? They never lost one night's sleep over it. They never had their ass in danger, and they never waited for the knock on the door telling them that their son was killed, all because some asshole with an Ivy League degree and a champagne glass in his hand decided that their boy did not need the money or weapons or even the fucking political support to stay alive.

Regarding politicians and military leaders: You know the difference between a politician and a statesman? Here is the LeMay definition: a politician is a high-profile hooker looking for money to fund a campaign so that he can be in position to be owned by a political party, doing their bidding like a slave. Johnson fit that category. A statesman is a politician whose allegiance is only to their nation, and who, despite the feelings of others, does what he believes in his gut is in the best interest of his country, politics be damned. That even means doing something that may cost him his career, but he takes the moral high ground as he sees it, to do what must be done. That was Churchill. That's the difference. Ronald Reagan is a statesman, and make a note of it—we may not have any more in the future. They are a damned dying breed.

That also applies to military commanders. You can have a charismatic, friendly, and amiable type of leader, but that is a difficult position to hold when you also have to maintain discipline. It can be done, but it is hard. Then there is the hard-ass, no-holds-barred, get-it-fucking-done leader who pushes his men to the limit and expects ever-better results afterward. The easygoing leader may be liked more by his men, but the hard-ass will sure as shit have their attention, and if he shares the dangers with them, he will have their respect. Respect is everything.

MacArthur was imperialistic, almost self-godlike, and he always remained aloof from his soldiers. You were never going to see old Mac sitting in the damned mud, swatting flies and mosquitoes, eating rancid chow in a pouring tropical rain. Oh no. His ass was in a nice house or office with water buffalo steaks and red wine. I have to say that he was just about the only senior flag officer I can say that about, from personal experience. All the others I have mentioned shared the misery, even Patton. He lived well per his rank, but he gave up his jeep to send wounded men back to an aid station in Sicily and walked on foot as the Germans shot at his men.

Bradley was always with the men when he could be. Same with Gavin, Ridgeway, Taylor, Walt, Smith, and the others. Even Stillwell, as much as I disliked that bastard for fucking with me, he shared the hardships and dangers with his men, and his troops loved him for it. That is enough for me to set my past feelings aside. Stillwell did what he thought he had to do, I just disagreed. They were all real leaders, and they had the respect of their men. MacArthur demanded respect, and it is not the same thing as earning it.

That's where the politicians in general continuously fail us all. They will issue their damned edicts, pass stupid-ass laws, and expect miracles while not providing resources, and then bitch and moan when shit comes up short due to their personal interference and incompetence. LBJ was the biggest political whore I ever knew; he would sell his own family out to secure votes. I learned that shit quickly. His entire image of this great savior for black America was all a fraud. He did not give a shit about black America, or anyone in America, unless they voted for him.

The only reason JFK chose him as a running mate was to get the southern votes. He thought that with Johnson's being a Texan, all the rednecks would vote for him [JFK] and not see him as a moral anti–Jim Crow Yankee carpetbagger. We all know that if it had not been for his father, Joseph, buying votes in Chicago and paying off and promising the Mob great legal leniency and turning a blind eye to their criminal shit, there would have never been a Kennedy Camelot, let alone a Lyndon Lounge.

By the way, and this is no shit: during the Cuban missile crisis [actually, during the Russian missile buildup around July and August],

Kennedy had to be reached by phone later at night because we had the U-2 pictures [later] proving that Soviet SAMs were in Cuba along with ships off-loading MiG fighters. There was no answer on his phone, but somehow they managed to track him through the Secret Service detail to a hotel, where he was fucking this chick who was married to a friend of his. Yes, and I know all about Marilyn Monroe and the forty others, including Phyllis McGuire.[64]

Sam Giancana would not have taken well to Kennedy screwing two of his women, especially McGuire. One Secret Service agent who was a former air force type, who lost a brother in Korea, told me that he knew personally that brother Bobby shared both women with his older brother. Once he was aware of a threesome with Marilyn. Some moral compasses they had. People wonder about the assassination of JFK, I say look to the Mob, because he no sooner took the oath of office than his brother began getting federal indictments against the very men who stole and bought votes for him. I am sure Sam Giancana was less than amused about Marilyn, Phyllis, and the Kennedy brothers also.[65]

I caught a lot of shit for being a part of George Wallace's election bid in 1968. I was reserved because of his previous position on race relations, and his advocacy of Jim Crow, and his being a Democrat segregationist. Nixon disappointed me, as he was no conservative. Wallace was a former air force enlisted man who flew in bombers against Japan during the war, and Nixon was a former naval officer. Both had the military credentials, but Wallace ran as an independent, not a Democrat. Nixon ran as a Republican who proved to be no conservative.

As far as what I am most proud of, besides leading men into combat, I guess it would be reorganizing SAC and taking care of our veterans and their families, especially widows. They really never get a lot of support, and I always thought about those women after their husbands died under my command.

I remember that one sergeant I saw who lived long enough to get back to our base but then died in the hospital. No one will ever understand what it feels like to watch a wounded man die, slowly, and in great pain, and you are the last person to hear his dying request, and he knew he was going to die. I promised that I would keep my word, and I did, because that shit is sacred to me. [Authors' note: LeMay cried and broke down during this part of the interview, then apologized.]

The last thing he asked me was to see that someone make sure his wife and son were cared for. That never left me. Ever. I had to write the letter to her. I would say writing the letters was the toughest part. I knew commanders who had their clerks type up generic form letters, then they would sign them. I found that disgusting and dishonoring the men who died. Their families deserved better. They were worthless shits as far as I was concerned. So, I focused upon that.[66]

Regarding our future, I really think that we as a nation need to select our involvements overseas with far more care than we did in Vietnam. Before we commit to action, the following questions should be asked, and serious criteria should be met: Is it in our national and geopolitical interests? What are our obligations? Are we going in to win or just be a presence? If we are in, are we prepared militarily and politically to commit all of our will and resources to winning? If those can be answered, then we will know what to do.

ACKNOWLEDGMENTS

This book came to life only due to the willingness and generosity of the men who provided their stories. I was not the first to interview them, nor in many cases the last. I began the interviews that form the first-person narratives of *Over the Reich* when I was still a teenager, but I hoped at some point in the future to create a series of books based on the words of those from many nations, both Allied and Axis, who saw combat in World War II. Over the years, I interviewed all of the subjects in this book multiple times, in person and by phone and email. The first, with Jimmy Doolittle, took place in April 1986; the last, with Bob Johnson, in July 1998. Throughout, I have been fortunate to have enjoyed the encouragement, aid, and goodwill of a great many people without whom this book would never have been completed in its present form.

The following persons were chief among many who assisted in making this book the very best it could be. I am grateful above all to Colonel Robert S. Johnson, Brigadier General Robin Olds, Colonel Edward R. "Buddy" Haydon, General Curtis E. LeMay, and General James H. Doolittle, all now deceased, for their trust and belief in me, for the seriousness with which all of them took the questions of a very ambitious young interviewer, and the way that several took me under their wings and became mentors—and even friends.

Other mentors and friends to whom I owe a debt of gratitude are the late historians Colonel Walter Boyne, Colonel Raymond F. Toliver, and Colonel Carroll V. Glines. Thanks also to friends and historians Barrett Tillman, Jon Guttman, Jay Stout, Bruce Henderson, and my good buddies and bestselling authors Adam Makos and Dr. Bryan Mark Rigg, who have offered practical help and collegial support along the years, and specifically while I completed the manuscript for the present volume.

A special mention goes to Robin Olds's daughter, the historian and author Christina Olds. She is a remarkable lady and a passionate advocate for the stories of the men who flew for our nation when duty called. Her book with her father and coauthor Ed Rasimus, *Fighter Pilot: The Memoirs of Legendary Ace Robin Olds,* clarified many things that Robin mentioned in his interviews, allowing me to make sense of many pages of notes and put names to persons I would otherwise have been obliged to neglect.

Once again, Anne-Marie Lewis has helped me put this book (one of many) together, reviewing material to simplify that which I make entirely too academic on occasion.

Finally, I would like to thank my agent, Dr. Gayle Wurst of Princeton International Agency for the Arts, for her stalwart support over many years and her sage advice on publishing this, our seventh book; and thanks to my editor, Brent Howard, and his team at Dutton, who have done so much to make an old dream come true.

This book is dedicated to our brave World War II veterans who are still alive, and to those who lie under the ground, including my grandfather and many other relatives. I just wish more people knew and appreciated what they did to save a world on fire.

Colin D. Heaton
New Bern, North Carolina

APPENDIX 1

Fig. 1 Eighth Air Force Heavy Bomber Aircraft Losses in the ETO[1]

BOMB GROUP	STATION	BOMBER TYPE	MISSIONS FLOWN	LOSSES
34th	Mendlesham	B-17	170	34
44th	Shipdham	B-24	343	153
91st	Bassingbourn	B-17	340	197
92nd	Podington	B-17	308	154
93rd	Hardwick	B-24	396	100
94th	Bury St. Edmunds	B-17	324	153
95th	Horham	B-17	320	157
96th	Snetterton Heath	B-17	321	189
100th	Thorpe Abbots	B-17	306	177
303rd	Molesworth	B-17	364	165
305th	Chelveston	B-17	337	154
306th	Thurleigh	B-17	342	171
351st	Polebrook	B-17	311	124
379th	Kimbolton	B-17	330	141
381st	Ridgewell	B-17	296	131
384th	Grafton Underwood	B-17	314	159
385th	Great Ashfield	B-17	296	129
388th	Knettishall	B-17	306	142
389th	Hethel	B-24	321	116
390th	Framlingham	B-17	300	144
392nd	Wendling	B-24	285	127
398th	Nuthampstead	B-17	195	58
401st	Deenethorpe	B-17	256	95
445th	Tibenham	B-24	282	95
446th	Bungay	B-24	273	58
447th	Rattlesden	B-17	257	97
448th	Seething	B-24	262	101

BOMB GROUP	STATION	BOMBER TYPE	MISSIONS FLOWN	LOSSES
452nd	Deopham Green	B-17	250	110
453rd	Old Buckenham	B-24	259	58
457th	Glatton	B-17	237	83
458th	Horsham Saint Faith	B-24	240	47
466th	Attlebridge	B-24	232	47
467th	Rackheath	B-24	212	29
486th	Sudbury	B-17	188	33
487th	Lavenham	B-17	185	48
489th	Halesworth	B-24	106	29
490th	Eye	B-17	158	40
491st	Metfield	B-24	187	47
492nd	North Pickenham	B-24	64	12
493rd	Deebach	B-17	158	41
Total			10,631	4,145

APPENDIX 2

Fig. 2 Eighth Air Force Heaviest Mission Losses in the ETO[1]

DATE	MISSION NUMBER	TARGET	DISPATCHED	ABORT	CROSSED COAST	LOST EN ROUTE	BOMBED	TOTAL LOST	CAT E	DAMAGED
17-AUG-43	84	Schweinfurt	230	21	209	21	188	36	3	118
17-AUG-43	84	Regensburg	146	5	141	14	127	24	1	50
17-AUG-43 TOTAL			**376**	**26**	**350**	**35**	**315**	**60**	**4**	**168**
6-SEP-43	91	Stuttgart (Various targets)	181	10	171	20	151	27	9	47
6-SEP-43	91	Stuttgart (Fw Factory)	157	28	129	18	111	18	1	69
6-SEP-43	91	B-24s (Diversion)	69	9	60	0	60	0	0	0
6-SEP-43 TOTAL			**407**	**47**	**360**	**38**	**322**	**45**	**10**	**116**
4-OCT-43	108	Wiesbaden / Frankfurt	104	7	97	0	97	5	0	45
4-OCT-43	108	Frankfurt	51	14	37	0	37	3	0	35
4-OCT-43	108	Saarlautern	115	10	105	0	105	4	4	19
4-OCT-43	108	Sarreguemines	53	6	47	0	47	0	0	2
4-OCT-43	108	Diversion (B-24s)	38	0	38	0	38	4	0	19
4-OCT-43 TOTAL			**361**	**37**	**324**	**0**	**324**	**16**	**4**	**120**
8-OCT-43	111	Bremen	118	13	105	0	105	9	0	61
8-OCT-43	111	Bremen	56	3	53	0	53	4	0	44
8-OCT-43	111	Vegesack (B-24s)	55	12	43	0	43	3	0	21
8-OCT-43	111	Bremen	170	14	156	0	156	14	2	110
8-OCT-43 TOTAL			**399**	**42**	**357**	**0**	**357**	**30**	**2**	**236**
9-OCT-43	113	Anklam	115	9	106	0	106	18	1	51
9-OCT-43	113	Marienberg	100	4	96	0	96	2	0	13
9-OCT-43	113	Gdynia	112	3	109	0	109	6	1	62

DATE	MISSION NUMBER	TARGET	DISPATCHED	ABORT	CROSSED COAST	LOST EN ROUTE	BOMBED	TOTAL LOST	CAT E	DAM*
9-OCT-43 TOTAL			**327**	**16**	**311**	**0**	**311**	**26**	**2**	**126**
10-OCT-43	114	Münster	274	38	236	0	236	30	3	102
10-OCT-43 TOTAL			**274**	**38**	**236**	**0**	**236**	**30**	**3**	**102**
14-OCT-43	115	Schweinfurt	291	37	254	32	222	60	7	138
14-OCT-43	115	Schweinfurt (B-24s Diversion)	60	31	0	0	0	0	0	0
14-OCT-43 TOTAL			**351**	**68**	**254**	**32**	**222**	**60**	**7**	**138**
11-JAN-44	182	Oschersleben	177		177	0	159	34	2	83
11-JAN-44	182	Halberstadt	114		114	0	107	8	1	42
11-JAN-44	182	Brunswick (Plus 1 B-24 tagalong)	234		234	0	219	16	1	47
11-JAN-44	182	Brunswick (B-24s)	138	70	68	2	66	2	1	7
11-JAN-44 TOTAL			**663**	**70**	**593**	**2**	**551**	**60**	**5**	**179**
6-MAR-44	250	Berlin	504		504	0	474	35	3	121
6-MAR-44	250	Berlin	226	12	226	0	198	16	1	54
6-MAR-44 TOTAL			**730**	**0**	**0**	**0**	**672**	**51**	**4**	**175**
GRAND TOTAL			**3,888**	**344**	**2,785**	**107**	**3,310**	**378**	**41**	**1,360**

The October 4, 1943, mission shows a deep France/shallow Germany mission and typical losses—just prior to the week the Eighth tried to hit lots of Luftwaffe production facilities ending in second Schweinfurt.

Category E is damaged beyond economical repair—these a/c were salvaged for parts only.

As a comparison, here are the fighter losses for the second Berlin raid (one group of B-17s and one squadron of P-38s actually got there on March 3 and bombed; the rest turned back due to weather.)

DATE	MISSION NUMBER	TARGET	DISPATCHED	ABORT	CROSSED COAST	LOST EN ROUTE	BOMBED	TOTAL LOST	CAT E	DAMAGED
6-MAR-44	250	Berlin (Fighters)	801	0	0	0	0	11	3	6

The Germans ignored the escorting fighters and just went after the bombers (actually a very bad tactic). The US fighters claimed 82-8-33: shot down, probable, damaged in the air, plus 1 destroyed on the ground and 12 damaged.

DATE	MISSION NUMBER	TARGET	DISPATCHED	ABORT	CROSSED COAST	LOST EN ROUTE	BOMBED	TOTAL LOST	CAT E	DAMAGED
1-AUG-43	0	Ploesti, Romania	179	2	175	1	174	55	2	0

SELECTED BIBLIOGRAPHY

Doolittle, James H., and Carroll V. Glines. *I Could Never Be So Lucky Again: An Autobiography of James H. "Jimmy" Doolittle.* Atglen, PA: Schiffer Military History, 1997.

Ethell, Jeffrey, and Alfred Price. *Target Berlin, Mission 250: 6 March 1944.* London: Jane's, 1981.

Gabreski, Francis S., and Carl Molesworth. *Gabby: A Fighter Pilot's Life.* New York: Bantam Doubleday Dell, 1991.

Hammel, Eric. *Air War Europa: America's Air War Against Germany in Europe and North Africa 1942–1945.* Pacifica, CA: Pacifica Press, 1994.

Heaton, Colin D. *Occupation and Insurgency: A Selective Examination of The Hague and Geneva Conventions on the Eastern Front, 1939–1945.* Algora, 2008.

Heaton, Colin D., and Anne-Marie Lewis. *The German Aces Speak: World War II Through the Eyes of Four of the Luftwaffe's Most Important Commanders.* Minneapolis: Zenith Press, 2011.

———. *The German Aces Speak II: World War II Through the Eyes of Four More of the Luftwaffe's Most Important Commanders.* Minneapolis: Zenith Press, 2014.

————. *The Me 262 Stormbird: From the Pilots Who Flew, Fought, and Survived It.* Minneapolis: Zenith Press, 2012.

————. *Night Fighters: Luftwaffe and RAF Air Combat over Europe, 1939–1945.* Annapolis, MD: Naval Institute Press, 2008.

————. *The Star of Africa: The Story of Hans Marseille, the Rogue Ace Who Dominated the World War II Skies.* Minneapolis: Zenith Press, 2012.

Johnson, Robert S. *Thunderbolt!* 6th ed. Spartanburg, SC: Honoribus Press, 1973.

Olds, Christina, and Robin Olds, with Ed Rasimus. *Fighter Pilot: The Memoirs of Legendary Ace Robin Olds.* New York: St. Martin's Griffin, 2010.

Rigg, Bryan Mark. *Flamethrower: Iwo Jima Medal of Honor Recipient and U.S. Marine Woody Williams and His Controversial Award, Japan's Holocaust and the Pacific War.* Addison, TX: Fidelis Historia, 2020.

Steinhoff, Johannes. *The Final Hours: A German Jet Pilot Plots Against Goering.* Baltimore: Nautical & Aviation, 1985.

Tillman, Barrett. *LeMay: A Biography.* New York: Palgrave Macmillan, 2007.

Toliver, Raymond F. *The Interrogator: The Story of Hanns Joachim Scharff, Master Interrogator of the Luftwaffe.* Atglen, PA: Schiffer, 1997.

NOTES

A Man Too Hard to Kill: Robert Samuel Johnson

1. Colonel Hubert "Hub" Zemke (March 14, 1914–August 30, 1994) was a career officer in the US Air Force, a fighter pilot in World War II, and a leading US Army Air Forces ace. General Jimmy Doolittle praised Zemke as his "greatest fighter group commander." He commanded the Fifty-Sixth Fighter Group (FG) in England, which came to be known as Zemke's Wolf Pack. Zemke was an innovator in fighter tactics, creating the "forward fan" in support of bomber escort missions, called Ramrods. He was shot down in 1944 and was joined by fellow Fifty-Sixth FG ace Francis S. Gabreski in the prisoner of war camp.

2. Lieutenant General Adolf Josef Ferdinand Galland (March 19, 1912–February 9, 1996) served during the Spanish Civil War with the Legion Condor (Condor Legion) and throughout the Second World War in Europe. He flew 705 combat missions and fought on the Western Front and in the Defense of the Reich. On four occasions, he survived being shot down, the last event being in an Me 262 jet, when USAAF P-47 fighter pilot Captain James Finnegan shot him down. Galland was one of ten pilots (out of twenty-seven military men) to be awarded the Diamonds to the Knight's Cross, Oak Leaves with Swords. He was credited with 104 aerial victories, all of them against the Western Allies. He was the second-youngest general in the German military, as well as the youngest lieutenant general of any nation during the war, becoming a flag officer in 1942 at age thirty.

3. Lieutenant General Gunther Rall (March 10, 1918–October 4, 2009) was a highly decorated German military aviator, officer, and general whose military career spanned nearly forty years. Rall was the third most successful fighter pilot in aviation history, with 275 victories, behind Major Gerhard Barkhorn with 301, who is second, and Major Erich Hartmann, who is first with 352. Rall became great friends with Hub Zemke, Francis S. Gabreski, Robert S. Johnson, and Shorty Powers, who shot down Rall, with Rall losing his right thumb. Rall ended the war with the Oak Leaves and Swords to the Knight's Cross. He became a postwar NATO general in the West German Air Force. See Rall interview in Colin D. Heaton and Anne-Marie Lewis, *The German Aces Speak II* (Minneapolis: Zenith Press, 2014).

4. "Pete" Everest would be shot down in the Pacific in his P-51 Mustang and end the war as a Japanese POW.

5. Brigadier General Charles Elwood "Chuck" Yeager (born February 13, 1923) was one of America's top aces in the ETO, scoring 11.5 victories, including the first Me 262 jet kill for the 357th FG. Yeager went on to break many other speed and altitude records. He was also one of the first American pilots to fly a MiG-15, after its pilot, No Kumsok, defected to South Korea. He later became a test pilot, breaking the sound barrier in level flight. Yeager became the first commandant of the USAF Aerospace Research Pilot School, which produced astronauts for NASA and the USAF, after its redesignation from the USAF Flight Test Pilot School. Having only a high school education he was not eligible to become an astronaut himself, although he trained them from December 1963 to January 1964. He is still alive and living in Northern California as this is written, not far from fellow 357th FG ace Bud Anderson.

6. Lieutenant General Gerald Walter Johnson (July 10, 1919–September 9, 2002) was credited with shooting down 16.5 enemy aircraft before being shot down and taken prisoner. After the war, he continued his military career, rising to command several fighter and bomber wings during the 1950s and 1960s. He commanded the Eighth Air Force for a period during the Vietnam War and retired in 1974 after serving as inspector general of the US Air Force.

7. Colonel David Carl Schilling (December 15, 1918–August 14, 1956) was credited with 22.5 confirmed victories, and was a leading advocate of long-range jet fighter operations. On December 23, 1944, he downed 5 German fighters to become one of the thirty-eight US Army Air Forces's "Ace-in-a-Day" pilots. Schilling flew 132 combat missions in two combat tours with the Fifty-Sixth. He also destroyed 10.5 enemy aircraft on ground while strafing enemy airfields. Schilling Air Force Base in Kansas was named in his memory. He raced cars with Curtis LeMay and died in a car crash in England. Today a replica P-47D flies bearing Schilling's aircraft's nickname, *Hairless Joe*.

8. Colonel Wolfgang Falck (August 19, 1910–March 13, 2007) was born in Berlin and called the "Father of the Night Fighters" for establishing the Luftwaffe's night fighter program. Working with Colonel General Joseph Kammhuber, he bolstered the nocturnal air defense network all over Europe, earning the Knight's Cross. Falck scored

seven kills during the war. After the war he was an aviation consultant with North American, McDonnell Douglas, and Republic aircraft manufacturers, where he worked with Robert S. Johnson. He lived with his wife, Gisela Hahn (widow of ace Hans "Assi" Hahn), at his home in St. Ulrich, Tirol, Austria. His interview is in Colin D. Heaton and Anne-Marie Lewis, *The German Aces Speak* (Minneapolis: Zenith Press, 2011).

9. Colonel Donald James Matthew Blakeslee (September 11, 1917–September 3, 2008) began flying in the Royal Canadian Air Force, piloting Spitfires during World War II. He then became a member of the Royal Air Force Eagle Squadrons before transferring to the US Army Air Forces in 1942. He flew more combat missions against the Luftwaffe than any other American fighter pilot, and by the end of the war scored 15.5 aerial victories. He also was one of the first fighter group leaders (Fourth FG) to fly escort "shuttle" missions for heavy bombers from England to the Soviet Union.

10. Lieutenant Colonel Egon Mayer (August 19, 1917–March 2, 1944) was credited with 102 enemy aircraft shot down in more than 353 combat missions all over the Western Front, which included 26 four-engine bombers, 51 Supermarine Spitfires, and 12 P-47 Thunderbolts. Mayer was the first fighter pilot to score 100 victories entirely on the Western Front. He was awarded the Knight's Cross, Oak Leaves and Swords. He was killed in action against Thunderbolts.

11. Captain Joseph H. Powers (June 8, 1920–January 18, 1951) was born in Tulsa, Oklahoma. He attended school in Tulsa and graduated Tulsa Central High School. He was attending the University of Oklahoma on December 7, 1941, when the Japanese attacked Pearl Harbor, causing the United States to enter World War II. He entered the US Army Air Forces through the US Army Air Forces' Aviation Cadet Program. He was commissioned a second lieutenant and assigned to the Sixty-First Fighter Squadron, Fifty-Sixth Fighter Group, Eighth Air Force, US Army Air Forces based at Halesworth, England. He became an ace in 1943, flying a P-47C. He was officially credited with 14.5 enemy aircraft shot down at the time World War II was over. He was just .5 aircraft short of being a triple ace. After the war, Powers remained in the USAAF, which in 1947 became the USAF. During the Korean War, he was assigned to the Sixty-Seventh Fighter-Bomber Squadron, Eighteenth Fighter-Bomber Group at the time of his death on January 18, 1951, when he was shot down. His remains were never recovered.

12. These were 16 Fw 190A fighters from III./JG-2 under the command of Major Egon Mayer. Mayer would not score a kill that day but would claim two damaged and one probable, which would not be confirmed. The *Kommodore* of JG-26, Major Josef Priller, scored a B-17 kill of the 384th Bomb Group, USAAF. It was his ninety-first victory. Mayer would be replaced by Captain Josef "Sepp" Wurmheller, who died in combat on June 22, 1944.

13. Second Lieutenant Louis Truett Barron was assigned to the Sixty-First FS, Fifty-Sixth FG. He failed to return from the escort mission for bombers targeting Villacoublay. Approaching the rendezvous at Forges, France, the squadron was pounced on by

Fw 190s from III Gruppe, JG-2. Second Lieutenant Barron was one of four squadron mates to be shot down on June 26, 1943, in P-47, serial number 41-6376. He was listed as killed in action.

14. Captain Merle C. Eby was also listed as killed in action in the same battle that cost the Fifty-Sixth their pilots that day and almost killed Robert S. Johnson.

15. Captain Robert H. Wetherbee (MIA, June 26, 1943; declared KIA, June 27, 1943) was a member of the Sixty-First Fighter Squadron of the Fifty-Sixth Fighter Group and flew the P-47C Thunderbolt HV-W, nicknamed *Little Butch*, serial number 41-6322. He was reported missing in action as of June 26, 1943. He was reported as one of 277 American soldiers missing in action on July 15, 1943, by the War Department. The WWII Memorial Registry reports that he died June 27, 1944, possibly as a prisoner of war. Captain Wetherbee is memorialized on the Tablets of the Missing at Cambridge American Cemetery, in Cambridge, England.

16. The Schweinfurt-Regensburg mission on August 17, 1943, was one of the worst days in Eighth Air Force history. On this mission, JG-11 used the Werfer-Granate, consisting of underwing rockets mounted on the Me 109s, to attack the bombers that survived the early attacks from JG-2, JG-300, and JG-26, and managed to get through the flak screen. Every German fighter on the Western Front within flying range was called up, flying an average of two sorties that day. The German pilots caught the bombers going in and returning. More than 300 enemy aircraft, including Me 110 twin-engine heavy fighters, likewise mounted with rockets, and even night fighter units, went up in force. Sixty-four heavy bombers were shot down, and another 55 were damaged for scrap, with another 40 damaged but repaired. The cost in American lives numbered more than 600. Three P-47s of the Fifty-Sixth Fighter Group and two RAF Spitfires were shot down attempting to protect the Schweinfurt force. The Spitfire pilots claimed 13 German fighters shot down, and P-47 pilots claimed 19 aircraft. Gunners on the bombers claimed 288 fighters shot down, but Luftwaffe records showed only 27 fighters were lost. The great discrepancy in the kill claims was due to the fact that many aircraft and gunners shot at the same aircraft during the massive melee. The later raid over the same targets on October 14, 1943, saw another 60 bombers lost over the target, and another 17 lost trying to return home, out of 291, for a loss of more than 20 percent of the attacking force. These two missions resulted in the suspension of deep raids into Germany until spring 1944. The senior leadership feared that another such loss would halt the daylight bombing program entirely.

17. Lieutenant Colonel Hans Philipp (March 17, 1917–October 8, 1943) scored 206 kills in more than 500 combat missions. The majority of his victories were claimed over the Eastern Front, with 29 kills over the Western Front. He received the Knight's Cross, Oak Leaves and Swords.

18. Boleslaw Michal (Mike) Gladych (May 17, 1918–July 12, 2011) was a Warsaw-born Polish fighter pilot who fled Poland and escaped Gestapo custody to arrive in England. He flew with the Free Polish 303 Squadron with Gabreski, who recruited him into the Fifty-Sixth FG in 1943. He had two encounters with Georg-Peter Eder, who, seeing him damaged, saluted and wagged his wings, then flew away. The two formally

met after the war and confirmed the events with each other. He flew further (unofficial) operations with an unnamed P-51 group, claiming an Me 262 jet downed, but this is not confirmed by USAAF records, and his ten credited kills were all made with the Sixty-First FS. It is also claimed that he intentionally understated the total of his air victories, lest he be promoted and transferred off combat duties.

Gladych was awarded the Virtuti Militari (Cross of Valour) with three bars by the Polish Air Force, the DFC by the RAF, and the Silver Star with two clusters and the Air Medal with three Oak Leaf clusters by the USAAF. He also claimed to have been awarded the Croix de Guerre for the sortie on March 8, 1944, when he strafed an airfield after shooting down an Fw 190. After the war ended, Gladych was allegedly involved in black-market smuggling across Europe, and in the early 1950s was recruited by the CIA to join a newly composed Project ARTICHOKE operating from Washington, DC.

He also located his brother, a Polish Resistance fighter, in a German POW camp in Austria that had been liberated by the Russians in 1945. Anticipating the fact that most of the Polish Resistance falling into the hands of the Soviets were likely to be deported to Siberia, Gladych used his USAAF status to visit the camp and managed to smuggle his brother out to the West. Afterward, Gladych emigrated to Seattle, obtaining a PhD degree in psychology and becoming a United States citizen. Until his death, he lived in the area where he practiced psychotherapy.

19. This would be Mike Gladych's first encounter with Luftwaffe ace Major Georg-Peter Eder, who was known to Allied pilots as "Lucky 13," for the blue "13" painted on the fuselage on both his Me 109G6 and his Fw 190A6 in 1943 and mid-1944, respectively. Eder would again spare Gladych's life when he encountered the Pole in his P-47D. After the war, they met and became friends.

20. James C. "Jimmy" Stewart (1919–2004) received the Distinguished Service Cross and the Silver Star for getting fourteen kills, but also for breaking up a couple of massive enemy fighter formations, saving a bomb group from having any losses. During the war, he was often confused with the other Jimmy Stewart, the famous actor who flew bombers. He often received bags of fan mail destined for the actor, which he had to give back to the postmaster.

21. Major Richard Ira Bong (September 24, 1920–August 6, 1945) was a Medal of Honor recipient and one of the most decorated American fighter pilots and the country's top flying ace in the war, credited with shooting down forty Japanese aircraft, all with the Lockheed P-38 Lightning fighter. He died in California while testing the Lockheed P-80 Shooting Star jet fighter shortly before the war ended.

Striking the First Blow for Freedom: James H. Doolittle

1. William Lendrum Mitchell (December 29, 1879–February 19, 1936) was a United States Army general who is regarded as the father of the United States Air Force.

2. Goodwin Jess "Goodie" Knight (December 9, 1896–May 22, 1970) was an American politician who was the thirty-first governor of California from 1953 until 1959. He

earned a bachelor of arts in law and business from Stanford University, where he was on the staff of the campus humor magazine, the *Stanford Chaparral*, in 1919. Knight also attended Cornell University. He served in the US Navy during World War I and later served as a California Superior Court judge.

3. Frank Russell Capra (born Francesco Rosario Capra in Palermo, Sicily, May 18, 1897–September 3, 1991) was an Italian American film director, producer, and writer who became the creative force behind some of the major award-winning films of the 1930s and 1940s. He was commissioned as a second lieutenant in artillery at Fort Sill, Oklahoma, during World War I but was later discharged after having survived the Spanish influenza. During World War II, Capra served in the US Army Signal Corps and produced propaganda films such as the *Why We Fight* series. The author Colin D. Heaton knew his son Frank Capra Jr. when he was president of Screen Gems Studios.

4. Glenn Hammond Curtiss (May 21, 1878–July 23, 1930) was an American aviation and motorcycling pioneer, and a major founder of the US aircraft industry. He began his career as a bicycle racer and builder before moving on to making motorcycles. As early as 1904, he began to manufacture engines for airships. In 1908 Curtiss joined the Aerial Experiment Association, a pioneering research group founded by Alexander Graham Bell at the famous inventor's Nova Scotia estate, Beinn Bhreagh, and began building aircraft. His name is legendary in the aviation world.

5. Eddie Campi (July 4, 1893–June 21, 1918) was a 105-pound member of San Francisco's Olympic Club in 1908. In 1913 he was working daily as an actor for the Kalem Moving Picture Company in Santa Monica, California. According to the June 20, 1918, issue of the Tacoma (WA) *News Tribune,* Campi was accidentally shot in the abdomen as a result of a June 18 hunting accident on his uncle's ranch near Hollister, California. He died three days later, on June 21. Reportedly, he was twenty-seven years old; however, record books list his birthday as July 4, 1893, which would have made him a few days short of twenty-five years of age.

6. John Gutenko (December 5, 1893–October 18, 1963), better known as Kid Williams, was a Danish boxer who held the bantamweight world championship during his career. Statistical boxing website BoxRec lists Williams as the number two bantamweight of all time, while *Ring* magazine founder Nat Fleischer placed him at number three. Williams was inducted into the *Ring* Hall of Fame in 1970 and the International Boxing Hall of Fame in 1996.

7. The Lafayette Escadrille was a group of American volunteer pilots flying for France in World War I.

8. Hugo Junkers (February 3, 1859–February 3, 1935) was a German aircraft engineer and aircraft designer who pioneered the design of all-metal airplanes and flying wings. His company, Junkers Flugzeug und Motorenwerke AG (Junkers Aircraft and Motor Works), was one of the mainstays of the German aircraft industry in the years between World War I and World War II. His multiengine, all-metal planes helped establish airlines in Germany and around the world. His designs included the Ju-87 Stuka, Ju-88 medium bomber, and Ju-52 trimotor transport, called the "Auntie Ju."

His designs also extended into engine development. The Junkers Jumo 008 was the final power plant for the Messerschmitt Me 262 jet, a design refined by Dr. Hans von Ohain.

9. Professor Dr. Kurt Waldemar Tank (February 24, 1898–June 5, 1983) was a German aeronautical engineer and test pilot who led the design department at Focke-Wulf from 1931 to 1945. He was responsible for the creation of several important Luftwaffe aircraft of World War II, including the Focke-Wulf series of fighters; Fw 190; Fw Ta 152 fighter-interceptor; and Fw 200 Condor airliner and maritime reconnaissance bomber. After the war, Tank spent two decades designing aircraft abroad, working first in Argentina and then India, before returning to Germany in the late 1960s to work as a consultant for Messerschmitt-Bölkow-Blohm.

10. Shangri-La is a fictional place first mentioned in a novel by James Hilton, published in 1933. It was also the presidential retreat, later renamed Camp David by President Eisenhower.

11. Elmer Ambrose Sperry Sr. (October 12, 1860–June 16, 1930) was an American inventor and entrepreneur most famous as the coinventor, with Hermann Anschütz-Kaempfe, of the gyrocompass and as founder of the Sperry Gyroscope Company. He was known as the "father of modern navigation technology." Sperry's compasses and stabilizers were adopted by the US military and used in both world wars. He also worked closely with the Japanese government and was honored after his death with a volume of reminiscences published in Japan. The Sperry Company continued after his death, using his futuristic designs, and created the ball turrets and top turrets that mounted the .50-caliber machine guns on all American medium and heavy bombers.

12. The Link Trainer, also known as the Blue Box and Pilot Trainer, was a flight simulator produced during the early 1930s from the concept developed in 1929 by Edwin Albert Link. The Link Trainer became famous during World War II and was used to train pilots in almost every nation.

13. General William Mitchell (December 28, 1879–February 19, 1936) is considered the father of the US Air Force. He was a powerful advocate for air power, and his efforts favored bomber aircraft inclusive of "pursuit"(fighter) aircraft.

14. The Junkers Ju-87 Stuka was a gull-winged dive bomber that excelled at close air support. Later, they were used extensively as antitank aircraft.

15. Master Sergeant Paul J. Leonard (June 19, 1912–January 5, 1943) received training as an airplane mechanic. After assignments to units at Kelly Field, Texas, Chanute Field, Illinois, and Lowry Field, Colorado, he was assigned to the Thirty-Seventh Bomb Squadron in May 1941. After the Tokyo raid, Leonard remained in the China-Burma-India theater until June 1942, at which time he returned to the States to become crew chief for General Doolittle. He served in England and North Africa from September 1942 until he was killed by enemy aircraft on January 5, 1943, at Youks-les-Bains, Algeria. Decorations include the Distinguished Flying Cross, Purple Heart (posthumous), and the Chinese Army, Navy, and Air Corps Medal, Class A, First Grade.

16. Lieutenant Colonel Richard Cole (September 7, 1915–April 9, 2019) was the last living member of the Doolittle Raiders.

17. Colonel Henry A. "Hank" Potter (September 22, 1918–May 27, 2002) was Doolittle's navigator on number one. He entered military service at Pierre on July 26, 1940, and attended Yankton College in South Dakota as well as the University of Oregon. Potter completed navigator training and was commissioned second lieutenant in June 1941. Following the Tokyo Raid, he had stateside service in Michigan, Colorado, Washington, DC, Florida, and California, and also served overseas in Germany from 1954 to 1958. Potter holds a rating as master navigator. Decorations include Distinguished Flying Cross, Air Medal with three Oak Leaf clusters, Army Commendation Medal, and the Chinese Army, Navy, and Air Corps Medal, Class A, First Grade. He retired as a full colonel.

18. Captain Fred A. Braemer (January 31, 1918–February 2, 1989) was the bombardier for number one. He later followed Doolittle around for the rest of the war on many assignments. He enlisted in the US Army on September 16, 1935 and served in the infantry and military intelligence until September 17, 1938, when he left the service for a year. Next, Braemer enlisted in the US Army Air Corps on September 16, 1939, and trained as a bombardier. Then Staff Sergeant Braemer was the bombardier on the first B-25 to take off from the aircraft carrier USS *Hornet* on April 18, 1942. After bombing Tokyo, his crew flew to China and bailed out when their aircraft ran out of fuel.

He remained in the China-Burma-India theater and flew twenty-six combat missions before returning to the United States to become a bombardier instructor in July 1943. Braemer was commissioned a second lieutenant in the USAAF on January 5, 1945, and was released from active duty and joined the Air Force Reserve on November 1, 1945. Lieutenant Braemer was recalled to active duty on September 24, 1951, and he flew twenty-eight combat missions as a B-29 Superfortress bombardier during the Korean War between December 1952 and June 1953.

After the war, Braemer served as a navigator, bombardier, and aircraft observer on B-47 Stratojet bombers until December 1957, when he reverted to enlisted status and was trained as an air traffic control operator. He served as an ATC operator at Wheelus AB, Libya, from January 1960 to September 1963, and then at Whiteman AFB, Missouri, from September 1963 to September 1965, when he regained his commission as a captain and was assigned to MacDill AFB, Florida. Braemer retired from the air force on September 30, 1966. He died on February 2, 1989, and was buried at Calvary Catholic Cemetery in Lincoln, Nebraska.

19. John Morrison Birch (May 28, 1918–August 25, 1945) was an American Baptist minister and missionary, and a US Army Air Forces captain who was a US military intelligence officer in China during World War II. Birch was killed in a confrontation with Chinese Communist soldiers a few days after the war ended. He was posthumously awarded the US Army Distinguished Service Medal. The John Birch Society, an American anti-Communist organization, was named in his honor by Robert H. W. Welch Jr. in 1958. Welch considered Birch to be a martyr and the first casualty of the Cold War.

20. B-25 number eight, and that aircraft landed in the Soviet Union, as it was closer than China. Their journey out was an odyssey.

21. Soong Mei-ling (March 5, 1898–October 23, 2003), also known as Madame Chiang Kai-shek or Madame Chiang, was a Chinese political figure who was first lady of the People's Republic of China, the wife of Generalissimo and President Chiang Kai-shek. Soong played a prominent role in the politics of the Republic of China and was the sister-in-law of Sun Yat-sen, the founder and leader of the Republic of China.

    She befriended the Doolittle Raiders and was a very welcoming hostess to the American Volunteer Group (AVG) pilots, known as the Flying Tigers. Having been good friends with Claire Chennault, she also intervened straight to President Roosevelt on behalf of Chennault and LeMay to halt General Joseph Stillwell from appropriating their fighters and heavy bombers, respectively.

    Fluent in English and speaking French, she was active in the civic life of her country and held many honorary and active positions, including chairwoman of Fu Jen Catholic University. During the Second Sino-Japanese War, she rallied her people against the Japanese invasion and in 1943 conducted an eight-month speaking tour of the United States to gain support.

22. The Doolittle Raiders assigned to each aircraft are as follows:

    CREW 1

    After conducting the raid, the crew bailed out over China and returned home safely.

    Pilot: Lieutenant Colonel James Doolittle (1896–1993)

    Copilot: Lieutenant Richard Cole (1915–2019)

    Navigator: Lieutenant Hank A. Potter (1918–2002)

    Bombardier: Staff Sergeant Fred Braemer (1918–1989)

    Engineer Gunner: Staff Sergeant Paul Leonard (1912–1943)

    CREW 2

    After conducting the raid, the crew survived a crash landing in China and returned home safely.

    Pilot: Lieutenant Travis Hoover (1917–2004)

    Copilot: Lieutenant William Fitzhugh (1915–1981)

    Navigator: Lieutenant Carl Wildner (1915–1994)

    Bombardier: Lieutenant Richard Miller (1916–1943)

    Engineer Gunner: Staff Sergeant Douglas Radney (1917–1994)

    CREW 3

    The crew bailed out over a mountainous hillside in China. One member of the crew, Corporal Leland Faktor, died after falling down a cliff.

    Pilot: Lieutenant Robert Gray (1919–1942)

    Copilot: Lieutenant Jacob Manch (1918–1958)

    Navigator: Lieutenant Charles Ozuk (1916–2010)

    Bombardier: Sergeant Aden Jones (1920–1983)

    Engineer gunner: Corporal Leland Faktor (1922–1942)

NOTES

CREW 4

The crew bailed out over China.

Pilot: Lieutenant Everett Holstrom (1916–2000)

Copilot: Lieutenant Nevelon Youngblood (1918–1949)

Navigator: Lieutenant Harry McCool (1918–2003)

Bombardier: Sergeant Robert Stephens (1915–1959)

Engineer Gunner: Corporal Bert Jordan (1919–2001)

CREW 5

The crew bailed out over China.

Pilot: Captain David Jones (1913–2008)

Copilot: Lieutenant Rodney Wilder (1917–1964)

Navigator: Lieutenant Eugene McGurl (1917–1942)

Bombardier: Lieutenant Denver Truelove (1919–1943)

Engineer gunner: Sergeant Joseph Manske (1921–1998)

CREW 6

The crew bailed out off the coast of China, resulting in two of them drowning. The remaining three swam to shore, were captured, and were interned as prisoners of war.

Pilot: Lieutenant Dean Hallmark (1914–1942), executed by the Japanese.

Copilot: Lieutenant Robert Meder (1917–1943), died in captivity as a result of torture, disease, and injuries.

Navigator: Lieutenant Chase Nielsen (1917–2007)

Bombardier: Sergeant William Dieter (1912–1942)

Engineer gunner: Corporal Donald Fitzmaurice (1919–1942)

CREW 7

The crew crash-landed on the coast of China and survived but sustained severe injuries.

Pilot: Lieutenant Ted Lawson (1917–1992)

Copilot: Lieutenant Dean Davenport (1918–2000)

Navigator: Lieutenant Charles McClure (1916–1999)

Bombardier: Lieutenant Robert Clever (1914–1942)

Engineer gunner: Sergeant David Thatcher (1921–2016)

CREW 8

After conducting the raid, the crew landed in Russia, where they were interned for more than a year. All returned safely home in 1943.

Pilot: Captain Edward York (1912–1984)

Copilot: Lieutenant Robert Emmens (1914–1992)

Navigator: Lieutenant Nolan A. Herndon (1918–2007)

Bombardier: Staff Sergeant Theodore Laban (1914–1978)

Engineer gunner: Sergeant David Pohl (1921–1999)

CREW 9

The crew bailed out over China.

Pilot: Lieutenant Harold Watson (1916–1991)

Copilot: Lieutenant James Parker (1920–1991)
Navigator: Lieutenant Thomas Griffin (1916–2013)
Bombardier: Sergeant Wayne Bissell (1921–1997)
Engineer gunner: Sergeant Eldred Von Scott (1907–1978)
CREW 10
The crew bailed out over China.
Pilot: Lieutenant Richard Joyce (1919–1983)
Copilot: Lieutenant J. Royden Stork (1916–2002)
Navigator bombardier: Horace E. "Sally" Crouch (1918–2005)
Engineer gunner: Sergeant George Larkin Jr. (1918–1942)
Gunner: Staff Sergeant Edwin Horton (1916–2008)
CREW 11
The crew bailed out over China.
Pilot: Captain Charles Greening (1914–1957)
Copilot: Lieutenant Kenneth Reddy (1920–1942)
Navigator: Lieutenant Frank Kappeler (1914–2010)
Bombardier: Staff Sergeant William Birch (1917–2006)
Engineer gunner: Sergeant Melvin Gardner (1920–1942)
CREW 12
The crew bailed out over China.
Pilot: Lieutenant William Bower (1917–2011)
Copilot: Lieutenant Thadd Blanton (1919–1961)
Navigator: Lieutenant William Pound (1918–1967)
Bombardier: Technical Sergeant Waldo Bither (1906–1988)
Engineer gunner: Staff Sergeant Omer Duquette (1916–1942)
CREW 13
The crew bailed out over China.
Pilot: Lieutenant Edgar McElroy (1912–2003)
Copilot: Lieutenant Richard Knobloch (1918–2001)
Navigator: Lieutenant Clayton Campbell (1917–2002)
Bombardier: Sergeant Robert Bourgeois (1917–2001)
Engineer gunner: Sergeant Adam Williams (1919–1993)
CREW 14
The crew safely bailed out over China.
Pilot: Major John Hilger (1909–1982)
Copilot: Lieutenant Jack Sims (1919–2007)
Navigator: Lieutenant James Macia (1916–2009)
Radio gunner: Staff Sergeant Edwin Bain (1917–1943)
Engineer gunner: Staff Sergeant Jacob Eierman (1913–1994)
CREW 15
The crew landed in waters off China's coast and made it safely to Chinese shores
in a life raft.
Pilot: Lieutenant Donald Smith (1918–1942)

Copilot: Lieutenant Griffith Williams (1920–1998)

Navigator bombardier: Lieutenant Howard Sessler (1917–2001)

Flight surgeon: Lieutenant Thomas White, MD (1909–1992)

Engineer gunner: Sergeant Edward Saylor (1920–2015)

CREW 16

The crew crash-landed near the China coast and were taken prisoners of war by Japanese forces.

Pilot: Lieutenant William Farrow (1918–1942), executed by the Japanese.

Copilot: Lieutenant Robert Hite (1920–2015)

Navigator: Lieutenant George Barr (1917–1967)

Bombardier: Corporal Jacob DeShazer (1912–2008)

Engineer gunner: Sergeant Harold Spatz (1921–1942), executed by the Japanese.

23. General of the Army George Catlett Marshall Jr. (December 31, 1880–October 16, 1959) rose through the US Army to become chief of staff under presidents Franklin D. Roosevelt and Harry S. Truman, then served as secretary of state and secretary of defense under Truman. After the war, as secretary of state, Marshall advocated a significant US economic and political commitment to postwar European recovery, including the Marshall Plan that bore his name. In recognition of this work, he was awarded the Nobel Peace Prize in 1953.

24. First Lieutenant William Glover Farrow (September 24, 1918–October 15, 1942) was captured by the Japanese, tried, and, along with two other crew members, Sergeant Harold Spatz and First Lieutenant Dean Hallmark, sentenced to death, and executed by firing squad. Most of the crew members' sentences were commuted to life imprisonment by Emperor Hirohito, but the sentences of the three men stood. The night before their execution, the men were permitted to write final letters. The International Red Cross was to mail the letters after receiving them from the Japanese. The Japanese did not pass on the letters, and they were never mailed. Lieutenant Farrow's ashes were recovered and interred in Arlington National Cemetery in 1946.

25. Sergeant Harold Althouse "Skinny" Spatz (July 14, 1921–October 15, 1942) was a top turret gunner and flight engineer, who was captured and executed.

26. First Lieutenant Dean Edward Hallmark (January 20, 1914–October 15, 1942), pilot of plane number six, was captured, tortured, and then executed by firing squad.

27. First Lieutenant Robert John Meder (August 23, 1917–December 11, 1943) died from starvation, beriberi, and dysentery while a prisoner of the Japanese on December 11, 1943.

28. Lieutenant Colonel Robert L. Hite (March 3, 1920–March 29, 2015) was commissioned as second lieutenant and rated as a pilot on May 29, 1941. He was captured after Tokyo Raid and liberated by American troops on August 20, 1945. Hite remained on active duty until September 30, 1947. He later returned to active duty during the Korean War, on March 9, 1951, and served overseas before relief from active duty again in November 1955. Decorations include the Distinguished Flying Cross, Purple Heart with one Oak Leaf cluster, and Chinese Breast Order of Pao Ting.

29. Lieutenant Colonel Chase Jay Nielsen (January 14, 1917–March 23, 2007) was a career officer in the US Air Force. He participated in the Doolittle Raid in 1942 and was one of the four surviving prisoners of war from that mission. He returned to testify at the trials of his captors in 1946. He served a decade in SAC with Curtis LeMay and others, and retired in 1961.

30. George Barr (April 6, 1917–July 12, 1967) survived the torture and years of captivity but suffered ill health afterward and was medically retired in 1947.

31. Staff Sergeant Jacob Daniel DeShazer (November 15, 1912–March 15, 2008) participated in the Doolittle Raid. Captured and tortured, he survived and later became a missionary in Japan. He was a great interview as well. During his captivity, DeShazer persuaded one of his guards to loan him a copy of the Bible. Although he had possession of the Bible for only three weeks, he saw its messages as the reason for his survival and resolved to become a devout Christian. His conversion included learning a few words of Japanese and treating his captors with respect, which resulted in the guards reacting in a similar fashion. After his release, DeShazer entered Seattle Pacific College, a Christian college associated with the Free Methodist denomination, and began studying to become a missionary, eventually returning to Japan with his wife, Florence, in 1948.

    DeShazer, the Doolittle Raider who bombed Nagoya, met Captain Mitsuo Fuchida, who led the attack on Pearl Harbor, becoming close friends. See *For That One Day: The Memoirs of Mitsuo Fuchida, Commander of the Attack on Pearl Harbor*, trans. Douglas T. Shinsato and Tadanori Urabe (Kamuela, HI: eXperience, 2011). Fuchida became a Christian in 1950 after reading a tract written about DeShazer titled "I Was a Prisoner of Japan," and spent the rest of his life as a missionary in Asia and the United States. DeShazer and Fuchida preached together as Christian missionaries in Japan. In 1959 DeShazer moved to Nagoya to establish a Christian church in the city he had bombed.

32. Marshal of the Royal Air Force Sir Arthur Travers Harris, 1st Baronet, GCB, OBE, AFC (April 13, 1892–April 5, 1984), commonly known as "Bomber" Harris by the press and often within the RAF as "Butcher" Harris, was air officer commanding-in-chief (AOC-in-C), RAF Bomber Command. In 1942 the British Cabinet agreed to the "area bombing" of German cities. Harris was given the task of implementing Churchill's policy and supported the development of tactics and technology to perform the task more effectively. Harris assisted Charles Portal, British chief of the air staff and marshal of the Royal Air Force, in carrying out the United Kingdom's most devastating attacks against the German infrastructure and population, including the bombing of Dresden. Curtis LeMay adopted the Harris method in his bombing of Japan.

33. The Vichy government in southern France under Marshall Henri Petain joined the Axis as an ally of Germany, dividing the country politically. Vichy forces occupied the French colonies in North Africa, the targets of Operation Torch.

34. Benito Mussolini (July 29, 1883–April 28, 1945) ruled Italy as a dictator from 1922 until he and his mistress were executed by anti-Fascist partisans.

35. Hideki Tōjō (December 30, 1884–December 23, 1948) was a Japanese politician and general of the Imperial Japanese Army who served as prime minister of Japan and president of the Imperial Rule Assistance Association for most of World War II. He was executed for war crimes.

36. The two primary Luftwaffe fighter units in northern France that Doolittle mentioned were Jagdgeschwader 2 (JG-2, Richthofen) and Jagdgeschwader 26 (JG-26, Schlageter). The Americans called the latter the "Yellow Nosed Bastards" as well as the "Abbeville Boys" (or "Kids").

37. These fighter recon missions had already started "unofficially" in 1943, when Colonel Zemke, commanding officer of the Fifty-Sixth Fighter Group, started his own Pathfinder probes without permission. He also started sending a squadron ahead of the main fighter group and the bombers, to draw the enemy up and engage them, so that when the rear echelon arrived, the Germans were already short on fuel, tired, and on the defensive.

38. Lieutenant General Archie J. Old Jr. (August 1, 1906–March 24, 1984) flew forty-three combat missions against Germany. On October 14, 1943, Old led the second raid on the Schweinfurt ball bearing factories. Of 291 B-17s that reached the target, 60 were downed by flak or enemy fighters, for a loss rate of 20 percent over target losses. A like number returned damaged and were scrapped or cannibalized. On June 21, 1944, Old led the second shuttle bombing run to Russia.

39. Stalin had actually stated that he wanted German and Eastern European industrial locations preserved for use by the USSR when the war was over. In fact, upon conquering half of Europe, entire factories were dismantled and taken back to the Soviet Union, along with all the civilian labor force they could capture. The Soviets, like the Germans, never developed a long-range bomber program.

40. William J. Donovan (January 1, 1883–February 8, 1959) served in both world wars and is the only person to have received all four of the United States' highest awards: the Medal of Honor, the Distinguished Service Cross, the Distinguished Service Medal, the National Security Medal, as well as the Silver Star, Purple Heart, and decorations from a number of other nations. He established the US Office of Strategic Services (OSS) and then founded the US Central Intelligence Agency (CIA).

41. David John Cawdell Irving (born March 24, 1938) is an English author and Holocaust denier who has written on the military and political history of World War II, with a focus on Nazi Germany. He was jailed in Austria for Holocaust denial, and, upon his release in 2006, he was banned from ever returning to Austria, with Canada, Italy, Germany, Poland, and New Zealand following suit.

42. Field Marshal Bernard Law Montgomery, 1st Viscount Montgomery of Alamein, KG, GCB, DSO, PC, DL (November 17, 1887–March 24, 1976), nicknamed "Monty," fought in both the First World War and the Second World War. His tactical maneuvers in North Africa against German general (and later field marshal) Erwin Rommel ("the Desert Fox") were legendary, as were his disagreements with Patton.

43. James David Graham Niven (March 1, 1910–July 29, 1983) was a legendary actor before the war. He served in Europe and later returned to acting, becoming a box office

megastar. He was the only A-list British actor to have served in the war, unlike the many Americans who signed up.

44. Robin Olds was told this same story as related by Doolittle.

The Ultimate Warrior: Robin Olds

1. Colonel Francis S. Gabreski, interview by Colin D. Heaton, 1996.
2. Colonel Hubert Zemke, interview by Colin D. Heaton, 1990.
3. General Curtis LeMay, interview by Colin D. Heaton, 1986.
4. Max Immelmann (September 21, 1890–June 18, 1916) scored fifteen victories and was the first German World War I ace. He was a pioneer in fighter aviation and is often mistakenly credited with the first aerial victory using a synchronized gun with the interrupter gear. Actually, this was achieved by German ace Kurt Wintgens on July 15, 1915. He was the first aviator to receive the Pour le Mérite (known as the "Blue Max" in his honor), and he received it at the same time as Oswald Boelcke. His name has become associated with a common flying tactic that he invented, called the Immelmann turn.
5. Gervais Raoul Victor Lufbery (March 14, 1885–May 19, 1918) was a French and American fighter pilot and flying ace in World War I. His service spanned both the French Air Force and US Army Air Service in World War I. Officially, all but one of his seventeen combat victories came while flying in French units.
6. Air Marshal William Avery Bishop, VC, CB, DSO & Bar, MC, DFC, ED (February 8, 1894–September 11, 1956) was a Canadian flying ace of the First World War. He scored seventy-two victories, making him the top Canadian and British Empire ace of the war. During the Second World War, he was instrumental in establishing the British Commonwealth Air Training Plan (BCATP) standardizing training manuals and methods for new pilots.
7. Major General Robert Olds (June 15, 1896–April 28, 1943) was an early supporter of and advocate for long-range bombers. He was an aide to General Billy Mitchell and mentored General Curtis LeMay. Olds remained at Mitchell's side during the sham court-martial, following his boss in proving that aerial bombing could sink capital ships.
8. Barnstormers were pilots who flew World War I–era aircraft and later biplane models around the country, doing flying maneuvers and offering spectators rides for money. Ernst Udet was a major attraction, as he was a sixty-four-victory ace from the First World War. He was the highest-scoring German ace to survive the war.
9. Robin was referring to the January 1945 "Fighters Revolt," when the leading fighter-wing commanders had a second meeting with Reichsmarschall and Commander in Chief of the Luftwaffe Hermann Göring in Berlin. There had been a previous meeting in November 1944, where the leaders addressed some of the accusations made against them, including cowardice. At that meeting, Galland was threatened with execution. In the January meeting, Galland was banned from attending, but this meeting went down even worse, requiring Hitler to intervene. See the recollections of Adolf

Galland and Luftwaffe officer Eduard Neumann in Heaton and Lewis, *German Aces Speak*, and Johannes Steinhoff in Heaton and Lewis, *German Aces Speak II*. Also, for a good overview, see Johannes Steinhoff, *The Final Hours: A German Jet Pilot Plots Against Goering* (Baltimore: Nautical & Aviation, 1985).

10. Brigadier General Benjamin Buckles "Ben" Cassiday Jr. (July 25, 1922–September 21, 2017) served with the Seventy-Ninth Fighter Group in Corsica, France, and Italy and completed 117 combat missions in P-47s. He flew from bases in North Africa and Italy in bomber escorts and ground support missions. At the end of World War II, as commander of the Eighty-Seventh Fighter Squadron, he remained with the Seventy-Ninth Fighter Group for two years in Austria. Cassiday began his next assignment in January 1950 as an exchange pilot with the US Navy. He flew 43 Korean combat missions in the Grumman F9F Panther from the carrier USS *Philippine Sea*. During his career, he flew with the Royal Air Force, the US Army Air Forces (later the USAF), and the US Navy.

His military decorations and awards include the Silver Star, Legion of Merit with two Oak Leaf clusters, Distinguished Flying Cross, Soldier's Medal with one Oak Leaf cluster, Air Medal with seven Oak Leaf clusters, two Navy gold stars, Presidential Unit Citation emblem with Oak Leaf cluster, Navy Unit Commendation ribbon, Navy Outstanding Service Medal, British Distinguished Flying Cross, Republic of Korea Presidential Unit Citation ribbon, and Philippine Presidential Unit Citation ribbon.

11. William Brooke Joyce (April 24, 1906–January 3, 1946), born in Brooklyn, New York, to an American father and English-born mother, was nicknamed "Lord Haw-Haw." As a child, his family relocated to Ireland. He was a Fascist politician and Nazi propaganda broadcaster under Propaganda Minister Joseph Goebbels. He transmitted his radio broadcasts to the United Kingdom during World War II. He became a German citizen in 1940. After the war, Joyce was convicted of one count of high treason in 1945 and sentenced to death, with the Court of Appeal and the House of Lords both upholding his conviction. He was hanged on January 3, 1946.

12. First noted in Christina Olds and Robin Olds with Ed Rasimus, *Fighter Pilot: The Memoirs of Legendary Ace Robin Olds* (New York: St. Martin's Griffin, 2010), 42.

13. Their interrogator was Hanns Scharff. For the full story, see Raymond F. Toliver, *The Interrogator: The Story of Hanns Joachim Scharff, Master Interrogator of the Luftwaffe* (Atglen, PA: Schiffer, 1997).

14. Major George Preddy (February 5, 1919–December 25, 1944) hailed from Greensboro, North Carolina. He was killed by friendly fire on Christmas Day, 1944. He was twenty-six. He had earned the Distinguished Service Cross (recommended for Medal of Honor), and two Silver Stars, seven Air Medals, and a Purple Heart. He scored 26.83 victories, making him the top P-51 Mustang ace in the ETO. His brother, William, a P-51 pilot with the 503rd Fighter Squadron, 339th Fighter Group, was later buried alongside him at the Lorraine American Cemetery in Saint-Avold, France. William died on April 17, 1945, from wounds sustained when he was shot down by enemy antiaircraft fire while strafing Ceske Budejovice Airfield in Czechoslovakia. Veterans

of Foreign Wars Post 2087 in Greensboro was named after George Preddy soon after World War II ended. In 1968 Business Interstate 85 through Greensboro, North Carolina, was renamed Preddy Boulevard in memory of both brothers. There is a memorial kiosk with video, photos, and models of planes flown by the Preddy brothers at Piedmont Triad International Airport.

15. The Focke-Wulf Fw 200 Condor was an early four-motor airliner converted later into a transport, maritime reconnaissance, and bomber aircraft. It specialized in maritime combat against Allied convoys, supplementing the U-boats due to its long range of about 1,860 miles. Only 276 were built.

16. Colonel Robert J. "Shorty" Rankin (October 23, 1918–March 14, 2013) flew P-47s with the Fifty-Sixth Fighter Group. He was credited with ten confirmed, one probable, and two damaged, and was the first P-47 pilot to achieve Ace-in-a-Day status by destroying five aircraft in one day. He shot down Major Gunther Rall, severing his right thumb.

17. Major Alton Glenn Miller (March 1, 1904–disappeared December 15, 1944) was an American trombonist, arranger, composer, and bandleader in the swing era. He was the bestselling recording artist from 1939 to 1942, leading one of the best-known big bands. While he was traveling to entertain US troops in France, his aircraft disappeared over the English Channel. Many Germans secretly listened to Miller's music, and fighter ace Hans-Joachim Marseille had a Glenn Miller record collection that he bought while stationed in France. That and his banned jazz collection were something of a controversy. See Colin D. Heaton and Anne-Marie Lewis, *The Star of Africa: The Story of Hans Marseille the Rogue Ace Who Dominated the World War II Skies* (Minneapolis: Zenith Press, 2012).

18. Two of Robin's victories may have been the following Germans: (1) 2./NAGr.1, Messerschmitt Bf 109G-6, Wnr.230146, Lieutenant Metzler; location, three miles north of Grave, near Nijmegen, the Netherlands. (2) 2./NAGr.1, Messerschmitt Bf 109G-6, Wnr.230174, Uffz. Sprünker; location: Bridge-Neumar, west of Cologne, Germany. Luftwaffe loss records courtesy of Walter Krupinski.

19. The jet Olds damaged was probably "White 8," flown by Hauptmann Tronicke of I/KG-54, a jet bomber unit. Tronicke landed the jet on the nacelles but died of his wounds. Olds should have been credited with the victory if this was the jet. The only other jet losses on April 7 were four Me 262s from JG-7, one of which collided with a B-24. The other two were crash-landed write-offs. Either way, Olds would have the victory if the jet he hit had been observed to crash-land. See Colin D. Heaton and Anne-Marie Lewis, *The Me 262 Stormbird: From the Pilots Who Flew, Fought and Survived It* (Zenith Press, Minneapolis, 2012), 263 (Olds), 290 (losses).

20. Hopefully, this victory record will be amended to accurately reflect Olds's Me 262 kill from April 7, 1945.

21. Brigadier General David Lee "Tex" Hill (July 13, 1915–October 11, 2007) is credited with 12.25 victories as a squadron leader with the Flying Tigers (Panda Bears Squadron) and another 6 as an officer in the US Army Air Forces in World War II. He retired as a brigadier general. Great man and interviewed by the author.

22. Lieutenant Colonel John C. "Pappy" Herbst (September 25, 1909–July 4, 1946) was an American flying ace of World War II who was officially the second-highest-scoring fighter pilot in the China-Burma-India theater, with eighteen confirmed victories scored during seven months with the Twenty-Third Fighter Group, Fourteenth Air Force. Tex Hill was his CO. Herbst died the day after getting married for the second time, flying with Olds.

23. Olds, *Fighter Pilot*, 126.

24. Colonel Leon W. Gray (October 18, 1913–November 26, 2007) was a Golden Gloves boxer as a young man. In World War II he served more than two years in the European theater, flying 420 combat hours in various types of fighters and fighter-bombers such as the P-51, Spitfire, Mosquito, and P-38. He received numerous decorations for bravery in combat, including the coveted Distinguished Service Cross for his "extraordinary heroism" piloting an unarmed P-38 (F-5 model) on critical photo reconnaissance missions. He once survived being shot down.

    In 1946 and 1947 Gray won the jet division of the famed Bendix Trophy Race, flying America's first operational jet fighter, the Lockheed P-80 Shooting Star. In 1959 his USAF team with Robin Olds, flying supersonic F-104s, won the prestigious William Tell missile competition. He is also credited with refining jet training methods while commanding units at various USAF bases, including Williams, Luke, and Davis-Monthan in Arizona. Leon Gray retired a colonel in 1967.

25. Laurance Spelman "Larry" Rockefeller (May 26, 1910–July 11, 2004), American venture capitalist and philanthropist, third of the five sons of John D. Rockefeller Jr.

26. Benjamin Oliver Davis Jr. (December 18, 1912–July 4, 2002) was commander of the World War II Tuskegee Airmen. On December 9, 1998, he was promoted to four-star general by President Bill Clinton. During World War II, Davis was commander of the Ninety-Ninth Fighter Squadron and the 332nd Fighter Group, which escorted bombers on air combat missions over Europe. Davis flew sixty missions in the P-39, P-40, P-47, and P-51. He followed in his father's footsteps in breaking racial barriers, as Benjamin O. Davis Sr. went to West Point and was the first African American general in the US Army.

27. The Warsaw Pact was a union formed under the auspices of the USSR after World War II in 1955. The Communist nations included Poland, Romania, Bulgaria, Hungary, Czechoslovakia, East Germany, and Albania.

28. Vermont Garrison (October 29, 1915–February 14, 1994), known as "the Gray Eagle," was an ace in both World War II and Korea. Garrison scored 17.33 victories combined, 7 victories in World War II and 10 victories in Korea, but he started his career in the Royal Air Force. He fought in Vietnam under Olds. Garrison earned the DSC, Silver and Bronze Stars, several DFCs, Legion of Merit, and a Purple Heart, among many other awards. He is buried in Arlington National Cemetery.

29. "Rapid Roger" missions were orders for each F-4 Phantom unit to fly their fighters round the clock, day and night, keeping up pressure on hard targets, such as the Ho Chi Minh Trail. They also flew ground attack and close air support missions for

ground units. As a result, more aircraft were being lost, many due to enemy action, but also due to the lack of required scheduled maintenance. Robin Olds killed it with a great ceremony.

30. General William Wallace Momyer (September 23, 1916–August 10, 2012) was a controversial figure and was no fan of Ben Davis and his black fighter pilots. He even pushed to have them removed from flying operations. He scored eight kills during World War II. He once engaged eighteen Ju-87 Stukas in North Africa, shooting down four. He later became commanding officer of Air Training Command, as well as the Seventh Air Force during the Vietnam War, and the Tactical Air Command (TAC). During his tour in Southeast Asia, he was concurrently the deputy commander of the Military Assistance Command, Vietnam (MACV) for air operations and thus responsible for Operation Rolling Thunder, the air campaign against North Vietnam, micromanaged by President Lyndon B. Johnson and Secretary of Defense Robert S. McNamara.

31. Olds and Olds with Rasimus, *Fighter Pilot*, 222.

32. Ibid., 271.

33. Ho Chi Minh (May 19, 1890–September 2, 1969), born Nguyễn Sinh Cung, also known as Nguyễn Tất Thành, Nguyễn Ái Quốc, Bác Hồ, was the Communist dictator of North Vietnam.

34. Lyndon Johnson was notorious for bullying fellow politicians into agreeing and voting with him on bills he felt were important. This included even following fellow senators or representatives into the men's room and pushing them up against the wall as a form of intimidation.

35. The KC-135 Stratotanker was a converted Boeing 707 airliner, refitted as a flying gas station.

36. Lieutenant Colonel John Robert Pardo (born March 10, 1934), along with Weapon System Officer First Lieutenant Steve Wayne and wingman Captain Earl Aman (with Weapon System Officer First Lieutenant Robert Houghton), was assigned to the Eighth Tactical Fighter Wing, 433rd Tactical Fighter Squadron, at Ubon Royal Thai Air Force Base, Thailand. In March 1967 they were trying to attack a steel mill in North Vietnam, just north of Hanoi.

37. The "Hanoi Hilton" was the nickname given to the Hỏa Lò Prison used by the French colonists in French Indochina for political prisoners, and later used by US prisoners of war during the Vietnam War

38. Olds and Olds with Rasimus, *Fighter Pilot*, 295.

39. Olds's wingman and his GIB were Jack Van Loan and Joe Milligan, respectively. Ibid., 309.

40. Pardo and Phil Combies each scored a kill on the mission.

41. Harold Brown (September 19, 1927–January 4, 2019) was an American nuclear physicist who served as US secretary of defense from 1977 to 1981 under President Jimmy Carter. Previously, in the John F. Kennedy and Lyndon B. Johnson administrations, he held the posts of director of defense research and engineering (1961–1965) and US secretary of the air force (1965–1969).

42. Jacksel Markham "Jack" Broughton (January 4, 1925–October 24, 2014) retired with the rank of colonel on August 31, 1968, with forty-three separate awards and decorations, including four Distinguished Flying Crosses, two Silver Stars, and the highest air force service decoration for heroism, the Air Force Cross. Broughton avowed that his proudest accomplishment was being combat qualified in every air force fighter, from the P-47 to the Convair F-106 Delta Dart. He authored two personal memoirs of the Vietnam War that were highly critical of the direction of the air war there and the rules of engagement.

43. The Paris Peace Accords of 1973 were an agreement for the United States to halt offensive operations. In trade, American POWs would be returned.

44. Karl Wendell Richter (October 4, 1942–July 28, 1967) was an officer in the US Air Force and an accomplished fighter pilot during the Vietnam War. At the age of twenty-three, he was the youngest pilot in that conflict to shoot down a MiG in air-to-air combat. His decorations included the Air Force Cross, Silver Star, Bronze Star, four Air Medals, and Purple Heart.

45. Stokely Standiford Churchill Carmichael (June 29, 1941–November 15, 1998) was an organizer in the civil rights movement in the United States and the global Pan-African movement. Born in Trinidad, he grew up in the United States from the age of eleven and became an activist while attending Howard University. He eventually developed the Black Power movement, first while leading the Student Nonviolent Coordinating Committee (SNCC), later serving as the "honorary prime minister" of the Black Panther Party (BPP), and lastly as a leader of the All-African People's Revolutionary Party (A-APRP).

46. The pilot of the damaged plane was Ron Catton (Olds and Olds with Rasimus, *Fighter Pilot*, 329). Wayne Hague disobeyed orders and flew into North Vietnamese airspace to rescue Catton with a top-off, allowing him to avoid ejecting over the target area due to fuel loss caused by damage.

47. The F-105 pilot was Lieutenant David Waldrop of the 388th Tactical Fighter Wing (Ibid., 322).

48. General John Paul McConnell (February 7, 1908–November 21, 1986) served in the China-Burma-India theater during World War II was later sixth chief of staff of the US Air Force. As chief of staff, McConnell served in a dual capacity. He was a member of the Joint Chiefs of Staff. He spent a year as director of plans at Strategic Air Command headquarters, Offutt Air Force Base, Nebraska.

49. Walt Whitman Rostow (also known as Walt Rostow or W. W. Rostow), OBE (October 7, 1916–February 13, 2003), was an American economist, professor, and political theorist who served as national security advisor to President Lyndon B. Johnson from 1966 to 1969. In World War II, he served in the Office of Strategic Services.

50. Robin was still married to Morgan when I initially interviewed him in 1989 and during the follow-ups in 1990 and 1993; by the time I interviewed him in 1994, the marriage was over.

51. My interviews with the German aces Rall, Galland, Hartmann, and Hrabak can be found in Heaton and Lewis, *German Aces Speak,* vols. I and II.

Cowboy on a Thoroughbred: Edward Ross "Buddy" Haydon

1. Cloyd Peart Clevenger (February 14, 1898–February 9, 1964) began flying gliders as a young boy in Oakland, California. He qualified as a fighter pilot and served as a second lieutenant during World War I. He was reputed to have been the first skywriter. Clevenger was a member of the barnstorming community and toured with Ernst Udet after the First World War. He gave flight lessons and was a rated certified instructor. He learned to fly in 1918 and logged over eleven thousand hours during his career. He held commercial pilot license number 141.

   Cloyd was an innovator, with his introduction to flight training broadcasts by Denver's KOA radio station in the late 1920s. He also wrote two books, *Modern Flight* and *Clevenger's Flight Manual*. He worked with the famous Ford Air Tours, promoting safe and dependable flying for the general public and the airlines. It was originally called the "Commercial Airplane Reliability Tour . . . they were subsequently promoted as 'The Commercial Airplane Reliability Tour for the Edsel B. Ford Trophy,' sometimes shortened to the Ford Reliability Tour and later, the National Air Tour," https://www.amazon.com/Ford-Air-Tours-1925-1931/dp/0972524916.

   Much of Clevenger's flying was in the Alexander Eaglerock planes and gliders. He was the chief pilot for the company and also an Alexander skywriter. Clevenger also flew with the Walter Varney Flying Circus and the Gates Flying Circus. Later, he flew for Frank Robertson Aircraft Corporation as a demonstration pilot and instructor. Cloyd flew as an airline pilot in Mexico and did aerial mapping for Pan American Aerial Surveys in the 1930s.

   Cloyd, an active member of the secretive Quiet Birdmen started in 1921 and the Military and Veteran Air Pilots Associations, was a World War I ace and later organized commuter airlines around the Caribbean. He was operations manager of Pan American World Airways Caribbean division.

   In 1938 he was jailed for a year and a day on charges of violating the US Neutrality Act by smuggling planes for use in the Spanish Civil War as a mercenary pilot. When World War II broke out, he joined Pan American again and ferried planes to Britain. Clevenger spent the war as a transport pilot. He moved to Mexico permanently in 1957 and died in Mexico City.

2. This was the top-secret rocket testing base commanded by Major General Walter Dornberger. Dr. Wernher von Braun was the chief rocket scientist, developing the V-1 "buzz bomb" (known as the "doodle bug" by the British), the Messerschmitt Me 163 Komet, and the V-2 ballistic missile. They also conducted many experiments that would later create the rocket and space programs for the United States.

3. Capt. Ernest "Red" Fiebelkorn (December 12, 1922–July 6, 1950) was credited with nine victories (including the half kill with Haydon) and is thought to have been one of the largest fighter pilots to see action in the ETO. At six foot four and 225 pounds, he must have had a difficult time getting himself into the cockpit of his P-51D, serial number 44-11161 (LC-N), nicknamed *June Nite* for his California-born wife, the former Ms. June Allyn, whom he had married in 1943. He was killed

in the Korean War flying North American F-82 Twin Mustangs out of Okinawa, Japan.

4. Standing less than a quarter mile away were Lieutenant General Adolf Galland and Captain Georg-Peter Eder. Eder was promoted to major on the spot and given temporary command of the *Kommando Nowotny Geschwader* (Wing).

5. January 20, 1945, was a maximum bombing effort, but no US fighter pilots filed any claims or kills for that day's missions. Only one Me 262 was damaged in the area where Haydon was working, and that crashed. Hence Haydon should have that victory added to his score sheet. The Me 262 belonged to 10./EJG-2 Werk Nr. 110286, flown by Sergeant Karl Hartung, who died in the crash while trying to land. See Heaton and Lewis, *Me 262 Stormbird*, 282. Luftwaffe jet loss records via Walter Krupinski.

6. The Volkssturm was the civilian auxiliary paramilitary force consisting primarily of older men and boys too young to be conscripted. Hitler ordered their expansion essentially as cannon fodder.

7. Colonel Clarence Emil "Bud" Anderson (born January 13, 1922) was the highest-scoring flying ace in his P-51 Mustang squadron, with 16.25 victories. Toward the end of Anderson's two combat tours in Europe in 1944, he was promoted to major at age twenty-two. His P-51D, named *Old Crow*, became one of the best-known airplanes in Europe. After the war, Anderson became a well-regarded fighter test pilot, and a fighter squadron and wing commander. He served as a wing commander during the Vietnam War. He retired as a full colonel in 1972, after which he worked in flight test management for McDonnell Douglas. A member of the National Aviation Hall of Fame, he is a true national treasure and a great gentleman, and he still loves to give interviews. Anderson is alive and well, living near Sacramento, California, at the time of this writing.

8. Brigadier General Charles Elwood "Chuck" Yeager (born February 13, 1923) was one of America's top aces in the ETO, scoring 11.5 victories, including the first Me 262 jet kill for the 357th FG. Yeager went on to break many other speed and altitude records. He was also one of the first American pilots to fly a MiG-15, after its pilot, No Kum-sok, defected to South Korea following the end of hostilities. He later became a test pilot, breaking the sound barrier in level flight. Yeager became the first commandant of the USAF Aerospace Research Pilot School, which produced astronauts for NASA and the USAF, after its redesignation from the USAF Flight Test Pilot School. Having only a high school education, he was not eligible to become an astronaut himself, although he trained them from December 1962 to January 1964. Yeager died December 7, 2020.

9. General John Charles Meyer (April 3, 1919–December 2, 1975), then a lieutenant colonel, deployed with the 352nd FG to a forward base in Belgium designated Y-29 in December 1944. His foresight in having the 487th Fighter Squadron preflighted and ready to take off on January 1, 1945, averted a major disaster when the field was attacked by fighters of Jagdgeschwader 11 (JG-11) in the massive aerial assault known as Operation Bodenplatte. Meyer led the takeoff under fire and scored against a strafing

Focke-Wulf Fw 190 before his landing gear had even retracted, earning him a Distinguished Service Cross that day. In Korea, he shot down two MiG-15s.

Later, a vehicle accident left him with a severe leg injury, thereby ending his combat flying with the 352nd after having flown 200 combat missions totaling 462 combat flying hours and having scored twenty-four aerial victories, with another thirteen credited to ground strafing. After the war, Meyer worked with Curtis LeMay and was once the commander in chief of the Strategic Air Command (SAC) and director of the Joint Strategic Target Planning Staff (JSTPS) at Offutt Air Force Base, Nebraska.

10. Major Theodor Weissenberger (December 21, 1914–June 11, 1950) scored 208 victories, with 8 of them scored in the jet. He was awarded the Knight's Cross with Oak Leaves and Swords, and spent much of his time with JG-5 Eismeer, flying in Finland and Norway with fellow jet pilot First Lieutenant Walter Schuck (206 kills, 4 in the jet, earning him Oak Leaves) and Major Heinrich Ehrler (206 kills, 5 in the jet, killed in action April 4, 1945). Weissenberger died in an auto racing accident on June 11, 1950, at the Nürburgring.

Weissenberger became the *Geschwaderkommodore*, and he had just arrived when he went head-to-head with Buddy Haydon. (Johannes Steinhoff had left JG-7 as acting CO, replacing Eder a short time later to help form Galland's Jagdverband 44 [JV-44].) Weissenberger's wingman is unknown for certain, but they were flying in support of 10. *Staffel* of *Erprobunungsjagdgeschwader* (Experimental Fighter Wing) Me 262s. It was Karl Hartung's jet that Haydon engaged and apparently shot down, but he never received the credit.

11. See endnote 3, above. Sergeant Karl Hartung was the only jet pilot with a damaged or a crashed jet on this day, which burned up less than a half mile from the engagement. Haydon should get credit for the kill.

Master of the Bombers: Curtis Emerson LeMay

1. LeMay's complete list of awards and decorations:
   Command pilot
   Distinguished Service Cross
   Distinguished Service Medal with two Oak Leaf clusters
   Silver Star
   Distinguished Flying Cross with two Oak Leaf clusters
   Air Medal with four Oak Leaf clusters
   Presidential Unit Citation with Oak Leaf cluster
   American Defense Service Medal
   American Campaign Medal
   European-African-Middle Eastern Campaign Medal with three Bronze
      Campaign Stars
   Asiatic-Pacific Campaign Medal with four Bronze Campaign Stars
   World War II Victory Medal

Army of Occupation Medal with Berlin Airlift Device
Medal for Humane Action
National Defense Service Medal with one Service Star
Armed Forces Expeditionary Medal
Vietnam Service Medal
Air Force Longevity Service Award with eight Oak Leaf clusters
British Distinguished Flying Cross
USSR—Order of the Patriotic War—First Degree
Legion of Honour (Commandeur) (France)
French Croix de Guerre avec Palme
Belgian Croix de Guerre avec Palme
Ecuador—Order of Aeronautical Merit, Knight Commander
Brazilian Order of Aeronautical Merit, Commander
Moroccan Order of Ouissam Alaouite, Commander
Argentina—Order of May of Aeronautical Merit—Grades of Grand Cross and
   Grand Commander
Brazilian Order of the Southern Cross, Grand Cross
Japanese Order of the Rising Sun, Grand Cordon
Swedish Commander Grand Cross of the Royal Order of the Sword
Chile—Order of Merit (degree unknown)
Chile—Medalla Militar de Primera Clase
Uruguay—Aviador Militar Honoris Causa (Piloto Commandante)

2. Barrett Tillman, *LeMay: A Biography* (New York: Palgrave-MacMillan, 2007), 4. During the interview, LeMay never mentioned his siblings by name.

3. Frank Luke Jr. (May 19, 1897–September 29, 1918) was an American fighter ace, ranking second among US Army Air Service pilots with eighteen victories, after Captain Eddie Rickenbacker with twenty-six victories. A specialist at shooting down German observation balloons. Between September 12 and September 29, 1918, Luke was credited with shooting down fourteen German balloons and four airplanes. Luke achieved these eighteen victories during just ten sorties in eight days, a feat unsurpassed by any pilot in World War I. Luke, killed on the ground after being shot down, was the first US airman to receive the Medal of Honor posthumously. Luke Air Force Base in Arizona is named in his honor.

4. Edward Corringham "Mick" Mannock (May 24, 1887–July 26, 1918) was an Irish-born British fighter pilot and flying ace in the Royal Flying Corps (later Royal Air Force) during the First World War. Mannock was an innovator of fighter aircraft tactics. Before he was killed in action, he had scored sixty-one victories, making him the fifth-highest-scoring pilot of the war. He was awarded the Victoria Cross (posthumously), the Distinguished Service Order with two Bars, and the Military Cross and Bar.

5. Captain Albert Ball (August 14, 1896–May 7, 1917) was an English fighter pilot during the First World War. At the time of his death, he was the United Kingdom's leading flying ace, with forty-four victories, and remained its fourth-highest scorer behind

Edward Mannock, James McCudden, and George McElroy. He received the Victoria Cross, Distinguished Service Order with two Bars, and the Military Cross. He was only twenty years old when he died. After hearing Ball had died, Baron Manfred von Richthofen said, "Such a shame, he was by far the best English flying man." Ball died due to engine failure, not wounds as a result of his last combat. His back was broken, and he had massive thoracic and limb fractures from the impact of the crash. The Germans gave him a memorable formal ceremony with a grave marker—such was the mutual respect between enemies. Over the grave of the man they dubbed "the English Richthofen," the Germans erected a cross bearing the inscription "*Im Luft-kampf gefallen für sein Vaterland Engl. Flieger-Hauptmann Albert Ball*, Royal Flying Corps" ("Fallen in air combat for his fatherland English pilot Captain Albert Ball").

6. Colonel General Ernst Udet (April 26, 1896–November 17, 1941) scored sixty-two victories in World War I and earned the Iron Cross in both classes, as well as the Pour le Mérite. He later became an integral part of Hitler's Luftwaffe, serving under fellow WWI ace and Blue Max recipient Hermann Göring. Both men flew under the command of Manfred von Richthofen, along with Manfred's brother, Lothar von Richthofen. Richthofen took command after the death of Blue Max recipient Oswald Boelcke, and Göring took command after Richthofen's death. Udet, never comfortable with his Nazi Party membership (since 1933), was always at odds with Göring. He committed suicide in his office in November 1941. Ironically, his direct subordinate, Colonel General Hans Jeschonnek (April 9, 1899–August 18, 1943), would do the same in 1943 after Göring used him as a scapegoat.

7. Manfred Albrecht Freiherr (Baron) von Richthofen (May 2, 1892–April 12, 1918) scored eighty confirmed victories, earning the Pour le Mérite as commander of his "Flying Circus." After his death, the Australian ground forces gave him an honored airman's funeral, with full military honors and grave marker, such was the respect.

8. Oswald Boelcke (May 19, 1891–October 28, 1916) scored forty victories as a flying ace of the First World War. He was one of the most successful and influential patrol leaders and tacticians. Boelcke is considered the father of the German fighter air force, and the "father of air fighting tactics." His treatise, the *Boelcke Dicta*, is still taught to combat fighter pilots. He and Max Immelmann were the two earliest recipients of the Pour le Mérite. Boelcke was killed in a midair collision with a squadron mate. Manfred von Richthofen took command of Jasta 1 upon his death.

9. Colonel Rene Paul Fonck (March 27, 1894–June 18, 1953) was the top French First World War fighter ace and is still considered the all-time Allied ace of aces. He received confirmation for 75 victories (72 solo and 3 shared) out of 142 claimed victories. Taking into account his probable claims, Fonck's final score could be 100 or more. He was made an officer of the Legion of Honor in 1918 and later a commander of the Legion of Honor after the war. He was also given the title of grand officer.

10. Douglas Campbell (June 7, 1896–October 16, 1990) was an American aviator and World War I flying ace. He was the first American aviator flying in an American-trained air unit to achieve the status of ace. Campbell was awarded the Distinguished Service Cross for bravery in aerial combat over Flirey, France, on May 19, 1918, and in

the next three weeks received four Oak Leaf clusters. He was also awarded the Croix de Guerre avec Palme by the French military. He scored his sixth and final victory on June 5, 1918, then he was wounded by shrapnel. He recuperated and returned to France but did not fly further combat before the war ended.

11. This school was operated by Harold Gatty, an Australian from Tasmania and a veteran of the Royal Australian Navy. See Tillman, *LeMay*, 7.

12. According to Tillman, there were sixty-eight crashes resulting in twelve deaths and another fifteen pilots badly injured. Ibid., 9.

13. LeMay was assisted by Lieutenant John W. Egan, who later joined him at Langley. Ibid., 10.

14. Andrews was demoted to colonel and sent to Texas for his open suggestion that there should be an independent air force. Ironically, like Billy Mitchell, his vision came true after World War II. Ibid., 15.

15. Mitchell proved his theory when he bombed the captured World War I battleship *Ostfriesland* and sank it on July 21, 1921, off the Virginia coast. The demonstration angered the navy brass who were proven wrong, that an aircraft can sink a capital ship.

16. The Munich Agreement was negotiated by Joachim von Ribbentrop and British prime minister Neville Chamberlain on September 30, 1938. This in effect gave Hitler freedom to invade the Sudetenland following his absorption of his native Austria. The weak British response emboldened him to attack Poland a year later, starting World War II.

17. Jesse Owens (September 12, 1913–March 31, 1980) set world records in the long jump that lasted 25 years, and won four gold medals at the 1936 Berlin Olympics in that event, as well as the 100-meter dash, 200-meter dash, and 400-meter relay.

18. Maximillian Adolph Otto Siegfried "Max" Schmeling (September 28, 1905–February 2, 2005) was the German heavyweight champion of the world between 1930 and 1932. His two fights with Joe Louis Barrow (known professionally as Joe Louis) in 1936 and 1938 were publicized worldwide because of their national associations. Hitler was so enraged after Schmeling's defeat in 1938 that he would not allow Schmeling's name to be mentioned. Schmeling served as a paratrooper in World War II and jumped into Crete during Operation Mercury in May 1941. Severely wounded, he was out for much of the war. Schmeling refused to join the Nazi Party and was openly opposed to its racial policies. Joe Louis became a close friend, and he financially supported him until Louis died, and he paid for the funeral. Schmeling also saved the lives of two Jewish brothers, sons of his friend David Lewin. Schmeling helped them get forged papers and paid for them to emigrate to the United States. He also admitted during an interview that he harbored more Jews after he learned about the death camps in 1943, but he trusted no one else with that information. After the war, the ex-champ became the largest distributor of Coca-Cola products in Germany, if not all of Europe. His interview was quite interesting.

19. Charles A. Lindbergh (February 4, 1902–August 26, 1974) was the first pilot to cross the Atlantic Ocean, in 1927, nonstop from New York to Paris. He became an international

celebrity. He again made world headlines in 1932, when his young son was kidnapped and murdered, which was called the "crime of the century" at that time.

20. The flight covered 11,000 miles in 63.5 hours' flying time at an average speed of 173 knots. See Tillman, *LeMay*, 18.

21. Robert Lee Scott Jr. (April 12, 1908–February 27, 2006) scored thirteen kills and retired from the US Air Force as a brigadier general on September 30, 1957. In total, General Scott wrote about a dozen books, including *God Is My Co-Pilot* and *The Day I Owned the Sky*.

22. Colonel Gregory "Pappy" Boyington (December 4, 1912–January 11, 1988) was a US Marines fighter pilot who broke service to join the American Volunteer Group (AVG, or Flying Tigers) in Burma and China. He received the Navy Cross and Medal of Honor, claiming twenty-eight kills. However, actual records account for only twenty-six, with four of his AVG kills unconfirmed. Many historians agree that his actual confirmed kills were twenty-two. Boyington was shot down on January 3, 1944, and spent the rest of the war as a POW.

23. John Richard "Dick" Rossi (April 19, 1915–April 17, 2008) resigned his navy commission in 1941 to join the American Volunteer Group (AVG) under the command of Colonel Claire Chennault. He arrived in Rangoon, Burma, on November 12, 1941, and was undergoing a training program in the P-40 Warhawk aircraft when Pearl Harbor was attacked. He scored 6.25 kills but made history by flying 735 missions (the most) over the Himalaya Mountains, called the Hump, as a transport pilot.

24. The American Volunteer Group, commanded by Colonel (later Lieutenant General) Claire Chennault (September 6, 1893–July 7, 1958) was supported by the Franklin Roosevelt administration to support China in its war against Japan, much like the American Eagle Squadrons flying in the British Royal Air Force against the Germans. The pilots were paid a salary plus $500 in US dollars for every victory confirmed. In nearly seven months of relentless combat (December 18, 1941 to July 4, 1942), the AVG men and machines shot down 296 confirmed enemy planes and 300 more probable kills. Japan lost 1,500 pilots, bombardiers, navigators, and gunners in air combat. The AVG also destroyed 573 bridges, 1,300 riverboats and innumerable road vehicles, and killed thousands of Imperial Japanese Army soldiers. They then became the Twenty-Third Fighter Group of the Fourteenth Air Force.

The total losses to the AVG were 69 planes and 25 pilots. Two crew chiefs, including mechanic John E. Fauth, were killed during Japanese bombing raids at various airfields. On the day the group was disbanded, there were just 30 well-used P-40s left to fly.

25. Colonel Francis S. Gabreski is another interview that will be a part of this ongoing series, and he is referenced throughout this book.

26. Tillman, *LeMay*, 19.

27. Thanks to Barrett Tillman's book, these details and names are clarified, which were not presented during the interviews. LeMay's former commander at Langley, Caleb V. Haynes, was working with Robert Olds on the Atlantic Ferrying Command, which

was part of the US Lend-Lease Act of 1941 to supply the British with war materiel by air and sea. See ibid., 19.

28. The Women Airforce Service Pilots (WASP) (also Women's Army Service Pilots or Women's Auxiliary Service Pilots) was a civilian women pilots' organization whose members were United States federal civil service employees. Members of WASP became trained pilots who tested aircraft, ferried aircraft, and trained other pilots. They served all over the world. Their luminary, Jacqueline Cochran, worked closely with Hap Arnold and many others to get women into the war as pilots.

29. George McGovern (July 19, 1922–October 21, 2012) was a US senator from South Dakota and the Democratic Party presidential candidate against Richard M. Nixon in 1972. He served as a B-24 pilot in missions over Italy as a member of the 455th Bomb Group of the Fifteenth Air Force.

30. Brigadier General James Maitland Stewart, USAF (May 20, 1908–July 2, 1997), was one of many Hollywood stars to join the military after war was declared. He was already an accomplished pilot, and he flew B-24 Liberators in World War II with the Second Bombardment Wing. He rose to the rank of colonel during the war. Hitler had a 100,000-reichsmark bounty on him to be paid to the fighter pilot who shot him down. Clark Gable had a similar bounty, as he was Eva Braun's favorite actor.

31. Group Captain Peter Wooldridge Townsend (November 22, 1914–June 19, 1995) scored nine kills and received the CVO, DSO, DFC and bar, RAF. A favorite of the royal family, Townsend even dated Princess Margaret.

32. James Harry "Ginger" Lacey (February 1, 1917–May 30, 1989) was one of the top-scoring Royal Air Force fighter pilots of the Second World War and the second-highest-scoring RAF fighter pilot of the Battle of Britain, behind Pilot Officer Eric Lock of Forty-One Squadron RAF. Lacey was credited with twenty-eight enemy aircraft destroyed, five probable kills, and nine damaged. He was awarded the DFM and bar.

33. The Pointblank Directive was a prioritized list of strategic targets for the strategic bombing campaign. The Casablanca Directive was a generalized targeting strategy for the Combined Bomber Offensive (CBO), which established the top priority as the destruction of German submarine construction yards, with the German aircraft industry second on the priority list. The Pointblank Directive put the German aircraft industry dedicated to the production of single-engine fighters at the top of the priority list. The Pointblank Directive identified nineteen critical industrial targets. Following is the list:

Single-engine fighter aircraft production—twenty-two targets
Ball bearing production—ten targets
Petroleum products/oil and refineries—thirty-nine targets
Grinding wheels and crude abrasives—ten targets
Nonferrous metals—thirteen targets
Synthetic rubber and rubber tires—twelve targets
Submarine construction plants and operational bases—twenty-seven targets
Military transport vehicle manufacturing centers—seven targets
Transportation (rail, barge, and surface roads)—no specific number

Coking plants—eighty-nine targets

Iron and steel works—fourteen targets

Machine tools—twelve targets

Electrical power/hydroelectric dams—fifty-five targets

Electrical equipment—sixteen targets

Optical precision instruments—three targets

Chemical plants—unknown number

Food—twenty-one targets

Nitrogen production—twenty-one targets

Antiaircraft and antitank artillery production/batteries

34. One of the primary fighter leaders involved was Major Walther Dahl (March 27, 1916–November 25, 1985), who shot down two B-17s on the October 14, 1943, Schweinfurt-Regensburg mission (which became known as Black Thursday for the USAAF), en route to the target as Stab III. JG-3, Udet. He also commanded II Gruppe JG-3 later. Dahl finished the war as a colonel with the Oak Leaves to the Knight's Cross with 128 kills, with 36 of his claimed victories being B-17 and B-24 heavy bombers; 30 heavy bombers were confirmed shot down without any discrepancy in the record. The remaining 6 may have been unknowingly damaged by other fighter pilots. He was also involved in the Fighters Revolt against Hermann Göring in January 1945.

35. Colonel Robert Knight Morgan (July 31, 1918–May 15, 2004) and his crew in the B-17F *Memphis Belle* were officially recognized as the first (although two other B-17s had just completed twenty-five missions before) bomber crew in the Eighth Air Force to complete the required twenty-five missions before rotating back to the United States. The author knew Morgan and his lovely wife, Linda, a remarkable lady, and met some of the surviving crew members.

36. On February 22, 1944, bad weather forced a stand-down, but not all the bomber wings received that order. First Bomb Division continued. Third Bomb Division aborted, while Second Bomb Division returned due to weather. The Americans lost forty-one bombers and eleven escort fighters to the Luftwaffe.

37. The top-secret unit Kampfgeschwader (KG)-200 operated and evaluated captured aircraft. Many of these were flown by German pilots, evaluated, and then used as support aircraft. A few of the bombers were used to infiltrate American bomber formations. They posed as a straggler, either monitoring a bomber formation or sometimes becoming a wolf in sheep's clothing, attacking other Allied aircraft. KG-200 was under the direct command of Colonel Werner Baumbach (December 27, 1916–October 20, 1953), a successful bomber pilot who received the Knight's Cross with Oak Leaves and Swords. He died in a flying accident in Argentina.

38. Charles André Joseph Marie de Gaulle (November 22, 1890–November 9, 1970) was a career French army officer who led the Free French forces during World War II. He later became president of France.

39. The North Atlantic Treaty Organization (NATO, also known as the Washington Treaty) was created in 1949 as a response to the growing Soviet threat to Western

Europe, and is still today a coalition of nations that has grown in numbers over the years.

40. On an academic level regarding a total analysis of wartime actions—whether war crime or perceived as such—see Colin D. Heaton, *Occupation and Insurgency: A Selective Examination of the Hague and Geneva Conventions on the Eastern Front, 1939–1945* (New York: Algora, 2008).

41. Major General Dr. Walter Robert Dornberger (September 6, 1895–June 27, 1980) was a German army artillery officer whose career spanned World War I and World War II. He was the military project leader for Germany's V-1 and V-2 rocket programs and other projects at the Peenemünde Army Research Center. The science director was Dr. Wernher von Braun.

42. Dr. Wernher Magnus Maximilian Freiherr (Baron) von Braun (March 23, 1912–June 16, 1977) was a German and later American aerospace engineer and space architect. He was the leading figure in the development of rocket technology in Germany regarding the V-1 and V-2 programs under the military director Major General Dr. Walter Dornberger. Von Braun pioneered rocket and space technology in the United States, creating the Redstone, Gemini, and Apollo space programs. He was instrumental in the development of the American rockets, in particular the Saturn V. It has been said that without von Braun, the United States would have never landed on the moon.

43. LaVerne G. "Blondie" Saunders (March 21, 1903–November 16, 1988) was a former American football coach at West Point. He was at Pearl Harbor on December 7, 1941, and he flew bomber missions thereafter. Saunders formed the Fifty-Eighth Bomb Wing, which was the first issued with the B-29. He assumed command of Twentieth Bomber Command. Upon LeMay's arrival, he was reassigned. In September 1944 his B-25 crashed upon takeoff in India. LeMay organized the search team that found the wreckage with Saunders trapped under an engine, his ankle crushed and requiring amputation of his leg. See Tillman, *LeMay*, 43–44.

44. Major General Charles W. Sweeney (December 27, 1919–July 16, 2004) was the pilot who flew *Bockscar*, the B-29 carrying the Fat Man atomic bomb to the Japanese city of Nagasaki on August 9, 1945.

45. General George Churchill Kenney (August 6, 1889–August 9, 1977) is best known as the commander of the Allied Air Forces in the Southwest Pacific Area (SWPA), a position he held between August 1942 and 1945. He was a World War I veteran and an innovator in fighter tactics.

46. Estimates range from 70,000 to 100,000 deaths on the night of March 9–10, 1945. Tillman, *LeMay*, 61, records the toll at 83,000 after 1,858 tons of incendiaries burned Tokyo and its surrounding districts.

47. Hideki Tōjō (December 30, 1884–December 23, 1948) was a Japanese politician and commanding general of the Imperial Japanese Army. He was also prime minister of Japan and president of the Imperial Rule Assistance Association for the majority of World War II. He was tried and executed for war crimes.

48. According to Tillman and the postwar evaluations, between 1944 and 1945, when LeMay was in command, Japan lost 330,000 people, the majority due to B-29 raids.

49. LeMay did not begin the program. Operation Starvation was launched by Brigadier General John H. Davies in command of the 313th Bomb Group, which had been laying mines. They were laid with great density and used magnetic, pressure, and acoustic detonators. Tillman, *LeMay*, 66.

50. Ibid.

51. Lieutenant General Leslie Groves (August 17, 1896–July 13, 1970) was the Army Corps of Engineers officer who oversaw the construction of the Pentagon. He was also the military project manager for the Manhattan Project, where he oversaw the work of J. Robert Oppenheimer, Enrico Fermi, and other top physicists who developed the atomic bomb.

52. The Portland-class heavy cruiser USS *Indianapolis* (CA-35), commanded by Captain Charles B. McVay III, was sunk on her return trip by Japanese sub I-58, commanded by Captain Mochitsura Hashimoto. Of the 1,196 crewmen, 900 were alive when the ship sank, but only 316 were picked up more than four days later, suffering from shark attacks. The navy never even listed the ship as overdue when it failed to reach port in Manila Bay on time after leaving Guam. McVay was court-martialed in a kangaroo show court ordered by Admiral Ernest J. King (long backstory there). Hashimoto was brought in as a prosecution witness, but he only assisted the defense. McVay was cleared of all serious charges and retired in 1949 as a rear admiral. He committed suicide in 1968.

53. For more on Operation Paperclip and Operation Lusty, see Heaton and Lewis, *Me 262 Stormbird*, 21, 219–221 (Paperclip), 213, 215 (Lusty). Paperclip was the gathering of top Germans in the science and aerospace fields; Lusty, the collection of hardware and technology, such as jets and rockets.

54. Albert Speer (March 19, 1905–September 1, 1981) was Adolf Hitler's chief architect from 1933 until the end of the war. Following the death of Fritz Todt, Speer was appointed minister of armaments on February 8, 1942, becoming responsible for war production. Because slave labor was used, he was convicted of war crimes and sentenced to 20 years in Spandau Prison. Of his several books written, *Inside the Third Reich* is considered benchmark reading, and became a television series in the 1980s starring Rutger Hauer and Sir Derek Jacobi.

55. Julius and Ethel Rosenberg were American citizens who were convicted of spying for the Soviet Union. They were accused of providing top-secret information about radar, sonar, jet propulsion engines, and valuable nuclear weapon designs. Convicted of espionage in 1951, they were executed in 1953 at Sing Sing Correctional Facility in Ossining, New York.

   Their son and relatives fought for years to clear their names, but after the fall of the USSR and the declassification of old KGB documents, the couple's guilt was quite clear. Other convicted coconspirators were sentenced to prison, including Ethel's brother, David Greenglass (who had made a plea agreement), Harry Gold, and Morton Sobell. Klaus Fuchs, a German scientist working in Los Alamos, New Mexico, at the Atomic testing and proving ground, was convicted in the United Kingdom.

56. SAC consisted of 50,000 personnel and 837 aircraft, 14 understrength wings, and no long-range air-to-air refueling capability, only 110 atomic bombs and 60 delivery-capable aircraft. Tillman, *LeMay*, 94.

57. Kim Il Sung (April 15, 1912–July 8, 1994) was the first Communist dictator of North Korea, starting a dynasty of totalitarian rulers. He invaded South Korea in 1950, starting the conflict.

58. Major General Orvil Arson Anderson (May 2, 1895–August 24, 1965) was a pioneer balloonist. In 1935 he and Albert William Stevens won the Mackay Trophy when they set a record of 72,395 feet in their balloon *Explorer II*. Anderson was a hawk on Korea, like MacArthur and LeMay, but he was forcibly retired after making this comment to a newspaper reporter: "Give me the order to do it, and I can break up Russia's five A-bomb nests in a week! And when I went up to Christ, I think I could explain to him why I wanted to do it now, before it is too late. I think I could explain to him that I had saved civilization."

59. Francis Gary Powers (August 17, 1929–August 1, 1977) was a former US Air Force pilot recruited by the Central Intelligence Agency as a pilot for the U-2 spy program. He was shot down by a surface-to-air missile, starting the famous "U-2 Incident."

60. When LeMay left SAC, it boasted 224,000 personnel, including almost 30,000 officers, 2,700 aircraft and 768 tankers, and 5,500 warheads, with more than 2,000 of them being strategic. Tillman, *LeMay*, 137–38.

61. Skunk Works was the nickname for Johnson's top-secret aircraft design department at Lockheed and its manufacturing program, much of it dedicated to the CIA and NASA.

62. The Lockheed A-12 was a high-altitude, Mach 3+ reconnaissance aircraft built for the United States Central Intelligence Agency (CIA) by Lockheed 's Skunk Works, based on the designs of Clarence "Kelly" Johnson. The aircraft was designated A-12, the twelfth in a series of internal design efforts for "Archangel," the aircraft's internal code name.

63. Muammar Mohammed Abu Minyar al-Gaddafi (c. 1942–October 20, 2011) was a colonel in the Libyan army who became the nation's dictator in 1969 until he was assassinated along with his son.

64. Phyllis McGuire (born February 14, 1931) was one of three sisters known as the McGuire Sisters, a famous singing trio.

65. Samuel Mooney Giancana, born Salvatore Giangana (May 24, 1908–June 19, 1975), was an American mobster, hit man, and boss of the criminal Chicago Outfit from 1957 to 1966. In 1960 Giancana and Joseph Kennedy Sr. had an arrangement to secure Illinois votes, in particular Chicago ballots, for his son, John F. Kennedy. Giancana, one of the original Five Family members, knew and worked with Al Capone and was a business partner with Joseph Kennedy when the Kennedy family patriarch made his fortune as a bootlegger during Prohibition. Joe Kennedy managed to coordinate the Sicilian and Irish mobs in a deal with boss Lucky Luciano.

66. LeMay helped create the Air Force Village Foundation in 1964, with assistance from many other well-known US Air Force types, including celebrities such as James Stewart. The first two were built around San Antonio, Texas, and plans for many others

were developed. He and Helen also started the General and Mrs. Curtis E. LeMay Foundation to assist the spouses of deceased air force veterans. See also Tillman, *LeMay,* 175.

Appendix 1

1. "Eighth Air Force Combat Losses," Penn State Personal Web Server, http://personal .psu.edu/kbf107/Losses.html.

Appendix 2

1. "Eighth Air Force Combat Losses," Penn State Personal Web Server, http://personal .psu.edu/kbf107/Losses.html.

INDEX

INDEX

Mountbatten, Lord Louis, 305, 306
Mussolini, Benito, 103, 375n34

N
Naumann, Johannes, 49
Nielsen, Chase Jay, 97, 120, 375n29
Nimitz, Chester, 306–307, 312, 321, 322
Niven, James David Graham, 117–118,
    185–186, 376n43
Nixon, Richard M., 300
No Kumsok, 364n5
North Atlantic Treaty Organization (NATO),
    299, 330, 391n39
Nowotny, Walter, 236, 244

O
Old, Archie J., Jr., 109, 376n38
Olds, Christina, 1–2, 124, 195
Olds, Christina Eloise, 189, 190
Olds, Eloise, 125
Olds, Robert, 125, 126, 127, 128, 130,
    134, 146, 377n7
Olds, Robin
  awards and medals, 176
  B-17s and, 262–263
  California duty, 183–185, 186, 187
  characteristics, 123, 124, 189, 250, 252,
    262–263
  childhood and education, 125, 130–131
  in England, 186–187, 194–196
  Falcon missiles, 218–219, 220
  flight training, 133, 134, 135–141, 143–144
  Haydon and, 231, 250
  as head of Air Force Academy, 229–231
  health, 190
  home on postwar leave, 183–184
  importance of air power, 5, 264
  Lyndon Johnson and, 228
  Robert Johnson and, 149
  Korean War, 187, 188–189
  LeMay and, 232, 233, 262, 264, 267, 346–347
  Lybia duty, 190–191
  marriages, 185–186, 190, 213, 232
  mentors, 127–128
  at Norton Air Force Base, 231
  Operation Bolo, 206–211
  ordered to stand down, 218
  Pardo's Push, 213–214
  Pentagon duty, 191–194
  promotions, 154, 176, 187, 229

Rall and, 233
retirement, 232
on US Air Force competition team, 380n24
on US entering World War II, 271, 272
West Germany duty, 190
at West Point, 131, 132–133, 134
Olds, Robin: Vietnam War
  bomber coverage during Vietnam War, 204
  characteristics, 222–223
  as commanding officer in Vietnam, 200–205
  Communist bounty on, 223
  end of tour, 227
  getting assignment, 196–199
  kills, 211, 221, 222
  monkey, 225
  number of missions flown, 232
  postmission lookovers, 212
  "Rapid Roger" missions and, 203
  refueling mid-air, 216, 217–218
  replacement pilots, 212–213, 221–222
  Rostow and, 228–229
  targets, 212, 214, 225–227
  Thai Nguyen Steel Works mission, 215–216
  Thud missions, 219–221
Olds, Robin: World War II
  desire for aerial combat, 153, 154
  early missions, 145
  forward sweep missions, 160–163
  in 479th Fighter Group, 143, 163
  home between tours, 174–176
  interdiction missions, 153, 154, 155, 178–179
  kills, 154, 156, 159–160, 163, 172, 177, 178,
    179, 379n18, 379n19, 379n20
  number of missions flown, 231
  photo recon mission over Stuttgart, 170–174
  preparation for fighting in Pacific, 181
  Ramrod missions, 146–149, 155–156, 165,
    166–169, 177–179
  tactical bombing missions, 157–160
  trip to and in England, 141–145
Olds, Stevan, 133, 136, 176
Olds, Susan Bird, 189, 190, 195
Operation Vittles, 331–332
Orr, Bob, 137
Owens, Jesse, 268, 388n17

P
P-38 Lightnings (Lockheed), 60, 61, 102, 106,
  136, 137, 138, 139, 140, 143, 150–151, 154,
  156, 163–164

403